THE CHRISTIAN FAITH

VOLUME I

Nor do I seek to understand, in order that I may believe, but I believe, in order that I may understand. — For he who does not believe, does not experience, and he who does not experience, does not understand.

—*Anselm,* Proslogion, *1*; de fide Trin., 2.

THE CHRISTIAN FAITH

English Translation of the Second German Edition

FRIEDRICH SCHLEIERMACHER

VOLUME I

Edited by

H. R. MACKINTOSH

and J. S. STEWART

Introduction to the Torchbook edition
by Richard R. Niebuhr

HARPER TORCHBOOKS

The Cloister Library

HARPER & ROW, PUBLISHERS, NEW YORK AND EVANSTON

THE CHRISTIAN FAITH

Volume I

Printed in the United States of America

The English translation of this Second German edition, edited by H. R. MacKintosh and J. S. Stewart, was originally published as one volume in 1928, with second and third printings in 1948 and 1956, by T. & T. Clark, Edinburgh, and is here reprinted by arrangement.

First HARPER TORCHBOOK edition published 1963 by
Harper & Row, Publishers, Incorporated
New York and Evanston

CONTENTS

VOLUME I

INTRODUCTION

FIRST PART OF THE SYSTEM OF DOCTRINE

FIRST SECTION

SECOND SECTION

INTRODUCTION TO THE TORCHBOOK EDITION

BY RICHARD R. NIEBUHR

The Christian Faith, presented systematically according to the fundamental doctrines of the Evangelical Church occupies in the history of theology a position analogous to that of Kant's critiques of reason in philosophy. It is the position and not the matter or manner of treatment that is similar, but nevertheless Friedrich Schleiermacher may justifiably be called the Kant of modern Protestantism, for it is his critical reflection on theological issues that sets the basic problems for the succeeding nineteenth century and the greater part of the twentieth. By no means all of Schleiermacher's fame and influence rest upon his systematic theology alone, for long before its appearance he had established his name as an apologist with the volume of essays entitled *On Religion, speeches to its cultured despisers,* written for his friends of the Romantic circle in Berlin at the close of the eighteenth century. But it is this last work of his maturity that gives to one of the most colorful and attractive churchmen of modern times an indisputable place in the development of Christian thought, and in keeping with this position *The Christian Faith* has never ceased to stimulate theological controversy in the Protestant world since its first publication in 1821/22 (revised edition upon which the English translation is based, 1830).

As so frequently happens in the storms of critical opinion that mark the arrival of a new intellectual climate in religious thought and theology proper, the source of the disturbance has not always been kept clearly in view. Despite the fact that Schleiermacher's name necessarily appears in every survey of modern religious thought, the interpretation of his mind is often beclouded and obscured by the passionate distrust that his central theme is capable of awakening. For Schleiermacher is the prototype of the theologian who takes seriously the Enlightenment and especially its discovery of religion as an historical, human phenomenon, and *The Christian Faith* is his classic effort to reconcile the empirical, descriptive (or, if the reader prefers, phenomenological) approach to Christianity as a human religion with the Christian faith in Jesus of Nazareth as the redeemer of mankind. During the great theological upheaval of the 1920's and 1930's, variously called today the period of "crisis theology" or "dialectical theology," the Karl Barth's and Emil Brunner's who protested against the liberal captivity of Protestantism attempted to emancipate their generation from the influence of Schleiermacher, because his position so little accorded with the revelation-oriented theology of those later times and its premise of the infinite, qualitative difference between eternity and time. Crisis theology, as it proclaimed that God is knowable only through God's self-disclosure (and not, therefore, through any innate human piety), cast Schleiermacher out in the name of its rejection of all anthropocentism. Nevertheless, the author of *The Christian Faith* still throws a long and inescapable shadow among the theologians of our own day. In part, the continuing effective presence of Schleiermacher is attributable to the cunning with which the thesis is always wont to live on in the antithesis, so that the affirmations of the dialectical theologians carry with themselves the echoes of that which they negate; in part it is due to the fact that Schleiermacher's theology really does not easily fit into the stereotype of liberalism with which commentators have been accustomed to dismiss the nineteenth century, so that the epithets aimed at the latter fail to cripple the power of his true thought; and finally, Schleiermacher's enduring influence is to be explained in part by the significant voices of such contemporaries as Rudolf Bultmann and Paul Tillich, men who never wholly accepted the Barthian revolution and still speak with a logic derived from, though not identical with, that of Schleiermacher and the religious milieu he helped to shape. Indeed, so firmly entrenched are Schleiermacher's ideas in the spirit of the times we call modern (reaching from the American and French revolutions to the present) that very little published today of a theological nature does not borrow consciously or otherwise from some facet of his thinking.

The Christian Faith was written by a man who well understood the historical interplay of minds and the fate of ideas. Furthermore, he never believed that scholarship and reflection were ends in themselves or that they could produce systems impervious to time. Schleiermacher conceived the purpose of theological thinking to be the edification of the church for its work in a particular time rather than the mapping out of the mind of God, just as the function of the school and university is to preserve, criticize and enrich the knowledge of reality that distinguishes the culture of a given nation. Such a theology must be rooted in the present quality of the church's faith—a present in the Augustinian sense that is informed by the remembered past—and seek both to express and to teach this faith. The texts from Anselm that are cited on the title page make clear this idea of theology: "Nor do I seek to understand in order that I may believe, but I believe in order that I may understand." (*Proslogion*, ch. 1) "For he who does not believe, does not experience, and he who does not experience, does not understand." (*de fide Trinitatis*, ch. 2) Schleiermacher's understanding of the nature of theology is not narrowly pragmatic in any sense but it is eminently practical and, despite the rigorous form in which it is cast, anti-intellectualist. Those words of Anselm stand for the fundamental principle of Schleiermacher's view of the historical cosmos, and whoever reads *The Christian Faith* is at the same time gaining an insight into the motives and considerations that guided one of the first modern men to rediscover the priority of historical existence, experience and the moral configuration of the self over all theoretical formulations about being and the Absolute.

Friedrich Daniel Ernst Schleiermacher (1768-1834) produced his great statement on the faith of the church against the background of a life spent in the pulpit and in the university. When, in later years, he wrote to the philosopher Jacobi that he would never give over his philosophizing to the direction of his piety nor his piety to his philosophy and that the work of both would for that reason doubtlessly remain unfinished, he was pronouncing not only the principle of his thought but of his personal history. Schleiermacher's temperament fitted him well for the role that more often than not he found himself enacting, namely that of ambassador and interpreter of one world to another, of the Christian to the secular, the Calvinist to the Lutheran, the academic or ecclesiastical to the political. It was not his way in this ambassadorial role to seek compromise or synthesis between the interests of the several worlds of which he was a citizen (save perhaps in the intra-Protestant disputes that inhibited the formation of the Union Church of Prussia) but rather to maintain the necessity of open communication between them and to promote recognition on the part of each of the integrity and proper sphere of the other. Where one sphere of life threatened to seize hegemony over the others, Schleiermacher was active in protest.

This was the spirit in which the young Schleiermacher forsook the close confines of the Moravian community in which he had been educated, as he became increasingly suspicious of its systematic exclusion of the new life of the intellect in the last years of the Enlightenment. At that time, and forever after, Schleiermacher was convinced that religous faith cannot flourish in a self-defensive and self-isolating posture. Despite his father's opposition, therefore, he enrolled in the university at Halle, an institution with a pietistic tradition but latterly more receptive to the ideas of the age, and there he prepared himself, albeit somewhat unenthusiastically, in theology and read in the new philosophy. Thence he departed for a position as a tutor in a noble Prussian family, but only after a further period of apprenticeship in the parish ministry did Schleiermacher begin to discover the particular personal equation that would enable him to move freely and creatively within the whole culture of his generation and people.

The epoch of his life arrived, however, only when he first settled in Berlin in 1796 and soon assumed the part of spokesman for Christianity to its Romantic sophisticates. This epoch opened with Schleiermacher's becoming a member of the circle of friends revolving about Henrietta Herz, a gifted Jewish patroness of the intellectual-social life of the city. Schleiermacher's prolific correspondence from these years gives us a better insight into his mind and its development at this juncture than at any other. Through this circle he met and made a friend of Friedrich von Schlegel, shared quarters with him, and in his company entered into the appropriation of the literary and philosophical Romanticism that then charged the air of Germany as political revolution swelled in France. These friends teased and reproached the unliterary Schleiermacher until he published *On Religion* (1799), in which the scope of his genius was first exhibited to the world. The then prevalent interest in Spinoza is clearly attested in these addresses but with a drastic qualification, for here religion instead of being sublimated into the affective element in the intellectual vision of the whole of being, is presented as an original and inalienable sense and taste for the infinite in the unique embodiment of finite beings. The organs of this sense and taste are "intuition" and "feeling," but they are presented with sufficient imprecision in the rhetorical style of the addresses to make an exact interpretation of the terms virtually impossible. Whether these addresses with their unorthodox equation of God and the universe are to be properly explained by their apologetic function or as the key to the real Schleiermacher is a question that will doubtlessly be debated so long as inaugural dissertations and doctoral theses must be written. The fundamental thing that Schleiermacher has to say is, however, beyond all discussion: religion is an intrinsic element in the self-consciousness of the fully developed man. *On Religion*'s statement of this principle became the most influential of all of Schleiermacher's subsequent work and is the chief basis on which he has customarily been identified as the theologian of Romanticism.

Nevertheless, in some ways, the *Soliloquies* of the following year provides a better insight into the author's mind. Here the reader encounters Schleiermacher giving a more critcal account of his ideas of individuality and of the self in relationship to the philosophy of Kant and Fichte. In retrospect, one can readily see that this latter concept constituted the really decisive idea in Schleiermacher's view of the cosmos and that "feeling" could emerge as a definite principle of his thought only as he gave the individual a clear and significant place in that cosmos. Despite the fact that the *Soliloquies* rings with a Fichtean heroism and Romantic disdain for the power and authority of conventional social forms, the most significant assertion in it is that of the fallacy of conceiving of the individual as an instance of rationality only quantitatively distinguished from other men. To become myself fully, Schleiermacher there confides in the confessional style of the book, I must empathetically enter into all alien forms of humanity. The self is not an incarnation of pure reason, but it is a member of an historically differentiated community. Contributions to the *Athenaeum,* written during these same years, offer more detailed information on his relations to the philosophy of the day.

Aside from the personal associations that led to the publications already cited, the Berlin period was important for another reason. As a consequence of his friendship wth Schlegel, Schleiermacher undertook the business of translating Plato, and Plato acquired a new disciple. With no other philosopher did Schleiermacher ever feel so profound an affinity. The work stretched out over the whole of his life and was never completed. It remains to this day something of a landmark in Plato scholarship, but more importantly for our purposes, it also provides the key to Schleiermacher's criticisms of Kant, Fichte and Schelling and to his own constructive position. Hereafter, Schleiermacher held that knowing depends on being and the love of being, that appearance is grounded in the thing itself, that progress in knowledge requires the mediation of other minds and moral appropriation—a dialogue, and that all of our knowing, although it presupposes and strives after the eternal truths, nevertheless begins *in mediis rebus* and cannot be deduced from or compressed into a single super-science. This combination of convictions sets him off from his idealist contemporaries and helps to explain how Schleiermacher could seek everywhere for the traces of ultimate unity and yet be content with, or rather insist on, the unfinished character of all thinking in time and place. His kinship to Plato on this archetectonic plane enables him to transcend his period and to stand with such men as St. Augustine, John Calvin and Jonathan

Edwards, who similarly combine a pathos for ultimate reality with a profound understanding of the moral nature of man.

An unhappy love affair drove Schleiermacher from the city of his first triumphs, and he took up residency in a northern rural parish. The removal from Berlin coincided with a slackening of the bond of sympathy for his early Romantic friends whose drift toward Catholicism, among other things, disgusted him, and in his new parish he plunged himself into the preparation of the foundation of his systematic work. Coincidentally with the last painful months between hope and despair over his beloved he moved to the university at Halle as professor. But two years later, in 1806, just when he realized he had found his *metier* as teacher and preacher to the university, Napoleon invaded the German lands and dissolved the faculty. When all hope for the restoration of the university had died, Schleiermacher returned to Berlin as a private scholar, and preacher, married the young widow of a close friend, and then, under Wilhelm von Humboldt, joined in the work of creating the University of Berlin, where he taught alongside Fichte and Hegel. As a consequence of this inner and outer tumult, he lived henceforth no less fully and sincerely in his many friendships, but the direction of his life was now unmistakably committed. He identified his fate with that of the great institutions on which the culture of the individual and the moral consciousness of the nation depend, the university and the church.

The thinking of Schleiermacher discovered the means of expressing its basic patterns in these times. While in his parish, he had written and published *Grundlinien einer Kritik der bisherigen Sittenlehre,* which was succeeded by his lectures on philosophical ethics at Halle and Berlin. *Die Weihnachtsfeier* (*The Christmas Eve*) (1805), his last effort to communicate through dramatic literary form, was a dialogue among close friends gathered on Christmas eve, concerning the significance of Christmas as a vehicle of the determining influence of the Redeemer on human nature. The dialogue anticipated the critical work of David Friedrich Strauss in its basic principles and briefly stated the interpretation of Jesus Christ and of the church upon which *The Christian Faith* itself was later premised. *Brief Outline of the Study of Theology* (1811) foreshadows the systematic articulation of the theological sciences in which *The Christian Faith* stands as the "dogmatic" element. Schleiermacher lectured as well on hermeneutics, history of philosophy, philosophy, ethics, political theory, psychology, church history, the New Testament, life of Jesus, Christian ethics and practical theology. Throughout his life in Berlin he preached regularly and nine volumes of his sermons are included in his collected works. Very early in his career he explained to his uncle, Stubenrauch, that he spoke from the pulpit with the assumption that the Christian community already existed before him and that he was addressing not unfaith but faith in need of instruction and nourishment. As a consequence, his sermons are marked by a directness and warmth, together with simplicity, that endow them with freshness even today. In addition to these activities, he also engaged energetically in the life and proceedings of the Prussian Academy of the Sciences, making considerable contributions to the history of classical philosophy and hermeneutics. All this while, however, Schleiermacher's inner being was deeply agitated by the political fortunes of Germany, and Prussia in particular. Ever since Napoleon's invasion of German territory, he was convinced that the fortunes of Protestantism and Prussia were intertwined and threatened alike by French imperialism. From his pulpits in Halle and Berlin, he delivered outspoken sermons that helped to create the rising national and liberal consciousness of Prussia and worked in other ways to encourage war with France and the restoration of German freedom. He was, however, by no means a simple nationalist but belonged to that group of men led by Baron von Stein who advocated a fundamental social and constitutional reform of Prussia and the institution of a system of national representation to supersede the organization by class and estates under an absolutist monarchy. These activities led to his suffering a period of official disgrace, along with many other leaders, after the political reaction settled down in 1819. Schleiermacher's role in church affairs, played from his position of prominence in The Trinity Church of Berlin, displayed the same liberal spirit. The two foci of his efforts in this quarter were the reform of the organization of the church on a basis of greater self-determination and the union of the Lutheran and Reformed Churches in Prussia. For the former end he was commissioned to draw up a constitution and did not hesitate to publish critcisms of the king's attempt to impose a uniform liturgy on the Prussian church; in connection with the latter, he shared in bringing the two communions together and entered the polemical lists against the orthodox Lutherans who felt that Luther's historic refusal to recognize the validity of the Reformed doctrine of the Lord's Supper was being compromised.

While the severe organization and execution of *The Christian Faith* wholly exclude every hint of the author's personal history, the book nevertheless obviously presents itself as the work of a mind seasoned in many another human science besides theology. Schleiermacher thought and wrote as a cosmopolitan, and the sharp, critical ability that he early acquired with his study of philosophy and historical criticism is everywhere evident. This cosmopolitanism and logical insight prevented him from entertaining as a Christian churchman ideas or beliefs he could not accept as a university professor. Indeed, the persistent tendency in Western Christianity to develop two different faiths, one for the intelligentsia and the other for the masses, was repugnant to the entirety of Schleiermacher's being, and *The Christian Faith* is his statement to the public of his time of the faith of the church in a fashion that requires neither particular scientific and philosophical presuppositions nor a renunciation of criticism and openmindedness. This intention of speaking precisely yet freely about the heart of the Christian religion in modern times is reflected at almost every level of the work.

The careful pains the author takes throughout to avoid every vestige of scholasticsm with its fine-spun distinctions concerning the properties of the Godhead is one example, for Schleiermacher was convinced that faith could no longer bear the burden of the speculative pretensions of the old Protestant orthodoxy. The new critical philosophy had made that way impossible. For similar reasons, and also because he foresaw the enormous authority that the natural sciences would shortly exercise, he rejected the nature/supernature schematism upon which Christian thought had rested since the middle ages. This natural/supernatural dichotomy could only lead to religious ruin, as the natural sciences encroached upon the old domain of theology. In the place of these orthodox supports for the Christian world view, Schleiermacher sought to substitute an analysis of piety and faith that disclosed religion as a mode of personal existence, a style of life, within which true self-consciousness evolves. The religous consciousness is the seed of all self-consciousness and sense of personal identity, and the specifically Christian religious consciousness does not prove itself by the relative success with which it vanquishes competing metaphysical systems or sciences based on the method of empirical study and criticism. Rather Christianity proves itself as it endows the individual with the confidence and freedom to play his own personal part in the divine economy of history.

This is the import of the famous formulae, *piety is a modification of feeling*, and, again, *the common element in all piety is a feeling of absolute dependence*, introduced in § 3 and § 4 of *The Christian Faith* (2nd edition). Hence, when Schleiermacher settled upon them, he was declaring the emancipation of theology (and piety) from the speculative philosophy of his own day and, by extension, from the philosophy of every other. To be sure, the author of *The*

Christian Faith was quite innocent of the ambition to isolate theological reflection from all contact with its sister disciplines and to recast it in the form of a purely esoteric science. (As already suggested, he regarded philosophizing as the natural business of the mind, just as he believed religion to be the affair of feeling, and he insisted that the dialogue between the two should be fostered.) But he was equally convinced that theology did not need to justify itself as a primitive form of philosophy, after the fashion of Hegel. Philosophy provides welcome conceptual tools for the purposes of religious self-criticism and clarity of expression, but religion itself does not arise in and through philosophical or proto-philosophical concepts. If we inspect our own existence in the world of time and space, we discover that our self-consciousness is informed by feelings of being acted upon or being stimulated, and by reciprocal feelings of action initiating in the self. Mutually implicated feelings of determination and freedom thus make up the rhythm of temporal life, but these feelings are clearly relative to each other, and they do not, therefore, exhaust the content of self-consciousness, for the subject of these feelings cannot be wholly identical with the sum of their content. Anterior to these feelings of freedom and dependence there is another species of feeling that is more accurately described as a feeling-form of consciousness and that, in its religious dimension, involves a sense of absolute dependence, a feeling of being placed, of receiving one's existence from a "whence." According to Schleiermacher's analysis, then, the self encounters itself at its deepest level as limited, as finite and as posited. This "whence" that structures the immediate self-consciousness is not the product of any philosophical or theological speculation; rather as it issues in the feeling of absolute dependence, it constitutes the most original expression in self-consciousness of the "immediate existence-relationship" in which selfhood or the person has its being.[1] The word, God, Schleiermacher adds, has no other original meaning than this.

Schleiermacher's point of departure in the analysis of self-consciousness is scarcely unique, since he was the contemporary of German idealism and such men as Fichte. But instead of discovering freedom at the heart of the self and a transcendental ego as the basis of consciousness, he discerned the relationship of dependence. "God-consciousness" is therefore a constitutive element of the total self-consciousness explicated by *The Christian Faith,* yet God and the self are not one; the creatureliness and finitude of the self remain unabrogated. Again, if the God-consciousness is an element of

[1] "Ueber seine Glaubenslehre an Dr. Lücke," *sämmtliche Werke,* I/2, p. 586.

self-consciousness, nevertheless it is not a faculty for the perception of God. Schleiermacher's whole position rests upon the premise that God cannot be thought or intuited as an object, for the relation to God underlies and includes all the specific relations of the self to its world within which the objectifying consciousness arises.

With Augustine and Kierkegaard, Schleiermacher envisioned the human problem, dictated by the constitution of self-hood, to be the problem of appropriating the God relationship and thereby true humanity. He arranged and characterized the various types of religion, fetishism, polytheism and monotheism, as exemplifications of the stages through which the self-consciousness passes on its way to full maturity and clarity. Fetishism and polytheism represent the confused self-consciousness, in which the dependence relationship to God still lies entangled in the relative dependencies of the self upon finite, natural objects and forces. Islam, a form of monotheism, embodies an aesthetic distortion of the self-consciousness or true humanity, insofar as it distinguishes between God and the world but nevertheless subordinates the God-relation to the world-relation by making pleasure the specification of religious joy or eternal happiness. (Schleiermacher showed little understanding of Judaism and he could make no significant place for it in his thought.) True humanity emerges only where the God-consciousness so informs the total self-consciousness that all particular relations to the world or in the world, whether they express free action or passive determination, pleasure or pain, are taken up into the God-consciousness without being annulled and are transformed into occasions for the further expression of and enjoyment of the self's utter dependence on its creator.

Without doubt, this account of feeling as the locus of religion is the best known of the many paragraphs that make up *The Christian Faith*. However, when examined closely, Schleiermacher's analysis of the phenomenon can be seen to be more suggestive than exact and exhaustive, and it is evident that the direction in which he was moving has only latterly been more thoroughly investigated, and that largely in phenomenological philosophy rather than in theological discussion, particularly in the recent examinations of the significance of human moods (*Stimmungen*), a term that Schleiermacher himself used on occasion as equivalent to feeling.

Nevertheless, it is not the concept of religious feeling alone that endows this work with its significance, but equally important to the understanding of the whole is the position that the figure of Jesus Christ occupies. In actuality, the direction of the argument of *The Christian Faith* evolves out of its Christology rather than out of its concept of feeling, or, more accurately perhaps, the concept of feeling receives its orientation from the doctrine of the person of Christ, and if the former element of the book reminds the reader of Schleiermacher the apologist speaking to the sophisticated despisers of religion and Christianity, in the treatment of Jesus Christ the Schleiermacher who preached regularly throughout a lifetime is also clearly reflected.

It would be too much to suggest that Schleiermacher was a Christo-centric thinker, at least in the sense that the doctrine about the person of Christ is the material center of his theology, from which everything else follows with an irresistible cogency. The "Christo-centrism" we find here is of another sort, for in *The Christian Faith,* Jesus of Nazareth is treated not as the object of faith, but as the mediator of faith. He is the reference point, the polestar, by which human nature finds its proper place with respect to God and the world. And, again, he is the sun from whom life is received; he is the very presupposition of life in faith. Everything in the Christian religious self-consciousness, Schleiermacher explains in § 11, is related to the redemption accomplished by Jesus of Nazareth. The terms, redemption and redeemer, are really not the most apt for Schleiermacher's view of Christ, and in the 89th paragraph of *The Christian Faith* he substitutes for the concept of redemption that of completion of the creation, so that, in effect, Jesus Christ becomes here the new man, the true man, the embodiment of humanity through whom a new form of self-consciousness and mode of existence is implanted in the world, and from whom, therefore, a new community arises, the Church. Schleiermacher's Christology draws most heavily upon the gospel of John and those elements in Paul assimilable to the Johanine theology. Quite literally for Schleiermacher, the Christian man is the one who has "the mind of Christ," that is to say, who receives his truly human self-consciousness at the hands of the community that has burgeoned forth in history out of the new life sown in Jesus of Nazareth by the eternal decree of God.

There are few works in Protestant theology that require as close attention as *The Christian Faith,* and correspondingly few since Calvin's *Institutes of the Christian Religion* that are as rewarding. Nevertheless, a number of difficulties inevitably arise, even for the most sympathetic reader. Perhaps that which one misses most of all in Schleiermacher is the spiritual astringency of his theological mentors, Augustine and Calvin, or of his late contemporary, Kierkegaard. This absence of any ascetic tendency, even the "intra-mundane asceticism" of Calvin, may well contribute to the disenchantment of contemporary theologians with this first of modern Protestants. Schleiermacher does not evince the slightest interest in weaning the religious consciousness away from its attachment to the world. This does not imply that Schleiermacher was blind to the leavening, criticising, prophetic office of the church in society, for he himself was involved in many efforts at reform, both political and ecclesiastical. Nevertheless, he prosecuted his theology with far too monolithic a conception of the self-consciousness that was so important to his thought as a whole. Schleiermacher could recognize development in human life, but not revolution, discontinuity and paradox. Therefore, the labyrinthine complexity of the self's relations to God and world, and the infinite opportunities therein for self-deception and concupiscence were also concealed to him. Dostoevsky would have been an alien spirit to Schleiermacher, and his view of human corruption is accordingly superficial and brittle. One could also hope for a more thorough exploration and interpretation of the upper side of the human religious self-consciousness, namely of joy and faith. But Schleiermacher never carried out the task here that his basic position so well equipped him to undertake, and he has yet to acquire an heir who fulfills this deficiency. Other, more familiar characteristics also disturb most readers of the book. The resolute refusal to speak of God in personal terms is the most serious and is actually not consonant at all with Schleiermacher's over-riding concern for human individuality and self-hood. He is, in this respect, a child of his idealistic times. Nevertheless, whoever applies himself to *The Christian Faith* enters into dialogue with the mind that still remains the master of modern theologians.

Cambridge, Massachusetts
April, 1963

EDITORS' PREFACE

THIS translation of Schleiermacher's chief dogmatic work was projected some years ago by a group of persons interested in the study of nineteenth-century theology, and anxious that one exceptionally influential source should be made accessible to English readers. Since the war, as everyone knows, the costs of publication have been high. It therefore was resolved in 1924 to send out an appeal for financial aid to Theological Colleges and Seminaries throughout the English-speaking world. To this appeal a response came so prompt and generous that the way for action opened up, and incidentally the urgency of the demand for a translation was made clearer than ever. A special debt of gratitude for timely assistance is due to the Hibbert Trustees and to a number of friends associated with Hartford Seminary, Connecticut.

In the opinion of competent thinkers the *Christian Faith* of Schleiermacher is, with the exception of Calvin's *Institutes*, the most important work covering the whole field of doctrine to which Protestant theology can point. To say this is not necessarily to adopt either his fundamental principles or the detailed conclusions to which these principles have guided him. On all such matters a nearly unbroken controversy has long prevailed. Indeed, at the moment a formidable attack is being delivered upon his main positions by a new and active school of thought in Germany. But, whether for acceptance or rejection, it is necessary for serious students to know what Schleiermacher has to say. Books devoted to the interpretation and criticism of his views have been not merely numerous but of unusually good quality. Surprise may not unnaturally be felt that during the century which has elapsed since the German original was issued, no attempt has been made to render it in English. For this delay, doubtless, good reasons could be assigned. But it was all the more desirable, in view of the growing sense of united purpose among Christian thinkers everywhere, that no more time should be lost before making Schleiermacher's great treatise available for a wider circle.

The translation has been executed by various hands. Paragraphs 1–31 were translated by the Rev. D. M. Baillie, M.A., of Cupar; 32–61 by the Rev. Professor W. R. Matthews, D.D., of King's College, London, and Miss Edith Sandbach-Marshall, M.A., B.D.; 62–85 by the Rev. Professor A. B. Macaulay, D.D., of the United Free Church College, Glasgow, and the late Rev. Alexander Grieve, Ph.D., of that city; 86–105 by the Rev. Professor J. Y. Campbell, M.A., of the Divinity School, Yale University; 106–125 by the Rev. R. W. Stewart, B.D., of Cambuslang; and 126–172 by the Rev. Professor H. R. Mackintosh, D.D., of New College, Edinburgh, who also has exercised a general supervision over the work as a whole. Dr. Grieve had promised to act as joint-editor, and the book would have gained much from his scholarly and unselfish care; but his too early death in 1927 broke off the plan. His place was taken by the Rev. J. S. Stewart, B.D., of Aberdeen, who assumed a full share in preparing the MS. for press and has collaborated in reading the whole proof.

The Editors wish to express their cordial thanks to the Publishers for the courteous and unfailing help they have given in the production of the book.

AUTHOR'S PREFACE TO THE SECOND EDITION

THERE lies before me, at this moment, the Preface with which I accompanied this work on its first appearance nine years ago. And just because I do not intend to reprint it, I dwell with pleasure on the wish expressed at its conclusion—namely, that, if possible by its own contents, but if not, then by the antagonism which its imperfections must excite, the book might contribute to an ever clearer understanding as to the meaning of our Evangelical Faith. That wish, thank God, has not remained unfulfilled; though I cannot quite make out how much of the excitement it has aroused among the theological public, or of the antagonism it has encountered, is to be set down to the truth it contains, and how much to its imperfections. This point facts will decide, as the controversy, now so vigorous, goes on its way. May this controversy keep its proper limits; and may no one suppose that acts of violence, even if perpetrated within the Church itself, are the fire which will most surely declare who has built with stubble, and who with precious stones. The issue of conflicts so alien in character can never guarantee the goodness of a cause.

My procedure in this new edition, in essentials, I have already explained elsewhere.[1] None the less, many readers may possibly find the difference between the two editions, even apart from the Introduction, greater than they had expected. Yet however great it may be, no leading proposition has been omitted, and none has had its specific content modified. With all my efforts, I have not on the whole succeeded in attaining greater brevity. Success, indeed, was hardly possible, for experience has shown that explanations themselves stood much in need of explanation. Still I did the best I could, and my hope is that many points have been put, if not with greater brevity, at least with greater clearness, and that misapprehensions have been eased or avoided. This chiefly has strengthened my confidence that the time is not far off when

[1] Cf. *Dr. Schleiermacher's Sendschreiben über seine Glaubenslehre an Dr. Lücke.*

it will no longer be necessary to write with fulness on topics many of which either are by now finally antiquated or even yet are misunderstood. When that time comes, some later thinker occupying the same standpoint will be able to write a much shorter Dogmatic. That in the future such a Dogmatic will be written, I have no doubt at all; though at the same time I must protest most emphatically against the honour recently done me in some quarters of bringing me forward as the head of a new theological school. I protest against this, because I am without either of the two requisite qualifications. In the first place, I have invented nothing, so far as I remember, except my order of topics and here or there a descriptive phrase; and similarly in my thinking I have never had any other aim than that of communicating my thoughts by way of stimulus, for each to use in his own fashion. Further, it is only in this sense—not as a mine of formulæ by the repetition of which members of a school might recognize each other—that I issue this book for the second and certainly the last time. Even if I am permitted longer life, I should prefer to attempt what would be at least brief outlines treating of other theological disciplines.

In my first edition I assumed too much when I said that my book was the first Dogmatic which had been composed with special reference to the Union of the two Protestant communions—the Lutheran and the Reformed. This honour I now gladly yield to my dear friend, Herr G. K. R. Schwarz, of Heidelberg; merely remarking that it ought to be regarded as a fundamental characteristic of the Union accomplished in these lands that there exists no necessity for any dogmatic adjustment between the two sides, still less for a new Confession; and that accordingly it was specially incumbent upon me, not only to proceed on this assumption, but also to the best of my power to give effect to it as a fixed principle, by a free and conciliatory treatment of the relevant documents.

Finally, I may observe that as the two volumes of the first edition proved so very unequal in size, I have included one part of the former second volume in the first volume of this edition; but this external change has no bearing on the inner structure of the whole work.

BERLIN, *April* 22, 1830.

THE CHRISTIAN FAITH

INTRODUCTION

§ 1. *The purpose of this Introduction is, first, to set forth the conception of Dogmatics which underlies the work itself; and secondly, to prepare the reader for the method and arrangement followed in it.*

1. It can never be superfluous to begin the treatment of any branch of study with a definition of that branch, except when complete agreement on the matter can be confidently taken for granted. And this can only be done when there has never been any controversy as to how the study is to be practised, or when it belongs to a larger scientific whole which is always delimited and articulated in the same way.

As regards the first of these conditions: we can, of course, start from the fact that most Christian churches have made use of Dogmatics in their internal tradition and in their external intercourse with other churches; but what it really is, and what gives propositions of religious and Christian import a dogmatic status—on these questions agreement would be hard to find. As regards the second condition: Dogmatics would indeed by general consent be placed in that province which we designate by the term 'theological sciences.' But one need only compare the most reputed of the encyclopædic surveys of this department to see how variously it is articulated, how differently different writers understand the individual disciplines, relate them to each other, and estimate their value; and this is true in an especial degree of Dogmatics. It would doubtless be a natural thing for me to take as my basis the definition of Dogmatics given in my own *Outline*; [1] but that book is so short and aphoristic that it is not superfluous to come to its aid with some elucidations. The very title of the present work, in which the name 'Dogmatics' is avoided, contains the

[1] *Kurze Darstellung*, § 3. [Eng. trans., *Brief Outline of the Study of Theology*, p. 92.]

elements of a definition, but not with completeness; and, moreover, the component parts of the title are themselves not beyond all need of definition. Therefore this part of the Introduction will go its own way independently, and only as the argument gradually unfolds itself will the reader be referred to the relevant passages of the *Brief Outline*. And since the preliminary process of defining a science cannot belong to the science itself, it follows that none of the propositions which will appear in this part can themselves have a dogmatic character.

2. The method and arrangement of a work, when the nature of the subject permits of diversities (and this is the case in a marked degree with Dogmatics, as the facts themselves show), will of course best justify themselves by the result. But the most favourable results can only be obtained if the reader is made acquainted with both method and arrangement at the outset. For that will make it possible for him to view each proposition at once in all its manifold relations. Moreover, the comparison of particular sections with the corresponding sections of similar works which have a different structure may under these conditions become instructive, while they would otherwise be merely confusing.

The greatest diversities in order and method will, of course, be those which follow from the particular way in which Dogmatics is conceived, and which thus disappear when a different conception of Dogmatics is taken as basis. But there are also lesser diversities among which choice may be exercised even by those who start from the same definition of the subject.

CHAPTER I

THE DEFINITION OF DOGMATICS

§ 2. *Since Dogmatics is a theological discipline, and thus pertains solely to the Christian Church, we can only explain what it is when we have become clear as to the conception of the Christian Church.*

NOTE.—Cf. the *Brief Outline*, Introduction, §§ 1, 2, 5, 22, 23; and in the First Part, Introd., §§ 1, 2, 3, 6, 7; First Section, §§ 1, 2. Also Sack's *Apologetik*, Introd., §§ 1–5.

1. The expression 'theological discipline' is here taken in the sense which is explicated in the first of the above-mentioned passages. From this it follows that the present work entirely disclaims the task of establishing on a foundation of general principles a Doctrine of God, or an Anthropology or Eschatology either, which should be used in the Christian Church though it did not really originate there, or which should prove the propositions of the Christian Faith to be consonant with reason. For what can be said on these subjects by the human reason in itself cannot have any closer relation to the Christian Church than it has to every other society of faith or of life.

2. Granted, then, that we must begin with a conception of the Christian Church, in order to define in accordance therewith what Dogmatics should be and should do within that Church: this conception itself can properly be reached only through the conception of 'Church' in general, together with a proper comprehension of the peculiarity of the Christian Church. Now the general concept of 'Church,' if there really is to be such a concept, must be derived principally from Ethics, since in every case the 'Church' is a society which originates only through free human action and which can only through such continue to exist. The peculiarity of the Christian Church can neither be comprehended and deduced by purely scientific methods nor be grasped by mere empirical methods.[1] For no science can by means of mere ideas reach and elicit what is individual, but must always stop short with what is

[1] Cf. *Brief Outline*, Introd., § 22; *Phil. Theol.*, § 1.

general. Just as all so-called *a priori* constructions in the realm of history come to grief over the task of showing that what has been in such-and-such wise deduced from above is actually identical with the historically given—so is it undeniably here also. And the purely empirical method, on the other hand, has neither standard nor formula for distinguishing the essential and permanent from the changeable and contingent. But if Ethics establishes the concept of the 'Church,' it can, of course, also separate, in that which forms the basis of these societies, the permanently identical from the changeable elements, and thus by dividing up the whole realm it can determine the places at which the individual forms could be placed as soon as they put in an appearance historically. And the task of thus exhibiting in a conceptually exhaustive way, according to their affinities and gradations, the totality of all those 'Churches' which are distinguished from each other by peculiar differences of basis—this task would be the business of a special branch of historical science, which should be exclusively designated Philosophy of Religion; just as, perhaps, the name Philosophy of Right would best be reserved for an analogous critical study which, as bearing on the general conception of the State as developed in Ethics, would have to do the same thing for the different individual forms of civic organization. The performance of this task of the Philosophy of Religion has, of course, been attempted in a variety of ways; but these attempts do not rest upon a sufficiently universal scientific method, nor do they sufficiently maintain the balance between the historical and the speculative, for us to be able to appeal to them in our theological studies as admittedly satisfactory. To begin with, these results of the Philosophy of Religion would have to be accepted by Apologetics, which, starting from that point, would lay down as foundation a description of the peculiar essence of Christianity and its relation to other 'Churches.' If, however, it were duly recognized that Apologetics is a theological discipline which needs to be refashioned for these present times, it would not be advisable to defer its appearance until the arrival of a satisfactory exposition of the Philosophy of Religion. Rather would Apologetics have to strike out in the interval upon an abbreviated course of its own. It would then begin at the same point as the Philosophy of Religion, and take the same road, but would leave aside, without working it out, all that does not directly contribute to the purpose of ascertaining the nature of Christianity. But now, since this discipline of Apologetics is only just beginning to come to life again, the following exposition has to perform this task for itself.

3. Thus this first part of our Introduction has only to collate and apply borrowed propositions, *i.e.* propositions which belong to other scientific studies, in this case to Ethics, Philosophy of Religion, and Apologetics. Of course, the results of an investigation which is put together out of such component parts cannot lay claim to any general recognition, except when that form of Ethics and of the Philosophy of Religion which underlies the investigation is likewise recognized. From this it is clear that even here at the very beginning there is plenty of opportunity for very diverse definitions and conceptions of Dogmatics, each of which can only regard itself as preparatory for a future one when the scientific studies of which it has to take account will be more firmly established, while, nevertheless, Christianity itself remains entirely the same.

Postscript 1.—In this connexion it is by no means intended to assert that these propositions must, in the independent treatment of the sciences to which they belong, occur in the same form in which they are here set forth. That is in itself improbable, since in this work we have before us none of the matter which would in those sciences lead up to the propositions.

Postscript 2.—By Ethics is here understood that speculative presentation of Reason, in the whole range of its activity, which runs parallel to natural science. By Philosophy of Religion is understood a critical presentation of the different existing forms of religious communion, as constituting, when taken collectively, the complete phenomenon of piety in human nature. The expression Apologetics is explained in the *Brief Outline*, § 39.

I. The Conception of the Church: Propositions borrowed from Ethics.

§ 3. *The piety which forms the basis of all ecclesiastical communions is, considered purely in itself, neither a Knowing nor a Doing, but a modification of Feeling, or of immediate self-consciousness.*

Note.—Cf. the *Speeches on Religion* (Eng. trans.), pp. 28 ff.

1. That a Church is nothing but a communion or association relating to religion or piety, is beyond all doubt for us Evangelical (Protestant) Christians, since we regard it as equivalent to degeneration in a Church when it begins to occupy itself with other matters as well, whether the affairs of science or of outward organization;

just as we also always oppose any attempt on the part of the leaders of State or of science, as such, to order the affairs of religion. But, at the same time, we have no desire to keep the leaders of science from scrutinizing and passing judgment from their own point of view upon both piety itself and the communion relating to it, and determining their proper place in the total field of human life; since piety and Church, like other things, are material for scientific knowledge. Indeed, we ourselves are here entering upon such a scrutiny. And, similarly, we would not keep the leaders of State from fixing the outward relations of the religious communions according to the principles of civil organization—which, however, by no means implies that the religious communion is a product of the State or a component part of it.

However, not only we, but even those Churches which are not so clear about keeping apart Church and State, or ecclesiastical and scientific association, must assent to what we have laid down. For they cannot assign to the Church more than an indirect influence upon these other associations; and it is only the maintenance, regulation, and advancement of piety which they can regard as the essential business of the Church.

2. When Feeling and Self-consciousness are here put side by side as equivalent, it is by no means intended to introduce generally a manner of speech in which the two expressions would be simply synonymous. The term 'feeling' has in the language of common life been long current in this religious connexion; but for scientific usage it needs to be more precisely defined; and it is to do this that the other word is added. So that if anyone takes the word 'feeling' in a sense so wide as to include unconscious states, he will by the other word be reminded that such is not the usage we are here maintaining. Again, to the term 'self-consciousness' is added the determining epithet 'immediate,' lest anyone should think of a kind of self-consciousness which is not feeling at all; as, *e.g.*, when the name of self-consciousness is given to that consciousness of self which is more like an objective consciousness, being a representation of oneself, and thus mediated by self-contemplation. Even when such a representation of ourselves, as we exist in a given portion of time, in thinking, *e.g.*, or in willing, moves quite close to, or even interpenetrates, the individual moments of the mental state, this kind of self-consciousness does appear simply as an *accompaniment* of the state itself. But the real immediate self-consciousness, which is not representation but in the proper sense

feeling, is by no means always simply an accompaniment. It may rather be presumed that in this respect everyone has a twofold experience. In the first place, it is everybody's experience that there are moments in which all thinking and willing retreat behind a self-consciousness of one form or another ; but, in the second place, that at times this same form of self-consciousness persists unaltered during a series of diverse acts of thinking and willing, taking up no relation to these, and thus not being in the proper sense even an accompaniment of them. Thus joy and sorrow—those mental phases which are always so important in the realm of religion—are genuine states of feeling, in the proper sense explained above ; whereas self-approval and self-reproach, apart from their subsequently passing into joy and sorrow, belong in themselves rather to the objective consciousness of self, as results of an analytic contemplation. Nowhere, perhaps, do the two forms stand nearer to each other than here, but just for that reason this comparison puts the difference in the clearest light.

NOTE.—Steffen's account of feeling is closely akin to mine, and the passage from it to mine is easy (*Falsche Theologie*, pp. 99, 100). 'The immediate presence of whole undivided personal existence, etc.' On the other hand, the account given by Baumgarten-Crusius (*Einleitung in das Studium der Dogmatik*, p. 56), apart from its antithesis between feeling and self-consciousness, (*a*) does not comprehend the whole, but only the higher regions, of feeling, and (*b*) seems to transfer feeling into the realm of the objective consciousness by using the word 'perception' (*Wahrnehmung*).

3. Our proposition seems to assume that in addition to Knowing, Doing, and Feeling, there is no fourth. This is not done, however, in the sense which would be required for an apagogic proof ; but those other two are placed alongside of Feeling simply in order that, with the exposition of our own view, we may at the same time take up and discuss those divergent views which are actually in existence. So that we might leave the question entirely aside whether there is a fourth such element in the soul, but for two reasons : namely, in the first place, that it is our duty to convince ourselves as to whether there is still another region to which piety might be assigned ; and, in the second place, that we must set ourselves to grasp clearly the relation which subsists between Christian piety in itself, on the one hand, and both Christian belief (so far as it can be brought into the form of knowledge) and Christian action, on the other. Now, if the relation of the three elements above-mentioned were anywhere set forth in a universally recognized way, we could simply appeal to that. But, as things are, we must

in this place say what is necessary on the subject ; though this is to be regarded as simply borrowed from Psychology, and it should be well noted that the truth of the matter (namely, that piety is feeling) remains entirely independent of the correctness of the following discussion. Life, then, is to be conceived as an alternation between an abiding-in-self (*Insichbleiben*) and a passing-beyond-self (*Aussichheraustreten*) on the part of the subject. The two forms of consciousness (Knowing and Feeling) constitute the abiding-in-self, while Doing proper is the passing-beyond-self. Thus far, then, Knowing and Feeling stand together in antithesis to Doing. But while Knowing, in the sense of possessing knowledge, is an abiding-in-self on the part of the subject, nevertheless as the act of knowing, it only becomes real by a passing-beyond-self of the subject, and in this sense it is a Doing. As regards Feeling, on the other hand, it is not only in its duration as a result of stimulation that it is an abiding-in-self : even as the process of being stimulated, it is not effected by the subject, but simply takes place in the subject, and thus, since it belongs altogether to the realm of receptivity, it is entirely an abiding-in-self ; and in this sense it stands alone in antithesis to the other two—Knowing and Doing.

As regards the question whether there is a fourth to these three, Feeling, Knowing, and Doing ; or a third to these two, abiding-in-self and passing-beyond-self : the unity of these is indeed not one of the two or the three themselves ; but no one can place this unity alongside of these others as a co-ordinate third or fourth entity. The unity rather is the essence of the subject itself, which manifests itself in those severally distinct forms, and is thus, to give it a name which in this particular connexion is permissible, their common foundation. Similarly, on the other hand, every actual moment of life is, in its total content, a complex of these two or these three, though two of them may be present only in vestige or in germ. But a third to those two (one of which is again divided into two) will scarcely be found.

4. But now (these three, Feeling, Knowing, and Doing being granted) while we here set forth once more the oft-asserted view that, of the three, Feeling is the one to which piety belongs, it is not in any wise meant, as indeed the above discussion shows, that piety is excluded from all connexion with Knowing and Doing. For, indeed, it is the case in general that the immediate self-consciousuess is always the mediating link in the transition between moments in which Knowing predominates and those in which Doing pre-

dominates, so that a different Doing may proceed from the same Knowing in different people according as a different determination of self-consciousness enters in. And thus it will fall to piety to stimulate Knowing and Doing, and every moment in which piety has a predominant place will contain within itself one or both of these in germ. But just this is the very truth represented by our proposition, and is in no wise an objection to it; for were it otherwise the religious moments could not combine with the others to form a single life, but piety would be something isolated and without any influence upon the other mental functions of our lives. However, in representing this truth, and thus securing to piety its own peculiar province in its connexion with all other provinces, our proposition is opposing the assertions from other quarters that piety is a Knowing, or a Doing, or both, or a state made up of Feeling, Knowing, and Doing; and in this polemical connexion our proposition must now be still more closely considered.

If, then, piety did consist in Knowing, it would have to be, above all, that knowledge, in its entirety or in its essence, which is here set up as the content of Dogmatics (*Glaubenslehre*): otherwise it must be a complete mistake for us here to investigate the nature of piety in the interests of our study of Dogmatics. But if piety *is* that knowledge, then the amount of such knowledge in a man must be the measure of his piety. For anything which, in its rise and fall, is not the measure of the perfection of a given object cannot constitute the essence of that object. Accordingly, on the hypothesis in question, the most perfect master of Christian Dogmatics would always be likewise the most pious Christian. And no one will admit this to be the case, even if we premise that the most perfect master is only he who keeps most to what is essential and does not forget it in accessories and side-issues; but all will agree rather that the same degree of perfection in that knowledge may be accompanied by very different degrees of piety, and the same degree of piety by very different degrees of knowledge. It may, however, be objected that the assertion that piety is a matter of Knowing refers not so much to the content of that knowledge as to the certainty which characterizes its representations; so that the knowledge of doctrines is piety only in virtue of the certainty attached to them, and thus only in virtue of the strength of the conviction, while a possession of the doctrines without conviction is not piety at all. Then the strength of the conviction would be the measure of the piety; and this is undoubtedly what those people have chiefly in mind who so love to paraphrase the word *Faith* as 'fidelity to one's convictions.' But in all other more typical fields of knowledge the only measure of conviction is the clearness and completeness of the thinking itself. Now if it is to be the same with *this* conviction, then we should simply be back at our old point, that he who thinks the religious propositions most clearly and completely, individually and in their connexions, must likewise be the most pious man, If, then, this conclusion is still to be rejected, but the hypothesis is to be retained (namely, that conviction is the measure of piety), the conviction in this case must be of a different kind and must have a different measure. However closely, then, piety may be connected with this conviction, it does not follow that it is connected in the same way with that knowledge. And if, nevertheless, the knowledge which forms Dogmatics has to relate itself to piety, the explanation of this is that while piety is, of course, the object of this knowledge, the knowledge can only be explicated in virtue of a certainty which inheres in the determinations of self-consciousness.

If, on the other hand, piety consists in Doing, it is manifest that the Doing which constitutes it cannot be defined by its content ; for experience teaches that not only the most admirable but also the most abominable, not only the most useful but also the most inane and meaningless things, are done as pious and out of piety. Thus we are thrown back simply upon the form, upon the method and manner in which the thing comes to be done. But this can only be understood from the two *termini*, the underlying motive as the starting-point, and the intended result as the goal. Now no one will pronounce an action more or less pious because of the greater or less degree of completeness with which the intended result is achieved. Suppose we then are thrown back upon the motive. It is manifest that underlying every motive there is a certain determination of self-consciousness, be it pleasure or pain, and that it is by these that one motive can most clearly be distinguished from another. Accordingly an action (a Doing) will be pious in so far as the determination of self-consciousness, the feeling which had become affective and had passed into a motive impulse, is a pious one.

Thus both hypotheses lead to the same point : that there are both a Knowing and a Doing which pertain to piety, but neither of these constitutes the essence of piety : they only pertain to it inasmuch as the stirred-up Feeling sometimes comes to rest in a thinking which fixes it, sometimes discharges itself in an action which expresses it.

Finally, no one will deny that there are states of Feeling, such as penitence, contrition, confidence, and joy in God, which we pronounce pious in themselves, without regard to any Knowing or Doing that proceeds from them, though, of course, we expect both that they will work themselves out in actions which are otherwise obligatory, and that the reflective impulse will turn its attention to them.

5. From what we have now said it is already clear how we must judge the assertion that piety is a state in which Knowing, Feeling, and Doing are combined. Of course we reject it if it means that the Feeling is derived from the Knowing and the Doing from the Feeling. But if no subordination is intended, then the assertion might just as well be the description of any other quite clear and living moment as of a religious one. For though the idea of the goal of an action precedes the action itself, at the same time it continues to accompany the action, and the relation between the two expresses itself simultaneously in the self-consciousness through a greater or less degree of satisfaction and assurance ; so that even here all three elements are combined in the total content of the state. A similar situation exists in the case of Knowing. For the thinking activity, as a successfully accomplished operation, expresses itself in the self-consciousness as a confident certainty. But simultaneously it becomes also an endeavour to connect the apprehended truth with other truths or to seek out cases for its application, and thus there is always present simultaneously the commencement of a Doing, which develops fully when the opportunity offers ; and so here also we find Knowing, Feeling, and Doing all together in the total state. But now, just as the first-described state remains, notwithstanding, essentially a Doing, and the second a Knowing, so piety in its diverse expressions remains essentially a state of Feeling. This state is subsequently caught up into the region of thinking, but only in so far as each religious man is at the same time inclined towards thinking and exercised therein ; and only in the same way and according to the same measure does this inner piety emerge in living movement and representative action. It also follows from this account of the matter that Feeling is not to be thought of as something either confused or inactive ; since, on the one hand, it is strongest in our most vivid moments, and either directly or indirectly lies at the

root of every expression of our wills, and, on the other hand, it can be grasped by thought and conceived of in its own nature.

But suppose there are other people who would exclude Feeling altogether from our field, and therefore describe piety simply as a Knowledge which begets actions or as a Doing which proceeds from a Knowing: these people not only would have to settle first among themselves whether piety is a Knowing or a Doing, but would also have to show us how a Doing can arise from a Knowing except as mediated by a determination of self-consciousness. And if they have eventually to admit this point, then they will also be convinced by the above discussion that if such a complex does bear the character of piety, nevertheless the element of Knowing in it has not in itself got the length of being piety, and the element of Doing is in itself no longer piety, but the piety is just the determination of self-consciousness which comes in between the two. But that relationship can always hold in the reverse order also: the Doing has not got the length of being piety in those cases in which a determinate self-consciousness only results from an accomplished action; and the Knowing is in itself no longer piety when it has no other content than that determination of self-consciousness caught up into thought.

§ 4. *The common element in all howsoever diverse expressions of piety, by which these are conjointly distinguished from all other feelings, or, in other words, the self-identical essence of piety, is this: the consciousness of being absolutely dependent, or, which is the same thing, of being in relation with God.*

Note.—For the word *schlechthinig* [translated 'absolute'], which occurs frequently in the following exposition, I am indebted to Professor Delbrück. I was unwilling to venture upon its use, and I am not aware that it has occurred anywhere else. But now that he has given it me, I find it very convenient to follow his lead in using it.

1. In any actual state of consciousness, no matter whether it merely accompanies a thought or action or occupies a moment for itself, we are never simply conscious of our Selves in their unchanging identity, but are always at the same time conscious of a changing determination of them. The Ego in itself can be represented objectively; but every consciousness of self is at the same time the consciousness of a variable state of being. But in this distinction of the latter from the former, it is implied that the variable does not proceed purely from the self-identical, for in

that case it could not be distinguished from it. Thus in every self-consciousness there are two elements, which we might call respectively a self-caused element (*ein Sichselbstsetzen*) and a non-self-caused element (*ein Sichselbstnichtsogesetzthaben*) ; or a Being and a Having-by-some-means-come-to-be (*ein Sein und ein Irgendwiegewordensein*). The latter of these presupposes for every self-consciousness another factor besides the Ego, a factor which is the source of the particular determination, and without which the self-consciousness would not be precisely what it is. But this other is not objectively presented in the immediate self-consciousness with which alone we are here concerned. For though, of course, the double constitution of self-consciousness causes us always to look objectively for an other to which we can trace the origin of our particular state, yet this search is a separate act with which we are not at present concerned. In self-consciousness there are only two elements : the one expresses the existence of the subject for itself, the other its co-existence with an other.

Now to these two elements, as they exist together in the temporal self-consciousness, correspond in the subject its *Receptivity* and its (spontaneous) *Activity*. If we could think away the co-existence with an other, but otherwise think ourselves as we are, then a self-consciousness which predominantly expressed an affective condition of receptivity would be impossible, and any self-consciousness could then express only activity—an activity, however, which, not being directed to any object, would be merely an urge outwards, an indefinite 'agility' without form or colour. But as we never do exist except along with an other, so even in every outward-tending self-consciousness the element of receptivity, in some way or other affected, is the primary one ; and even the self-consciousness which accompanies an action (acts of knowing included), while it predominantly expresses spontaneous movement and activity, is always related (though the relation is often a quite indefinite one) to a prior moment of affective receptivity, through which the original 'agility' received its direction. To these propositions assent can be unconditionally demanded ; and no one will deny them who is capable of a little introspection and can find interest in the real subject of our present inquiries.

2. The common element in all those determinations of self-consciousness which predominantly express a receptivity affected from some outside quarter is the *feeling of Dependence*. On the other hand, the common element in all those determinations which

predominantly express spontaneous movement and activity is the *feeling of Freedom.* The former is the case not only because it is by an influence from some other quarter that we have come to such a state, but particularly because we *could* not so become except by means of an other. The latter is the case because in these instances an other is determined by us, and without our spontaneous activity could not be so determined. These two definitions may, indeed, seem to be still incomplete, inasmuch as there is also a mobility of the subject which is not connected with an other at all, but which seems to be subject to the same antithesis as that just explained. But when we become such-and-such from within outwards, for ourselves, without any other being involved, that is the simple situation of the temporal development of a being which remains essentially self-identical, and it is only very improperly that this can be referred to the concept 'Freedom.' And when we cannot ourselves, from within outwards, become such-and-such, this only indicates the limits which belong to the nature of the subject itself as regards spontaneous activity, and this could only very improperly be called 'Dependence.'

Further, this antithesis must on no account be confused with the antithesis between gloomy or depressing and elevating or joyful feelings, of which we shall speak later. For a feeling of dependence may be elevating, if the 'having-become-such-and-such' which it expresses is complete ; and similarly a feeling of freedom may be dejecting, if the moment of predominating receptivity to which the action can be traced was of a dejecting nature, or again if the manner and method of the activity prove to be a disadvantageous combination.

Let us now think of the feeling of dependence and the feeling of freedom as *one,* in the sense that not only the subject but the corresponding other is the same for both. Then the total self-consciousness made up of both together is one of *Reciprocity* between the subject and the corresponding other. Now let us suppose the totality of all moments of feeling, of both kinds, as one whole : then the corresponding other is also to be supposed as a totality or as one, and then that term 'reciprocity' is the right one for our self-consciousness in general, inasmuch as it expresses our connexion with everything which either appeals to our receptivity or is subjected to our activity. And this is true not only when we particularize this other and ascribe to each of its elements a different degree of relation to the twofold consciousness within us, but also when we think of the total 'outside' as one, and moreover (since it contains other receptivities and activities to which we have a relation) as one together with ourselves, that is, as a *World*. Accordingly our self-consciousness, as a consciousness of our existence in the world or of our co-existence with the world, is a series in which the feeling of freedom and the feeling of dependence are divided. But neither an absolute feeling of dependence, *i.e.* without any feeling of freedom in relation to the co-determinant, nor an absolute feeling of freedom, *i.e.* without any feeling of dependence in relation to the co-determinant, is to be found in this whole realm. If we consider our relations to Nature, or those which exist in human society, there we shall find a large number of objects in regard to which freedom and dependence maintain very much of an equipoise: these constitute the field of equal reciprocity. There are other objects which exercise a far greater influence upon our receptivity than our activity exercises upon them, and also *vice versa*, so that one of the two may diminish until it is imperceptible. But neither of the two members will ever completely disappear. The feeling of dependence predominates in the relation of children to their parents, or of citizens to their fatherland; and yet individuals can, without losing their relationship, exercise upon their fatherland not only a directive influence, but even a counter-influence. And the dependence of children on their parents, which very soon comes to be felt as a gradually diminishing and fading quantity, is never from the start free from the admixture of an element of spontaneous activity towards the parents: just as even in the most absolute autocracy the ruler is not without some slight feeling of dependence. It is the same in the case of Nature: towards all the forces of Nature—even, we may say, towards the heavenly bodies—we ourselves do, in the same sense in which they influence us, exercise a counter-influence, however minute. So that our whole self-consciousness in relation to the World or its individual parts remains enclosed within these limits.

3. There can, accordingly, be for us no such thing as a feeling of absolute freedom. He who asserts that he has such a feeling is either deceiving himself or separating things which essentially belong together. For if the feeling of freedom expresses a forth-going activity, this activity must have an object which has been somehow given to us, and this could not have taken place without an influence of the object upon our receptivity. Therefore in every such case there is involved a feeling of dependence

which goes along with the feeling of freedom, and thus limits it. The contrary could only be possible if the object altogether came into existence through our activity, which is never the case absolutely, but only relatively. But if, on the other hand, the feeling of freedom expresses only an inward movement of activity, not only is every such individual movement bound up with the state of our stimulated receptivity at the moment, but, further, the totality of our free inward movements, considered as a unity, cannot be represented as a feeling of absolute freedom, because our whole existence does not present itself to our consciousness as having proceeded from our own spontaneous activity. Therefore in any temporal existence a feeling of absolute freedom can have no place. As regards the feeling of absolute dependence which, on the other hand, our proposition does postulate: for just the same reason, this feeling cannot in any wise arise from the influence of an object which has in some way to be *given* to us; for upon such an object there would always be a counter-influence, and even a voluntary renunciation of this would always involve a feeling of freedom. Hence a feeling of absolute dependence, strictly speaking, cannot exist in a single moment as such, because such a moment is always determined, as regards its total content, by what is *given*, and thus by objects towards which we have a feeling of freedom. But the self-consciousness which accompanies all our activity, and therefore, since that is never zero, accompanies our whole existence, and negatives absolute freedom, is itself precisely a consciousness of absolute dependence; for it is the consciousness that the whole of our spontaneous activity comes from a source outside of us in just the same sense in which anything towards which we should have a feeling of absolute freedom must have proceeded entirely from ourselves. But without any feeling of freedom a feeling of absolute dependence would not be possible.

4. As regards the identification of absolute dependence with 'relation to God' in our proposition: this is to be understood in the sense that the *Whence* of our receptive and active existence, as implied in this self-consciousness, is to be designated by the word 'God,' and that this is for us the really original signification of that word. In this connexion we have first of all to remind ourselves that, as we have seen in the foregoing discussion, this 'Whence' is not the world, in the sense of the totality of temporal existence, and still less is it any single part of the world. For we have a feeling of freedom (though, indeed, a limited one) in relation

to the world, since we are complementary parts of it, and also since we are continually exercising an influence on its individual parts; and, moreover, there is the possibility of our exercising influence on all its parts; and while this does permit a limited feeling of dependence, it excludes the absolute feeling. In the next place, we have to note that our proposition is intended to oppose the view that this feeling of dependence is itself conditioned by some previous knowledge about God. And this may indeed be the more necessary since many people claim to be in the sure possession of a concept of God, altogether a matter of conception and original, *i.e.* independent of any feeling; and in the strength of this higher self-consciousness, which indeed may come pretty near to being a feeling of absolute freedom, they put far from them, as something almost infra-human, that very feeling which for us is the basic type of all piety. Now our proposition is in no wise intended to dispute the existence of such an original knowledge, but simply to set it aside as something with which, in a system of Christian doctrine, we could never have any concern, because plainly enough it has itself nothing to do directly with piety. If, however, word and idea are always originally one, and the term 'God' therefore presupposes an idea, then we shall simply say that this idea, which is nothing more than the expression of the feeling of absolute dependence, is the most direct reflection upon it and the most original idea with which we are here concerned, and is quite independent of that original knowledge (properly so called), and conditioned only by our feeling of absolute dependence. So that in the first instance God signifies for us simply that which is the co-determinant in this feeling and to which we trace our being in such a state; and any further content of the idea must be evolved out of this fundamental import assigned to it. Now this is just what is principally meant by the formula which says that to feel oneself absolutely dependent and to be conscious of being in relation with God are one and the same thing; and the reason is that absolute dependence is the fundamental relation which must include all others in itself. This last expression includes the God-consciousness in the self-consciousness in such a way that, quite in accordance with the above analysis, the two cannot be separated from each other. The feeling of absolute dependence becomes a clear self-consciousness only as this idea comes simultaneously into being. In this sense it can indeed be said that God is given to us in feeling in an original way; and if we speak of an original revelation of

God to man or in man, the meaning will always be just this, that, along with the absolute dependence which characterizes not only man but all temporal existence, there is given to man also the immediate self-consciousness of it, which becomes a consciousness of God. In whatever measure this actually takes place during the course of a personality through time, in just that measure do we ascribe piety to the individual. On the other hand, any possibility of God being in any way *given* is entirely excluded, because anything that is outwardly given must be given as an object exposed to our counter-influence, however slight this may be. The transference of the idea of God to any perceptible object, unless one is all the time conscious that it is a piece of purely arbitrary symbolism, is always a corruption, whether it be a temporary transference, *i.e.* a theophany, or a constitutive transference, in which God is represented as permanently a particular perceptible existence.

§ 5. *What we have thus described constitutes the highest grade of human self-consciousness; but in its actual occurrence it is never separated from the lower, and through its combination therewith in a single moment it participates in the antithesis of the pleasant and the unpleasant.*

1. The relation between these two forms of self-consciousness, namely, the feeling of absolute dependence and the self-consciousness which, as expressing the connexion with perceptible finite existence, splits up into a partial feeling of dependence and a partial feeling of freedom, will best be seen if we bring in yet a third form. If we go back to the first obscure period of the life of man, we find there, all over, the animal life almost solely predominating, and the spiritual life as yet entirely in the background; and so we must regard the state of his consciousness as closely akin to that of the lower animals. It is true, indeed, that the animal state is to us really entirely strange and unknown. But there is general agreement that, on the one hand, the lower animals have no knowledge, properly so called, nor any full self-consciousness which combines the different moments into a stable unity, and that, on the other hand, they are nevertheless not entirely devoid of consciousness. Now we can hardly do justice to this state of affairs except by postulating a consciousness of such a sort that in it the objective and the introversive, or feeling and perception, are not really distinct from each other, but remain in a state of unresolved

confusion. The consciousness of children obviously approximates to this form, especially before they learn to speak. From that time on, this condition tends more and more to disappear, confining itself to those dreamy moments which form the transition between sleep and waking ; while in our wide-awake hours feeling and perception are clearly distinct from each other, and thus make up the whole wealth of man's sensible life, in the widest sense of the term. In that term we include (speaking simply of the consciousness, and leaving out action proper), on the one hand, the gradual accumulation of perceptions which constitute the whole field of experience in the widest sense of the word, and, on the other hand, all determinations of self-consciousness which develop from our relations to nature and to man, including those which we described above (§ 4, 2) as coming nearest to the feeling of absolute dependence ; so that by the word 'sensible' we understand the social and moral feelings no less than the self-regarding, since they all together have their place in that realm of the particular which is subject to the abovementioned antithesis. The former division [*i.e.* the accumulation of perceptions] which belongs to the objective consciousness, we pass over, as it does not concern us here. But in the whole of the latter class, consisting of feelings which we have designated sensible, the corresponding co-determinant to which we trace the constitution of the present state belongs to the realm of reciprocal action ; so that, whether we are at the moment more conscious of dependence or of freedom, we take up towards it, in a sense, an attitude of equal co-ordination, and indeed set ourselves as individuals (or as comprised within a larger individual, as, *e.g.*, in our patriotic feelings) over against it as another individual. Now it is in this respect that these feelings are most definitely distinguished from the feeling of absolute dependence. For while the latter from its very nature negatives absolute freedom (§ 4, 3), though it does it under the form of self-consciousness, this is not the consciousness of ourselves as individuals of a particular description, but simply of ourselves as individual finite existence in general ; so that we do not set ourselves over against any other individual being, but, on the contrary, all antithesis between one individual and another is in this case done away. Hence there seems to be no objection to our distinguishing three grades of self-consciousness : the confused animal grade, in which the antithesis cannot arise, as the lowest ; the sensible self-consciousness, which rests entirely upon the antithesis, as the middle ; and the feeling of absolute dependence, in which the antithesis again disappears and the subject unites and identifies itself with everything which, in the middle grade, was set over against it, as the highest.

2. If there did exist a feeling of absolute freedom, in it also the above antithesis would be done away. Only, such a subject could never stand in any relation with other similarly constituted subjects, but whatever is given to it must be given as purely susceptible or passive material. And since, for this reason alone, such a feeling is never found in man, the only immediate self-consciousness in man on that grade is the feeling of absolute dependence which we have described. For every moment which is made up of a partial feeling of freedom and a partial feeling of dependence places us in a position of co-ordinate antithesis to a similar other. But now there remains the question, whether there exists any other self-consciousness, not immediate but accompanying some kind of knowledge or action as such, which can be ranked along with that which we have described. Let us then conceive, as the act or state of an individual, a highest kind of knowledge in which all subordinate knowledge is comprised. This, indeed, in its province is likewise elevated above all antithesis. But its province is that of the objective consciousness. However, it will of course be accompanied by an immediate self-consciousness expressive of certainty or conviction. But since this concerns the relation of the subject as knower to the known as object, even this self-consciousness which accompanies the highest knowledge remains in the realm of the antithesis. In the same way, let us conceive a highest kind of action, in the form of a resolve which covers the whole field of our spontaneous activity, so that all subsequent resolves are developed out of it, as individual parts,[1] which were already contained in it. This also in its province stands above all antithesis, and it is likewise accompanied by a self-consciousness. But this also concerns the relation of the subject as agent to that which may be the object of its action, and thus has its place within the antithesis. And since obviously this must be equally true of every self-consciousness which accompanies any particular knowledge or action, it follows that there is no other self-consciousness which is elevated above the antithesis, and that this character belongs exclusively to the feeling of absolute dependence.

3. While the lowest or animal grade of consciousness gradually disappears as the middle grade develops, the highest cannot develop

[1] See *Ueber die Behandlung des Pflichtbegriffs*, 1824, pp. 4–6.

at all so long as the lowest is present ; but, on the other hand, the middle grade must persist undiminished even when the highest has reached its perfect development. The highest self-consciousness is in no wise dependent on outwardly given objects which may affect us at one moment and not at another. As a consciousness of absolute dependence it is quite simple, and remains self-identical while all other states are changing. Therefore, in itself it cannot possibly be at one moment thus and at another moment otherwise, nor can it by intermission be present at one moment and absent at another. Either it is not there at all, or, so long as it is there, it is continuously there and always self-identical. Now if it were impossible for it to co-exist with the consciousness of the second grade (as it cannot with that of the third), then either it could never make an appearance in time, but would always remain in the concealment in which it lay during the predominance of the lowest grade, or it must drive out the second and exist alone, and, indeed, in ever-unchanging identity. Now this latter supposition is controverted by all experience, and indeed is manifestly impossible unless our ideation and action are to be entirely stripped of self-consciousness, which would irrevocably destroy the coherence of our existence for our own minds. It is impossible to claim a constancy for the highest self-consciousness, except on the supposition that the sensible self-consciousness is always conjoined with it. Of course, this conjunction cannot be regarded as a fusion of the two : that would be entirely opposed to the conception of both of them which we have established. It means rather a co-existence of the two in the same moment, which, of course, unless the Ego is to be split up, involves a reciprocal relation of the two. It is impossible for anyone to be in some moments exclusively conscious of his relations within the realm of the antithesis, and in other moments of his absolute dependence in itself and in a general way ; for it is as a person determined for this moment in a particular manner within the realm of the antithesis that he is conscious of his absolute dependence. This relatedness of the sensibly determined to the higher self-consciousness in the unity of the moment is the consummating point of the self-consciousness. For to the man who once recognizes what piety is, and appropriates it as a requirement of his being, every moment of a merely sensible self-consciousness is a defective and imperfect state. But even if the feeling of absolute dependence in general were the entire content of a moment of self-consciousness, this also would be an imperfect state ; for it would lack the definiteness and clearness which spring from its being related to the determination of the sensible self-consciousness. This consummation, however, since it consists in the two elements being related to each other, may be described in two different ways. Described from below it is as follows: when the sensible self-consciousness has quite expelled the animal confusion, then there is disclosed a higher tendency over against the antithesis, and the expression of this tendency in the self-consciousness is the feeling of absolute dependence. And the more the subject, in each moment of sensible self-consciousness, with his partial freedom and partial dependence, takes at the same time the attitude of absolute dependence, the more religious is he. Described from above it is as follows: the tendency which we have described, as an original and innate tendency of the human soul, strives from the very beginning to break through into consciousness. But it is unable to do so as long as the antithesis remains dissolved in the animal confusion. Subsequently, however, it asserts itself. And the more it contributes to every moment of sensibly determined self-consciousness without the omission of any, so that the man, while he always feels himself partially free and partially dependent in relation to other finite existence, feels himself at the same time to be also (along with everything towards which he had that former feeling) absolutely dependent—the more religious is he.

4. The sensibly determined self-consciousness splits up of itself, in accordance with its nature, into a series of moments that differ in their content, because our activity exercised upon other beings is a temporal one, and their influence upon us is likewise temporal. The feeling of absolute dependence, on the other hand, being in itself always self-identical, would not evoke a series of thus distinguishable moments; and if it did not enter into relation with such a series in the manner described above, either it could never become an actual consciousness in time at all, or else it must accompany the sensible self-consciousness monotonously without any relation to the manifold rising and falling variations of the latter. But, as a matter of fact, our religious consciousness does not take either of these forms, but conforms to the description we have given above. That is to say: being related as a constituent factor to a given moment of consciousness which consists of a partial feeling of freedom and a partial feeling of dependence, it thereby becomes a particular religious emotion, and being in another moment related to a different datum, it becomes a different religious emotion;

yet so that the essential element, namely, the feeling of absolute dependence, is the same in both, and thus throughout the whole series, and the difference arises simply from the fact that it becomes a different moment when it goes along with a different determination of the sensible self-consciousness. It remains always, however, a moment of the higher power; whereas, where there is no piety at all, the sensible self-consciousness breaks up (as was likewise described) into a series of moments of the lower power, while in the period of animal confusion there does not even take place a definite separation and antithesis of the moments for the subject.

It is the same with the second part of our proposition. That is to say: the sensible self-consciousness splits up also, of itself and from its very nature, into the antithesis of the pleasant and the unpleasant, or of pleasure and pain. This does not mean that the partial feeling of freedom is always pleasure, and the partial feeling of dependence always pain, as seems to be assumed by those who wrongly think that the feeling of absolute dependence has, of its very nature, a depressing effect. For the child can have a feeling of perfect well-being in the consciousness of dependence on its parents, and so also (thank God) can the subject in his relation to the government; and other people, even parents and governments, can feel miserable in the consciousness of their freedom. So that each may equally well be either pleasure or pain, according to whether life is furthered or hindered by it. The higher self-consciousness, on the other hand, bears within it no such antithesis. Its first appearance means, of course, an enhancement of life, if a comparison arises with the isolated sensible self-consciousness. But if, without any such reference, we think of it in its own self-identity, its effect is simply an unchanging identity of life, which excludes any such antithesis. This state we speak of under the name of the Blessedness of the finite being as the highest summit of his perfection. But our religious consciousness, as we actually find it, is not of that character, but is subject to variation, some pious emotions approximating more to joy, and others to sorrow. Thus this antithesis refers simply to the manner in which the two grades of self-consciousness are related to each other in the unity of the moment. And thus it is by no means the case that the pleasant and the unpleasant, which exist in the sensible feeling, impart the same character to the feeling of absolute dependence. On the contrary, we often find, united in one and the same moment (as a clear sign that the two grades are not fused into each other or neutralized by each other so as to become a third) a sorrow of the lower and a joy of the higher self-consciousness ; as, *e.g.*, whenever with a feeling of suffering there is combined a trust in God. But the antithesis attaches to the higher self-consciousness, because it is the nature of the latter to become temporal, to manifest itself in time, by entering into relation with the sensible self-consciousness so as to constitute a moment. That is to say : as the emergence of this higher self-consciousness at all means an enhancement of life, so whenever it emerges *with ease*, to enter into relation with a sensible determination, whether pleasant or unpleasant, this means an easy progress of that higher life, and bears, by comparison, the stamp of joy. And as the disappearance of the higher consciousness, if it could be perceived, would mean a diminution of life, so whenever it emerges *with difficulty*, this approximates to an absence of it, and can only be felt as an inhibition of the higher life.

Now this alternation undeniably forms the feeling-content of every religious life, so that it seemed superfluous to illustrate these formulæ by examples. But we may now go on to ask how this usual course of the religious life is related to that which we have at an earlier point described, if only problematically, as the highest development of it. Suppose that the opposite characters are both continuously being strongly imprinted upon the individual religious emotions, so that both alternately rise to a passionate level : this gives to the religious life an instability which we cannot regard as of the highest worth. But suppose that the difficulties gradually disappear, so that facility of religious emotions becomes a permanent state ; and that gradually the higher grade of feeling comes to preponderate over the lower, so that in the immediate self-consciousness the sensible determination asserts itself rather as an opportunity for the appearance of the feeling of absolute dependence than as containing the antithesis, which is therefore transferred into the realm of mere perception : then this fact, that the antithesis has almost disappeared again from the higher grade of life, indisputably means that the latter has attained its richest content of feeling.

5. From the above it follows directly that (and in what sense) an uninterrupted sequence of religious emotions can be required of us, as indeed Scripture actually requires it ; and it is confirmed every time a religious soul laments over a moment of his life which is quite empty of the consciousness of God (since no one laments the absence of anything which is recognized to be impossible). Of course, it goes without saying in this connexion that the feeling of

absolute dependence, when it unites with a sensibly determined self-consciousness, and thus becomes an emotion, must vary as regards strength. Indeed, there will naturally be moments in which a man is not directly and definitely conscious of such a feeling at all. And yet, indirectly, it can be shown that in these moments the feeling was not dead; as, *e.g.*, when such a moment is followed by another in which the feeling strongly asserts itself, while the second is not felt to be of a different character from the first or a definite departure from it, but to be linked up with it tranquilly as a continuation of its essentially unchanged identity (which is not the case when the preceding moment was one from which the feeling was definitely excluded). Also, of course, the different formations assumed by the sensible self-consciousness in virtue of the highly manifold minglings of the feeling of freedom and the feeling of dependence, differ in the degree in which they evoke or encourage the appearance of the higher self-consciousness; and in the case of those which do it in a lesser degree, a weaker appearance of the higher need not be felt as an inhibition of the higher life. But there is no determination of the immediate sensible self-consciousness which is incompatible with the higher; so that there is no kind of necessity for either of the two ever to be interrupted, except when the confused state of consciousness gains ground, and both retire behind it.

Postscript.—If thus the direct inward expression of the feeling of absolute dependence is the consciousness of God, and that feeling, whenever it attains to a certain clearness, is accompanied by such an expression, but is also combined with, and related to, a sensible self-consciousness: then the God-consciousness which has in this way arisen will, in all its particular formations, carry with it such determinations as belong to the realm of the antithesis in which the sensible self-consciousness moves. And this is the source of all those anthropomorphic elements which are inevitable in this realm in utterances about God, and which form such a cardinal point in the ever-recurring controversy between those who accept that fundamental assumption and those who deny it. For those who rejoice in the possession of an original idea of the Supreme Being derived from some other quarter, but who have no experience of piety, will not tolerate the statement that the expression of that feeling posits the action of the very same thing which is expressed in their original idea. They assert that the God of feeling is a mere fiction, an idol, and they may perhaps even hint that such a fancy is more tenable in the form of Polytheism. And those who will not admit either a conception of God or a feeling which represents Him, base their position on the contention that the representation of God which is put together out of such utterances, in which God appears as human, destroys itself. Meanwhile, religious men know that it is only in speech that they cannot avoid the anthropomorphic: in their immediate consciousness they keep the object separate from its mode of representation, and they endeavour to show their opponents that without this integration of feeling no certainty is possible even for the strongest forms of objective consciousness or of transitive action, and that, to be consistent, they must limit themselves entirely to the lower grade of life.

§ 6. *The religious self-consciousness, like every essential element in human nature, leads necessarily in its development to fellowship or communion; a communion which, on the one hand, is variable and fluid, and, on the other hand, has definite limits,* i.e. *is a Church.*

1. If the feeling of absolute dependence, expressing itself as consciousness of God, is the highest grade of immediate self-consciousness, it is also an essential element of human nature. This cannot be controverted on the ground that there is for every individual man a time when that consciousness does not yet exist. For this is the period when life is incomplete, as may be seen both from the fact that the animal confusion of consciousness has not yet been overcome, and from the fact that other vital functions too are only developing themselves gradually. Nor can it be objected that there are always communities of men in which this feeling has not yet been awakened; for these likewise only exhibit on a large scale that undeveloped state of human nature which betrays itself also in other functions of their lives. Similarly it cannot be argued that the feeling is accidental (non-essential), because even in a highly developed religious environment individuals may be found who do not share it. For these people cannot but testify that the whole matter is not so alien to them but that they have at particular moments been gripped by such a feeling, though they may call it by some name that is not very honouring to themselves. But if anyone can show, either that this feeling has not a higher value than the sensible, or that there is besides it another of equal value—only then can anyone be entitled to regard it as a merely accidental form, which, while it

may perhaps exist for some people in every age, is nevertheless not to be reckoned as part of a complete human nature for everybody.

2. The truth that every essential element of human nature becomes the basis of a fellowship or communion, can only be fully explicated in the context of a scientific theory of morals. Here we can only allude to the essential points of this process, and then ask everybody to accept it as a fact. Fellowship, then, is demanded by the *consciousness of kind* which dwells in every man, and which finds its satisfaction only when he steps forth beyond the limits of his own personality and takes up the facts of other personalities into his own. It is accomplished through the fact that everything inward becomes, at a certain point of its strength or maturity, an outward too, and, as such, perceptible to others. Thus feeling, as a self-contained determination of the mind (which on the other side passes into thought and action, but with that we are not here concerned), will, even *qua* feeling, and purely in virtue of the consciousness of kind, not exist exclusively for itself, but becomes an outward, originally and without any definite aim or pertinence, by means of facial expression, gesture, tones, and (indirectly) words ; and so becomes to other people a revelation of the inward. This bare expression of feeling, which is entirely caused by the inward agitation, and which can be very definitely distinguished from any further and more separate action into which it passes, does indeed at first arouse in other people only an idea of the person's state of mind. But, by reason of the consciousness of kind, this passes into living imitation ; and the more able the percipient is (either for general reasons, or because of the greater liveliness of the expression, or because of closer affinity) to pass into the same state, the more easily will that state be produced by imitation. Everybody must in his own experience be conscious of this process from both its sides, the expressing and the perceiving, and must thus confess that he always finds himself, with the concurrence of his conscience, involved in a multifarious communion of feeling, as a condition quite in conformity with his nature, and therefore that he would have co-operated in the founding of such a communion if it had not been there already.

As regards the feeling of absolute dependence in particular, everyone will know that it was first awakened in him in the same way, by the communicative and stimulative power of expression or utterance.

3. Our assertion that this communion is at first variable and fluid follows from what we have just been saying. For as individuals in general resemble each other in variable degrees, both as regards the strength of their religious emotions and as regards the particular region of sensible self-consciousness with which their God-consciousness most easily unites, each person's religious emotions have more affinity with those of one of his fellows than with those of another, and thus communion of religious feeling comes to him more easily with the former than with the latter. If the difference is great, he feels himself attracted by the one and repelled by the others; yet not repelled directly or absolutely, so that he could not enter into any communion of feeling with them at all; but only in the sense that he is more powerfully attracted to others; and thus he could have communion even with these, in default of the others, or in circumstances which specially drew them together. For there can hardly exist a man in whom another would recognize no religious affection whatever as being in any degree similar to his own, or whom another would know to be quite incapable of either moving or being moved by him. It remains true, however, that the more uninterrupted the communion is to be, *i.e.* the more closely the kindred emotions are to follow each other, and the more easily the emotions are to communicate themselves, so much the smaller must be the number of people who can participate. We may conceive as great an interval as we like between the two extremes, that of the closest and that of the feeblest communion; so that the man who experiences the fewest and feeblest religious emotions can have the closest kind of communion only with those who are equally little susceptible to these emotions, and is not in a position to imitate the utterances of those who derive religious emotion from moments where he himself never finds it. A similar relation holds between the man whose piety is purer, in the sense that in every moment of it he clearly distinguishes the religious content of his self-consciousness from the sensible to which it is related, and the man whose piety is less pure, *i.e.* more confused with the sensible. However, we may conceive the interval between these extremes as being, for each person, filled up with as many intermediate stages as we like; and this is just what constitutes the fluidity of the communion.

4. This is how the interchange of religious consciousness appears when we think of the relation of individual men to each other But if we look at the actual condition of men, we also find

well-established relationships in this fluid, and therefore (strictly speaking) undefined communion or fellowship. In the first place, as soon as human development has advanced to the point of a domestic life, even if not a completely regulated one, every family will establish within itself such a communion of the religious self-consciousness—a communion which, however, has quite definite limits as regards the outside world. For the members of the family are bound together in a peculiar manner by definite congruity and kinship, and, moreover, their religious emotions are associated with the same occasions, so that strangers can only have an accidental and transitory, and therefore a very unequal, share in them.

But we also find families not isolated but standing collectively in distinctly defined combinations, with common language and customs, and with some knowledge or inkling of a closer common origin. And then religious communion becomes marked off among them, partly in the form of predominating similarity in the individual families, and partly by one family, which is particularly open to religious emotions, coming to predominate as the paramountly active one, while the others, being as it were scarcely out of their nonage, display only receptivity (a state of affairs which exists wherever there is a hereditary priesthood). Every such relatively closed religious communion, which forms an ever self-renewing circulation of the religious self-consciousness within certain definite limits, and a propagation of the religious emotions arranged and organized within the same limits, so that there can be some kind of definite understanding as to which individuals belong to it and which do not—this we designate a *Church*.

Postscript.—This will be the best place to come to an understanding, from our own point of view, as to the different senses in which the word *Religion* is customarily used—though indeed, as far as possible, we here confine ourselves to an occasional and cursory employment of the word for the sake of variety.[1] In the first place, then, when people speak of *a particular religion*, this is always with reference to one definite 'Church,' and it means the totality of the religious affections which form the foundation of such a communion and are recognized to be identical in the various members, in its peculiar content as set forth by

[1] [That is to say, Schleiermacher normally uses the word *Frömmigkeit*, which we *usually* translate 'piety,' while we translate the adjective *fromm* sometimes by 'pious' and sometimes by 'religious.'—TRANSL.]

contemplation and reflection upon the religious emotions. Correspondingly, the individual's susceptibility (which admits of different degrees) to the influence of the fellowship or communion, as also his influence upon the latter, and thus his participation in the circulation and propagation of the religious emotions—this is designated *Religiosity* (*Religiosität*). Now if a man, on the analogy of 'Christian Religion' and 'Mohammedan Religion,' begins to speak also of '*Natural Religion*,' he is again abandoning the rule and confusing the use of words, because there is no natural 'Church' and no definite compass within which the elements of natural religion can be sought. If the expression '*Religion in general*' be employed, it again cannot signify such a whole. Nothing can fitly be understood by it but the tendency of the human mind in general to give rise to religious emotions, always considered, however, along with their expression, and thus with the striving for fellowship, *i.e.* the possibility of particular religions (but without regard to the distinction between fluid and defined fellowships). It is only that tendency, the general susceptibility of individual souls to religious emotion, that could be called 'religion in general.' These expressions, however, are seldom clearly distinguished in actual use.

Now, in so far as the constitution of the religious affections of the individual contains more than can be recognized as uniform in the communion, this purely personal element is usually, in regard to its content, called *Subjective Religion*, while the common element is called *Objective Religion*. But this usage becomes in the highest degree inconvenient whenever (as is now the case among ourselves) a large Church splits up into several smaller communions without entirely giving up its unity. For the peculiarities of the smaller Churches would then also be 'subjective religion' in comparison with what was recognized as common to the larger Church, while they would be 'objective' in comparison with the peculiarities of their particular members. Finally, in the religious emotions themselves, a distinction can be made between the inner determination of self-consciousness and the manner of its outward expression, though these are closely connected; and thus the organization of the communicative expressions of piety in a community is usually called *Outward Religion*, while the total content of the religious emotions, as they actually occur in individuals, is called *Inward Religion*.

Now, while these definitions may well be the best, as comprehending the various and very arbitrary usages, we have only to compare the expressions with the explanations given, in order to realize how indeterminate it all is. Therefore it is really better to avoid these designations in scientific usage, especially as the term 'religion,' as applied to Christianity, is quite new in our language.

II. The Diversities of Religious Communions in General: Propositions borrowed from the Philosophy of Religion.

§ 7. *The various religious communions which have appeared in history with clearly defined limits are related to each other in two ways: as different stages of development, and as different kinds.*

1. The religious communion which takes the form of household worship within a single family cannot fitly be regarded as an appearance in the realm of history, because it remains in the obscurity of an inner circle. Moreover, the transition from this to a really historical appearance is often very gradual. The beginning of it is seen in the large style of the patriarchal household, and the persisting association between families of sons and grandsons that live near each other; and it is out of these alone that the two fundamental forms previously mentioned (§ 6, 4) can be developed. In these transitions, if several of them are placed beside each other, both kinds of difference can be found at least in germ.

Now in the first place, as regards the different stages of development: the historical appearance is in itself a higher stage, and stands above the mere isolated household worship, just as the civic condition, even in its most incomplete forms, stands above the formless association of the pre-civic condition. But this difference by no means relates only to the form or the compass of the fellowship itself, but also to the constitution of the underlying religious affections, according as they attain to clearness in conscious antithesis to the movements of the sensible self-consciousness. Now this development depends partly on the whole development of the mental powers, so that for that reason alone many a communion cannot continue longer in its own peculiar mode of existence; as, *e.g.*, many forms of idol-worship, even though they might claim a high degree of mechanical skill, are incompatible with even a moderate scientific and artistic education, and perish when confronted by it. Yet it is also partly true that the development takes its own course ; and there is no contradiction in saying that, in one and the same whole, the piety may develop to its highest consummation, while other mental functions remain far behind.

But all differences are not to be thus regarded as distinct stages or levels. There are communal religions (Greek and Indian polytheism are good cases in point), of which one might well seem to be at the same point in the scale as the other, but which are yet very definitely different from each other. If, then, several such exist which belong to the same stage or level, the most natural course will be to call them different kinds or species. And indisputably it can be shown, even at the lowest stage, that most religious communions which are geographically separated from each other are also divided by inner differences.

2. But of course these two distinctions, into stages of development and into kinds (genera) or species, cannot in this realm, or indeed generally in the realm of history or of so-called moral 'persons,' be maintained so definitely or carried through so surely as in the realm of Nature. For we are not here dealing with invariable forms which always reproduce themselves in the same way. Each individual communion is capable of a greater or lesser development within the character of its kind or genus. Let us, now, consider that in this way, just as the individual may pass from a more imperfect religious communion to a higher one, so a particular communion might, without prejudice to its generic character, develop beyond its original level, and that this may happen equally to all. Then the idea of stages would naturally disappear, for the last phase of the lower and the first of the higher might be continuously connected, and it would then be more correct to say that each genus works itself up by a series of developments from the imperfect to the more perfect. But, on the other hand, we may take the fact that, just as we say an individual becomes in a certain sense a new man by passing to a higher form of religion, so the generic character of a communion must be lost when it rises to a higher level. Then even on any one level, if the inner development is to go on, the generic character would become uncertain and altogether unstable, while the levels or stages would be all the more sharply and definitely distinguished.

This variability, however, does not discredit the reality of our twofold distinction. For every religious communion which appears in history will be related to the others in this twofold way. It will be co-ordinate with some, and subordinate or superior to others; and thus it is distinguished from the former in the one manner and from the latter in the other. And if those who busy themselves most with the history and criticism of religions have given less attention to the task of fitting the different forms into this framework, this may be partly because they confine themselves almost exclusively to the individual, and partly also because it may be difficult in particular cases to lay bare these relationships and properly to distinguish and separate co-ordinates and subordinates. It may here suffice us to have established the twofold distinction in a general way, since our sole concern is to investigate how Christianity is related, in both respects, to other religious communions and forms of faith.

3. Our proposition does not assert, but it does tacitly presuppose the possibility, that there are other forms of piety which are related to Christianity as different forms on the same level of development, and thus so far similar. But this does not contradict the conviction, which we assume every Christian to possess, of the exclusive superiority of Christianity. In the realm of Nature also we distinguish perfect and imperfect animals as different stages of the development of animal life, and again on each of these stages different genera, which thus resemble each other as expressions of the same stage; but this does not mean that one genus of the lower stage may not be nearer to the higher, and thus more perfect, than the others. Similarly, though several kinds of piety belong to the same stage as Christianity, it may yet be more perfect than any of them.

Our proposition excludes only the idea, which indeed is often met with, that the Christian religion (piety) should adopt towards at least most other forms of piety the attitude of the true towards the false. For if the religions belonging to the same stage as Christianity were entirely false, how could they have so much similarity to Christianity as to make that classification requisite? And if the religions which belong to the lower stages contained nothing but error, how would it be possible for a man to pass from them to Christianity? Only the true, and not the false, can be a basis of receptivity for the higher truth of Christianity. The whole delineation which we are here introducing is based rather on the maxim that error never exists in and for itself, but always along with some truth, and that we have never fully understood it until we have discovered its connexion with truth, and the true thing to which it is attached. With this agrees what the apostle says when he represents even Polytheism as a perversion of the original consciousness of God which underlies it, and when, in this evidence of the longing which all these fancies have failed to satisfy, he finds an obscure presentiment of the true God.[1]

§ 8. *Those forms of piety in which all religious affections express the dependence of everything finite upon one Supreme and Infinite Being,* i.e. *the monotheistic forms, occupy the highest level; and all others are related to them as subordinate forms, from which men are destined to pass to those higher ones.*

1. As such subordinate stages we set down, generally speaking, Idol-worship proper (also called Fetichism) and Polytheism; of which, again, the first stands far lower than the second. The idol-worshipper may quite well have only one idol, but this does not give such Monolatry any resemblance to Monotheism, for it ascribes to the idol an influence only over a limited field of objects or processes, beyond which its own interest and sympathy do not extend. The addition of several idols is merely an accident, usually caused by the experience of some incapacity in the original one, but not aiming at any kind of completeness. Indeed, the main reason why people remain on this level is that the sense of totality has not yet developed. The old ξόανα of the original Greek tribes were probably idols in the proper sense, each being something in itself alone. The unification of these different worships, by which one Being was substituted for several such idols, and the rise of several cycles of myths by which these creations were brought into connexion with each other—this was the development through which the transition from Idol-worship to Polytheism proper took place. But the more the idea of a multiplicity of local habitations clung to the Beings thus constituted, the more did Polytheism continue to savour of Idol-worship. Polytheism proper is present only when the local references quite disappear, and the gods, spiritually defined, form an organized and coherent plurality, which, if not exhibited as a totality, is nevertheless presupposed and striven after as such. The more, then, any single one of these Beings is related to the whole system of them, and this system, in turn, to the whole of existence as it appears in consciousness, the more definitely is the dependence of everything finite, not indeed on a Highest One, but on this highest totality, expressed in the religious self-consciousness. But in this state of religious faith there

[1] Rom. 1$^{21ff.}$, Acts 17$^{27-30}$.

cannot fail to be here and there at least a presentiment of One Supreme Being behind the plurality of higher Beings; and then Polytheism is already beginning to disappear, and the way to Monotheism is open.

2. As for this difference, of believing in one God on whom the religious man regards himself as being (along with the world of which he is a part) absolutely dependent, or in a group of gods to whom he stands in different relations according as they divide the government of the world among them, or finally in particular idols which belong to the family or the locality or the particular occupation in which he lives: it seems at first, indeed, to be only a difference in the mode of representation, and therefore, from our point of view, only a derivative difference. And only a difference in the immediate self-consciousness can for us be a fit measure of the development of religion. But it is also very easy to show that these different representations depend on different states of self-consciousness. Idol-worship proper is based upon a confused state of the self-consciousness which marks the lowest condition of man, since in it the higher and the lower are so little distinguished that even the feeling of absolute dependence is reflected as arising from a particular object to be apprehended by the senses. So, too, with Polytheism: in its combination of the religious susceptibility with diverse affections of the sensible self-consciousness, it exhibits this diversity in such a very preponderant degree that the feeling of absolute dependence cannot appear in its complete unity and indifference to all that the sensible self-consciousness may contain; but, instead, a plurality is posited as its source. But when the higher self-consciousness, in distinction from the sensible, has been fully developed, then, in so far as we are open in general to sensible stimulation, *i.e.* in so far as we are constituent parts of the world, and therefore in so far as we take up the world into our self-consciousness and expand the latter into a general consciousness of finitude, we are conscious of ourselves as absolutely dependent. Now this self-consciousness can only be described in terms of Monotheism, and indeed only as we have expressed it in our proposition. For if we are conscious of ourselves, as such and in our finitude, as absolutely dependent, the same holds true of all finite existence, and in this connexion we take up the whole world along with ourselves into the unity of our self-consciousness. Thus the different ways of representing that existence outside of us to which the consciousness of absolute dependence refers, depend

partly on the different degrees of extensiveness of the self-consciousness (for as long as a man identifies himself only with a small part of finite existence, his god will remain a fetich); and partly on the degree of clearness with which the higher self-consciousness is distinguished from the lower. Polytheism naturally represents in both respects an indeterminate middle stage, which sometimes is very little different from Idol-worship, but sometimes, when in the handling of the plurality there appears a secret striving after unity, may border very closely on Monotheism; whether it be that the gods rather represent the forces of Nature, or that they symbolize the human qualities which are operative in social relationships, or that both these tendencies are united in the same cult. Otherwise it could not in itself be explained how the correlative term in the feeling of absolute dependence could be reflected as a plurality of beings. But if the higher consciousness has not become quite distinct from the lower, then the correlative can only be conceived in a sensible way, and then for that very reason it contains the germs of plurality. Thus it is only when the religious consciousness expresses itself as capable of being combined with all the states of the sensible self-consciousness without discrimination, but also as clearly distinct from the latter, in such a way that in the religious emotions themselves no sharper distinction appears than that between the joyful and the depressing tone—it is only then that man has successfully passed beyond those two stages, and can refer his feeling of absolute dependence solely to one Supreme Being.

3. It can therefore justly be said that as soon as piety has anywhere developed to the point of belief in one God over all, it may be predicted that man will not in any region of the earth remain stationary on one of the lower planes. For this belief is always and everywhere very particularly engaged, if not always in the best way, in the endeavour to propagate itself and disclose itself to the receptive faculties of mankind; and this succeeds eventually, as we can see, even among the rudest human races, and by a direct transition from Fetichism without any intermediate passage through a stage of Polytheism. On the other hand, there is nowhere any trace, so far as history reaches, of a relapse from Monotheism, in the strict sense. In the case of most of those Christians who under persecution went back to heathenism, it was only an apparent return. Where it was a matter of real earnest, these people must, previously, at their conversion to Christianity, have been simply carried on by a general movement, without having appropriated

the essence of this belief into their own personal consciousness. However, we must not, from all this, draw the conclusion that the existence of Fetichism requires for its explanation the assumption of a still lower stage, in which religious emotion would be altogether lacking. Many have, indeed, described the original state of mankind as such a brute-existence ; but, even if we cannot deny all trace of such a state, it can be neither proved historically nor imagined in a general way how of itself this state should have given rise to the development of something higher. No more can it be shown that Polytheism has anywhere transformed itself, by a sheer process from within, into genuine Monotheism ; although this can at least be conceived as possible, as has been indicated above. In any case, we must secure ourselves against the demand that, since we have definitely exhibited such a gradation, we are bound also to give a definite account of such an original state of religion ; for in other connexions also it is the case that we never get back to origins. If, then, we keep simply to our presuppositions, without resorting to any historical statements about a period which is altogether prehistoric, we are left with a choice between two ways of conceiving it. Either that quite obscure and confused form of religion was everywhere the original form, and advanced to Polytheism through the concentration of several small tribes into one larger community ; or a childish Monotheism (which for that very reason was subject to a confused mingling of the higher and the lower) was the original stage, and among some people darkened completely into idol-worship, while among others it clarified into a pure belief in God.

4. On this highest plane, of Monotheism, history exhibits only three great communions—the Jewish, the Christian, and the Mohammedan ; the first being almost in process of extinction, the other two still contending for the mastery of the human race. Judaism, by its limitation of the love of Jehovah to the race of Abraham, betrays a lingering affinity with Fetichism ; and the numerous vacillations towards idol-worship prove that during the political heyday of the nation the monotheistic faith had not yet taken fast root, and was not fully and purely developed until after the Babylonian Exile. Islam, on the other hand, with its passionate character, and the strongly sensuous content of its ideas, betrays, in spite of its strict Monotheism, a large measure of that influence of the sensible upon the character of the religious emotions which elsewhere keeps men on the level of Polytheism. Thus Christianity,

because it remains free from both these weaknesses, stands higher than either of those other two forms, and takes its place as the purest form of Monotheism which has appeared in history. Hence there is strictly no such thing as a wholesale relapse from Christianity to either Judaism or Mohammedanism, any more than there is from any monotheistic religion to Polytheism or idol-worship. Individual exceptions will always be connected with pathological states of mind; or, instead of religion, it will prove to be simply one form of irreligion that is exchanged for another, which indeed is what always happens in the case of renegades. And so this comparison of Christianity with other similar religions is in itself a sufficient warrant for saying that Christianity is, in fact,[1] the most perfect of the most highly developed forms of religion.

Postscript 1.—The above account is at variance with the view which sees no real piety at all, but only superstition, in the religions of the lower levels, mainly because they are supposed to have had their source simply in fear. But the honour of Christianity does not at all demand such an assertion. For since Christianity itself affirms [2] that only perfect love casts out all fear, it must admit that imperfect love is never entirely free from fear. And likewise it is always the case, even in idol-worship, if the idol is worshipped as a protector at all, and not as an evil being, that the fear is by no means quite without any impulses of love, but is rather an adaptation, corresponding to the imperfect love, of the feeling of absolute dependence. Moreover (quite apart from the fact that many of these religions are too cheerful to be explicable by fear), if we should set out to discover for them a quite different origin from that of true religion, it would be difficult to show what sort of tendency this is in the human soul, and what its inner aim is, which engenders idol-worship, and which must again be lost when the latter gives place to Religion. The truth is, rather, that we must never deny the homogeneity of all these products of the human spirit, but must acknowledge the same root even for the lower powers.

Postscript 2.—But for the assonance of the names there would scarcely be any occasion for us expressly to remark that it is not at all our present business to say anything about that way of thinking which is called Pantheism. For it has never been the confession of a religious communion which actually appeared in history, and it is only with these that we are concerned. Moreover, this name was not originally used even by individuals to designate their own

[1] Cf. § 7, 3. [2] 1 John 4^{18}.

views, but crept in as a taunt and nickname; and in such cases it always remains difficult to hold consistently to any one meaning. The one thing concerning the subject which can be discussed in this place (and indeed *only* in such a place as this) is the question of the relation of this way of thinking to piety. It is admitted that it does not, like the three above-described theories, spring from the religious emotions, by direct reflection upon them. But it may be asked whether, having once arisen in some other way—by the way of speculation or simply of reasoning—it is yet compatible with piety. To this question an affirmative answer may be given without hesitation, provided that Pantheism is taken as expressing some variety or form of Theism, and that the word is not simply and solely a disguise for a materialistic negation of Theism. If we look at idol-worship, and consider how it is always conjoined with a very limited knowledge of the world, and is also full of magic and sorcery of every sort, it is very easy to see that in very few cases can one speak of a clear distinction on this level between what is assigned to God and what is assigned to the world. And why could not a Hellenic polytheist, embarrassed by the entirely human shapes of the gods, have identified his great gods with the evolved gods of Plato, leaving out the God whom Plato represents as addressing them, and positing only the enthroned Necessity? This would not imply any change in his piety, yet his representation of it would have become pantheistic. But let us think of the highest stage of religion, and let us accordingly hold Pantheism fast to the usual formula of One and All: then God and world will remain distinct at least as regards function, and thus such a man, since he reckons himself as belonging to the world, can feel himself, along with this All, to be dependent on that which is the corresponding One. Such states of mind can scarcely be distinguished from the religious emotions of many a Monotheist. At any rate, the distinction (always rather a curious one, and, if I may say so, roughly drawn) between a God who is outside of and above the world, and a God who is in the world, does not particularly meet the point, for nothing can strictly be said about God in terms of the antithesis between internal and external without imperilling in some way the divine omnipotence and omnipresence.

§ 9. *The widest diversity between forms of piety is that which exists, with respect to the religious affections, between those forms which subordinate the natural in human conditions to the moral and those which, on the contrary, subordinate the moral to the natural.*

1. It is primarily in the interests of Christianity, and therefore only for the highest level, that we shall here attempt a conceptual division of religions which appear as co-ordinate (a cross-division, *i.e.*, in relation to our division of the whole field). Whether this division holds for the subordinate stages too, is a question that does not here concern us. But for the highest stage the attempt is necessary. For even if this stage is, as a matter of history, exhausted in the three above-mentioned communions, yet we need a more exactly defined position in which to fix Christianity; for otherwise we could only distinguish it empirically from the other two, and could never be certain whether the more essential differences were being brought to light or whether we were only getting hold of accidental characteristics. Hence our attempt cannot be held to have succeeded until we find a basis of division by which Christianity is either clearly distinguished, in itself, from the two others, or along with one of the others distinguished from the third.

Now, since the feeling of absolute dependence is in itself perfectly simple, and the conception of it provides no basis of differentiation, such a basis can be derived only from the fact that that feeling, in order to realize itself in an actual moment, must first unite with a sensible stimulation of self-consciousness, and that these sensible stimuli must be regarded as infinitely various. Now it is true that the feeling of absolute dependence in itself is equally related to all these stimulations, and is highly susceptible to them all alike. But nevertheless it may, by analogy, be assumed that this relationship in actual reality differentiates itself variously not only in individual men but also in larger masses. And thus with some people a certain class of sensible feelings develops easily and surely into religious emotion, and another opposite class with difficulty or not at all, while with other people the case is precisely reversed. Or it may be that the same sensible states of self-consciousness develop into religious moments with some people in one set of conditions, and with other people in the opposite set of conditions. As regards the former alternative, we might first of all divide these states into the more physical and the more spiritual, into those which arise through the influence of men and their actions and those which arise through the influence of external Nature. But this could only hold of individual men, that some are more susceptible to religious emotion through the impressions of external Nature, and others through social relationships and the temper which they produce. The difference between one religious communion and another cannot be thus explained, since every such communion includes all these diversities, and none excludes from its pale either the one or the other kind of emotion, or even makes the one less prominent than the other to any significant extent. Again, we might point to the fact that, our whole life being an interpenetration and succession of activity and passivity, a man is sometimes more conscious of himself as active and sometimes more as passive. And this might be held better to provide a common constitution for larger masses of people—the fact that in certain quarters the active form of self-consciousness more easily rises into religious emotion, and the passive remains on the sensible level, while in other quarters this is reversed. Only, of course, this so simply conceived distinction remains a merely fluid one between a more and a less, so that the same moment may be conceived as either more active or more passive according as it is compared with one or with another. If a grand division of universal application is to be made between the different forms of piety, the above fluid distinction must be transformed into such a subordination as is indicated in our proposition. This subordination is on the one side most strongly marked when the passive states (whether pleasant or unpleasant, whether occasioned by external Nature or by social relationships) only arouse the feeling of absolute dependence in so far as they are referred to the spontaneous activity, *i.e.* in so far as we know that some particular thing (just because we stand in that relation to the totality of existence which is expressed in our passive state) has to be done by us, so that the action which depends on and proceeds from that state has thus precisely this God-consciousness as its impulse. Thus where piety has taken this form, the passive states, having risen into religious emotion, become simply an occasion for the development of a definite activity which can only be explained as the result of a God-consciousness of that particular description. And in the realm of such religious emotions all passive relations of man to the world appear as simply means for evoking the totality of his active states, whereby the antithesis between the sensibly pleasant and the unpleasant therein is overcome and retires into the background; while, on the contrary, it of course remains predominant in the cases in which the sensible feeling does not rise into religious emotion. This subordination we designate *teleological* Religion ; an expression which indeed is elsewhere somewhat differently used, but which is here meant to signify simply that a predominating reference to the moral task constitutes the fundamental type of the religious affections. Now if the action which is prefigured in the religious emotion is a practical contribution to the advancement of the Kingdom of God, the mental state is an elevating one, whether the feeling which occasioned it be pleasant or unpleasant. But if the action is a retreat into oneself, or a seeking for help to relieve a perceptible obstruction of the higher life, the mental state is a subduing one, whether the feeling which occasioned it was pleasant or unpleasant. The reverse form of this subordination appears in its completeness when the self-consciousness of a state of activity is taken up into the feeling of absolute dependence only in proportion as the state itself appears as a result of those relations which exist between the subject and all the rest of existence, and is thus referred to the passive side of the subject. But every individual state of activity is simply a particular expression of the disposition of common human faculties which exists in the subject and constitutes his personal peculiarity. Consequently, in every religious emotion of this sort, that disposition itself is posited as the result of the influences, ordered by the Supreme Being, of all things upon the subject ; and thus in the elevating emotions, as harmony, *i.e.* as beauty of the individual life, and in the unpleasant or subduing emotions, as discord or ugliness. Now this form of piety, in which each moment of spontaneous activity, simply as a determination of the individual by the whole of finite existence, and thus as referred to the passive side, is taken up into the feeling of absolute dependence, we will call *æsthetic* Religion. These two fundamental forms are definitely opposed to each other, in virtue of the opposite subordination of the elements which are common to both ; and every kind of religious fellow-feeling or sympathy is naturally found in both forms, just as is the personal feeling, since the former is simply an expanded, the latter a contracted, self-consciousness.

2. A general demonstration as to whether the actual historical faiths can best be classified according to this antithesis would be the business only of a general critical History of Religions. Here we are simply concerned as to whether the division so far justifies itself, as to provide a means of distinguishing Christianity from religions co-ordinate with it, and by more narrowly determining its position to facilitate the task of isolating its peculiar essence.

As a matter of fact, the religion which is chiefly present to our minds, as being sharply opposed in this respect to Christianity, is not co-ordinate with it, but belongs to a lower level, namely, Greek Polytheism. In this religion the teleological trend falls entirely into the background. Neither in their religious symbols nor even in their Mysteries is there any considerable trace of the idea of a totality of moral ends to which a man's mental states are in general to be related. On the contrary, what we have called the æsthetic outlook very definitely predominates, inasmuch as even the gods are principally intended to exhibit different dispositions of the activities of the human soul, and thus a peculiar form of inward beauty. Now no one can well deny that Christianity, even apart from the fact that it belongs to a higher level, is sharply opposed to this type. In the realm of Christianity the consciousness of God is always related to the totality of active states in the idea of a Kingdom of God. As for the idea of a beauty of the soul, regarded as the result of all the influences of Nature and the world, this has always remained so foreign to Christianity (in spite of Christianity's early absorption of Hellenism *en masse*) that it has never been adopted into the cycle of current expressions in the realm of Christian piety, and has never been maintained in any treatise of Christian morals. But that figure of a Kingdom of God, which is so important and indeed all-inclusive for Christianity, is simply the general expression of the fact that in Christianity all pain and all joy are religious only in so far as they are related to activity in the Kingdom of God, and that every religious emotion which proceeds from a passive state ends in the consciousness of a transition to activity.

But now we have to determine whether the above-mentioned antithesis between the teleological and the æsthetic trend is not, after all, necessarily bound up with the distinction between the two levels, so that all Polytheism would necessarily belong to the æsthetic side and all Monotheism to the teleological. To this end we must simply take our stand upon the highest level, and ask whether the two other monotheistic faiths are like Christianity in this respect or not. As for Judaism, then, though it relates the passive states to the active rather in the form of divine punishments and rewards than in the form of moral challenge and influence, nevertheless the predominating form of God-consciousness is that of the commanding Will; and thus, even when it proceeds from passive states, it necessarily turns to the active. Islam, on the other hand, in no way shows this subordination of the passive to the active. Rather does this form of piety come to complete rest in the consciousness of immutable divine appointments, and even the consciousness of spontaneous activity is only united with the feeling of absolute dependence in the sense that its determination is supposed to rest upon those appointments. And this fatalistic character reveals in the clearest manner a subordination of the moral to the natural. Thus the monotheistic stage appears divided, the teleological type being most expressed in Christianity, and less perfectly in Judaism, while Mohammedanism, which is quite as monotheistic, unmistakably expresses the æsthetic type. All this points us for our present task to a definitely limited field, and what we are going to establish as the peculiar essence of Christianity must no more deviate from the teleological line than it may descend from the monotheistic level.

§ 10. *Each particular form of communal piety has both an outward unity, as a fixed fact of history with a definite commencement, and an inward unity, as a peculiar modification of that general character which is common to all developed faiths of the same kind and level; and it is from both of these taken together that the peculiar essence of any particular form is to be discerned.*

NOTE.—Cf. *Speeches on Religion* (Eng. trans.), pp. 210 ff.

1. The first part of this proposition would be false if it could be shown, or even conceived as possible, that Christian piety could anywhere arise, as it were of itself, quite apart from any historical connexion with the impulse which proceeded from Christ. The same thing would in that case be true of Mohammedan and Jewish piety too, with reference to Moses and Mohammed. But the possibility of it will be admitted by nobody. Of course this outward unity is not so rigid on the subordinate levels of religion; partly because in these cases the starting-point often falls in the prehistoric period (as it does in the case of the pre-Mosaic monotheistic worship of Jehovah); partly because many of these historical forms, such as the Greek, and still more the Roman, Polytheism, present to us a composite whole which, from many very diverse starting-points, has gradually been woven together or even grown together of itself. The same might indeed be said of the Norse and Indian systems. But these apparent exceptions rather confirm the rule laid down in our proposition. For the less the outward unity can be definitely exhibited, the more precarious

becomes the inward unity too. It appears that, just as in the realm of Nature the species are less definite on the lower levels of life, so in this realm of religion also the uniform consummation of the outward and the inward unity is reserved for the higher development; and thus in the most perfect form (which we may say in advance is Christianity) the inward peculiarity must be most intimately bound up with that which forms the historical basis of the outward unity.

The second part of our proposition would be false if it could be asserted that the different religious communions were really separated only by space and time without having any genuinely inward difference. But this would imply that whenever two such communions came into contact spatially they would necessarily recognize their identity with each other, and so become one, and that nothing could hinder this except (to a certain extent) a foolish self-will which was anxious to cling to the name of the founder. It would also imply that each individual could, without undergoing any inward change, pass from his own religious communion to a quite different one, simply by dissolving the one historical connexion and entering into another. But this would be contrary to all experience. Indeed it would, on this hypothesis, be impossible that one religious communion should spring up within another and break away from it; for if nothing new came in, there could be no new beginning where the same elements had been already present.

2. With respect to the actual beginning of each religious communion there need be no further discussion. Whether a new variety of the feeling of absolute dependence takes shape first simply in one individual or in several simultaneously, is a matter of indifference, though everyone will see that the latter is, generally speaking, less probable than the former. It would also be futile to try to distinguish the different ways in which such a new form can arise in the soul, since the communion can only arise through its communication and transmission. But what our proposition says about the inward difference requires some further discussion. Our proposition makes the statement (which, however, in accordance with our present purpose, we are going to apply only to the religious communions of the highest level) that the same thing is present in all, but present in a quite different way in each. The prevailing view, on the contrary, is that the greater part is the same in all communions of the highest level, and that to this common matter

there is simply added in each some special element of its own; so that perhaps, to give a rough illustration, the belief in one God, with all that it involves, is the element common to all these communions, but in the one there is added obedience to commandment, in another the belief in Christ, and in a third the belief in the prophets. But if the belief in Christ had no influence upon the separately pre-existing consciousness of God and on its mode of uniting with the sensible emotions, either that belief would stand quite outside the realm of religion, and would consequently (since no other realm can be assigned to it) be a mere nothing, or Christ would at any rate be only one particular object producing impressions which could be united with the consciousness of God, in which case also one could not properly speak of a belief in Christ. Suppose however the meaning is that the belief in Christ has an influence only on *some* of the religious emotions, while the majority of them take exactly the same form in Christianity as in other monotheistic faiths. This would involve the assertion that this belief has not so much an influence on the consciousness of God (which, after all, must be the same in all religious emotions of the same man at the same time, *i.e.* so long as he belongs to the same religious communion), but rather has an influence merely upon the sensibly stimulated consciousness; and such an influence could not be the basis of a distinctive way of faith. Hence there remains for us only the view adopted in our proposition, which implies that in each really distinctive religious communion the self-consciousness itself must have a different determination, since only on this condition can the religious emotions be all differently determined. Now just as each individual instance necessarily makes it clear that the presence of an absolutely identical element in two different ways of faith can be only in appearance, if the God-consciousness itself is differently determined in the two: so also it is only in appearance that each faith has some element which is entirely absent in others. Otherwise, if in other faiths also we find God becoming Man, and a communication of the Divine Spirit, what would be the absolutely new thing in Christianity? But the same thing may be seen in a general way. For if, on the supposition of a quite similarly determined consciousness of God, some element is found in one faith which is not found in another, this could only be caused by a different field of experience, and so the whole difference would necessarily disappear if the experiences were brought into line with each other.

3. Though it was only in a somewhat indefinite way that we were able to establish the conception of *kind* in our present province, the conception of the *Individual* has here a firmer basis, and the formula set up in our proposition is the same which holds for all individual differences within the same kind. For every man has in him all that another man has, but it is all differently determined; and the greatest similarity is only a diminishing or (relatively) vanishing difference. So also every species has the same characteristics as every other species of its genus, and everything which is really additional is merely accidental. But the discovery of this differentiating matter in any individual existence is a task which can never be perfectly, but only approximately, discharged in words and sentences. And hence naturalists and historians are wont to bring forward only certain marks as distinguishing signs, without meaning to assert that these express everything distinctive and characteristic; and the man who describes religion must in most cases be content with the same procedure. But if we must make an attempt at some kind of general statement, in order that the apologist of any particular faith may be the less likely to fall into error, we should be content with saying this: in every individual religion the God-consciousness, which in itself remains the same everywhere on the same level, is attached to some relation of the self-consciousness in such an especial way that only thereby can it unite with other determinations of the self-consciousness; so that all other relations are subordinate to this one, and it communicates to all others its colour and its tone. If it should seem that by this we are expressing merely a different rule for the *connecting* of religious moments, rather than a difference of form or of content, we have only to note that every moment is itself a connexion, as being the transition from the preceding to the following moment, and thus must become a different moment when the religious self-consciousness is placed in a different connexion.

Postscript.—It is only by means of the two points set up in our proposition (namely, the distinctive beginning to which each religious communion goes back, and the peculiar form which the religious emotions and their utterances take in each communion) that it is possible to regulate the usage of the familiar terms '*positive*' and '*revealed.*' It is well known that these terms are used somewhat confusedly, being often applied in exactly the same manner at one moment to the individual doctrines, at another to the faith in general, and being at one time opposed to the natural, at another to the rational. Hence it would be a difficult task so to fix their meaning as to secure for them a uniformly consistent usage in the realm of scientific theology. For the former of the two terms we are given a good lead by the use made of it in the theory of Law, where positive rights are contrasted with natural rights. If we compare the two, one finds that natural right never appears in the same sense as positive, namely, as the basis of a civic community. Even the simplest and most original relationships, such as paternal authority or the marriage union, are in each society defined in a distinctive manner—in the developed State by express legislation, and in earlier stages by prevailing custom. Natural right, however, is simply what can be abstracted in a similar manner from the legislation of all societies. And even if, as pure knowledge, it were to come into existence in another way, yet everyone would admit that when you come to the application of it, it must first be more precisely defined, and therefore, as applicable to practice, can only be traced back to this act of more precise definition. Now it is the same with Natural Religion. It never appears as the basis of a religious communion,[1] but is simply what can be abstracted uniformly from the doctrines of all religious communions of the highest grade, as being present in all but differently determined in each. Such a natural religion would mark out the common elements in all religious affections which are found in the ecclesiastical communions, and if we conceive of all religious communions as already given, and also of all the different philosophical systems as having adjusted their differences as regards the terminology of such a doctrine, this natural religion would be everywhere the same, and would remain ever self-identical. But it would never anywhere be more than a mere private possession, which would belong, in addition to their definite type and manner of piety and its expression in doctrine, to those individuals in the various religious communions who, acknowledging from their own standpoint the other communions in their inter-relation, were able to view together in a higher unity things which are separated in actuality. Moreover, it would not be difficult to show that what is called natural religion did actually arise in this way, and, further, that any attempt to make this secondary product the basis of an ecclesiastical communion has always failed, and must always fail. But that is hardly our business here. Agreed, then, that in any case, even if it should have arisen in a different way, such a natural

[1] Cf. § 6, *Postscript*.

religion, or rather, properly speaking, natural theology, being a mere collocation of doctrines, would be simply the common element in all monotheistic faiths : then the positive element in each would be seen to be the individualized element, which, as shown above, is found in each of them not simply here and there but, strictly considered, all over them, though it may be more prominent at one point than at another. It simply betrays a misapprehension when people attempt to distinguish the actually existing religious communions from each other by the principle that the positive element is found in one at one point and in another at another point, as, *e.g.*, that in Christianity it is the doctrines, in Judaism the commandments.[1] For if in one communion the commands are more elaborated and the doctrines less, and in another *vice versa*, it is simply that in the one case the doctrine is concealed in the command as in a symbol, and in the other the doctrine itself appears as a command that it be expressed and confessed. Moreover, it would be equally false to deny that the precepts of Christian morals are positive and to deny that the doctrine of Jehovah in Judaism is positive. In any case, neither the command, as the expression of a common mode of action, nor the doctrine, as the expression of a common mode of representation, is an original element : both are based on a common distinctive quality of the religious emotions. Now since without this the particular communion itself could not have come into existence, and since it has maintained an existence dating from, and in relation to, the fact which marked its beginning, it must be dependent on that fact for the peculiar stamp of its religious emotions. This, then, is what is to be signified by the term '*positive*' : the individual content of all the moments of the religious life within one religious communion, in so far as this content depends on the original fact from which the communion itself, as a coherent historical phenomenon, originated.

The words '*reveal*,' '*revealed*,' '*revelation*,' present still further difficulties, since even originally they sometimes signify the illumination of what was obscure, confused, unobserved, and sometimes rather the disclosing and unveiling of what was hitherto concealed and kept secret, and still further confusion has been introduced by the distinction between mediate and immediate (direct and indirect) revelation. To begin with, all will at once agree that the word 'revealed' is never applied either to what is discovered in the realm of experience by one man and handed on to others, or to

[1] See M. Mendelssohn's *Jerusalem*.

what is excogitated in thought by one man and so learned by others; and further, that the word presupposes a divine communication and declaration. And in this sense we find the word very generally applied to the origin of religious communions. For of what religious mysteries and varieties of worship, either among the Greeks or among the Egyptians and Indians, would it not be asserted that they originally came from heaven or were proclaimed by Deity in some way which fell outside the human and natural order? Not seldom, indeed, we find even the beginning of civic communities (just as from the beginning we often find the moral and the religious unseparated) traced to a divine sending of the man who first gathered the tribe together into a civic union, and so the new organization of life is based on a revelation. Accordingly we might say that the idea of revelation signifies the *originality* of the fact which lies at the foundation of a religious communion, in the sense that this fact, as conditioning the individual content of the religious emotions which are found in the communion, cannot itself in turn be explained by the historical chain which precedes it.

Now the fact that in this original element there is a divine causality requires no further discussion; nor does the fact that it is an activity which aims at and furthers the salvation of man. But I am unwilling to accept the further definition that it operates upon man as a cognitive being. For that would make the revelation to be originally and essentially *doctrine*; and I do not believe that we can adopt that position, whether we consider the whole field covered by the idea, or seek to define it in advance with special reference to Christianity. If a system of propositions can be understood from their connexion with others, then nothing supernatural was required for their production. But if they cannot, then they can, in the first instance, only be apprehended (we need only appeal for confirmation to the first principles of Hermeneutics) as parts of another whole, as a moment of the life of a thinking being who works upon us directly as a distinctive existence by means of his total impression on us; and this working is always a working upon the self-consciousness. Thus the original fact will always be the appearing of such a being, and the original working will always be upon the self-consciousness of those into whose circle he enters. That this does not exclude doctrine, but implies it, is obvious. For the rest, it always remains very difficult, indeed almost impossible, to give definite limits to this idea, and, if it is thus definitely grasped, to explain its rise wherever it appears. For everywhere in the realm of mythology, Greek as well as Oriental and Norse, these divine communications and declarations border so closely on the higher states of heroic and poetic inspiration that it is difficult to distinguish them from each other. And thus it becomes difficult to avoid a widened application of the idea, to the effect that every original ideal which arises in the soul, whether for an action or for a work of art, and which can neither be understood as an imitation nor be satisfactorily explained by means of external stimuli and preceding mental states, may be regarded as revelation. For the fact that the one is greater and the other less cannot here make a dividing line. And, indeed, the inward generation of a new and peculiar idea of God in a moment of inspiration has often been one and the same thing with the rise of a distinctive worship. Indeed, it would be difficult to draw any clear dividing line at all between what is revealed and what comes to light through inspiration in a natural way, unless we are prepared to fall back on the position that revelation is only to be assumed when not a single moment but a whole existence is determined by such a divine communication, and that what is then proclaimed by such an existence is to be regarded as revealed. This, in the polytheistic religions, would include not only the divine declarations and oracles attached to certain holy places which the divinity has made known to be his specially chosen habitations, but also those persons who, because they are descended from the divinity, make known the divine archetype in a human life in an original way which cannot be explained by the historical context. In this same sense Paul calls even the world the original revelation of God.[1] But this may again lead us to the conclusion that no particular thing, since it always belongs to the world, can in itself be regarded as divine revelation. For just as the dawning of an archetypal idea in an individual soul, even if it cannot be explained by the previous states of that very soul, can certainly be explained by the total state of the society to which the individual belongs: so even the men who are credited with divine descent always appear as determined by the character of their people, and thus it is from the total energy of the people that their existence is to be explained or comprehended. Hence even if we do venture to establish, in the way we have done above, the relation of the idea of 'revelation' and 'revealed' to the idea of the 'positive' for the whole realm of historically actual religious communions, we shall nevertheless naturally and inevitably find

[1] Rom. 1[20].

that the application of the idea to the fact which forms the basis of any particular religious communion will be contested by all other communions, while each will claim it for its own basal fact.

Finally, this must be added: that if one faith wishes to establish the validity of its own application of the idea as against the others, it cannot at all accomplish this by the assertion that its own divine communication is pure and entire truth, while the others contain falsehood. For complete truth would mean that God made Himself known as He is in and for Himself. But such a truth could not proceed outwardly from any fact, and even if it did in some incomprehensible way come to a human soul, it could not be apprehended by that soul, and retained as a thought; and if it could not be in any way perceived and retained, it could not become operative. Any proclamation of God which is to be operative upon and within us can only express God in His relation to us; and this is not an infra-human ignorance concerning God, but the essence of human limitedness in relation to Him. On the other hand, there is the connected fact that a consciousness of God which arose in a realm of complete barbarity and degradation might be really a revelation, and might nevertheless, through the fault of the mind in which it arose, become, in the form in which it was apprehended and retained, an imperfect one. And therefore it may truly be said even of the imperfect forms of religion, so far as they can be traced, in whole or in part, to a particular starting-point and their content cannot be explained by anything previous to that point, that they rest upon revelation, however much error may be mingled in them with the truth.

III. Presentation of Christianity in its Peculiar Essence: Propositions borrowed from Apologetics.

§ 11. *Christianity is a monotheistic faith, belonging to the teleological type of religion, and is essentially distinguished from other such faiths by the fact that in it everything is related to the redemption accomplished by Jesus of Nazareth.*

1. The only pertinent way of discovering the peculiar essence of any particular faith and reducing it as far as possible to a formula is by showing the element which remains constant throughout the most diverse religious affections within this same communion, while it is absent from analogous affections within other communions. Now since we have little reason to expect that this peculiarity is equally strongly marked in all the different varieties of

emotions, there is all the greater possibility of our missing the mark in this attempt, and so coming in the end to the opinion that there is no hard-and-fast inward difference at all, but only the outward difference as determined by time and place. However, we may with some certainty conclude from what has been said above,[1] that we shall be least likely to miss the peculiarity if we keep principally to what is most closely connected with the basal fact, and this is the procedure which underlies the formula of our proposition. But Christianity presents special difficulties, even in this fact alone, that it takes a greater variety of forms than other faiths and is split up into a multiplicity of smaller communions or churches ; and thus there arises a twofold task, first, to find the peculiar essence, common to all these communions, of Christianity as such, and secondly, to find the peculiar essence of the particular communion whose right is to be authenticated or whose system of doctrine is to be established. But still further difficulty lies in the fact that even in each particular ecclesiastical communion almost every doctrine appears with the most multifarious variations at different times and places ; and this implies as its basis, not indeed, perhaps, an equally great diversity in the religious affections themselves, but always at least a great diversity in the manner of understanding and appraising them. Indeed, the worst of all is that, owing to this variation, the bounds of the Christian realm become a matter of dispute even among Christians themselves, one asserting of this form of teaching, and another of that form, that though it was indeed engendered within Christianity it is nevertheless really un-Christian in content. Now, if he who wishes to solve our problem belongs himself to one of these parties, and assumes at the outset that only what is found within the realm of that one view ought to be taken into account in ascertaining what is distinctive of Christianity, he is at the outset taking controversies as settled, for the settlement of which he professes to be only discovering the conditions. For only when the peculiar essence of Christianity has been ascertained can it be decided how far this or that is compatible or incompatible with it. But if the investigator succeeds in freeing himself from all partiality, and therefore takes into account everything, however opposed, so long as it professes to be Christian, then on the other hand he is in danger of reaching a result far scantier and more colourless in its content, and consequently less suitable to the aims of our present task. That is the present state of affairs, and it

[1] § 10, *Postscript*.

cannot be concealed. Now since each man, the more religious he is, usually brings his individual religion the more into this investigation, there is a large majority of the people who form their idea of the peculiar essence of Christianity according to the interests of their party. But for the interests of Apologetics as well as of Dogmatics it seems advisable rather to be content with a scanty result at the beginning and to hope for its completion in the course of further procedure, than to begin with a narrow and exclusive formula, which is of necessity confronted by one or more opposing formulæ, with which there must be a conflict sooner or later. And it is in this sense that the formula of our proposition is set up.

2. It is indisputable that all Christians trace back to Christ the communion to which they belong. But here we are also presupposing that the term *Redemption* is one to which they all confess : not only that they all *use* the word, with perhaps different meanings, but that there is some common element of meaning which they all have in mind, even if they differ when they come to a more exact description of it. The term itself is in this realm merely figurative, and signifies in general a passage from an evil condition, which is represented as a state of captivity or constraint,[1] into a better condition—this is the passive side of it. But it also signifies the help given in that process by some other person, and this is the active side of it. Further, the usage of the word does not essentially imply that the worse condition must have been preceded by a better condition, so that the better one which followed would really be only a restoration : that point may at the outset be left quite open. But now apply the word to the realm of religion, and suppose we are dealing with the teleological type of religion. Then the evil condition can only consist in an obstruction or arrest of the vitality of the higher self-consciousness, so that there comes to be little or no union of it with the various determinations of the sensible self-consciousness, and thus little or no religious life. We may give to this condition, in its most extreme form, the name of *God-lessness*, or, better, *God-forgetfulness*. But we must not think this means a state in which it is quite impossible for the God-consciousness to be kindled. For if that were so, then, in the first place, the lack of a thing which lay outside of one's nature could not be felt to be an evil condition ; and in the second place, a re-creating in

[1] [This does not apply as precisely to the English word *redemption* as to the German word *Erlösung*, which primarily means release or deliverance.—Transl.]

the strict sense would then be needed in order to make good this lack, and that is not included in the idea of redemption. The possibility, then, of kindling the God-consciousness remains in reserve even where the evil condition of that consciousness is painted in the darkest colours.[1] Hence we can only designate it as an absence of facility for introducing the God-consciousness into the course of our actual lives and retaining it there. This certainly makes it seem as if these two conditions, that which exists before redemption and that which is to be brought about by redemption, could only be distinguished in an indefinite way, as a more and a less ; and so, if the idea of redemption is to be clearly established, there arises the problem of reducing this indefinite distinction to a relative opposition. Such an opposition lies in the following formulæ. Given an activity of the sensible self-consciousness, to occupy a moment of time and to connect it with another : its 'exponent' or 'index' will be greater than that of the higher self-consciousness for uniting itself therewith ; and given an activity of the higher self-consciousness, to occupy a moment of time through union with a determination of the sensible, its 'exponent' or 'index' will be less than that of the activity of the sensible for completing the moment for itself alone. Under these conditions no satisfaction of the impulse towards the God-consciousness will be possible ; and so, if such a satisfaction is to be attained, a redemption is necessary, since this condition is nothing but a kind of imprisonment or constraint of the feeling of absolute dependence. These formulæ, however, do not imply that in all moments which are so determined the God-consciousness or the feeling of absolute dependence is at zero, but only that in some respect it does not dominate the moment ; and in proportion as that is the case the above designations of Godlessness and God-forgetfulness may fitly be applied to it.

3. The recognition of such a condition undeniably finds a place in all religious communions. For the aim of all penances and purifications is to put an end to the consciousness of this condition or to the condition itself. But our proposition establishes two points which in this connexion distinguish Christianity from all other religious communions. In the first place, in Christianity the incapacity and the redemption, and their connexion with each other, do not constitute simply one particular religious element among others, but all other religious emotions are related to this, and this

[1] Rom. $1^{18\text{ff.}}$

accompanies all others, as the principal thing which makes them distinctively Christian. And secondly, redemption is posited as a thing which has been universally and completely accomplished by Jesus of Nazareth. And these two points, again, must not be separated from each other, but are essentially interconnected. Thus it could not by any means be said that Christian piety is attributable to every man who in all his religious moments is conscious of being in process of redemption, even if he stood in no relation to the person of Jesus or even knew nothing of Him—a case which, of course, will never arise. And no more could it be said that a man's religion is Christian if he traces it to Jesus, even supposing that therein he is not at all conscious of being in process of redemption—a case which also, of course, will never arise. The reference to redemption is in every Christian consciousness simply because the originator of the Christian communion is the Redeemer ; and Jesus is Founder of a religious communion simply in the sense that its members become conscious of redemption through Him. Our previous exposition ensures that this will not be understood to mean that the whole religious consciousness of a Christian can have no other content than simply Jesus and redemption, but only that all religious moments, so far as they are free expressions of the feeling of absolute dependence, are set down as having come into existence through that redemption, and, so far as the feeling appears still unliberated, are set down as being in need of that redemption. It likewise goes without saying that, while this element is always present, different religious moments may and will possess it in varying degrees of strength or weakness, without thereby losing their Christian character. But it *would*, of course, follow from what has been said, that if we conceive of religious moments in which all reference to redemption is absent, and the image of the Redeemer is not introduced at all, these moments must be judged to belong no more intimately to Christianity than to any other monotheistic faith.

4. The more detailed elaboration of our proposition, as to how the redemption is effected by Christ and comes to consciousness within the Christian communion, falls to the share of the dogmatic system itself. Here, however, we have still to discuss, with reference to the general remarks we made above,[1] the relation of Christianity to the other principal monotheistic communions. These also are traced back each to an individual founder. Now if the difference of founder were the only difference, this would be a

[1] § 10.

merely external difference, and the same thing would be true if these others likewise set up their founder as a redeemer and thus related everything to redemption. For that would mean that in all these religions the religious moments were of like content, only that the personality of the founder was different. But such is not the case : rather must we say that only through Jesus, and thus only in Christianity, has redemption become the central point of religion. For inasmuch as these other religions have instituted particular penances and purifications for particular things, and these are only particular parts of their doctrine and organization, the effecting of redemption does not appear as their main business. It appears rather as a derivative element. Their main business is the founding of the communion upon definite doctrine and in definite form. If, however, there are within the communion considerable differences in the free development of the God-consciousness, then some people, in whom it is most cramped, are more in need of redemption, and others, in whom it works more freely, are more capable of redemption ; and thus through the influence of the latter there arises in the former an approximation to redemption ; but only up to the point at which the difference between the two is more or less balanced, simply owing to the fact that there exists a communion or fellowship. In Christianity, on the other hand, the redeeming influence of the Founder is the primary element, and the communion exists only on this presupposition, and as a communication and propagation of that redeeming activity. Hence within Christianity these two tendencies always rise and fall together : the tendency to give pre-eminence to the redeeming work of Christ, and the tendency to ascribe great value to the distinctive and peculiar element in Christian piety. And the same is true of the two opposite tendencies : the tendency to regard Christianity simply as a means of advancing and propagating religion in general (its own distinctive nature being merely accidental and secondary), and the tendency to regard Christ principally as a teacher and the organizer of a communion, while putting the redeeming activity in the background.

Accordingly, in Christianity the relation of the Founder to the members of the communion is quite different from what it is in the other religions. For those other founders are represented as having been, as it were, arbitrarily elevated from the mass of similar or not very different men, and as receiving just as much for themselves as for other people whatever they do receive in the way of divine doctrine and precept. Thus even an adherent of those faiths will hardly deny that God could just as well have given the law through another as through Moses, and the revelation could just as well have been given through another as through Mohammed. But Christ is distinguished from all others as Redeemer alone and for all, and is in no wise regarded as having been at any time in need of redemption Himself; and is therefore separated from the beginning from all other men, and endowed with redeeming power from His birth.

Not that we mean here to exclude at the outset from the Christian communion all those who differ from this presentation of the matter (which is itself capable of manifold shades of variation) in holding that Christ was only later endowed with redeeming power, provided only that this power is recognized as something different from the mere communication of doctrine and rule of life. But if Christ is regarded entirely on the analogy of the founders of other religions, then the distinctive peculiarity of Christianity can only be asserted for the content of the doctrine and rule of life, and the three monotheistic faiths remain separate only in so far as each holds unflinchingly to what it has received. But now suppose them all together capable of advancing still to perfection, and suppose they were able to find for themselves, sooner or later, the better doctrines and precepts of Christianity: then the inward difference would entirely disappear. Suppose that finally the Christian Church is likewise to move on beyond what has been received from Christ: then nothing else remains for Christ but to be regarded as an outstanding point in the development, and this in such a sense that there is a redemption *from* Him as well as a redemption through Him. And since the perfecting principle can only be Reason, and this is everywhere the same, all distinction between the progress of Christianity and that of other monotheistic faiths would gradually disappear, and all alike would only have a validity limited to a definite period, so far as their distinctive character was concerned.

In this way the difference becomes clear between two widely divergent conceptions of Christianity. But at the same time the lines leading from the one to the other become visible. If the latter of the two conceptions were ever to present itself as a complete doctrine, such a communion would perhaps of its own accord sever its connexion with the other Christian communions. But otherwise it could still be recognized as a Christian communion, unless it actually declared itself to be now freed from the necessity of adherence to Christ. Still less should participation in the Christian communion be denied to *individuals* who approximate to that view, so long as they desire to maintain in themselves a living consciousness of God along with, and by means of, that communion.

5. This development of the argument will, it is hoped, serve to confirm what we have established for the purpose of determining the distinctive element of Christianity. For we have tried, as it were by way of experiment, to single out from among the common elements of Christian piety that element by which Christianity is most definitely distinguished externally ; and in this attempt we were guided by the necessity of regarding the inner peculiarity and the outward delimitation in their interconnexion. Perhaps in a universal Philosophy of Religion, to which, if it were properly recognized, Apologetics could then appeal, the inner character of Christianity in itself could be exhibited in such a way that its particular place in the religious world would thereby be definitely fixed. This would also mean that all the principal moments of the religious consciousness would be systematized, and from their interconnexion it would be seen which of them were fitted to have all the others related to them and to be themselves a constant concomitant of all the others. If, then, it should be seen that the element which we call 'redemption' becomes such a moment as soon as a liberating fact enters a region where the God-consciousness was in a state of constraint, Christianity would in that case be vindicated as a distinct form of faith and its nature in a sense construed. But even this could not properly be called a proof of Christianity, since even the Philosophy of Religion could not establish any necessity, either to recognize a particular Fact as redemptive, or to give the central place actually in one's own consciousness to any particular moment, even though that moment should be capable of occupying such a place. Still less can this present account claim to be such a proof ; for here, in accordance with the line we have taken, and since we can only start from a historical consideration, we cannot even pretend to do as much as might be done in a complete Philosophy of Religion. Moreover, it is obvious that an adherent of some other faith might perhaps be completely convinced by the above account that what we have set forth is really the peculiar essence of Christianity, without being thereby so convinced that Christianity is actually the truth, as to feel compelled to accept it. Everything we say in this place is

relative to Dogmatics, and Dogmatics is only for Christians ; and so this account is only for those who live within the pale of Christianity, and is intended only to give guidance, in the interests of Dogmatics, for determining whether the expressions of any religious consciousness are Christian or not, and whether the Christian quality is strongly and clearly expressed in them, or rather doubtfully. We entirely renounce all attempt to prove the truth or necessity of Christianity ; and we presuppose, on the contrary, that every Christian, before he enters at all upon inquiries of this kind, has already the inward certainty that his religion cannot take any other form than this.

§ 12. *Christianity does indeed stand in a special historical connexion with Judaism ; but as far as concerns its historical existence and its aim, its relations to Judaism and Heathenism are the same.*

1. We here take Judaism to mean primarily the Mosaic institutions, but also, as preparing the way for these, every earlier usage which helped to separate the people from other peoples. With this Judaism, then, Christianity has an historical connexion through the fact that Jesus was born among the Jewish people, as indeed a universal Redeemer could scarcely spring from any other than a monotheistic people, once such a people was in existence. But we must not represent the historical connexion in a too exclusive manner. At the time of the appearance of Christ the religious thought of the people was no longer based exclusively on Moses and the prophets, but had been in many ways remoulded through the influence of non-Jewish elements which it had absorbed during and after the Babylonian Dispersion. And, on the other hand, Greek and Roman Heathendom had been in many ways prepared for Monotheism, and in these quarters the expectation of a new phase was most intense ; while contrariwise among the Jews the Messianic promises had been partly given up and partly misunderstood. So that when one puts together all the historical circumstances, the difference becomes much smaller than it appears at the first glance. And Christ's descent from Judaism is largely counterbalanced by the facts that so many more heathen than Jews went over to Christianity, and that Christianity would not have been received by the Jews even as much as it was, had they not been permeated by those foreign elements.

2. The truth rather is that the relations of Christianity to

Judaism and Heathenism are the same, inasmuch as the transition from either of these to Christianity is a transition to another religion. The leap certainly seems greater in the case of Heathenism, since it had first to become monotheistic in order to become Christian. At the same time, the two processes were not separated, but Monotheism was given to the heathen directly in the form of Christianity, as it had been previously in the form of Judaism. And the demand made upon the Jews, to give up their reliance upon the law, and to put a different interpretation upon the Abrahamitic promises, was just as large a demand. Accordingly we must assume that Christian piety, in its original form, cannot be explained by means of the Jewish piety of that or of an earlier time, and so Christianity cannot in any wise be regarded as a remodelling or a renewal and continuation of Judaism. Paul does indeed regard the faith of Abraham as the prototype of Christian faith, and represents the Mosaic Law simply as something slipped in between ;[1] and from this it might, of course, be inferred that he meant to represent Christianity as a renewal of that original and pure Abrahamitic Judaism. But his meaning was only that Abraham's faith was related to the promise as ours is to the fulfilment, and not by any means that the promise was the same to Abraham as the fulfilment is to us. Where he expressly speaks of the relation of the Jews and the Heathen to Christ, he represents it as being exactly the same :[2] he represents Christ as being the same for both, and both as being alike very far from God and so in need of Christ. Now if Christianity has the same relation to Judaism as to Heathenism, it can no more be regarded as a continuation of the former than of the latter : if a man comes from either of them to Christianity, he becomes, as regards his religion, a new man. But the promise to Abraham, so far as it has been fulfilled in Christ, is represented as having had its reference to Christ only in the divine decree, not in the religious consciousness of Abraham and his people. And since we can only recognize the self-identity of a religious communion when there is a uniformity of the religious consciousness, we can no more recognize an identity between Christianity and Abrahamitic Judaism than between it and the later Judaism or Heathenism. And neither can it be said that that purer original Judaism carried within itself the germ of Christianity, so that it would have developed of itself by natural progress from Judaism without the intervention of any new factor ; nor

[1] Gal. $3^{9. 14. 23-25}$.

[2] Rom. $2^{11. 12}$ 3^{21-24}, 2 Cor. $5^{16. 17}$, Eph. 2^{13-18}.

that Christ Himself lay in the line of this progress in such a way that a new communal life and existence could not begin with Him.

3. The widely prevalent notion of one single Church of God, existing from the beginning of the human race to the end of it, is opposed to our proposition more in appearance than in reality. If the Mosaic Law belongs to the one chain of this divine economy of salvation, then we must, according to approved Christian teachers, include also the Greek philosophy,[1] especially that which tended towards Monotheism ; and yet we cannot, without quite destroying the peculiarity of Christianity, assert that its teaching forms a single whole with the heathen philosophy. If, on the other hand, this doctrine of the one Church is chiefly intended to express the fact that Christ's active relation to all that is human knows no limits, even with regard to the time that was past, this is an intention upon which we cannot yet pass judgment, but which is quite compatible with our proposition. And even in Old Testament prophecy there is ascribed to the New Covenant a different character from the Old,[2] and this direct antithesis expresses the inward separation in the most definite way. Hence the rule may be set up that almost everything else in the Old Testament is, for our Christian usage, but the husk or wrapping of its prophecy, and that whatever is most definitely Jewish has least value. So that we can find rendered with some exactness in Old Testament passages only those of our religious emotions which are of a somewhat general nature without anything very distinctively Christian. For those which are distinctively Christian, Old Testament sayings will not provide a suitable expression, unless we think certain elements away from them and read other things into them. And that being the case, we shall certainly find quite as near and accordant echoes in the utterances of the nobler and purer Heathenism ; as indeed the older Apologists were no less glad to appeal to what they held to be heathen Messianic prophecies, and thus recognized there a striving of human nature towards Christianity.

§ 13. *The appearance of the Redeemer in history is, as divine revelation, neither an absolutely supernatural nor an absolutely supra-rational thing.*

1. As regards revelation, it has already [3] been granted that the starting-point of any entity which has a distinctive constitu-

[1] Εἰκότως οὖν Ἰουδαίοις μὲν νόμος Ἕλλησι δὲ φιλοσοφία μέχρι τῆς παρουσίας· ἐντεῦθεν δὲ ἡ κλῆσις ἡ καθολικὴ εἰς περιούσιον δικαιοσύνης λαόν. Clemens Alex., *Strom.* vi.

[2] Jer. 31^{31-34}

[3] § 10, *Postscript.*

tion of its own, still more of any communion and especially a religious communion, can never be explained by the condition of the circle in which it appears and operates; for if it could, it would not be a starting-point, but would itself be the product of a spiritual process. But though its existence transcends the nature of the circle in which it appeared, there is no reason why we should not believe that the appearing of such a life is the result of the power of development which resides in our human nature—a power which expresses itself in particular men at particular points according to laws which, if hidden from us, are nevertheless of divine arrangement, in order through these men to help the others forward. And indeed, apart from such a supposition, any progress of the human race as a whole or any part of it would be inconceivable. Every outstanding endowment of an individual, through whose influence any spiritual institution within a particular circle takes shape anew, is such a starting-point; only, the more such expressions are temporally and spatially limited in their influence, the more do they appear, if not explicable by what went before, yet conditioned by it. Therefore when we designate all these men as heroes, each in his own sphere, and ascribe to them a higher inspiration, this is what is meant: that for the good of the definite circle in which they appear they have been quickened and inspired from the universal fountain of life. And the fact that such men appear from time to time must be regarded as due to the working of a law, if we are to maintain the higher significance of human nature at all. The case of all such individuals is therefore analogous to that of the idea of revelation, which it is better to apply only to the region of the higher self-consciousness. No one will object to the supposition that in all founders of religions, even on the subordinate levels, there is such an endowment, if only the doctrine and communion which proceed from them have a distinctive and original character. But if this is to be applied in the same sense to Christ, it must first of all be said that, in comparison with Him, everything which could otherwise be regarded as revelation again loses this character. For everything else is limited to particular times and places, and all that proceeds from such points is from the very outset destined to be submerged again in Him, and is thus, in relation to Him, no existence, but a non-existence; and He alone is destined gradually to quicken the whole human race into higher life. Anyone who does not take Christ in this universal way as divine revelation cannot desire that Christianity should be an enduring phenomenon. But notwithstanding, it must be asserted that even the most rigorous view of the difference between Him and all other men does not hinder us from saying that His appearing, even regarded as the incarnation of the Son of God, is a natural fact. For in the first place: as certainly as Christ was a man, there must reside in human nature the possibility of taking up the divine into itself, just as did happen in Christ. So that the idea that the divine revelation in Christ must in this respect be something absolutely supernatural will simply not stand the test. Even the Protevangelium,[1] by linking the prediction of Christ directly to the Fall, declares entirely against the idea that human nature is somehow incapable of taking up into itself the restorative divine element and that the power to do so must first be introduced into it. But secondly: even if only the *possibility* of this resides in human nature, so that the actual implanting therein of the divine element must be purely a divine and therefore an eternal act, nevertheless the temporal appearance of this act in one particular Person must at the same time be regarded as an action of human nature, grounded in its original constitution and prepared for by all its past history, and accordingly as the highest development of its spiritual power (even if we grant that we could never penetrate so deep into those innermost secrets of the universal spiritual life as to be able to develop this general conviction into a definite perception). Otherwise it could only be explained as an arbitrary divine act that the restorative divine element made its appearance precisely in Jesus, and not in some other person. But the supposition of divine arbitrariness in particular matters belongs to an anthropopathic view of God, and Scripture does not declare itself in favour of such a view, but rather seems itself to point to our view that the act is conditioned.[2]

2. We now come to the supra-rational. Christ could not in any way be distinguished as Redeemer from the totality of mankind if those phases of His life by which He accomplishes redemption were explicable by means of the reason which dwells equally in all other men. For then those conditions would also be found in the others, and they also could work redemption. We may further take for granted that in redeemed people there are states of mind which are conditioned solely by Christ's communication or influence, and apart from this, one could not say that redemption has taken place in them. Consequently, these states cannot

[1] [*i.e.* Gen. 3^{15}.] [2] Gal. 4^{4}.

be explained solely by the reason which has dwelt in them from their birth—though, indeed, this does play an indispensably necessary part, since such states can never exist in a soul devoid of reason. Accordingly, the supra-rational certainly has a place in the Redeemer and the redeemed, and consequently in the whole compass of Christianity; and anybody who refused to recognize this in any form would be incapable of understanding redemption in the proper sense, and could only acknowledge Christianity as an institution, to continue until a better appeared, for the transmission of the influence of a human reason which, especially in the form of its self-consciousness, was affected in a remarkable and superior manner. This supra-rational quality is also recognized almost without exception in the utterances of those who confess Christ, and is expressed in various forms as an indwelling (either from the beginning, or coming in later and continuing, or confined to one moment) of God or of the λόγος in Christ, and as a moving of the redeemed by the Holy Spirit. But however great a difference we make between this supra-rational and the common human reason, it can never, without falling into self-contradiction, be set up as an *absolutely* supra-rational element. For the highest goal that is set for these workings of redemption is always a human state which not only would obtain the fullest recognition from the common human reason, but in which also it is impossible always to distinguish, even in the same individual, between what is effected by the divine Spirit and what is effected by the human reason. Inasmuch, then, as the reason is completely one with the divine Spirit, the divine Spirit can itself be conceived as the highest enhancement of the human reason, so that the difference between the two is made to disappear. But further: even at the very outset, whatever opposes the movements of the divine Spirit is the same as what conflicts with human reason; for otherwise there could not exist in man (as there does), before the entry of those divine influences, a consciousness of the need of redemption, which these very influences set at rest. If, then, the human reason itself in a sense contains that which is produced by the divine Spirit, the latter does not in this connexion, at least, go beyond the former. Now what is true of the redeemed may also be said of the Redeemer. For even the people who do not assume any kind of divine indwelling in Him do nevertheless, for their part, extol the very same activities, ideas, and practical precepts of His (which others explain by divine indwelling) as being the highest pitch of the rational, and thus with their human reason apprehend them with approval; which apprehension, again, those others do not reproach or reject, but likewise recognize with approval.

Postscript.—According to the view of religion which we have taken as our basis, the peculiar being of the Redeemer and of the redeemed in their connexion with Him is the original point at which this question of the supernatural and the supra-rational in Christianity emerges; so that there is no ground whatever for admitting anything supernatural or supra-rational which is not connected with the appearing of the Redeemer but would in itself form another original element. The question is usually handled, partly with reference to the individual facts for which a supernatural quality is especially claimed (we cannot yet speak of them here), and partly with reference to the Christian doctrines, which are for us nothing but the expressions given to the Christian self-consciousness and its connexions. But if the supernatural in the Christian self-consciousness consists in the fact that it cannot, in the form in which it actually exists, be produced by the activity of reason, it by no means follows from this that the expressions given to this self-consciousness must also be supra-rational. For in the same sense in which the Christian self-consciousness is supra-rational, the whole of Nature is supra-rational too, and yet we do not apply that epithet to the things we say *about* Nature, but call them purely rational. But the whole process of formulating our expressions concerning the religious self-consciousness is just as much a rational process as in the case of Nature; and the difference is merely that this objective consciousness is given at first hand only to him who is affected by Nature, while that (Christian) self-consciousness is given only to him who is affected by the Redeemer in the manner which is peculiar to His followers. Now this itself makes plain what we are to think of the prevalent view that Christian doctrine consists partly of rational and partly of supra-rational dogmas. It is, indeed, of itself obvious that this can be no more than a juxtaposition, and that these two kinds of dogmas cannot form one whole. Between the rational and the supra-rational there can be no connexion. This further becomes pretty clearly evident in all treatises upon Christian doctrine which divide themselves into a natural theology, purely rational and thus valid not only within, but also outside of Christianity, and a positive supra-rational theology, valid only within the compass of Christianity. For then the two are and remain separate from each other. The apparent practicability of a union of the two arises from the fact that there are, of course, Christian dogmas in which the peculiarly Christian element retreats considerably into the background, so that they may be taken to be purely rational in those respects in which the others are recognized as supra-rational. But if that peculiarly Christian element were not in them at all, they would, of course, not be Christian dogmas. Hence the truth of the matter is as follows. In one respect all Christian dogmas are supra-rational, in another they are all rational. They are supra-rational in the respect in which everything experiential is supra-rational. For there is an inner experience to which they may all be traced: they rest upon a *given*; and apart from this they could not have arisen, by deduction or synthesis, from universally recognized and communicable propositions. If the reverse were true, it would mean that you could instruct and demonstrate any man into being a Christian, without his happening to have had any experience. Therefore this supra-rationality implies that a true appropriation of Christian dogmas cannot be brought about by scientific means, and thus lies outside the realm of reason: it can only be brought about through each man willing to have the experience for himself, as indeed it is true of everything individual and characteristic, that it can only be apprehended by the love which wills to perceive. In this sense the whole of Christian doctrine is supra-rational. It may, however, be further asked whether the dogmas which give expression to the religious affections of the Christian and their connexions are not subject to the same laws of conception and synthesis as regulate all speech, so that the more perfectly these laws are satisfied in such a presentation, the more will each individual be constrained to apprehend correctly what is thought and intended, even if he cannot, for lack of the fundamental inward experience, convince himself of the truth of the matter. It must be answered that in this sense everything in Christian doctrine is entirely according to reason. Accordingly, the supra-rationality of all particular Christian dogmas is the measure by which it can be judged whether they succeed in expressing the peculiarly Christian element; and again, their rationality is the test of how far the attempt to translate the inward emotions into thoughts has succeeded. But to assert that it cannot be demanded that what goes beyond reason should be rationally presented, appears to be only a subterfuge designed to cover up some imperfection in the procedure; just as the opposite view that in Christian doctrine everything must be, in every sense, based on reason, is simply meant to cover up the lack of a fundamental experience of one's own.

The usual formula, that the supra-rational in Christianity must not be contrary to reason, seems intended to say the same thing as our proposition. For it implies, on the one hand, the recognition of the supra-rational, and, on the other hand, the task of showing that it is not contrary to reason, and this can only be achieved by means of a rational presentation.

§ 14. *There is no other way of obtaining participation in the Christian communion than through faith in Jesus as the Redeemer.*

1. To participate in the Christian communion means to seek in Christ's institution an approximation to the above-described [1] state of absolute facility and constancy of religious emotions. No one can wish to belong to the Christian Church on any other ground. But since each can only enter through a free resolve of his own, this must be preceded by the certainty that the influence of Christ puts an end to the state of being in need of redemption, and produces that other state ; and this certainty is just faith in Christ. That is to say, this term always signifies, in our present province, the certainty which accompanies a state of the higher self-consciousness, and which is therefore different from, but not for that reason less than, the certainty which accompanies the objective consciousness. In the same sense we spoke above [2] of faith in God, which was nothing but the certainty concerning the feeling of absolute dependence, as such, *i.e.* as conditioned by a Being placed outside of us, and as expressing our relation to that Being. The faith of which we are now speaking, however, is a purely factual certainty, but a certainty of a fact which is entirely inward. That is to say, it cannot exist in an individual until, through an impression which he has received from Christ, there is found in him a beginning—perhaps quite infinitesimal, but yet a real premonition—of the process which will put an end to the state of needing redemption. But the term 'faith in Christ' here (as the term 'faith in God' formerly) relates the state of redemption, as effect, to Christ as cause. That is how John describes it. And so from the beginning only those people have attached themselves to Christ in His new community whose religious self-consciousness had taken the form of a need of redemption, and who now became assured in themselves

[1] § 5, 4. [2] § 4, 4.

of Christ's redeeming power.[1] So that the more strongly those two phases appeared in any individual, the more able was he, by representation of the fact (which includes description of Christ and His work) to elicit this inward experience in others. Those in whom this took place became believers, and the rest did not.[2] This, moreover, is what has ever since constituted the essence of all direct Christian preaching. Such preaching must always take the form of testimony; testimony as to one's own experience, which shall arouse in others the desire to have the same experience. But the impression which all later believers received in this way from the influence of Christ, *i.e.* from the common Spirit communicated by Him and from the whole communion of Christians, supported by the historical representation of His life and character, was just the same impression which His contemporaries received from Him directly. Hence those who remained unbelieving were not blamed because they had not let themselves be persuaded by reasons, but simply because of their lack of self-knowledge, which must always be the explanation when the Redeemer is truly and correctly presented and people show themselves unable to recognize Him as such. But even Christ Himself represented this lack of self-knowledge, *i.e.* of the consciousness of needing redemption, as the limit to His activity. And so the ground of unbelief is the same in all ages, as is also the ground of belief or faith.

2. The attempt has often been made to demonstrate the necessity of redemption, but always in vain. We need not, however, appeal to these cases, for it is clear in itself that the thing is impossible. Any man who is capable of being satisfied with himself as he is will always manage to find a way out of the argument. And no more can it be demonstrated, once the consciousness of this need has been awakened, that Christ is the only One who can work redemption. In His own time there were many who did believe that redemption was near, and yet did not accept Him. And even when we have a more correct idea of the end to be sought, it is not easy to see how it could be proved that any particular individual is in a position to achieve the desired effect. For in this matter we are concerned with amount of spiritual power, which we have no means of calculating; and even if we had, we should also require some fixed datum against which the calculation could be set. It cannot even be proved in a general way that such a redemption is bound to come, even if we presuppose a general know-

[1] John 1$^{45, 46}$ 6$^{68, 69}$, Matt. 16$^{15-18}$. [2] Acts 2$^{37, 41}$.

ledge not only of what men are like but also of what God is like. There would still be plenty of room for different sophistical arguments to draw opposite conclusions from the same data, according as God's purpose for man was conceived in one way or in another.

Agreed, then, that we must adhere to the kind of certainty which we have just described, and that faith is nothing other than the incipient experience of the satisfaction of that spiritual need by Christ: there can still be very diverse ways of experiencing the need and the succour, and yet they will all be faith. Moreover, the consciousness of need may be present for a long time in advance, or it may, as is often the case, be fully awakened only by the contrast which the perfection of Christ forms with our own condition, so that the two things come into existence simultaneously, the supreme consciousness of need and the beginning of its satisfaction.

3. It is true that in the Scriptures themselves proofs are often mentioned, which the witnesses of the Gospel employed.[1] Yet it is never asserted that faith sprang from the proof, but from the preaching. Those proofs were only applied among the Jews, with reference to their current ideas of the coming Messiah, in order to repulse the opposition presented by these ideas to the witness of the Gospel, or to anticipate any such opposition. This was an indispensable line of defence for witnesses of Christ who were Jews and who were dealing with Jews. If they wished to assert that they themselves had never expected any other kind of redemption than this, or that their expectations had been transformed by the appearing and the influence of Christ, they must either break with the whole Jewish religion, which they had no warrant for doing, or show that the prophetic representations were applicable to this Jesus as Redeemer. If we took the other view of the matter, it would mean that the faith of the Gentile Christians was not the same as that of the Jewish Christians; and then it would not have been possible for these two to become really one, but the Gentiles would have had to become Jews first, in order then to be brought to Christ by the authority of the prophets.

Postscript.—Our proposition says nothing of any intermediate link between faith and participation in the Christian communion, and is accordingly to be taken as directly combining the two, so that faith of itself carries with it that participation; and not only as depending on the spontaneous activity of the man who has become a believer, but also as depending on the spontaneous

[1] Acts $6^{9.\,10}$ 9^{20-22}, also $18^{27.\,28}$.

activity of the communion (Church), as the source from which the testimony proceeded for the awakening of faith. At the same time, in shutting up the whole process between these two points, the witness or testimony and its effect, our proposition is intended to make an end of everything which, in the form of demonstration, is usually brought to the aid of the proper witness or even substituted for it. This refers principally to the attempts to bring about a recognition of Christ by means of the miracles which He performs, or the prophecies which predicted Him, or the special character of the testimonies originally borne to Him, regarded as the work of divine inspiration. In all this there seems to be more or less illusion on the following point: that the efficacy of these things somehow always presupposes faith, and therefore cannot produce it.

First consider *Miracle,* taking the word in its narrower sense, so that prophecy and inspiration are not included, but simply phenomena in the realm of physical nature which are supposed not to have been caused in a natural manner. Whether we confine ourselves to those performed by Jesus Himself, or include those which took place in connexion with Him, these miracles cannot bring about a recognition of Him at all. In the first place, we know of these miracles only from those same Holy Scriptures (for the miracles related in less pure sources are never adduced along with them) which relate similar miracles of people who did not adhere to Christianity at all, but are rather to be reckoned among its enemies; and Scripture gives us no marks for distinguishing evidential miracles from non-evidential. But further, Scripture itself bears witness that faith has been produced without miracles, and also that miracles have failed to produce it; from which it may be concluded that even when it has existed along with miracles it was not produced by miracles but in its own original way. Hence if the purpose of miracles had been to produce faith, we should have to conclude that God's breaking into the order of Nature proved ineffectual. Accordingly, many find the purpose of miracles simply in the fact that they turn the attention to Christ. But this, again, is at least so far contradicted by Christ's oft-repeated command not to make the miracles more widely known, that we should have to limit their efficacy to the immediate eye-witnesses, and thus this efficacy would no longer exist to-day. But, finally, the following question cannot be avoided. In any other context than that of such faith and its realm, we may encounter any number of facts which we cannot explain naturally, and yet we never think of miracle, but simply regard the explanation as deferred until we have a more exact knowledge both of the fact in question and of the laws of Nature. But when such a fact occurs in connexion with some faith-realm which has to be established, we think at once of miracle ; only, each man claims miracle as real for the realm of his own faith alone, and sets down the others as false. On what is this distinction based ? The question can hardly be answered except as follows. In general we do, perhaps, assume so exclusive a connexion between miracles and the formation of a new faith-realm, that we only admit miracle for this kind of case ; but the state of each individual's faith determines his judgment of the alleged miracle, and so the miracle does not produce the faith. As regards that universal connexion, however, the state of the case seems to be as follows. Where a new point in the development of the spiritual life, and indeed primarily of the self-consciousness, is assumed to exist, new phenomena in physical Nature, mediated by the spiritual power which is manifested, are also expected, because both the contemplative and the outwardly active spiritual states all proceed from the self-consciousness, and are determined by its movements. Thus, once Christ is recognized as Redeemer, and consequently as the beginning of the supreme development of human nature in the realm of the self-consciousness, it is a natural assumption that, just because at the point where such an existence communicates itself most strongly, spiritual states appear which cannot be explained from what went before, He who exercises such a peculiar influence upon human nature around Him will be able, in virtue of the universal connexion of things, to manifest also a peculiar power of working upon the physical side of human nature and upon external Nature. That is to say, it is natural to expect miracles from Him who is the supreme divine revelation ; and yet they can be called miracles only in a relative sense, since our ideas of the susceptibility of physical Nature to the influence of the spirit and of the causality of the will acting upon physical Nature are as far from being finally settled and as capable of being perpetually widened by new experiences as are our ideas of the forces of physical Nature themselves. Now, since, in connexion with the divine revelation in Christ, phenomena presented themselves which could be brought under this concept of miracle, it was natural that they should actually come to be regarded from this point of view, and adduced as confirmation of the fact that this was a new point of development. But this confirmation will be effectual only where there is already present a beginning of faith ; failing that, the miracle would either be declared false or be reserved, as regards the understanding of it, for some natural explanation which the future would reveal. Still less could it be proved from the miracles which accompanied it that Christianity is the supreme revelation, since similar phenomena are on the same grounds to be expected in the lower faiths too, and miracles themselves cannot, as such, be divided into higher and lower. Indeed, the possibility cannot be excluded that similar phenomena might occur even apart from all connexion with the realm of religion, whether as accompanying other kinds of development or as signalizing deeper movements in physical Nature itself. Similarly, on the other hand, it seems to be a matter of course that such supernatural phenomena, which accompany revelation, disappear again in proportion as the new development, freed from its point of origin in the external realm, is organized, and so becomes Nature.

The same thing may be said with regard to *Prophecies*, in case anyone should wish to assign to them a more powerful rôle than that which we have granted above. Let us confine ourselves to the prophecies of the Jewish prophets regarding Christ, for in more recent times the heathen prophecies have been universally set aside, and we are not here immediately concerned with the prophecies of Christ and His apostles. Suppose, then, that we wished to make more use of those prophetic utterances among Jews. It is quite conceivable that a Jew should become a Christian because he came to see that those prophecies were to be referred to Jesus, and that nevertheless he should possess neither the real faith nor the true participation in the Christian communion, understanding it all, perhaps, in a quite different way, because he did not feel any need of redemption. But suppose these prophecies were to be universally set before unbelievers, in order to produce in them the will to enter into communion with Christ. It might be made out at the start that these prophecies are all to be regarded as belonging together, that they all have in view an individual, and indeed one and the same individual (for otherwise the fulfilment of them all in one and the same person would really be a non-fulfilment), and further that they have all come to fulfilment in Christ, each in the sense in which it was meant, not those figuratively meant being fulfilled in a literal sense and those literally meant in a figurative sense (for that also would not be a real fulfilment). But, after all, it always comes to this in the end : that Jesus must be taken to be the

Redeemer, because the Redeemer was predicted with descriptive details which are found in Him. But this argument presupposes that people already have faith in the prophets who predicted, as such; and it is impossible to imagine how an unbeliever outside of Judaism should come to have such a faith, except on the supposition that the inspiration of the prophets is proved to him, and with this we shall deal below. Without such a faith the collocation of prophecies and their fulfilments would be a mere signpost, giving an impulse to seek fellowship with Christ only to those people who were already feeling the need of redemption; and this only in so far as the need expressed in the prophecies is analogous to their own, and at the same time the thing prophesied has a manifest connexion with that need;[1] that is to say, in so far as each man could himself have prophesied the same thing out of his own need. The impulse, however, could only issue in his seeking to have the experience for himself,[2] and only when this attempt succeeded would there be faith. And certainly this impulse can now, when facts speak so loud, be given much more powerfully and surely in other ways than by means of the prophecies. This becomes especially clear when we reflect how the case really stands with regard to the above-mentioned presuppositions; namely, that it can never be proved that those prophets foresaw Christ as He really was, and still less the Messianic kingdom as it really developed in Christianity. Thus it must be admitted that a proof from prophecy of Christ as the Redeemer is impossible; and in particular, the zealous attempt to seek out for this purpose prophecies or prototypes which relate to accidental circumstances in the story of Christ must appear simply as a mistake. A clear distinction must, therefore, be made between the apologetical use which the apostles made of the prophecies in their intercourse with the Jews, and a general use which might be made of them as evidences. When, however, faith in the Redeemer is already present, then we can dwell with great pleasure on all expressions of the longing for redemption awakened by earlier and inadequate revelations. And this is the real significance (and it has, of course, a confirmative and corroborative value) of Messianic prophecies, wherever they appear and in however obscure presentiments they are shrouded: they disclose to us a striving of human nature towards Christianity, and at the same

[1] In this sense perhaps the prophecy quoted in Matt. 12$^{19, 20}$ is the most pregnant prophecy.

[2] John 1$^{41, 46}$.

time give it as the confession of the best and most inspired of earlier religious communions, that they are to be regarded only as preparatory and transitory institutions. As for the prophecies made by Christianity itself, it is, of course, natural that at the beginning of the development of a new thing the outlook is directed very much towards the future, *i.e.* towards its completion, and so one can understand the questions of the disciples, to which answers —on the basis of which they afterwards made further prophecies— could not altogether be denied. But Christ's prophecies cannot serve as a proof of His unique office and His exclusive vocation as Redeemer, for the simple reason that others also have admittedly prophesied. Again, it was equally natural that the more the new dispensation became established as an historical phenomenon, the more the interest in the future decreased and prophecy disappeared.

Now from all this it follows that, if faith in the revelation of God in Christ and in redemption through Him has not already arisen in the direct way through experience as the demonstration of the Spirit and of power, neither miracles nor prophecies can produce it, and indeed that this faith would be just as immovable even if Christianity had neither prophecies nor miracles to show. For the lack of these could never refute that demonstration, or prove a mere delusion the experience of need satisfied in the fellowship of Christ. From the lack of these, indeed, nothing could be concluded except that those natural assumptions do not always prove true, and that the beginning of the most perfect form of religious self-consciousness appeared more suddenly, and confined its working more closely to its own immediate realm.

We come finally to *Inspiration*. In Christianity this conception has a wholly subordinate significance. It cannot be related at all to Christ, since the divine revelation through Him, however it is conceived, is always conceived as identical with His whole being, and not as appearing fragmentarily in sporadic moments. And as for what the apostles received from the Spirit, Christ traces that entirely to His own instruction, and those who through their testimony became believers did not believe because the testimony sprang from inspiration, for of that they knew nothing. The conception therefore relates only in the first place to the prophets of the Old Covenant, and in the second place to the composition of the New Testament Scriptures; and so we have to deal with it here only in so far as concerns the attempt to compel faith demonstratively by means of Holy Scripture, when this is first assumed to be inspired. But as regards the Old Testament, Prophecy cannot be understood alone without Law and History; and this whole, taken all together, is so consistently theocratic that (while we can indeed distinguish in it two 'poles,' one of which exercises attraction, the other repulsion, towards the New Testament), if, apart from the New Testament, we succeeded in making anyone believe in the prophetic inspiration (which, however, could hardly be accomplished except upon their own testimony that the word of God came to them), yet from this there could not be developed a faith in Christ as the end of the Law. We shall rather express the whole truth if we say that we believe in the prophetic inspiration simply because of the use which Christ and His apostles make of the utterances of the prophets. As regards the New Testament, the faith had been disseminated for two hundred years before that Testament was unanimously established as having peculiar validity. And, moreover, it was not a matter of Christian faith being in the meantime always mediated by faith in the Old Testament, for among the great mass of the heathen, who went over to Christianity without having been previously Judaized, this was by no means the case. But even now, and even supposing that the inspiration of the New Testament Scriptures can be proved from these Scriptures themselves, this would nevertheless presuppose a very perfect understanding of these Scriptures. And thus, since this is possible only for a few, we should still require some other way in which faith might arise, so that there would be two kinds of faith. And further, it is still impossible to see how an objective conviction of this kind could exercise such an influence on the self-consciousness, that, from the mere knowledge that those people were inspired who asserted that men need redemption and that Christ is their Redeemer, this assertion would immediately come to contain for all an inward truth. All that this conviction in itself can do is merely to give an impulse towards the awakening of a fuller self-consciousness and towards the winning of a total impression of Christ; and only from this will faith then proceed.

IV. The Relation of Dogmatics to Christian Piety.

§ 15. *Christian doctrines are accounts of the Christian religious affections set forth in speech.*

Note.—Cf. § 3, 5.

1. All religious emotions, to whatever type and level of religion they belong, have this in common with all other modifications of

the affective self-consciousness, that as soon as they have reached a certain stage and a certain definiteness they manifest themselves outwardly by mimicry in the most direct and spontaneous way, by means of facial features and movements of voice and gesture, which we regard as their expression. Thus we definitely distinguish the expression of devoutness from that of a sensuous gladness or sadness, by the analogy of each man's knowledge of himself. Indeed, we can even conceive that, for the purpose of maintaining the religious affections and securing their repetition and propagation (especially if they were common to a number of people), the elements of that natural expression of them might be put together into sacred signs and symbolical acts, without the thought having perceptibly come in between at all. But we can scarcely conceive such a low development of the human spirit, such a defective culture, and such a meagre use of speech, that each person would not, according to the level of reflection on which he stands, become in his various mental states likewise an object to himself, in order to comprehend them in idea and retain them in the form of thought. Now this endeavour has always directed itself particularly to the religious emotions ; and this, considered in its own inward meaning, is what our proposition means by an account of the religious affections. But while thought cannot proceed even inwardly without the use of speech, nevertheless there are, so long as it remains merely inward, fugitive elements in this procedure, which do indeed in some measure indicate the object, but not in such a way that either the formation or the synthesis of concepts (in however wide a sense we take the word ' concept ') is sufficiently definite for communication. It is only when this procedure has reached such a point of cultivation as to be able to represent itself outwardly in definite speech, that it produces a real doctrine (*Glaubenssatz*), by means of which the utterances of the religious consciousness come into circulation more surely and with a wider range than is possible through the direct expression. But no matter whether the expression is natural or figurative, whether it indicates its object directly or only by comparison and delimitation, it is still a doctrine.

2. Now Christianity everywhere presupposes that consciousness has reached this stage of development. The whole work of the Redeemer Himself was conditioned by the communicability of His self-consciousness by means of speech, and similarly Christianity has always and everywhere spread itself solely by preaching. Every proposition which can be an element of the Christian preaching

(κήρυγμα) is also a doctrine, because it bears witness to the determination of the religious self-consciousness as inward certainty. And every Christian doctrine is also a part of the Christian preaching, because every such doctrine expresses as a certainty the approximation to the state of blessedness [1] which is to be effected through the means ordained by Christ. But this preaching very soon split up into three different types of speech, which provide as many different forms of doctrine: the poetic, the rhetorical (which is directed partly outwards, as combative and commendatory, and partly inwards, as rather disciplinary and challenging), and finally the descriptively didactic. But the relation of communication through speech to communication through symbolic action varies very much according to time and place, the former having always retreated into the background in the Eastern Church (for when the letter of doctrine has become fixed and unalterable, it is in its effect much nearer to symbolic action than to free speech), and having become ever more prominent in the Western Church. And in the realm of speech it is just the same with these three modes of communication. The relation in which they stand to each other, the general degree of richness, and the amount of living intercourse in which they unfold themselves, as they nourish themselves on one another and pass over into one another—these things testify not so much to the degree or level of piety as rather to the character of the communion or fellowship and its ripeness for reflection and contemplation. Thus this communication is, on the one hand, something different from the piety itself, though the latter cannot, any more than anything else which is human, be conceived entirely separated from all communication. But, on the other hand, the doctrines in all their forms have their ultimate ground so exclusively in the emotions of the religious self-consciousness, that where these do not exist the doctrines cannot arise.

§ 16. *Dogmatic propositions are doctrines of the descriptively didactic type, in which the highest possible degree of definiteness is aimed at.*

NOTE.—Cf. § 3, 4 and 5; and § 13, 1 and 2.

1. The poetic expression is always based originally upon a moment of exaltation which has come purely from within, a moment of enthusiasm or inspiration; the rhetorical upon a moment whose exaltation has come from without, a moment of stimulated interest

[1] See § 5, 4.

which issues in a particular definite result. The former is purely descriptive (*darstellend*), and sets up in general outlines images and forms which each hearer completes for himself in his own peculiar way. The rhetorical is purely stimulative, and has, in its nature, to do for the most part with such elements of speech as, admitting of degrees of signification, can be taken in a wider or narrower sense, content if at the decisive moment they can accomplish the highest, even though they should exhaust themselves thereby and subsequently appear to lose somewhat of their force. Thus both of these forms possess a different perfection from the logical or dialectical perfection described in our proposition. But, nevertheless, we can think of both as being primary and original in every religious communion, and thus in the Christian Church, in so far as we ascribe to everyone in it a share in the vocation of preaching. For when anyone finds himself in a state of unusually exalted religious self-consciousness, he will feel himself called to poetic description, as that which proceeds from this state most directly. And, on the other hand, when anyone finds himself particularly challenged by insistent or favourable outward circumstances to attempt an act of preaching, the rhetorical form of expression will be the most natural to him for obtaining from the given circumstances the greatest possible advantage. But let us conceive of the comprehension and appropriation of what is given in a direct way in these two forms, as being now also wedded to language and thereby made communicable: then this cannot again take the poetic form, nor yet the rhetorical; but, being independent of that which was the momentary element in those two forms, and expressing as it does a consciousness which remains self-identical, it becomes, less as preaching than as confession (ὁμολογία), precisely that third form —the didactic—which, with its descriptive instruction, remains distinct from the two others, and is made up of the two put together, as a derivative and secondary form.

2. But let us confine ourselves to Christianity, and think of its distinctive beginning, namely, the self-proclamation of Christ, Who, as subject of the divine revelation, could not contain in Himself any distinction of stronger and weaker emotion, but could only partake in such a diversity through His common life with others. Then we shall not be able to take either the poetic or the rhetorical form of expression as the predominating, or even as the really primary and original, form of His self-proclamation. These have only a subordinate place in parabolic and prophetic discourses. The essential

thing in His self-proclamation was that He had to bear witness regarding His ever unvarying self-consciousness out of the depths of its repose, and consequently not in poetic but in strictly reflective form ; and thus had to set Himself forth, while at the same time communicating His alone true objective consciousness of the condition and constitution of men in general, thus instructing by description or representation, the instruction being sometimes subordinate to the description, and sometimes *vice versa*. But this descriptively didactic mode of expression used by Christ is not included in our proposition, and such utterances of the Redeemer will hardly be set up anywhere as dogmatic propositions ; they will only, as it were, provide the text for them. For in such essential parts of the self-proclamation of Christ the definiteness was absolute, and it is only the perfection of the apprehension and appropriation which reproduces these, that can be characterized by the endeavour after the greatest possible definiteness. Subordinate to these, however, there do appear genuinely dogmatic propositions in the discourses of Christ, namely, at those points at which He had to start from the partly erroneous and partly confused ideas current among His contemporaries.

3. As regards the poetic and rhetorical forms of expression, it follows directly from what we have said, that they may fall into apparent contradiction both with themselves and with each other, even when the self-consciousness which is indicated by different forms of expression is in itself one and the same. And a solution will only be possible, in the first place, when it is possible in interpreting propositions that are apparently contradictory to take one's bearings from the original utterances of Christ (a thing which can in very few cases be done directly), and, in the second place, when the descriptively didactic expression, which has grown out of those three original forms put together, is entirely or largely free from those apparent contradictions. This, however, will not be possible of achievement so long as the descriptively didactic expression itself keeps vacillating between the emotional and the didactic, in its presentation to the catechumens or the community, and approaches sometimes more to the rhetorical and sometimes more to the figurative. It will only be possible in proportion as the aim indicated in our proposition underlies the further development of the expression and its more definite separation from the rhetorical and the poetic, both of which processes are essentially bound up with the need of settling the conflict. Now, of course,

this demand, that the figurative expression be either exchanged for a literal one or transformed into such by being explained, and that definite limits be imposed on the corresponding element in the rhetorical expressions, is unmistakably the interest which science has in the formation of language ; and it is mainly with the formation of religious language that we are here concerned. Hence dogmatic propositions develop to any considerable extent and gain recognition only in such religious communions as have reached a degree of culture in which science is organized as something distinct both from art and from business, and only in proportion as friends of science are found and have influence within the communion itself, so that the dialectical function is brought to bear on the utterances of the religious self-consciousness, and guides the expression of them. Such a union with organized knowledge has had a place in Christianity ever since the earliest ages of the Church, and therefore in no other religious communion has the form of the dogmatic proposition evolved in such strict separation from the other forms, or developed in such fulness.

Postscript.—This account of the origin of dogmatic propositions, as having arisen solely out of logically ordered reflection upon the immediate utterances of the religious self-consciousness, finds its confirmation in the whole of history. The earliest specimens of preaching preserved for us in the New Testament Scriptures already contain such propositions ; and on closer consideration we can see in all of them, in the first place, their derivation from the original self-proclamation of Christ, and, in the second place, their affinity to figurative and rhetorical elements which, for permanent circulation, had to approximate more to the strictness of a formula. Similarly in later periods it is clear that the figurative language, which is always poetic in its nature, had the most decided influence upon the dogmatic language, and always preceded its development, and also that the majority of the dogmatic definitions were called forth by contradictions to which the rhetorical expressions had led.

But when the transformation of the original expressions into dogmatic propositions is ascribed to the logical or dialectical interest, this is to be understood as applying only to the form. A proposition which had originally proceeded from the speculative activity, however akin it might be to our propositions in content, would not be a dogmatic proposition. The purely scientific activity, whose task is the contemplation of existence, must, if it is to come to anything, either begin or end with the Supreme Being ; and so there may be forms of philosophy containing propositions of speculative import about the Supreme Being which, in spite of the fact that they arose out of the purely scientific interest, are, when taken individually, difficult to distinguish from the corresponding propositions which arose purely out of reflection upon the religious emotions, but have been worked out dialectically. But when they are considered in their connexions, these two indubitably show differences of the most definite kind. For dogmatic propositions never make their original appearance except in trains of thought which have received their impulse from religious moods of mind; whereas, not only do speculative propositions about the Supreme Being appear for the most part in purely logical or natural-scientific trains of thought, but even when they come in as ethical presuppositions or corollaries, they show an unmistakable leaning towards one or other of those two directions. Moreover, in the dogmatic developments of the earliest centuries, if we discount the quite unecclesiastical Gnostic schools, the influence of speculation upon the content of dogmatic propositions may be placed at zero. At a later time, certainly, when the classical organization of knowledge had fallen into ruins, and the conglomerate-philosophy of the Middle Ages took shape within the Christian Church, and at the same time came to exercise its influence upon the formation of dogmatic language, a confusion of the speculative with the dogmatic, and consequently a mingling of the two, was almost inevitable. But this was for both an imperfect condition, from which philosophy freed itself by means of the avowal, growing ever gradually louder, that at that time it had stood under the tutelage of ecclesiastical faith, and therefore under an alien law. Having, however, since then made so many fresh starts in its own proper development, it was able to escape from the wearisome task of inquiring exactly as to what kind of speculative propositions were at that time taken to be dogmatic, and *vice versa*. For the Christian Church, however, which is not in a position ever and anon to begin the development of its doctrine over again from the start, this separation is of the greatest importance, in order to secure that speculative matter (by which neither the poetic and rhetorical nor the popular expression can consent to be guided) may not continue to be offered to it as dogmatic. The Evangelical (Protestant) Church in particular is unanimous in feeling that the distinctive form of its dogmatic propositions does not depend on any form or school of philosophy, and has not proceeded at all from a speculative interest, but simply from the interest of satisfying the immediate self-consciousness solely through the means ordained by Christ, in their genuine and uncorrupted form. Thus it can consistently adopt as dogmatic propositions of its own no propositions except such as can show this derivation. Our dogmatic theology will not, however, stand on its proper ground and soil with the same assurance with which philosophy has so long stood upon its own, until the separation of the two types of proposition is so complete that, *e.g.*, so extraordinary a question as whether the same proposition can be true in philosophy and false in Christian theology, and *vice versa*, will no longer be asked, for the simple reason that a proposition cannot appear in the one context precisely as it appears in the other: however similar it sounds, a difference must always be assumed. But we are still very far from this goal, so long as people take pains to base or deduce dogmatic propositions in the speculative manner, or even set themselves to work up the products of speculative activity and the results of the study of religious affections into a single whole.

§ 17. *Dogmatic propositions have a twofold value—an ecclesiastical and a scientific; and their degree of perfection is determined by both of these and their relation to each other.*

1. The ecclesiastical value of a dogmatic proposition consists in its reference to the religious emotions themselves. Every such emotion, regarded singly, is indeed for description an infinite, and all dogmatic concepts, as well as all concepts of psychology, would have to be used to describe one moment of life. But just as in such a moment the religious strain may be the dominant one, so again in every such strain some one relation of the higher self-consciousness stands out as determinative; and it is to this strain, uniformly for all analogous moments of religious emotion, that the dogmatic propositions refer. Thus, in all completely expressed dogmatic propositions, the reference to Christ as Redeemer must appear with the same measure of prominence which it has in the religious consciousness itself. Naturally, however, this is not equally strongly the case in all religious moments, any more than in the life of any civic state the distinctive character of its constitution can appear equally strongly in all moments. Accordingly, the less strongly the reference to Christ is expressed in a dogmatic proposition, as, *e.g.*, in the religious emotions mediated by our relation to the external world, the more easily may it resemble a

doctrinal proposition of another religious communion, in cases where the distinctive character of that communion too remains for the most part in the background. Now this occurs even within the Christian Church itself, in respect of the various modifications of the Christian consciousness which separate into larger or smaller groups. Now, if a dogmatic proposition is so formed that it satisfies the Christian consciousness for all alike, then it actually holds good in a larger circle, but it is not calculated to show up differences, which are thus indirectly marked as unimportant or in process of disappearing. If, on the other hand, it has respect only to one of these different modifications, then it holds good only within this smaller compass. Sometimes the former kind of dogma may seem colourless, and the latter be the right kind; at other times the latter may be factious or sectarian, and the former be the right kind. But such differences in dogmatic propositions dealing with the same subject, which do not represent any differences at all in the immediate religious self-consciousness, are of no significance for their ecclesiastical value.

2. The scientific value of a dogmatic proposition depends in the first place upon the definiteness of the concepts which appear in it, and of their connexion with each other. For the more definite these become, the more does the proposition pass out of the indefinite realm of the poetic and rhetorical, and the more certain will it be that the proposition cannot enter into apparent contradiction with other dogmatic propositions belonging to the same form of religious consciousness. But in forming its concepts Dogmatics has not succeeded—indeed, one might say that from the nature of the subject it cannot succeed—in everywhere substituting the exact expression for the figurative; and thus the scientific value of dogmatic propositions depends, from this side, for the most part simply upon the highest possible degree of precision and definiteness in explaining the figurative expressions which occur. And we can the more readily leave it at that, since, even if the exact expression could throughout be substituted for the figurative, the latter is the original, and therefore the identity of the two would have to be shown, which would come to the same thing in the end. In the second place, the scientific value of a dogmatic proposition consists in its fruitfulness, that is to say, its many-sidedness in pointing us towards other kindred ones; and not so much in a heuristic way (since no dogmatic proposition is based on another, and each one can only be discovered from contemplation of the Christian self-

consciousness) as in a critical way, because then it can be the more easily tested how well one dogmatic expression harmonizes with others. For it is undeniable that, of a number of dogmatic expressions which are supposed to refer to the same fact of the Christian consciousness, that one will deserve the preference which opens up and enters into combination with the largest range of other expressions referring to kindred facts. And when we find a realm or system of dogmatic language which is closely bound together and forms a self-contained whole, that is an account of the facts which we may presume to be correct.

A proposition which lacks the first of these two properties, and which thus belongs entirely to the poetic or the rhetorical realm of language, has not got the length of being a dogmatic proposition. A proposition which, as regards the second of the two properties, goes beyond the principle we have set up, and seeks to establish anything objectively without going back to the higher self-consciousness, would not be a religious doctrine (*Glaubenssatz*) at all, and would simply not belong to our field.

3. Now since every doctrine of the faith has, as such, an ecclesiastical value, and since these doctrines become dogmatic when they acquire a scientific value, dogmatic propositions are the more perfect the more their scientific character gives them an outstanding ecclesiastical value, and also the more their scientific content bears traces of having proceeded from the ecclesiastical interest.

§ 18. *The collocation of dogmatic propositions, for the purpose of connecting them and relating them to each other, proceeds from the very same need which led to the formation of them, and is simply a natural sequel to it.*

1. We distinguish Christ's own preaching (which was the starting-point of everything) from dogmatic material, chiefly because when He went didactically into particular details, He verged upon the poetic and the rhetorical, and when He proclaimed Himself in precise and unfigurative language, He never went beyond a quite summary presentation of His being and His work.[1] But every religious emotion which was the direct effect of that preaching became, in the given life-context of the moment, a particular emotion, and therefore the apprehension of it in thought, as an appropriation of that original self-proclamation, was only

[1] Cf. John 3^{17} 8^{12} 10^{30} 12^{45}.

partial and imperfect; so that the total mass of the doctrines which thus arose and were worked out with the greatest possible definiteness as dogmatic propositions, is simply, taken all together, the unfolding, ever more and more complete, of that original preaching. Therefore each individual proposition which has so arisen implies a striving after the remaining ones, and thus an endeavour to connect each with others; and each, just in so far as it is definitely one individual proposition, obtains its place only on the presupposition that it has other more or less kindred propositions beside it and around it.

2. Let us begin with the rhetorical and poetic preaching both of Christ Himself and of His witnesses, which did go into particular details. From this point the didactic form of expression certainly arises mainly out of the problem of settling the apparent conflict between individual metaphors and figures, but partly too out of the need for freeing the expression from the ambiguity and uncertainty which attach to it outside of the given context, and of setting it forth more independently as the same for all. But every apparent contradiction of that sort makes one apprehensive of a number of others, because each casts suspicion upon the whole realm of language in which it occurs, as possibly concealing contradictions. Thus if in a given case an exact and didactic form of expression is set up, by which one may orientate oneself in relation to the apparent opposition, our assurance depends entirely upon the condition that the reconciling expression does not in turn stand in apparent contradiction with itself, but that this whole realm of language is immune from any such danger. But certainty on this point can only be gained by the relating of several such expressions to each other, and by ever repeated attempts to connect them together. Now, although the didactic expression is both more definite and in itself more comprehensible, yet it is always a combination of general ideas which become perfectly definite only when considered along with the higher ones above them and the lower ones under them; just as every such idea, as subject, can only be fully contemplated in the totality of its predicates, and as predicate, only in the whole range of its applicability. So that every such proposition points towards others, in which occur both kindred ideas and the same ideas in other connexions.

3. Thus it is unthinkable that the religious self-consciousness should be sufficiently alive to utter and communicate itself, without at the same time fashioning for itself the didactic form of expression,

whether in the looser form of popular usage or in the stricter form of the schools. And it is equally unthinkable that the particular elements of this expression should exist in any religious communion without forming themselves into a wealth of thought-series, which would partly aim at the original object of describing the religious emotions themselves in a real succession or in their natural connexion, and partly at working out the didactic expression itself into the greatest possible lucidity.

When we speak of Christian *Preaching*, we mean chiefly the utterance and presentation which have a directly rousing effect. But when we speak of Christian *Teaching* or *Doctrine* (*Lehre*), we mean rather that communication which employs the didactic form of expression, whether in order to rouse by bringing the idea in its clarity home to the consciousness, as happens in homiletic practice, or in order to isolate more definitely, through the clarity of the idea, the immediate religious self-consciousness, and reliably to establish its independence, which is the business of the dogmatic schools. But manifestly this can only reach a satisfactory conclusion when the system of doctrine has become a complete system, in which every essential moment of the religious and Christian consciousness is given its developed dogmatic expression, and all the dogmatic propositions are brought into relation with each other. Hence it is far from praiseworthy when respected theologians, perhaps confounding the thing itself with a perversion of it, reckon the scholarly study of doctrine as a degeneracy of the Christian communion or as a result of such degeneracy. Rather is it, on the one hand, the more necessary for the preaching office itself, as modes of presentation multiply with the variety of languages, that there should be a system of doctrine elaborated with dialectical precision. And on the other hand, it is natural that the more the Christian communion recruits and renews itself out of its own resources, the more does preaching itself take the form of popular *teaching* or *doctrine*, and the more does this doctrine (which itself in turn, however, requires the scholarly teaching as norm and limit) become the most important means to promote the living circulation of the religious consciousness.

Postscript.—If from this position we survey the whole procedure proper for dogmatic propositions, which indeed is just the subject of Dogmatic Theology, we arrive at the conclusion that it may begin at any point, wheresoever the requirements most demand it. The syntheses are, then, in part, of the kind which by preference are occasional, immediately serving the purpose of directly communicating the religious consciousness, and claiming only ecclesiastical value for the propositions in question, as doctrine which belongs to the realm of preaching and edification. But they are also, in part, of the kind where more depends upon their scientific value, and which keep strictly to the realm of Dogmatic Theology itself. These may take the form of *Monographs, i.e.* explications of some single proposition in its various relations as these may be surveyed from the standpoint of the proposition itself. Or they may take the form of *loci theologici* (*i.e.* collections of such monographs), which, of course, may be complete, so as to include the whole range of propositions which can be connected with each other, though this will be seen to be merely accidental, since such completeness has nothing to do with the form. Or, finally, they may take the form of a complete *System of Doctrine*, such as has been already described. Such a system, again, may be purely positive, and in that case either merely aphoristic or provided with an apparatus of explanations. Or it may include the polemical element, by taking account of other modifications of the religious and Christian consciousness, or other expressions of the same modification. Or, finally, it may also include the historical, by taking account of the development of dogmatic propositions and the changes which have occurred in the realm of dogmatic terminology.

§ 19. *Dogmatic Theology is the science which systematizes the doctrine prevalent in a Christian Church at a given time.*

NOTE.—See *Brief Outline*, §§ 3, 15, 18, 19, 26, 27.

1. This definition does not seem to exclude the possibility that a person could be a master of Dogmatic Theology and could even communicate it to others without himself believing in what he expounded, just as a man may have knowledge of the interconnexion of propositions in philosophical systems which he does not himself accept. But since the dogmatic procedure has reference entirely to preaching, and only exists in the interests of preaching, all who busy themselves therewith must be assumed to possess the relevant faith, if they are to offer anything profitable, because otherwise it would be a case of a professed reference and relation without any real congruity. The thing, however, is inconceivable except on the supposition that the exponent was not conscious of any religious emotions, even of a different variety. For otherwise no one could, without doing violence to himself, conceal the

contradiction between the position which he expounds as internally coherent and derived from the Christian consciousness, and the position which he himself accepts. And so a dogmatic presentation which takes no sides but is purely historical will always be sufficiently distinct from a presentation which is also apologetic—the only kind now in view. Moreover, it can hardly be denied that those dogmatic presentations (perhaps not uncommon even in our own Church) which, without any firm personal conviction, keep strictly to what is ecclesiastically received, either lack rigorous coherence and inward harmony, or involuntarily betray a weakening of the conviction.

2. Limitation to the doctrine of one particular Church is not a characteristic universally valid, for Christendom has not always been divided into a number of communions definitely separated by diversity of doctrine. But for the present this characteristic is indispensable ; for, to speak only of the Western Church, a presentation suitable for Protestantism cannot possibly be suitable for Catholics, there being no systematic connexion between the doctrines of the one and those of the other. A dogmatic presentation which aimed at avoiding contradiction from either of these two parties would lack ecclesiastical value for both in almost every proposition.

That each presentation confines itself to the doctrine existing at a certain time, is indeed seldom expressly avowed, but it nevertheless seems to be a matter of course ; and this seems, for the most part, to be the only possible explanation of the large number of dogmatic presentations which follow upon each other. It is obvious that the text-books of the seventeenth century can no longer serve the same purpose as they did then, but now in large measure belong merely to the realm of historical presentation ; and that in the present day it is only a different set of dogmatic presentations that can have the ecclesiastical value which these had then ; and the same fate will one day befall the present ones too. But of course it is only from the more universal crises of development that large alterations in doctrine arise, while the alterations which are continually going on amount to so little that it takes a long time to render them perceptible.

3. Now 'the prevalent doctrine' is not by any means to be taken as signifying merely what is expressed in (confessional) Symbols, but rather all doctrines which are dogmatic expressions of that which, in the public proceedings of the Church (even if only

in certain regions of it), can be put forward as a presentation of its common piety without provoking dissension and schism. Hence this characterization admits of considerable variety in the dogmatic presentations. None the less it might be held that this makes the definition too narrow, partly because it seems as if no alterations could ever come into the dogmatic presentations unless at some time or other something not yet prevalent were adopted, and partly because in this way everything individually distinctive is excluded. But, in the first place, everyone will admit that a system, however coherent, of purely and entirely individual opinions and views, which, even if really Christian, did not link themselves at all to the expressions used in the Church for the communication of religion, would always be regarded as simply a private confession and not as a dogmatic presentation, until there came to be attached to it a like-minded society, and there thus arose a public preaching and communication of religion which found its norm in that doctrine. Consequently it may in a general way be said that the less there is of publicly accepted matter in any such presentation, the less does it answer to the conception of a Dogmatic. Yet this does not mean that the individuality of the author may not have an influence upon the form and manner of treatment, and even assert itself at particular points by intentional correction of the usual position. And this of itself makes it clear that our definition by no means excludes improvements and new developments of Christian doctrine. But this becomes still clearer when we add the fact that such improvements and developments hardly ever proceed directly from the dogmatic discussions themselves, but are for the most part occasioned, in one way or another, by the proceedings of public worship or by popular literature for the dissemination of religion.

4. The correctness of our definition is also made clear by the following considerations: that when a presentation of Christian doctrine lacks one of the above characteristics, it no longer falls within the real field of Dogmatics; and that the most fundamental aberrations in the dogmatic field are caused by some one of these requirements being torn out of its natural connexions and taken by itself as the only rule for the treatment of the subject.

As for the popular presentation of doctrine, in catechisms and similar works, for the general instruction of the Church, this does indeed require completeness and coherence, but it makes no claim to erudition and systematic arrangement and connexion; and therefore we separate this from the properly dogmatic field. Further, many religious books which aim either at mystical depth or at rational clarity are more of the descriptively didactic type than of the directly rousing, and these too handle doctrine with a certain completeness ; but they lack the historical attitude, and the reference to the public ecclesiastical understanding of the faith, so that they inform us only about the individual, or one isolated fragment of the whole ; and therefore we do not give them the title of dogmatic, however coherently systematic they may be in themselves. Finally let us take the canonical and symbolical definitions of doctrine which have from time to time entered into the traffic of dogmatics. These, of course, should always presuppose the science of the complete systematization of doctrine, and in that sense they of course belong to dogmatic theology. Only they do not themselves go so far as to give a complete presentation of this systematic coherence, but are concerned only with particular points of doctrine.

Similarly, the most fundamental aberrations in the dogmatic field are accounted for by the one-sided attention paid to one or other of the characteristics which we established. If from time to time dogmatic presentations of doctrine come to appear as pretty much a mere tradition which has become static, this happens because people aim at no more than establishing the doctrine which is already publicly accepted, and thus look upon it as an absolutely given quantity. If, on the other hand, there are to be found dogmatic presentations which in their time enjoyed a widespread acceptance, but which, viewed from some distance and compared with earlier and later ones, appear entirely arbitrary, these are the ones which, having sprung from some transient and confused movement in the ecclesiastical realm, comprehended that movement alone, and thus were one-sided, never getting any further than the one particular phase ; in which circumstances it is easy for arbitrary caprice and sophistry to take the place of scientific rigour. Finally, if there are presentations which, while they of course handle Christian doctrine and profess to be dogmatic, do not go back at all to the religious affections, these are the ones which aim only at satisfying the demand for scientific system and coherence, as if that could at the same time produce what a genuinely dogmatic presentation must presuppose, namely, faith. Thus they attempt either directly to deduce and prove what is distinctively Christian from the universal reason, or to make it disappear, as an imperfect thing, in a purely rational and universally valid doctrine of religion.

Postscript.—Many theologians are in complete agreement with the definition of dogmatic theology which we have here established, but assign this actual Dogmatic to a pretty low level, as being only concerned with the presentation of ecclesiastical opinions, and assert that there must stand above it another and higher theology which, even with disregard of these ecclesiastical opinions, would bring out and make evident the essential truths of religion.[1] But the Christian science of God and Salvation cannot possibly recognize such a distinction between ecclesiastical doctrines and essential truths of religion (which are yet supposed to be Christian, for otherwise there can be no talk of them in this connexion at all), either in the sense that these truths of religion have another source, or in the sense that their content is of a different type. For there is only one source from which all Christian doctrine is derived, namely, the self-proclamation of Christ ; and there is only one type of doctrine, for, whether more perfect or less perfect, it all arises out of the religious consciousness itself and its direct expression. Therefore, if anybody is disposed to say that the ecclesiastical doctrine of any given time and place is mere opinion, because it does not remain ever self-identical and is not unmixed with error, it must be replied that nevertheless there is nothing else superior to it in the realm of Christian knowledge, except the purer and more perfect ecclesiastical doctrine which may be found in some other period and in other presentations. But this purifying and perfecting is just the work and the task of Dogmatic Theology.

But let us suppose this task to have been fully discharged, and Dogmatic Theology thus to have reached its completion. Even then we could not agree with those other theologians who make Dogmatics the whole of Christian theology, and who thus regard all the other branches of theological study, Scriptural Exegesis and Church History, both in their widest range and with all their accessories, as merely auxiliary sciences to Dogmatics. For even though both of these are necessary to Dogmatics, nevertheless their whole value does not consist in the service they render to it : each of them has also its own peculiar value directly for the advancement and guidance of the Church, which is the ultimate purpose of all

[1] See, among other works, Bretschneider's *Entwicklung*, § 25, and *Handbuch der Dogmatik*, § 5, where in the end one is in doubt whether Dogmatics belongs to Christian theology at all.

Christian theology, Dogmatics included. Rather would we say that, though Scriptural Exegesis and Church History are, each in its own peculiar office, dependent on the study of Dogmatics, and suffer when Dogmatics is neglected, so that all these different branches can only approach completion by reciprocally influencing each other, yet it would be a very suspicious thing if it were just Dogmatics that principally set the tone in this progress, because it depends more than the other branches (if only in form) upon Philosophy (*Weltweisheit*). For philosophy makes frequent new beginnings, and most of these revolutions engender new combinations and new expressions for the field from which Dogmatics draws its vocabulary; hence it is in this branch of theology that those variations most easily arise which provoke irrelevant controversy, and also those restatements which do not exactly represent progress but rather hinder than advance the theoretic development.

CHAPTER II

THE METHOD OF DOGMATICS

§ 20. *Since every system of doctrine, as a presentation of Dogmatic Theology, is a self-contained and closely-connected whole of dogmatic propositions, we must, with regard to the existing mass of such propositions, establish in the first place a rule according to which some will be adopted and others excluded; and in the second place, a principle for their arrangement and interconnexion.*

1. It is here presupposed that the individual propositions are the original, and are in existence earlier than the systematizing tendency itself; and this is entirely in line with the foregoing discussion. Thus it is by no means the case that first of all a principle is either somehow given externally or invented specially by each investigator, and that the individual propositions only proceed from the explication of this principle. That is indeed conceivable in the speculative realm, but not here. For the Christian self-consciousness must be already developed in the community before really dogmatic elements come to be formed, and it is only through the fragmentary, and perhaps chaotic, presence of these, that the task of making an orderly connexion arises. This last, however, only fulfils its purpose when it makes the collocation so complete that we can be certain we have in the doctrine a record of all the common elements of the Christian consciousness. Such completeness is, therefore, the aim of every system of doctrine. For without it we could not even have the assurance that our dogmatic expression of the distinctive essence of Christianity was correct, since the very region which was omitted might furnish proof of the contrary. This conviction of being correct can only proceed from having an outline of the whole, which clearly exhibits a comprehensive and exhaustive division.

2. It is undeniable that there has been great diversity in systems of doctrine even at the same times and in the same Churches. And since this is at least partly due to the differences of procedure in

adopting and connecting doctrines, it is only in very indefinite form that rules can be established for these two processes. But each individual system of doctrine characterizes itself best when, within these forms, it shows its own distinctive point of view with the greatest possible definiteness.

A double method naturally presents itself here. We could, starting from our general conception of the Christian consciousness, sketch an outline of the different ways in which it can express itself according to the nature of the human soul and of human life, and seek to fill in this outline with the existing doctrinal material ; and with this method the only concern would be to make sure that we were not adopting any mutually incompatible elements. But we could also take the line of bringing together all expressions of religious emotion which had developed in one particular region of Christianity and belonged to one and the same type ; and then it would only remain to arrange this material in the most convenient and synoptical way. To place the methods thus side by side is enough to show that we must combine the two, because each finds only in the other a security for what it lacks itself.

I. The Selection of the Dogmatic Material.

§ 21. *In order to build up a system of doctrine, it is necessary first to eliminate from the total mass of dogmatic material everything that is heretical, and to retain only what is ecclesiastical.*

1. If we think of the Christian Church as being what we call a moral Person, *i.e.* as being, though of course made up of many personalities, nevertheless a genuine individual life, then it must at once be admitted that in every such life, just as in individual lives in the narrower sense, there is a distinction between healthy and diseased conditions. The latter are always conditions which do not arise from the inward foundation of the life and in its clear course, but are to be explained only by foreign influences. So when among any race of people individuals arise who exhibit a quite alien physiological type, so that they do not take very kindly to the majority and their mode of life, or when in a republican state citizens arise with monarchist sentiments, or *vice versa*, we regard this as a disease of the whole, and also assume that it can only be explained by foreign influences. Now, even if this last point might not be admitted by everybody, yet everybody will reserve the name of 'heretical' in the realm of Christian doctrine for that which he cannot explain from his idea of the distinctive essence of

Christianity, and cannot conceive as accordant therewith, but which nevertheless gives itself out as Christian and seeks to be regarded as such by others. Now, it is a matter of fact that during the period of the actual development of Christian doctrine a multitude of such elements appeared which the majority persistently rejected as of alien type, while they recognized the remainder, as self-consistent and as forming a coherent continuum, under the name of Catholic, *i.e.* common to the whole Church. In this connexion it may, of course, sometimes be the case that the religious emotions set forth in the doctrine are themselves at variance with the true essence of Christian piety ; but sometimes it is only in the working out of the doctrine that this variance arises, so that the religious affections themselves are not diseased, and only misunderstanding or false method produces an appearance of heresy. Now these two cases are of course seldom properly distinguished, and therefore many things have been too hastily declared heretical. But, nevertheless, real heresy has not been lacking ; and in its case foreign influences will readily be admitted, when one reflects that the Christian Church originally sprang solely from people who belonged before to other faiths, so that alien matter could easily creep in unawares.

2. It is undeniable that this makes the determination of what is heretical, and must therefore be excluded from the system of doctrine, appear a very uncertain thing, and people will all fix it differently who start from different formulæ of the distinctive essence of Christianity. But that cannot be otherwise, as the whole course of events in the Christian Church proves. For new heresies no longer arise, now that the Church recruits itself out of its own resources ; and the influence of alien faiths on the frontier and in the mission-field of the Church must be reckoned at zero so far as regards the formation of doctrine, though there may long remain in the piety of the new converts a great deal which has crept in from their religious affections of former times, and which, if it came to clear consciousness and were expressed as doctrine, would be recognized as heretical. But concerning the earlier heresies, on the other hand, there are the most diverse judgments, just as there are different ways and modes of conceiving the essence of Christianity. Hence anyone who aims at setting up a system of doctrine can only follow the rule of our proposition in the sense that he will not adopt anything which, according to the fundamental type of Christian doctrine which he has established, can only be traced to a foreign

source. If, however, we are not to proceed by haphazard but with due certainty, we cannot hold by the antithesis of Catholic and heretical as it presented itself in history down to a certain point, especially as subsequent revindications of this or that heresy have not been unheard-of. We must rather start from the essence of Christianity, and seek to construe the heretical in its manifold forms by asking in how many different ways the essence of Christianity can be contradicted and the appearance of Christianity yet remain. Conducted in this way, the inquiry into the heretical serves to supplement the inquiry into the essence of Christianity, and the two confirm each other. The more it turns out that what is thus set up problematically as heretical is also actually given in history, the more ground have we to regard the formula upon which the construction is based as a correct expression of the essence of Christianity. And the more naturally there develops out of this same formula the form of doctrine which Christianity has constantly professed, the more ground have we to regard as really diseased and worthy of rejection whatever conflicts on any side with that formula.

§ 22. *The natural heresies in Christianity are the Docetic and the Nazarean, the Manichean and the Pelagian.*

1. If in using these expressions we think only of the historical phenomena which have been so called, the choice of them as designating the whole range of heresy may seem very arbitrary and very disproportionate. For while the last two have been very widespread and have frequently recurred, the first two were very transitory and confined to narrow circles, and there are other names which are far more important and far more in everybody's mouth. But these names are here intended only to denote universal forms which we are here going to unfold, and the definitions of which they are intended to remind us proceed from the general nature of the situation, even if, *e.g.*, Pelagius himself should not be a Pelagian in our sense. But the nature of the situation means primarily the number of different ways in which the distinctive fundamental type of Christian doctrine can be contradicted while the appearance of Christianity yet remains. The question, from what foreign influences these can have sprung, is a matter of purely historical investigation, which does not properly concern us here; though, of course, the conviction that all alien material, if it is to lay claim at all to the name of Christian, must fit into one of these

forms, would be the only complete security for the truth of our presentation of the matter.

2. Now, if the distinctive essence of Christianity consists in the fact that in it all religious emotions are related to the redemption wrought by Jesus of Nazareth, there will be two ways in which heresy can arise. That is to say: this fundamental formula will be retained in general (for otherwise the contradiction would be manifest and complete, so that participation in Christian communion could not even be desired), but *either* human nature will be so defined that a redemption in the strict sense cannot be accomplished, *or* the Redeemer will be defined in such a way that He cannot accomplish redemption. But each of these two cases, again, can appear in two different ways. As regards the former: if men are to be redeemed, they must both be in need of redemption and be capable of receiving it. Now, if one of these conditions is openly posited, but the other covertly denied, the contradiction at the same time touches the fundamental formula itself, only this is not directly apparent. If, then, in the first place, the need of redemption in human nature, *i.e.* its inability to bring the feeling of absolute dependence into all human states of consciousness, is posited in such an absolute way that the ability to receive redeeming influences is made actually to disappear, so that human nature is not simultaneously in need of redemption and capable of receiving it, but only becomes capable of receiving it after a complete transformation, this is equivalent to an annulling of our fundamental formula. Now this is the unfailing consequence, if we suppose an Evil-in-itself as being original and opposed to God, and think of human nature as suffering from that inability by reason of a dominion which this original Evil exercises over it; and therefore we call this deviation the Manichean. But, on the other hand, suppose the ability to receive redemption is assumed so absolutely, and consequently any hindrance to the entry of the God-consciousness becomes so utterly infinitesimal, that at each particular moment in each individual it can be satisfactorily counterbalanced by an infinitesimal overweight. Then the need of redemption is reduced to zero, at least in the sense that it is no longer the need of one single Redeemer, but merely, for each person in one of his weak moments, the need of some other individual who, if only for the moment, is stronger as regards the eliciting of the God-consciousness. Thus redemption would not need to be the work of one particular Person, but would be a common work of all for all, in which, at most, some would only

have a greater share than others ; and this aberration we may with good reason call, as above, the Pelagian.

Turn now to the other kind of heresy. If Christ is to be the Redeemer, *i.e.* the real origin of constant living unhindered evocation of the God-consciousness, so that the participation of all others in it is mediated through Him alone, it is, on the one hand, necessary that He should enjoy an exclusive and peculiar superiority over all others, and, on the other hand, there must also be an essential likeness between Him and all men, because otherwise what He has to impart could not be the same as what they need. Therefore on this side also the general formula can be contradicted in two different ways, because each of these two requisites may be conceived so unlimitedly that the other no longer remains co-posited, but disappears. If the difference between Christ and those who are in need of redemption is made so unlimited that an essential likeness is incompatible with it, then His participation in human nature vanishes into a mere appearance ; and consequently our God-consciousness, being something essentially different, cannot be derived from His, and redemption also is only an appearance. Now though the Docetics, properly so called, directly denied only the reality of the body of Christ, yet this likewise excludes the reality of human nature in His Person generally, since we never find body and soul given in separation from each other ; and therefore we may fitly call this aberration the Docetic. Finally, if on the other hand the likeness of the Redeemer to those who are to be redeemed is made so unlimited that no room is left for a distinctive superiority as a constituent of His being, which must then be conceived under the same form as that of all other men, then there must ultimately be posited in Him also a need of redemption, however absolutely small, and the fundamental relationship is likewise essentially annulled. This aberration we call by the name given to those who are supposed first to have regarded Jesus entirely as an ordinary man, the Nazarean or Ebionitic.

Other kinds of heresy than can be comprehended under one or other of these four forms cannot be conceived, if the conception of the Christian religion (piety) is to remain unchanged. For there are no more points at which the conception can be indirectly attacked. And if the conception of redemption is roundly denied, or another redeemer is set up, and thus it is roundly asserted either that men are not in need of redemption or that there is no redeeming power in Jesus, then the assertion is no longer heretical but anti-Christian.

3. These concepts of the natural heresies likewise serve, from our point of view, in the construction of any system of Christian doctrine, as limiting points which one must avoid if the agreement of particular details with the remainder is not to be destroyed. But then this also implies that no formula, in whatever division of the system it may occur, which avoids the two opposite aberrations, is to be regarded as heretical: however disproportionate the one side may appear as compared with the other, so long as neither completely disappears, the formula is still ecclesiastical or catholic. On the other hand, every formula must be suspect which can be identified with any one of these aberrations. Only, let everybody guard in this matter against the illusions so easily produced by the 'foreshortening' natural to distance. For the nearer a man stands to the Pelagian line himself, the more easily will he believe that he sees actually on the Manichean side the man who really is still standing almost in the middle; and so, too, with other cases. And therefore, unless the confusion is to grow ever greater, it is highly important that people should go to work with the greatest caution when it comes to declaring anything heretical.

But further, these heresies are specially bound up in pairs. That is to say, in their relation to the essence of Christianity the Manichean and the Docetic belong together, and so again do the Pelagian and the Ebionitic. For if human nature is essentially infected with positively original Evil, then the Redeemer cannot have any real participation in human nature; and if the higher self-consciousness is hindered by the lower in Christ in the same way as in all other men, then His contribution to redemption can only be related to any other man's contribution as the more to the less. But if, on the other hand, we have regard to the fact that what cannot be understood from the essence of Christianity must have arisen through foreign influences, and that in the period of the original development of doctrine Christianity came into contact almost exclusively with Judaism and Greek Heathenism, then the Manichean and the Nazarean seem rather to belong together, as being of Judaizing tendency, the one in a purer form, and the other rather imbued with Orientalism; while the Docetic and the Pelagian seem to be of Hellenizing tendency, since mythology led to the former, and the ethical trend of the Mysteries to the latter.

Postscript.—We are far from wishing to drag in here the antithesis, at present so intense, between Supernaturalism and Rationalism. But nevertheless let us note that since in accordance with the above discussion we have to admit, even within the range of the ecclesiastical, manifold approximations to these heretical extremes, they also are divided between those two modes of treatment; and that in supernaturalistic presentations—not only in the properly dogmatic ones, but in the popular ones too—echoes may be found of the Docetic and Manichean, just as rationalistic presentations may with some justice be reproached with approximating to the Ebionitic and Pelagian. And the fact that any treatment of doctrine which does not escape one-sidedness altogether, necessarily inclines to one or other of these two sides, seems to testify to the correctness of this account of the heretical.

§ 23. *A system of doctrine drawn up at the present time within the Western Church cannot be indifferent to the antithesis between Roman Catholic and Protestant, but must adhere to one or the other.*

1. Some justification seems to be required for our here making the antithesis between the Eastern and the Western Church greater than the antithesis which we have expressed (between Roman Catholic and Protestant), and then, nevertheless, passing over the former. The first of these two steps seems to have against it the fact that the Eastern Church, as anti-Papal, appears to stand on the side of Protestantism. But suppose it were admitted that that antithesis *is* greater: then to pass over it seems inconsistent; and the common character of the Western Church would first have to be specified, in order that we might discover within it the principle for the subordinate antithesis between Romanism and Protestantism. As against this, however, it is to be noted that this cannot at all be the place to construe these antitheses in a completely graduated scale, but only in their relation to the study of doctrine. And how little the anti-Papal character of the Eastern Church signifies in this respect, may be seen from the facility with which individual fragments of that Church acknowledge the Roman Primacy without giving up their Eastern type, and especially without making any considerable alteration in their doctrine. The antithesis *is* indeed a greater one in the precise connexion with which we are here concerned, in the sense that a lively activity in the realm of doctrine has remained common to the two Western Churches even since their separation, whereas the Eastern Church since its break-away has in this realm become more and more torpid, and in it the combination of knowledge about religion

with a really scientific organization is almost entirely destroyed. But just because of this purely negative character there was the less to be said here about that Church, since it cannot be determined whether it will again step back more into connexion with the world's intellectual intercourse, and so have the strength to elicit and develop within itself an antithesis analogous to the Western one.

2. This antithesis has not affected the whole range of doctrine, for alongside of the doctrines over which the two Churches are avowedly in conflict there are others for which they set up the same formulæ, and yet others about which analogous differences are found within both Churches. And the antithesis itself, like every similar one within the Christian communion, must be regarded as destined some day and somehow to disappear. So one can certainly conceive of very different modes of procedure in the construction of the system of doctrine, according as one believes that the antithesis has not yet reached its culminating-point, or that it has already passed it. In the latter case, it would be a true progress if we were to seek for, or prepare in advance, mediating formulæ in the controversial doctrines, in order to facilitate and help to bring about, from every standpoint, the approaching abrogation of the antithesis. Then it would likewise be the correct thing to establish as firmly as possible the common matter in the non-controversial doctrines, in order to make it as difficult as possible for well-meaning zealots who misconceived the whole condition of the Church, to delay unnecessarily the union of its two parts by stirring up new and unprofitable controversies. But, in the other case, we should have to assume the probability that, if the tension between the two parts is destined still to increase generally, it will also increase in the realm of doctrine. And in that case we should, in the same spirit (namely, with a view to accelerating the whole process in a steady course as much as possible), have to adopt the opposite line of procedure. A Protestant system of doctrine has in that case to aim at exhibiting the antithesis in those portions of doctrine where it has not hitherto appeared; for only when it had been developed in all portions could we be quite sure that it had reached its culminating-point in doctrine. Now since the course of such an antithesis is seldom quite direct, the main trend being from time to time interrupted by reactions towards the opposite side, there may easily arise in the first half of the course an appearance of one's being in the second, and *vice versa*. Therefore, both modes of treatment are usually found simultaneously

alongside of each other; but in both there is also found sometimes more consciousness, sometimes less, of the particular point at which they stand.

3. The proposition which we have set up therefore excludes neither of these two modes of treatment. For even he who regards the tension as now decreasing, and prepares means of accommodation, cannot (if he remains within the realm of Dogmatics) help putting forward the distinction as still valid, and professing the side which corresponds to the rest of his presentation of Christian doctrine. A system of doctrine could only remain neutral on controversial points if it went back to older formulæ, and that means, of course, to less definite ones, out of which the more definite ones have only developed in the course of controversy. But it is impossible in a scientific exposition to confine oneself to the indefinite when the definite is already given.

We, however, cannot regard the tension as already on the decrease. For when there arises in the Evangelical (Protestant) Church a variety of views regarding any portion of doctrine, the result of it is never a greater approximation to Roman formulæ; and similarly in the Roman Church those movements which take an anti-Protestant direction seem to be the most successful. It is therefore rather to be presumed that, even when the doctrines sound the same, there are still hidden differences, than that, when the formulæ diverge considerably, the difference in the religious affections themselves is inconsiderable.

§ 24. *In so far as the Reformation was not simply a purification and reaction from abuses which had crept in, but was the origination of a distinctive form of the Christian communion, the antithesis between Protestantism and Catholicism may provisionally be conceived thus: the former makes the individual's relation to the Church dependent on his relation to Christ, while the latter contrariwise makes the individual's relation to Christ dependent on his relation to the Church.*

1. If we confine our attention to the rise of Protestantism, it is certainly undeniable that the Reformers and their first adherents were conscious only of the wish to purify. They had no intention whatsoever of forming a Church of their own, but were simply driven to it. If, on the other hand, we confine our attention to the present time, and reflect that the Evangelical (Protestant) Church never exercises an organized missionary activity upon the

Catholic Church, and indeed never expresses, as part of its essential nature, the desire to bring over the whole Catholic Church into the Evangelical; and if we reflect that we could not help doing these things if we regarded all elements which are alien to us and peculiar to Roman Catholicism, whether doctrines or institutions and usages, as simply corruptions of Christianity; then it follows that, while we do not cease to combat by word and deed what we really reckon as corruptions, we at the same time assume that other matter, which is indigenous there but equally alien to us, is yet of such a kind that we feel we may leave it standing alongside of our own religion, as being of a different formation but equally Christian. It will also be evident that even supposing the Catholic Church leant towards our definitions in all doctrines that have become controversial, this would not cause a reunion of the two Churches; and this can only be explained by the existence of a spirit alien to ours, which repels us. But it is plain that the two conclusions go together: we ascribe such a peculiarity of character to our own Church, just as we do to the Catholic. And in case we should be disposed to keep solely to the idea of purification, this also must be added: in the first place, that, as a universal rule, what has previously existed never recurs at a later time in quite the same form; and, in the second place, that no one particular point of time could be given, all over, to which the Church should have been brought back by the Reformation. For the Apostolic Age cannot be brought back, partly because we cannot sacrifice the dogmatic precision of our ideas, partly because we can as little re-establish the then relations to Judaism and Heathenism as we can the political passivity. Some things in the Evangelical Church may point to earlier periods, and some to later; but its self-reproducing unity is of a kind which did not formerly exist, though there may have been individuals whose religion was analogous to it.

2. Now this naturally creates for the Evangelical theologian the task of bringing to clear consciousness the distinctive character of Protestantism in antithesis to Catholicism, and thus fixing the antithesis itself, if possible, in a formula. Otherwise he will no more be able to perform his work with some degree of security and completeness than will the Christian theologian in general who has similarly failed to fix the distinctive essence of Christianity. Now it is of course very natural that such a formula should not arise out of the controversy between the two parties themselves; but unfortunately even we Protestants among ourselves have by no

means come to agree upon such a formula. Usually we reduce the antithesis to some one salient point which does not explain everything, and we do it in such a way that one of the two parties appears only negatively defined; or we treat the antithesis as a more or less accidental aggregate of individual differences. Some people, perhaps, have thought that for Evangelical Dogmatics it is already, unfortunately, too late for such a formula, because the doctrine of our Church is completely settled in our Symbols, so that no new element can be gained for it. And others, perhaps, have thought it is not yet time for such a formula, because the spirit of Protestantism has not yet in doctrine fully developed itself on all sides. But, as a matter of fact, the relation of the two Churches is at present such that it is now possible, and also now necessary, to come to a complete orientation on the point; and, for another thing, we have to provide against un-Protestant matter creeping in unawares even into our own further development. Since, however, so little has yet been done upon this task, the attempt here made can claim to be no more than a provisional one.

3. Just as the distinctive essence of Christianity could never be discovered from the mere concept of religion and of the religious communion, so the distinctive essence of Protestantism cannot be discovered from the general expression which we have given to Christianity. And just as the essence of Christianity could not be discovered by a merely empirical method, so it would be difficult to arrive in that way at the principle of the inner unity of the Evangelical Church. Here, indeed, the difficulty would be still greater. For, on the one hand, at the rise of Protestantism the purificatory aim alone appeared definitely, and the distinctive spirit which began to develop lay unconscious and concealed behind that aim. And, on the other hand, even the outward unity of the new Church is much more difficult to define, because there was no unity of starting-point, and yet there did not arise as many new communions as there were starting-points. Hence amid the great mass of very diverse and independently developed personal peculiarities, it must be almost impossible to determine what there was to unite them apart from that purificatory aim, and how far they belonged together. Now since the antithesis can be most clearly seen from the present consolidated existence of the two Churches alongside of each other, it seemed best to attempt the solution of the problem by considering what kind of qualities of the one communion most strongly arouse in the common mind of the other the consciousness

of the antithesis. Now it is the charge most generally made by the Roman Church against Protestantism, that it has so much destroyed the old Church, and yet, by reason of its own fundamental principles, is not in a position to build up again a stable and durable communion, but leaves everything uncertain and in solution, and each individual standing by himself. The main reproach which we, contrariwise, bring against Catholicism is that, in ascribing everything to the Church and tracing everything to the Church, it deprives Christ of the honour due to Him, and puts Him in the background, and even in a measure subordinates Him to the Church. To this add the fact, that ecclesiastical Protestantism is as little chargeable in the latter respect as Catholicism in the former; and consider how nevertheless each party is disposed to point out in the other chiefly what could most easily lead it astray from the common ground of Christianity. Plainly the opinion of the Catholics is that, even though we were to hold fast the reference to Christ, we should nevertheless be in danger of giving up the Christian principle by dissolving the communion; and our opinion of the Roman Church is that, however fast it may hold this communion, it is nevertheless in danger of becoming un-Christian by neglecting the reference to Christ. Now add to this the further fact that the spirit of Christianity which rules in both Churches does not allow either of them ever to reach that extreme. Then there follows from this the formula which we have set up. In the controversial doctrines themselves this formula can only justify itself gradually in the course of the further discussion (unless we want to anticipate in a fragmentary way a large part of our system of doctrine). Here we can only make some preliminary remarks in support of the formula, and draw some conclusions from it regarding the treatment of Evangelical Dogmatics.

4. In support of our formula it may be said (though we could not take this as our starting-point) that it ascribes to the two parties antithetical characters which modify the essence of Christianity in antithetical ways. For since Christian piety never arises independently and of itself in an individual, but only out of the communion and in the communion, there is no such thing as adherence to Christ except in combination with adherence to the communion. That the two should be subordinated to each other in opposite ways is only possible because the same fact which *we* regard as the institution of the Church, to serve the work or influence of Christ, is regarded by *them* as a transference to the Church of the

work of Christ. So this, too, speaks well for our formula, that here, where we are primarily seeking to define the antithesis for the *theoretic* side of the doctrine, the formula fastens mainly upon the concept of the Church. This makes it probable that what is opposed in the *practice* of the two Churches and in the principles of their constitution can also be evolved out of this formula.

But as regards the treatment of Evangelical Dogmatics, what follows is that in those portions of doctrine to which the formula can be most directly applied, the greatest care must be taken not to carry the antithesis too far, lest we should fall into un-Christian positions. And, on the other hand, that in those doctrines in which the antithesis is least prominent, especial care must be taken not to set up formulæ which have never got rid of the antithetical character, or which have perhaps even taken on something of it once again. In this way it can best be ascertained how far the distinctive Evangelical spirit has everywhere become developed in doctrine. At the same time it seems natural that that Church which places the communion above the relation to Christ also most easily takes over matter from the earlier religious communions, and consequently that whatever has a certain flavour of the Jewish or the Heathen is more in keeping with the Roman Church, just as every opposition to these elements, even in earlier times, contained something akin to Protestantism.

Postscript.—What has been said about the indefiniteness of the outward unity of the Evangelical (Protestant) Church refers especially to the different branches of it, and in particular to the separation between the Reformed and the Lutheran Church. For the original relation was such that, notwithstanding their different starting-points, they might just as well have grown together into an outward unity as have come to separate from each other. Now this presentation of doctrine, even in its very title, professes adherence only to the Protestant Church in general, without naming either of those two in particular. Thus it starts from the assumption that the separation of the two has lacked sufficient grounds, inasmuch as the differences in doctrine are in no sense traceable to a difference in the religious affections themselves, and the two do not diverge from each other, either in morals and moral theory or in constitution, in any way which at all corresponds to those differences of doctrine. Therefore we can only treat of such differences in the same way as writers in other subjects take notice of divergent presentations by different teachers—in short, simply as an academic matter.

§ 25. *Every Evangelical (Protestant) Dogmatic ought to contain a peculiar and distinctive element; only, this will be more prominent in some systems than in others, and sometimes more in some points of doctrine, sometimes in others.*

NOTE.—Cf. *Brief Outline*, p. 118.

1. We could not at all grant the name of Dogmatics to a presentation composed purely of original doctrines peculiar to itself. Even the earliest coherent presentations of the Evangelical Faith could only bear that name, in so far as they linked themselves to what went before, and had most of their system in common with what was ecclesiastically given. And so an epitome of doctrine which claimed no connexion with that which at the time of the Reformation either took shape or was for the Evangelical Church recognized anew, could not by any means pass as an Evangelical system of doctrine, however opposed all its contents might be to Romanism. And if we had nothing to show but such an epitome, then indeed the unity and identity of our Church would not appear at all in its doctrine, and there would, from this side, be no guarantee whatever of the mutual kinship of those who call themselves Protestants. If, on the other hand, our system of doctrine were so perfectly and precisely definite that there could be no divergence unless one were willing to exclude oneself from the communion of the Church, then new presentations of the system of doctrine within our Church would be entirely superfluous and useless. If repetitions of a hard-and-fast letter are to mean anything, there must at least be change in the turns of expression or in the arrangement of the propositions. But both of these really always indicate characteristic alterations, since there never are two expressions meaning exactly the same thing, and since every proposition acquires a somewhat different meaning when it is placed in a different context. And so even where there was only a slight tinge of difference in a number of different presentations, there would always likewise be divergent and distinctive doctrines. As a matter of fact, however, our system of doctrine is very far from having such a thoroughgoing definiteness, for even in the different confessional documents the same thing is not always comprehended in the same letters, and these solely official and perhaps universally recognized presentations have, after all, only individual parts of the system

of doctrine as their subject. And just as in the Reformation age this common matter sprang simply out of the free agreement of individuals, it is still true, since the Protestant Church has become firmly established, that there is no other way in which anything can become generally accepted than by the free concurrence of the results obtained by individuals who are engaged upon the same subject. The fact that, notwithstanding, common doctrine is not lacking, sufficiently proves that the individuals are united by something distinctive which they have in common; and anything more than this, as regards unity of doctrine, is not to be expected in the Evangelical Church, nor is it required.

2. Let us then start from the facts that the system of doctrine in our Church all over is not a thing absolutely settled, and that it may indeed be asserted that its distinctive character has not yet become fully manifest in doctrine. Then we can only proceed on the supposition that in the further development also of the system of doctrine in the future these two elements will appear together, and will penetrate each other—matter which is common to all, and which makes good its claim as a pure and universally recognizable expression of .the distinctive Protestant spirit; and peculiar matter which expresses the personal views of its exponents. And every particular presentation of the substance of the doctrine, which lays claim to an ecclesiastical character, will be the more perfect the more inwardly it unites in itself and relates together the common and the peculiar. The common matter naturally starts from, and becomes most prominent in, those portions of doctrine which are most akin to the original efforts to purify the faith. Now if this effort at the time of the Reformation itself did not transform the whole tenor of doctrine, but allowed much to be simply taken over unaltered from earlier definitions, this realm will naturally become a controversial one, and much of what has hitherto passed as common matter will gradually become obsolete. The element of peculiarity lies originally in the arrangement of the individual doctrines, in which there is, and can be, practically nothing which would be recognized as necessarily of general acceptance. But further, all points of doctrine, even while keeping within the universally recognized mode of expression, permit of more exact definition in many ways; and everyone achieves something who makes people recognize this capacity for modification, and in his own way makes use of his rights in the matter. Finally, the element of peculiarity in the presentation touches also

the area of what is gradually becoming antiquated, with a view to remodelling individual doctrines in a way more true to the Protestant spirit. But even the most lively originality cannot aim at anything higher than to set the common doctrine in the clearest light ; just as, again, for the common element there is no higher aim than to encourage the peculiar and original development of doctrine without disturbing the communion, by establishing as definitely as possible the Protestant character of the system. The more the two elements thus interpenetrate each other, the more ecclesiastical, and at the same time the more favourable to progress, is the presentation. The more they are detached from each other, and merely stand side by side as unconnected, the more does the element which clings to the historical, and is set up as of common acceptance, appear to be of merely antiquarian interest, and the original element to be simply ultra-modern.

Postscript.—The terms *orthodox* and *heterodox*, which even etymologically do not form a proper antithesis, are too uncertain for me to have any great desire to employ them. Consider, however, how much there is which was originally decried as heterodox in our Church, and which afterwards came to pass muster as orthodox, but always through an earlier orthodoxy becoming obsolete. Then it becomes plain how this antithesis refers solely to what professes to be common matter. The name of orthodox is then given to what is in unmistakable conformity with the matter fixed in the confessional documents ; and what is not thus in conformity is heterodox. But now, if heterodox matter succeeds in vindicating itself as being more accordant with the spirit of the Evangelical Church than is the letter of the confessional documents, then the latter becomes antiquated and the former becomes orthodox. Now, since such changes in our Church can never by a special act be declared universally valid, the employment of these two terms, for things which are still subject to discussion, is always doubtful policy. The situations which occasion it will probably never cease to arise, because what is fixed in the confessional documents contains exegeses of Scripture, and thus the progress of the art of exegesis may render doubtful that part of the Symbols. And similarly, on the other hand, even if the heterodox cannot be definitely distinguished in content and expression from the heretical of older times, yet it must not be regarded as heretical, if only it seeks to make good its claim in connexion with the commonly accepted elements of our Church's system of doctrine.

For, in the case of those people who do not desire to separate themselves from our Church's system of doctrine, we must not, even when there are such divergences, put them down to anything more than misunderstandings, which are sure to disappear again through scientific interchange of views within the Church itself. And especially we must not think there has been any hidden influence of principles which belong to other religious communions.

§ 26. *In the Evangelical (Protestant) Church the Science of Christian Doctrine and that of Christian Morals have long been separated: and so here too, for the purposes of our presentation, we eliminate from the totality of the dogmatic material such propositions as are elements of the Science of Christian Morals.*

NOTE.—Cf. *Brief Outline*, §§ 31 ff.

1. Even the propositions of the Science of Christian Morals are in the above sense propositions or doctrines of the faith. For the modes of action which they describe under the form of theorems or precepts (for the two come to the same thing) are likewise expressions of the religious affections of the Christian. That is to say, every religious emotion is essentially a modification of human existence, and if it is understood as a quiescent state, there arises a proposition which belongs to the Science of Christian Doctrine. But every such emotion, unless it either gets interrupted in its natural course or is too weak from the beginning (and we cannot here take account of either of these cases), issues just as essentially in activity; and if the different modifications of the Christian's religious consciousness are understood as activities which arise in different ways in accordance with the circumstances which at the time occasion and determine them, there arise propositions which belong to the Science of Christian Morals. But rules of life and formulæ for modes of action which were not of that type would not belong to the Science of Christian Morals, but either to the purely rational Science of Morals or to some special technical or practical study.

2. Now it is clear that only the two taken together represent the whole reality of the Christian life. For it is inconceivable that a man should everywhere and always have in his self-consciousness the emotions which are expressed in the doctrines of the Christian faith, without also acting, everywhere and always, in the way set forth by Christian morals. And it is equally easy to

understand how the two could have been for a long time unified in presentation, so that they formed a single discipline. For the issues of the religious emotions in activity can always, when taken together at suitable points, be described in a supplemental way even in the Science of Doctrine, as natural consequences of the described states themselves ; as, *e.g.*, what are called duties to God may come after the treatment of the Divine Attributes. Similarly there are doctrines which in themselves belong equally to both studies, and which thus provide in the Science of Doctrine a place where particular parts of the Science of Morals, or even the whole of it, could easily be introduced. Such are the portions of doctrine which treat of Sanctification and of the Church. But in the nature of the case the Science of Doctrine could equally well be introduced into the Science of Morals, and in the same twofold manner ; *i.e.* the religious affections could be described, each as something which preceded the developing activities in general, but which also accompanied and was, as it were, echoed in these ; but they could also be described at particular points. For since the expression of the self-consciousness is a moral activity, it would be possible in a treatment of this latter to introduce the whole Science of Doctrine as an explication of the thing which is to be expressed. But (when the two were united) the relation was always a purely one-sided one, the treatment of the Science of Morals being included in the Science of Doctrine. The Science of Doctrine in this way became shapeless in consequence of unevenly distributed appendices, and the need for viewing as a connected whole the modes of action accepted in the Christian Church was not satisfied. Hence it was inevitable that the ethical interest should sooner or later lead to the two studies being separated from each other.

II. The Formation of the Dogmatic System.

§ 27. *All propositions which claim a place in an epitome of Evangelical (Protestant) doctrine must approve themselves both by appeal to Evangelical confessional documents, or in default of these, to the New Testament Scriptures, and by exhibition of their homogeneity with other propositions already recognized.*

1. It may seem strange that here the confessional documents of the Evangelical Church, collectively, are, as it were, given a prior place to the New Testament Scriptures themselves. But this

must not by any means be taken as establishing a precedence for these documents. That, indeed, would contradict the documents themselves, since they always appeal to Scripture. Thus the appeal to them in fact always implies indirectly an appeal to Scripture. But the appeal to Scripture can directly prove only that a proposition which has been set up is Christian, while its distinctively Protestant content is not decided upon, except in the few cases where it can be shown that the Catholic Church has sanctioned an opposite use of the same passages of Scripture. Thus for the Protestant content there remain only the other two kinds of proof; and, of these, the first place is assured to the proof from the confessional documents, in virtue of the general demand made upon Dogmatics to set forth doctrine prevalent in the Church. For these documents are plainly the first common possession of Protestantism; and just as all Protestant communities grew together into the Church primarily through attachment to these, so every system of doctrine which desires to pass as Protestant must strive to attach itself to this history. Indeed, this holds of its original and distinctive elements as much as of its common elements, only that for the former, it is naturally enough to have an indirect demonstration that its propositions are compatible with the Symbols. Thus the direct appeal to Scripture is only necessary either when the use which the confessional documents make of the New Testament books cannot be approved of (and we must at least admit the possibility that in individual cases all the testimonies adduced, even if not falsely applied, may nevertheless be unsatisfying, since other passages of Scripture must be applied as means of proof), or when propositions of the confessional documents do not themselves seem sufficiently scriptural or Protestant, and these must accordingly be superannuated and other expressions substituted, which will then certainly the more easily find acceptance, the more it is shown that Scripture on the whole favours them or even perhaps demands them. Therefore this method of always going back in the first instance to the confessional documents affords at the same time the advantage, that the ecclesiastical status of any proposition thereby at once becomes clear, and consequently the significance of the whole presentation for the further development of the system of doctrine is much more easily perceived.

From this it follows that, if we look at individual cases, the proving of a proposition by exhibiting its relation to other propositions already proved in another way is a merely subordinate matter, and only suitable to propositions of second rank, which neither appear directly in the Symbols nor are represented in any definite way in Scripture. But, on the other hand, when this reference is added at each point to that original method of proof, it does properly illuminate for the first time the suitability both of the arrangement of the system of doctrine and of the terminology which prevails in it.

2. Now, as we here class together all confessional documents of the Evangelical Church, in both its main branches, as of equal right, there is for us no single one which could have proceeded from the whole Church or even have been recognized by it. And so the distinction between the greater and more universal authority of some, and the more doubtful and scantier authority of others, vanishes as of no significance at all. Indeed, since in the confessional documents, at least of the second stage, Reformed modes of presentation are directed against Lutheran, and *vice versa,* it must be admitted at the outset that only that part of the confessional documents in which they all agree can be really essential to Protestantism ; and indeed that, through this conflict between the different particular confessional documents, the right of holding different views on all non-essential points has itself, as it were, received symbolic recognition for the whole Evangelical Church. Further, it is unquestionable that in a certain sense all our Symbols, though some more than others, are merely occasional documents, in which therefore the precise mode of statement of many points depends upon time and place ; and we have no reason to suppose that the authors themselves would offer the selected expression as the only perfectly right one. And here is another related point : the authors themselves (certainly quite in accordance with their then convictions, but nevertheless too precipitately for the character of a confessional document, since they were still engaged in inquiry) repudiated views then held to be heretical, and, in all points which had not yet become definitely controversial, testified to their agreement with the then prevalent doctrine. That sentence of condemnation may have fallen on many a divergence which had proceeded from the same spirit as the Reformation itself, because this spirit had not learnt to recognize itself promptly. And similarly many an older doctrinal view might be taken over, simply because people failed to see at once how it conflicted with the essence of Protestantism. From this it follows that, in going back to the Symbols, if we are to avoid making that procedure a

hindrance to the further development of doctrine, we must, in the first place, rather have regard to the spirit than cling to the letter, and, in the second place, we must apply the exegetical art to the letter itself, in order to make a right use of it.

3. Our proposition mentions only the New Testament Scriptures, not the Bible in general. We have already to some extent prepared the reader for this in what we said above about the relation of Christianity to Judaism.[1] But, further, everyone must admit that if a doctrine had neither direct nor indirect attestation in the New Testament, but only in the Old, no one could have much confidence in regarding it as a genuinely Christian doctrine; whereas if a doctrine is attested by the New Testament, no one will object to it, because there is nothing about it in the Old. Hence the Old Testament appears simply a superfluous authority for Dogmatics. Now it is indeed true that even New Testament passages can demonstrate no more than that a proposition or doctrine is Christian. But, nevertheless, this is a thoroughly Protestant mode of procedure, in the case of every dogmatic proposition to go back to Scripture itself, and to human claims only in so far as they are attested by Scripture, but in this use of Scripture to allow everyone the free application of the exegetical art, as based on linguistic science. Naturally, however, the use made of Scripture varies itself a great deal, according to the differing character of the propositions. When the original trend towards purification of the Church is uppermost, the agreement must be so exact that Scripture can be used polemically against the assertions of the Roman Church. When it is rather the distinctive character of Protestantism that is concerned, it is enough to show that this more particularized form of doctrine is embraced within what Scripture says, without having to show that this particular form is the only scriptural one. And, similarly, all that the original and peculiar element in the presentation can with certainty venture to assert is, that it contains nothing demonstrably contrary to Scripture; the common element, on the other hand, must definitely attach itself to Scripture.

But this must not by any means be understood to mean that the Biblical vocabulary should itself be adopted in the system of doctrine. For since the New Testament is but partially didactic in form, and is nowhere properly systematic, a mode of expression which there is perfectly suitable would in most cases only very

[1] See § 12, 2 and 3.

imperfectly answer the demands which are made of a system of doctrine. And, further, the didactic parts of Scripture are for the most part occasional discourses and writings, and therefore full of special references which in a dogmatic presentation must simply cause confusion. Hence our task cannot be anything like perfectly discharged by the adducing of some passages of Scripture under each proposition. This procedure has actually become hurtful in many ways, to Dogmatics on the one hand, and to Scriptural exegesis on the other. The relating of particular passages of Scripture to particular dogmatic propositions can therefore only be done indirectly, by showing that the former are based on the same religious emotions which are set forth in the latter, and that the differences of expression are only such as are occasioned by the different connexions in which they appear. But since this can only be done by explaining these connexions, there ought to be developed more and more in this branch of study a large-viewed use of Scripture, not stressing individual passages torn out of their context, but only taking account of larger sections, and these particularly fruitful ones, so as to exhibit in the trains of thought of the sacred writers those same combinations on which the dogmatic results also are based. Such an application of Scripture can, however, only be made allusively in the system of doctrine itself, and its success depends entirely upon agreement in hermeneutic principles and methods. Therefore, on this side, Dogmatics can only reach its consummation simultaneously with the theory of Scriptural exegesis.

4. Thus there is room for great variety on this side too, so that Protestant systems of doctrine may be of very different stamp without losing their ecclesiastical character. When in a Dogmatic the appeal to the confessional documents and to analogy falls very much into the background, while the reference to Scripture predominates throughout, we have what I should call, for the most part, a *Scriptural Dogmatic*. In such a Dogmatic, the arrangement will be the thing of least importance ; but it will be a perfectly ecclesiastical arrangement, except where (say) the recognizedly common Protestant element is sacrificed to what is merely local and temporary in Scripture, or even to an eccentric interpretation of Scripture, or where it gives up the dialectical development of the ideas and goes back to the often indefinite and ambiguous language of the Bible. On the other hand, I should give the name of *Scientific Dogmatic* preferably to a Dogmatic which, starting from some recognized principal points, would make everything clear by its

orderly sequence, the parallelism of its members, and the coherence of its individual propositions, in which case citation from Scripture and application of the Symbols, of course, falls automatically into the background. Only, of course, those principal points must be none other than the fundamental facts of the religious self-consciousness conceived in a Protestant spirit. For if they were speculations, the system of doctrine might indeed be very scientific, but it would not be Christian doctrine. Finally, if a Dogmatic attaches itself principally to the confessional documents alone, and contents itself with proving everything from these and making everything dependent on these, without either going back to Scripture in details or linking up everything more closely by strict arrangement, this would be a *Symbolical Dogmatic* ; and in such we cannot fail to see a certain approximation to the Roman Catholic Church, since it lays the whole stress on every detail being recognized by the Church. But so long as it does not, on the one hand, set up the principle that Scriptural exegesis is subject to authority, and does not, on the other hand, ascribe to its own propositions a value independent of their expressing the inner experience of each individual, its Protestant character is not endangered. Since, however, each of these forms exposes itself the more to its own peculiar danger, the more it steers clear of the others, it would certainly seem that the common aim of all must be to diverge from each other as little as possible.

Postscript.—Our proposition is completely silent as to the very general custom of appealing in dogmatic systems to the dicta of other teachers, from the Church Fathers down to the most recent ; and this certainly means declaring such a procedure to be non-essential. Nevertheless, these citations may have a value, though not always the same value. In so far as what is established in our confessional documents passes over into a system of doctrine, citation of later theologians cannot increase the conviction of the ecclesiastical character of the propositions ; and it has a value only in compendiums, for the purpose of referring the reader to the most outstanding of later developments. Even ancient Patristic citations can in this case be of use only in an apologetical or polemical connexion as against the Roman Church. But it is different in cases of divergence, whether only in terminology or in content as well, from the symbolical documents. For the more a proposition has made itself heard from different quarters, the more claim has it to present itself as current in the Church. In particular, when a system of doctrine belongs definitely to one of the three above-mentioned forms, it becomes the more complete the more closely it connects itself with systems which bear equally strongly the stamp of one of the other forms.

§ 28. *The dialectical character of the language and the systematic arrangement give Dogmatics the scientific form which is essential to it.*

NOTE.—Cf. § 13, *Postscript*; § 16, § 18.

1. The term 'dialectical' is here taken in exactly the ancient sense. The dialectical character of the language therefore consists simply in its being formed in a technically correct manner, that it may be used in all intercourse for the communication and correction of the knowledge in question. Now this cannot be said of either the poetic or the rhetorical form of expression, nor even of the descriptively didactic, which, having sprung from the other two, has not become quite separate from them. Thus the expressions amid which the system of doctrine moves, form (inasmuch as they go back to the religious feeling) a special realm of language within the didactically religious, *i.e.* the strictest region of it. The questions of how religious feeling becomes diversified, and what object it refers to, encroach upon the ground of Psychology, Ethics, and Metaphysics; and the proper language of Dogmatics is distinguished more definitely from the didactically religious in general by its affinity to the scientific terminology of those realms: a terminology which is as sedulously avoided in the homiletical and poetical communication of the religious consciousness as it is eagerly sought after in the dogmatic. Hence the great diversity of views and of their expressions in all these philosophical realms makes the suitable management of language in dogmatic presentation a most difficult problem. However, the only views which are primarily unfit for use in dogmatic language are those which make no separation between the conceptions of God and the World, admit no contrast between good and evil, and thus make no definite distinction in man between the spiritual and the sensible. For these distinctions are the original presuppositions of the religious self-consciousness, because without these the self-consciousness, when widened into a world-consciousness, could not be set in antithesis to the God-consciousness,[1] nor could one speak of a distinction between a free and an inhibited higher self-consciousness, nor, consequently, of redemption and the need for it.[2] Now the more frequently philo-

[1] § 8, 2. [2] § 11, 2.

sophical systems change within those limits, the more frequent also are the revolutions in dogmatic language. These revolutions are indeed inevitable only when a system has become antiquated, *i.e.* when thinking really no longer conforms to its type. But they often take place earlier through the more intense zeal of theologians who have been caught away by a rising system, and who hope that the new system will be better fitted than any previous one to make an end of all divisions and misunderstandings in the realm of Dogmatics. Others again, by the spectacle of that very zeal, are made apprehensive lest one particular philosophical system should set itself up as lord and judge in theological matters. But the apprehension is, as a rule, as unfounded as the hope. The hope is illusory, because the important misunderstandings are always there before the expressions used upon the controversial points take on a strictly dogmatic complexion, and consequently the change resulting from the influence of another system does not in itself touch the origin of the misconceptions, unless the language should thereby gain a higher degree of clearness and definiteness. And it is the same with the apprehension referred to. For, in the first place, a system never, at least in our day, continues to have sole supremacy for a sufficiently long time. And secondly, as a general consideration, so long as it is really an interest in Christian piety that evokes the dogmatic presentation, this latter can never turn against that interest : such a danger can only arise when the whole procedure has not sprung from that interest, but is alien in type. Apart from this, there are two other opposite complaints which one sometimes hears made concerning the language used by theologians, as regards its connexion with philosophy. The more frequent complaint is that the language is too abstract and too far removed from the immediate language of religion, for the sake of which alone Dogmatics exists. The other one is less frequent—that one cannot tell from the language used which philosophical system the theologian assumes as his starting-point. Both complaints appear to be unfounded. For in our Church it is only the scientifically educated who can be expected to take their bearings from Dogmatics for the realm of popular religious teaching, and the key for this they are bound to have. And as regards the other complaint, for this purpose it is neither necessary nor profitable to know which philosophical system a theologian adheres to, so long as his language is correct and self-consistently formed. In all sciences the Schools always more or less discard their own language for the universal language of educated people, and yet the language of the Schools does always tend to keep itself distinct. Now the more a theologian keeps to the strictest language of the Schools, the more readily will he give occasion for the first complaint ; and for the second, the more use he makes of the elements which have been adopted into the universal language of humanity. In this latter, indeed, there remain for long enough elements collected from different periods and systems. But even out of these, by means of skilful selection and due explanation, there can be formed a whole which is perfectly well adapted for dogmatic usage. And thus the danger of an influence hurtful to the interests of Christian piety completely disappears, and a balance is maintained amid the influences of various contemporary systems.

2. If, however, Dogmatics is to fulfil its proper vocation, *i.e.* both to clear up the misconceptions which ever and again tend to arise in the whole business of making communications from the immediate religious life of the Christian, and also, so far as in it lies, to prevent such misconceptions by the norm it has established, not only is a dialectically formed vocabulary indispensable in the establishing of the system of doctrine, but also as strict and systematic an arrangement of the subject-matter as possible. For the more indefinite and more imperfectly formed material offered by every fragmentary opinion can only be rightly appraised by comparison with the perfectly definite and ordered material of the self-contained system, and only so can it be rectified. For even the most definite idea and the clearest proposition do not lose every trace of instability until they have been placed in an absolute context, for the simple reason that the sense of any proposition is not fully given except in some definite context. But this is the very essence of systematic arrangement, that by comprehensive co-ordination and exhaustive subordination each proposition should be brought into a perfectly definite relation with all others. Now a dogmatic system of doctrine is capable of this in so far as the subject treated of forms a self-contained whole, *i.e.*, on the one hand, in so far as all Christian religious emotions of the Protestant type, wherever they appear, can be represented in a complex of coherent formulæ, and, on the other hand, in so far as it is true that facts of consciousness which can be subsumed under these formulæ are not to be found anywhere outside of this communion. Now in this sense the Evangelical (Protestant) Church, it is true, is not so perfectly self-contained that there might not be doctrines which

the Roman Church expresses in exactly the same way, or that, on the other hand, its doctrines might not for the most part be also found in other anti-Roman communions which do not form a single whole with the Evangelical Church. But this latter contingency is due simply to the fact that outward unity does not depend solely on doctrine. As far as doctrine is concerned, those small communions do for us really form a single whole with the Evangelical Church. And the former case disappears when we come to regard the propositions, not by themselves alone, but in their context; and thus at suitable points an Evangelical Dogmatic may legitimately set itself to dispel that impression. In Dogmatics, however, the arrangement of material can have no resemblance to that employed in those sciences which are built upon some fundamental principle or can be developed from within themselves, or in those either which comprise a definite field of external perception and in this sense are historical. Instead of a fundamental law, Dogmatics has simply the fundamental inner fact of Christian piety which it postulates; and what it has to arrange consists simply in the different modifications of this fact which emerge, according to its differing relations with the other facts of consciousness.[1] Thus the task of arrangement consists simply in so comparing and so distinguishing those different relations that the different modifications themselves appear as a complete whole, and that consequently, by means of the formulæ all taken together, the infinite multiplicity of the particular can be synoptically viewed in a definite plurality. But the dialectical language and the systematic arrangement require one another, and also they promote one another. The dialectical language is too sharply defined for any other kind of religious communication, and outside of the complete doctrinal system itself it is permissible only in passages which are extensions of or outflows from the latter. But a systematic arrangement would never stand out so clearly, and still less could it win recognition, if it did not make use of language which admits of a strict calculus-like procedure for the trying and testing of all connexions of ideas. But it is self-evident how very much the task of systematic arrangement is facilitated when the particulars are given in dialectical language of uniform consistency, and also how the most precise expression for the particular is more easily found when a schematism of sharp distinctions and close connexions has already been fashioned for that purpose.

[1] § 10, 3.

3. After all we have already said on this point, it seems superfluous now expressly to remark or to demonstrate that there is no other connexion than that which we have exhibited between Christian Dogmatics and speculative philosophy ; especially since, in a treatment of the subject developed on the lines we have described above, there scarcely remains any point at which speculation could force its way into the system of doctrine. Our method indeed would seem to be the one that will most easily get rid of all traces of the Scholastic mode of treatment, by which philosophy (transformed as it was by the spread of Christianity) and real Christian Dogmatics were frequently mingled in one and the same work. There is only one point remaining for discussion here. Those members of the Christian communion through whose agency alone the scientific form of Dogmatics arises and subsists are also those in whom the speculative consciousness has awakened. Now as this is the highest objective function of the human spirit, while the religious self-consciousness is the highest subjective function, a conflict between the two would touch essential human nature, and so such a conflict can never be anything but a misunderstanding. Now it is certainly not sufficient merely that such a conflict should not arise : the man of knowledge is bound to reach the positive consciousness that the two are in agreement ; only, this is not the work of Dogmatics, since even for the same religious standpoint the procedure would necessarily vary with every different type of philosophy. If, on the other hand, such a conflict does arise, and some one rightly or wrongly finds the occasion of misunderstanding to be on the religious side, that circumstance may of course lead to his giving up religion altogether, or at least the Christian religion. But to guard against this, otherwise than by taking care not to occasion misunderstandings by unconsidered formulæ—that again is not the business of Dogmatics, which has nothing whatever to do with those who do not admit the fundamental fact. It is rather the business of Apologetics.

Postscript.—Those expositions of Christian doctrine which have long flourished under the name of Practical Dogmatics or Popular Dogmatics do indeed dispense both with dialectical language and with systematic arrangement. But these lie outside of the realm to which we here appropriate the name of Dogmatics. They are sometimes compromises between a system of doctrine and a catechism, and sometimes adaptations of Dogmatics to homiletical ends. The former have for the most part the aim of communicating the results of dogmatic developments with a certain coherence to those who would not find it easy to follow a scientific argument. But as that aim is itself somewhat arbitrary, the undertaking seems to lead to too much confusion and to foster too great superficiality for anything really useful to be achieved. As for the latter kind, its place will be completely filled if in Practical Theology the needful general directions are added concerning the matter of religious communications as well as concerning the form.

§ 29. *We shall exhaust the whole compass of Christian doctrine if we consider the facts of the religious self-consciousness, first, as they are presupposed by the antithesis expressed in the concept of redemption, and secondly, as they are determined by that antithesis.*

NOTE.—Cf. §§ 8, 9, and 11.

1. It is clear, to begin with, that the antithesis between the inability to inform all moments of life with the feeling of absolute dependence and the corresponding ability communicated to us by the Redeemer, presupposes that feeling itself and a knowledge of it. For since it is never presented to us except in man, we cannot know about it except in so far as it exists in ourselves ; and without knowing about it we could not know about an incapacity for it, nor even about the difference between the Redeemer and ourselves. Thus the state which precedes the communication of the capacity cannot be either absolute forgetfulness of God or a mere empty striving after the God-consciousness, but must somehow contain this last as a datum in the self-consciousness. It might, however, be said that such facts of the religious self-consciousness, which precede fellowship with the Redeemer, cannot belong to the system of *Christian* doctrine, but only to some general system of doctrine, or to the system of some religious communion from which one could pass to Christianity. To this we must reply that these states of the religious mind do not disappear when the mind has been laid hold of by Christianity, but are facilitated and encouraged in proportion as the communicated capacity is less or more. Thus they belong to the religious consciousness of the Christian too, and they might have been described as states not determined by that antithesis but remaining unchanged on all its different levels ; while the facts which are determined by the antithesis itself must differ in their content according as the incapacity or the communicated capacity has the preponderance. Only, the former kind of facts,

remaining as they do ever self-identical, will never by themselves alone occupy completely any moment of the religious life in the realm of Christian piety, but only partially; and it is for that reason, and because none the less we have to consider these facts in themselves, on account of their different nature, that the mode of expression used in our proposition has been preferred.

2. If, then, this first element in our proposition does thus belong to Christian piety, because it necessarily appears in combination with the second, we further venture to assert that the two taken together enclose the whole realm of Christian piety. For even if we assume that by degrees the incapacity disappears completely, this will not give rise to any new modifications of the religious self-consciousness, but will simply bring the reality nearer to the formulæ which express the condition in its purity. And so our only concern is to measure out the provinces of the two elements precisely and completely, that we may be sure of the completeness of the whole. The two will, then, of course, be so related to each other that the first part will contain those doctrines (the possibility in general of which has already been admitted) in which the distinctively Christian element is less prominent, and which may therefore most easily be coincident in expression with those of other faiths. These doctrines, however, are by no means constituent parts of a universal or so-called natural theology. Not only are they in every case expressions of the religious self-consciousness, and thus genuinely dogmatic propositions, but they are also definitely Christian, in virtue of the distinctively Christian reference which is inherent in the arrangement of the whole, and which we might repeat in every proposition. But apart from this, it certainly could be said—especially as all that belongs to the realm of the Science of Christian Morals remains excluded—that there are dogmatic propositions which only express monotheism in general, without making it clear whether they belong to the teleological or the æsthetic point of view. Therefore it is necessary that, if general allusions to the Science of Christian Morals are not given in Dogmatics, we should nevertheless always keep in mind the fact that to a system of Christian doctrine, of whatever form, there essentially belongs also a system of Christian morals developing in harmony with it.

3. These two, then, may be identified with each other: facts which are presupposed by the antithesis, and facts which remain unchanged throughout the whole development of the antithesis; and we have further asserted that these, together with the facts

which are determined by the antithesis, comprise the whole of Christian doctrine. Now from this it follows that, strictly considered, nothing which belongs exclusively to a period preceding the Christian development of that antithesis, and also nothing which belongs to a period which will only begin when the incapacity has been completely overcome and has disappeared, can be brought within the compass of Christian doctrine in the proper sense. No matter can be thus introduced except in so far as it has a demonstrable and definite connexion with the religious affections which are found within the antithesis. Now since all Christian piety rests upon the appearing of the Redeemer, the same thing is true of Him too, namely, that nothing concerning Him can be set up as real doctrine unless it is connected with His redeeming causality and can be traced to the original impression made by His existence. Whatever falls outside these limits either must have its proper place elsewhere or can make good its position only in virtue of some more distant relationship to be demonstrated in a special way.

§ 30. *All propositions which the system of Christian doctrine has to establish can be regarded either as descriptions of human states, or as conceptions of divine attributes and modes of action, or as utterances regarding the constitution of the world; and all three forms have always subsisted alongside of each other.*

1. Since the feeling of absolute dependence, even in the realm of redemption, only puts in an appearance, *i.e.* becomes a real self-consciousness in time, in so far as it is aroused by another determination of the self-consciousness and unites itself therewith,[1] every formula for that feeling is a formula for a definite state of mind; and consequently all propositions of Dogmatics must be capable of being set up as such formulæ. But any such sensible determination of the self-consciousness points back to a determinant outside of the self-consciousness. Now since, in virtue of the general coherence always postulated in every human consciousness, this determinant always appears as a part thereof, any modification which has so arisen of the feeling of absolute dependence may be known if we can get a description of that element of existence on which the state in question is based. Thus conceived, the dogmatic propositions become utterances regarding the constitution of the world, but only for the feeling of absolute dependence and with

[1] Cf. § 5.

reference to it. Finally, not only is the feeling of absolute dependence in itself a co-existence of God in the self-consciousness, but the totality of being from which, according to the position of the subject, all determinations of the self-consciousness proceed, is comprehended under that feeling of dependence; and therefore all modifications of the higher self-consciousness may also be represented by our describing God as the basis of this togetherness of being in its various distributions.

2. If we compare these three possible forms with each other, it is clear that descriptions of human states of mind with this content can only be taken from the realm of inner experience, and that therefore in this form nothing alien can creep into the system of Christian doctrine; whereas, of course, utterances regarding the constitution of the world may belong to natural science, and conceptions of divine modes of action may be purely metaphysical; in which case both are engendered on the soil of science, and so belong to the objective consciousness and its conditions, and are independent of the inner experience and the facts of the higher self-consciousness. Thus these two forms (the first of which includes, of course, all propositions of a generally anthropological content) do not in themselves afford any guarantee that all propositions so conceived are genuinely dogmatic. Hence we must declare the description of human states of mind to be the fundamental dogmatic form; while propositions of the second and third forms are permissible only in so far as they can be developed out of propositions of the first form; for only on this condition can they be really authenticated as expressions of religious emotions.

3. If, then, all propositions which belong to the system of Christian doctrine can indisputably be expressed in the fundamental form, and propositions which assert attributes of God and qualities of the world must be reduced to propositions of that first form before we can be safe from the creeping in of alien and purely scientific propositions, then it would seem that Christian Dogmatics has only to carry through consistently that fundamental form in order to complete the analysis of Christian piety, while the other two forms might be entirely set aside as superfluous. But if anyone were to attempt at the present time to treat Christian Dogmatics in this way, his work would be left isolated without any historical support; and not only would it lack a really ecclesiastical character, but, however perfectly it rendered the content of Christian doctrine, it could not fulfil the real purpose of all

Dogmatics. For since dogmatic language only came to be formed gradually out of the language which was current in the public communication of religion, the rhetorical and hymnic elements in this latter must have been especially favourable to the formation of conceptions of divine attributes, and indeed these became necessary in order that those expressions should be kept within due proportions. Similarly there arose, partly out of these, and partly out of the need for fixing the relation between the Kingdom of God and the world, utterances regarding the constitution of the world. Then, as the habit increased of treating Metaphysics in combination with Dogmatics, these two kinds of proposition became more numerous through the addition of similar ones of alien content, whereas the fundamental form naturally came to be left behind, and scarcely found any place except in presentations of a less scientific character. Hence a work which at the present time tried to confine itself entirely to the proper fundamental form would have no link with the past, and just for that reason would be of little practical use, either for purging the doctrinal system of alien elements, or for maintaining the clarity and verity of the rhetorical and poetic communications.

§ 31. *Thus the division outlined above will have to be fully worked out according to all these three forms of reflection upon the religious affections; but always and everywhere on this same basis, namely, the direct description of the religious affections themselves.*

1. As the elements of Dogmatics have taken shape in a fragmentary manner, and the science itself has therefore been fitted together externally out of these elements rather than generated organically, it is easy to understand how, generally speaking, propositions of all three kinds have been placed together without distinction, while none of the forms has been worked out with completeness and perspicuity. But such a state of affairs by no means satisfies the demands which may justly be made of dogmatic science; and in place of that we must of necessity (since, as we have seen, we cannot confine ourselves to the fundamental form alone) introduce that completeness of treatment which our proposition indicates. Nothing else can satisfy the present need. Now the general description of the Christian religion given above [1] underlies this whole presentation so fundamentally that even our

[1] See § 11.

division of the subject-matter rests upon it. And so each individual section will have to be prefaced by a similar general description, to which in turn the further articulation of that section will have reference ; and with this the ecclesiastical doctrines belonging to the same province will be brought into connexion : first, those which come nearest to the direct exposition of the religious affections, and then those which express the same thing in the form of divine attributes and qualities of the world.

2. From this it follows that the doctrine of God, as set forth in the totality of the divine attributes, can only be completed simultaneously with the whole system : whereas it is usually treated continuously and without a break, and before any other points of doctrine. But this divergence from the usual order can hardly be viewed as a disadvantage. For, not to mention the fact that divine attributes and modes of action which bear exclusively on the development of human soul-states (and this can be said of all the so-called moral attributes of God) cannot be understood without previous knowledge of these states, it is in general undeniable that the usual arrangement is peculiarly apt to conceal the relation of those doctrines both to the feeling of absolute dependence in general and to the fundamental facts of the Christian religion, and to give the impression of a quite independent speculative theory. Whereas our method not only makes that connexion most luminous, but also places in closer juxtaposition things which can only be understood alongside of and by means of each other.

Postscript.—Further comparison of the schematism here set forth with those more common in our older and newer textbooks and systems would exceed the limits of an Introduction which is not obliged to be polemical. The method here adopted can only be justified by the finished argument itself.

FIRST PART OF
THE SYSTEM OF DOCTRINE

FIRST PART

The Development of that Religious Self-Consciousness which is always both presupposed by and contained in every Christian Religious Affection.

INTRODUCTION

§ 32. *The finding of one's self in immediate self-consciousness as absolutely dependent is always presupposed and also accordingly contained in every Christian religious self-consciousness, and this is the only way that, in general, our own being and the infinite being of God can be one in self-consciousness.*

1. The fact that the whole Christian religious consciousness is here presupposed is entirely legitimate, for here we abstract entirely from the specific content of the particular Christian experiences, and what we have stated is in no way affected by these differences. Hence nothing can be deduced from the above proposition either for or against any dogmatic formulation of such specific content. But if anyone should maintain that there might be Christian religious experiences in which the Being of God was not involved in such a manner, *i.e.* experiences which contained absolutely no consciousness of God, our proposition would certainly exclude him from the domain of that Christian belief which we are going to describe. Our proposition appeals, therefore, against such a person to the religious self-consciousness as it appears and is recognized everywhere in the Evangelical (Protestant) Church : that is, we assert that in every religious affection, however much its special contents may predominate, the God-consciousness must be present and cannot be neutralized by anything else, so that there can be no relation to Christ which does not contain also a relation to God. At the same time, we also assert that this God-consciousness, as it is here described, does not constitute by itself alone an actual moment in religious experience, but always in connexion with other particular determinations ; so that this God-consciousness maintains its identity through its particular moments in all mani-

festations of Christian piety, just as in life generally the self-consciousness of an individual does in the different moments of his existence. Hence the view that in every Christian affection there must be a relation to Christ does not in the least contradict our proposition. Much more is this the case when the pious feeling comes to expression as an actual moment in the form of pleasure or pain. For the Christian faith, however, the incapacity implied in religious pain must be ascribed to lack of fellowship with the Redeemer, while, on the other hand, the ease in evoking pious feeling which goes along with religious pleasure is regarded as a possession which comes to us from this fellowship. Thus it is evident that, within the Christian communion, there can be no religious experience which does not involve a relation to Christ.

2. It is possible to give a non-religious explanation of this sense of absolute dependence ; it might be said that it only means the dependence of finite particulars on the whole and on the system of all finite things, and that what is implied and made the centre of reference is not God but the world. But we can only regard this explanation as a misunderstanding. For we recognize in our self-consciousness an awareness of the world, but it is different from the awareness of God in the same self-consciousness. For the world, if we assume it to be a unity, is nevertheless in itself a divided and disjointed unity which is at the same time the totality of all contrasts and differences and of all the resulting manifold determinations, of which every man is one, partaking in all the contrasts. To be one with the world in self-consciousness is nothing else than being conscious that we are a living part of this whole ; and this cannot possibly be a consciousness of absolute dependence ; the more so that all living parts stand in reciprocal interaction with each other. This oneness with the whole in each several part is essentially twofold : a feeling of dependence, indeed, so far as the other parts act spontaneously upon it, but also a feeling of freedom in so far as it likewise reacts spontaneously on the other parts. The one is not to be separated from the other.

The feeling of absolute dependence, accordingly, is not to be explained as an awareness of the world's existence, but only as an awareness of the existence of God, as the absolute undivided unity. For neither is there in relation to God an immediate feeling of freedom, nor can the feeling of dependence in relation to Him be such that a feeling of freedom can be its counterpart. On the contrary, at the highest point of Christian devotion and with the clearest consciousness of the most unimpeded self-activity, the absoluteness of the feeling of dependence remains undiminished. This is what is indicated by the statement that the realization of oneself as absolutely dependent is the only way in which God and the ego can co-exist in self-consciousness. If we abolish this distinction and mistake the self-consciousness which refers to God as referring only to the world, then we must dispute in the latter the reality of this feeling of freedom and, indeed, consequently entirely reject it, since there is no moment in self-consciousness in which we do not think of ourselves as one with the world. This non-religious explanation, which casts aside what we hold to be the characteristic of the religious consciousness as a deception, comes sometimes from those who explain all feeling of freedom as illusion and sometimes even from those who, maintaining that there is nothing upon which we could feel ourselves absolutely dependent, reject all distinction between the ideas of God and the world.

3. It is obvious that, as we are no longer moving outside the province of Christian piety, we do not here concern ourselves with the only partially developed and differentiated religious feeling which constitutes polytheistic types of belief ; the Christian feeling can only exist side by side with monotheism. On the other hand, it may be objected that the foregoing statement is not pertinent to our subject, because it is not so much peculiarly Christian as characteristic of monotheism in general. The answer is that there is no purely monotheistic piety in which the God-consciousness alone and by itself forms the content of religious experiences. Just as there is always present in Christian piety a relation to Christ in conjunction with the God-consciousness,[1] so in Judaism there is always a relation to the Lawgiver, and in Mohammedanism to the revelation given through the Prophet. In our Holy Scriptures for this reason God is constantly referred to by the name of the Father of our Lord Jesus Christ. The saying of Christ also (John 14^{7-9}) implies that every relation to Christ includes also the God-consciousness.

§ 33. *This feeling of absolute dependence, in which our self-consciousness in general represents the finitude of our being (cf. § 8, 2), is therefore not an accidental element, or a thing which varies from person to person, but is a universal element of life ; and the recognition of this fact entirely takes the place, for the*

[1] Quare in omni cogitatione de Deo et omni invocatione mentes intueantur Christum, etc. Melanchthon, *Loc. de Deo.*

system of doctrine, of all the so-called proofs of the existence of God.

Melanchth., *loc. de Deo*: Esse Deum et praecipere obedientiam juxta discrimen honestorum et turpium impressum humanis mentibus.—Zwingl., *d. ver. et fals. rel.*, p. 9. Fucus ergo est et falsa religio, quicquid a Theologis ex philosophia, quid sit Deus, allatum est.—Clem., *Strom.* vii. p. 864, πίστις μὲν οὖν ἐνδιάθετόν τί ἐστιν ἀγαθὸν, καὶ ἄνευ τοῦ ζητεῖν τὸν θεὸν ὁμολογοῦσα τοῦτον εἶναι καὶ δοξάζουσα ὡς ὄντα· ὅθεν χρὴ ἀπὸ ταύτης ἀναγόμενον τῆς πίστεως, καὶ αὐξηθέντα ἐν αὐτῇ χάριτι θεοῦ τὴν περὶ αὐτοῦ κομίσασθαι ὡς οἷόν τέ ἐστι γνῶσιν.

1. One cannot concede the postulated self-consciousness with the content we have already described, and yet maintain that it is something unessential, *i.e.* that it may or may not be present in a man's life according to whether, in the course of his life, he meets with this or that experience. For its emergence does not depend at all upon the fact that something definite and objective is given in the experience of a partially developed subject, but only on the fact that in some way or other the sensory consciousness has been stimulated from without. But what is presupposed on the subjective side is only that which is common to all—the intelligence in its subjective function, in which the disposition towards God-consciousness is a constituent element.

That the feeling of absolute dependence as such is the same in all, and not different in different persons, follows from the fact that it does not rest upon any particular modification of human nature but upon the absolutely general nature of man, which contains in itself the potentiality of all those differences by which the particular content of the individual personality is determined.

Further, if a difference is admitted between perfection and imperfection as measured by greater or less development, this arises from the fact that the emergence of this feeling depends upon a contrast having been apprehended in consciousness; the lack of development is simply the lack of differentiation of functions. For when the objective consciousness and self-consciousness are not yet clearly differentiated in such a way as nevertheless to be distinctly connected together, in that case the consciousness as a whole has not yet become genuinely human. And if sensuous self-consciousness and the higher self-consciousness are not thus differentiated from one another and related to one another, development is incomplete.

2. We may conclude then that godlessness within the Christian community has its cause simply in defective or arrested development. Should it occur however in spite of a complete development,

we can only regard this as illusion and appearance. It is nevertheless possible to distinguish in the main three types of godlessness.

The first is the childish complete lack of God-consciousness, which as a rule disappears in the course of the natural development of the individual, and only in exceptional cases degenerates into brutal godlessness in such as bitterly resist their own wider development. Both things are to be met with outside the Christian community for the most part among peoples that innocently or voluntarily remain on the lowest grade of development. The existence of this type, however, is hardly to be proved historically.

The second type of godlessness is the sensual. This occurs when a feeling of absolute dependence actually appears, but intimately associated with awareness of that on which there can be no absolute dependence ; since what is conceived as capable of passion can give no absolute dependence, for it implies the possibility of self-initiated activity upon it. Face to face with this contradiction, it may be doubted whether the disposition towards God-consciousness has really been operative, the appearance merely being obscured by perverted reflexion, or whether the inner reflexion corresponds to the original, inner fact, so that the latter does not really belong to the province of piety. But a comparison of the way in which in childhood the God-consciousness at first manifests itself shows that here certainly the disposition to God-consciousness is already effective ; it is only on account of the imperfect development of self-consciousness that the process cannot fully be carried to its conclusion. This condition is obviously akin to Polytheism,[1] for the same germ of multiplicity is there also, only it is restrained by opposing influences ; further, this anthropomorphic conception is sometimes of a more pure and spiritual kind and sometimes verges on Fetichism.

Finally, the third type of godlessness is the so-called definite denial of God—Atheism, which is propounded as a speculative theory in the midst of a Christian society, in a condition of full development and even in the highest stage of culture. This again is twofold. In part it is a wicked fear of the sternness of the God-consciousness, and hence, though moments of enlightenment intervene, clearly a product of licentiousness and thus a sickness of the soul usually accompanied by contempt of everything intellectual ; and of this (godlessness) it can be said that it is naught, because it entirely lacks inner truth. And in part it is simply a

[1] § 8, 2.

reasoned opposition to the current and more or less inadequate representations of the religious consciousness. Moreover, the atheism of the eighteenth century was, for the most part, a struggle against the petrified, anthropomorphic presentations of doctrine, a struggle provoked by the tyranny of the Church. But when, over and above the defects of representation, the inner facts of self-consciousness themselves are thus wholly misconstrued, this serious misunderstanding is none the less merely a disease of the understanding which may revive sporadically and from time to time, but never produces anything that is historically permanent. This fact cannot therefore be pled against our assertion that the feeling of absolute dependence, as here expounded, and the God-consciousness contained in it are a fundamental moment of human life.

3. But even supposing its universality could be disputed, still no obligation would arise for the system of doctrine to prove the existence of God ; that would be an entirely superfluous task. For since in the Christian Church the God-consciousness should be developed in youth, proofs, even if youth were capable of understanding them, could only produce an objective consciousness, which is not the aim here, nor would it in any way generate piety. We are not concerned here with the question whether there are such proofs, and whether, if we have no immediate certitude of God, then that of which we do have immediate certitude, and by which God could be proved, must not itself be God. Our point simply is that these proofs can never be a component part of the system of doctrine ; for that is only for those who have the inner certainty of God, as we have already described it, and of that they can be directly conscious at every moment. On our interpretation of Christian doctrine it would be quite unnecessary to enlarge on this point did it not seem essential to protest against the general custom of furnishing Dogmatics at this point with such proofs, or at least of referring to them as already familiar from other sciences. It is obvious that for the purpose of Dogmatics this reference is quite useless : for neither in catechetical nor in homiletical nor in missionary work can such proofs be of any value. Experience, too, shows how little can be accomplished by such a polemic against theoretical atheism as above described. Dogmatics must therefore presuppose intuitive certainty or faith ; and thus, as far as the God-consciousness in general is concerned, what it has to do is not to effect its recognition but to explicate its content. That such proofs are not the concern of Dogmatics is obvious also from

the fact that it is impossible to give them dogmatic form ; for we cannot go back to Scripture and symbolical books, since they themselves do not prove, but simply assert. Moreover, he for whom such assertion is authoritative needs no further proof.

The prevalent method of inflating Christian doctrine with rational proofs and criticism had its origin in the confusion of Dogmatics and philosophy in old Patristic times.[1] Closely related to this, and therefore to be named here, is the equally erroneous view that Christian theology, to which Dogmatics also belongs, is differentiated from Christian religion by its sources of knowledge. Religion, for instance, it is argued, draws from Scripture only, but theology draws also from the Fathers, reason and philosophy. But as theology itself draws from Scripture, and the Scriptures themselves have arisen out of the Christian religion, what originates in reason and philosophy cannot be Christian theology. It is certainly a great gain here, and elsewhere, to banish all material of this kind from the Christian system of doctrine, for only thus is a uniformity of method to be established. Such a difficult choice as that between moral proofs, geometrical proofs, and probable proofs [2] is not a task for any dogmatic theologian to take up, even if it be only for his own personal satisfaction.

Postscript.—Though it lies outside our present scheme we may remark here that there can be a precisely similar awareness of God in the objective consciousness, an awareness which in itself does not take the form of a temporal consciousness, but which in a like manner can be aroused and brought into existence through sense-perception ; and in fact all scientific construction, whether in the sphere of nature or of history, is based upon it. But just as it could only injure science to employ expressions belonging to the religious consciousness or to mingle with science anything belonging to that sphere, so it can only be harmful to faith and the system of doctrine to intersperse them with scientific propositions or to make them dependent on scientific foundations. For the system of doctrine has as little to do immediately with the objective consciousness as pure science with the subjective.

§ 34. *The feeling of absolute dependence is contained in every Christian religious affection, in proportion as in the latter,*

[1] Augustin., *d. ver. rel.* 8: Sic enim creditur et docetur, quod est humanae salutis caput, non aliam esse philosophiam, id est sapientiae studium, et aliam religionem.

[2] Reinhard's *Dogmatik*, § 7 and § 30.

through its co-determining stimuli, we become conscious that we are placed in a universal nature-system, i.e. *in proportion as we are conscious of ourselves as part of the world.*

1. To be conscious of oneself as part of the world is the same thing as to find oneself placed in a universal nature-system. In every actual self-consciousness there is either an awareness of a relation of our being to some object opposed to it or the comprehension at one and the same time of a being and a having. That which is set in opposition to us must naturally decrease as our self-consciousness widens. Whether we widen it to the self-consciousness of the human race or are simply aware of ourselves as finite spirit, in either case there is nothing set over against us except what the spirit does not possess. The expansion takes place only in virtue of a partial identity (between subject and object), and hence in virtue of a system of nature ; thus in every such process we discover ourselves to be in a nature-system of spiritual being.

But though in our self-consciousness we constantly distinguish the system of relations from the spirit in ourselves, nevertheless the system is seated in the spirit as its original possession, original just because there is a system of nature. It exists in our self-consciousness always as influenced by being other than itself and thus as co-existent with such being in the system of nature. This system, however, is not posited as having limits ; hence it contains within itself all finite being, only in undeveloped form. If we extend our self-consciousness to that of the human species, then the whole earth co-posited with its external relations is equally undeveloped, partly as that which is possessed by us and partly as that which stands over against us. But that which stands over against us is only in self-consciousness so far as it affects us, and consequently exists along with us in a nature-system ; and thus also the whole system of nature or the world exists in our self-consciousness in so far as we recognize ourselves to be a part of the world. But this must be the case in every Christian and religious emotion because it is (at each moment) accompanied by the sensuous self-consciousness. Even if we were known to ourselves only as presentational activity (*vorstellende Thätigkeit*)—that is to say, as being centres for ideas—even so the self-consciousness is a centre for truth ; and that implies a relation of being in the self-consciousness, corresponding to the relation of ideas in the objective consciousness.

It is true, one frequently encounters the view that the more prominent the system of nature is in self-consciousness, the more the feeling of absolute dependence recedes ; and that, on the other hand, the latter is most in evidence when something is posited which abrogates the systematic connexion of nature, *i.e.* something miraculous. This we can only regard as an error. The real fact is that we most abrogate the systematic connexion of nature when we posit either a dead mechanism or chance and arbitrariness ; and in both cases the God-consciousness recedes—a clear proof that it does not exist in inverse proportion to our consciousness of the relatedness of nature. But the miraculous obviously presupposes the system of nature : for universal chance excludes everything miraculous. If, then, the miraculous really aroused the God-consciousness in a special degree, we should have to find the cause in the fact that many people only become aware of the rule through the exception. But this view in itself would justify the conclusion that this universal God-consciousness emerges more strongly and frequently in the religious experience of the Roman Church than in ours : because its adherents, properly speaking, are all immersed in the miraculous and may expect it at any moment. The proportion in which the God-consciousness appears is in fact the reverse of this.

Our proposition can be verified also in detail. The daily revolution of the atmospheric changes frequently appears to us as a mechanism ; on the other hand, it is pre-eminently the abode of the seemingly contingent ; whereas the periodical renewing of life's functions gives us the most vivid feeling of nature, but obviously the God-consciousness is more clearly posited in the latter than in the former.

3. Moreover, no Christian religious emotion can be imagined in experiencing which we do not find ourselves placed in a nature-system. Whatever the emotion may express, and whether it issue in action or in speculation, we must always be conscious of ourselves in this manner, and this consciousness must also be united to the God-consciousness ; because otherwise the moment would be at one and the same time religious and non-religious. The only thing to which we ought still to call attention is that this element of our pious moments, so far as their content is concerned, is the same at each stage of Christian development. It will certainly occur more frequently when a soul in fellowship with Christ has already attained a very marked facility in the development of the

God-consciousness; and will occur very little in one whom the sensuous impulse sways so quickly from moment to moment that such a development can rarely follow. The content, however, is always the same, for it does not at all depend on any definite relation or condition, but the individual regards his absolute dependence as exactly the same as that of every other finite being.

All we have to do in the first part of our exposition is, to the best of our ability, to describe this religious feeling of nature in general, apart from the specifically Christian content which is always attached to it.

§ 35. *According to the criterion of the three forms established in* § 30 *we shall have to treat, first, the relation present in the religious self-consciousness between the finite being of the world and the infinite Being of God; then, in the second section, the attributes of God in relation to the world as they appear in that self-consciousness; and lastly, in the third section, the constitution of the world as therein conceived in virtue of its absolute dependence on God.*

1. Considered as finite being and hence as representing all finite being, this consciousness of the absolute dependence of the self as an inward permanent datum which can be made apparent at any moment, is a state of our heart or soul (*Gemüthszustand*): so that the first part of our proposition entirely corresponds with what we expect of the dogmatic basal form. In it must be expressed the relation of the world (regarded as absolutely dependent on God) and God (regarded as the Being on Whom the world absolutely depends), and if the propositions still to be established keep within these limits it cannot be said that they go outside the real province of Dogmatics.

2. But that danger certainly does exist in the other two forms. For these do not immediately reflect the religious self-consciousness, in which are given only the antithesis and the relation of the antithetic entities to each other; but since the one makes God the subject of its thesis, and the other the world, great discrimination must be used lest either of them should express concerning their subject anything in excess of the immediate content of that self-consciousness.

The second dogmatic form, which treats of the divine attributes, is based proximately on the poetical and theoretical expressions which occur in hymns and sermons. Since it does not sufficiently conform these expressions to dialectical usage, it may easily be led into saying something about the Infinite Being which would contradict the antithesis contained in self-consciousness and represent the Infinite Being as dependent on the finite, while in fact the latter was posited as absolutely dependent on the Infinite. Those expressions would then not correspond to the religious self-consciousness which they ought to set forth.

From another point of view the third form needs careful thought. For here the world is made the subject of dogmatic propositions; and for various reasons—partly on account of the customary confusion between speculative thought and dogmatic, and partly because those who are ignorant of science like to borrow from it those general conceptions which they think desirable and which make clearer their own higher self-consciousness—for such reasons it can easily occur that, through weak compliance with these mistaken demands, objective statements should find their way into catechetical and homiletic utterances, and that these again should pass, in a slightly different form, into Dogmatics.

3. If, then, the statements of these two latter forms have gone beyond the sphere of Dogmatics, and if in practice they have come to predominate, it is only too natural that statements of the first form should be more and more assimilated to them, and in this manner should partake of errors which by themselves they would have escaped. How far this has occurred up to the present time in the development of Dogmatics the following argument will show.

FIRST SECTION

A Description of our Religious Self-Consciousness in so far as the Relation between the World and God is expressed in it.

INTRODUCTION

§ 36. *The original expression of this relation,* i.e. *that the world exists only in absolute dependence upon God, is divided in Church doctrine into the two propositions—that the world was created by God, and that God sustains the world.*

NOTE.—πιστεύω εἰς θεὸν παντοκράτορα is also the original simple expression of the Roman Symbol.—Docent . . . Deum . . . semper adorandum ut omnium Dominum ac regem summum in aevum regnantem ; ab eoque solo pendere omnia. *Conf. Bohem.*, Art. iii.—Omnia ipsum habere sub potestate et manu. *Catech. Genev.*

1. The proposition that the totality of finite being exists only in dependence upon the Infinite is the complete description of that basis of every religious feeling which is here to be set forth. We find ourselves always and only in a continuous existence ; our life is always moving along a course ; consequently just so far as we regard ourselves as finite being, apart from all other things, our self-consciousness can represent this being only in its continuity. And this in so complete a sense that (the feeling of absolute dependence being so universal an element in our self-consciousness) we may say that in whatever part of the whole or at whatever point of time we may be placed, in every full act of reflection we should recognize ourselves as thus involved in continuity, and should extend the same thought to the whole of finite being. The proposition that God sustains the world, considered in itself, is precisely similar. At least it only seems to have acquired another and lesser content because we have grown accustomed to think of preservation and creation together, and thus a beginning is excluded from the range of the idea of preservation. On the other hand, the proposition, 'God has created,' considered in itself, lays down absolute dependence, but only for the beginning, with the exclusion of development ;

and whether the creation is conceived as taking place once for all or in the manner of one part after another, it lays down something which is not immediately given in our self-consciousness. Thus this proposition appears to belong to Dogmatics only so far as creation is complementary to the idea of preservation, with a view of reaching again the idea of unconditional all-inclusive dependence.

2. Thus there is no sufficient reason for retaining this division instead of the original expression which is so natural. And there can have been no reason for bringing this distinction into Dogmatics originally except that it was already to be found in traditional religious teaching, and that both the suitability of such expressions and the right measure of their use could be better guarded and established if the distinction were also adopted in the system of doctrine. Thus it did not originally arise on purely dogmatic grounds; and not only so, but it is not the outcome of any purely religious interest (which would find complete satisfaction in the simple expression); and thus, left to itself, the distinction between creation and preservation would fall into oblivion.

But for a human imagination only partially awakened, the beginning of all spatial and temporal existence is a subject which it cannot leave alone; consequently the treatment of the question is older than the abstract scientific phase of speculation, and belongs to the period of mythology. The question is linked up for us with the Mosaic account of creation, but that by itself does not give it a religious or Christian character any more than other things in the Pentateuch which have been brought over in the same way from primitive and prehistoric times. Yet for a long time this representation had to submit to being used for purposes of speculation and of science as well, and, indeed, for the purpose of supporting opposing theories or even as their source.

§ 37. *As the Evangelical (Protestant) Church has adopted both doctrines, but has not in her confessional documents given to either of them any distinctive character, it behoves us so to treat them that, taken together, they will exhaust the meaning of the original expression.*

NOTE.—*Augsburg Conf.* i.: 'A Creator and Sustainer of all things—visible and invisible.'—*Ibid.* xix.: 'Almighty God has created the whole of Nature and sustains it, etc.'—*Conf. et expos. simpl.* iii.: Deum credimus . . . creatorem rerum omnium cum visibilium tum invisibilium . . . et omnia vivificantem et conservantem.'—*Conf. Gall.* vii.: Credimus Deum cooperantibus tribus personis—condidisse universa, non tantum coelum et terram omniaque

iis contenta, sed etiam invisibiles spiritus.—*Conf. Angl.* i.: Unus est Deus . . . creator et conservator omnium tum visibilium tum invisibilium.—*Conf. Scot.* i.: . . . unum Deum . . . per quem confitemur omnia in coelo et in terra tam visibilia quam invisibilia creata in suo esse retineri, etc.—*Conf. Hung.*: Confitemur Deum verum esse et unum auctorem et conservatorem omnium.

1. These juxtapositions of creation and preservation are all derived from the later additions made in the Roman creed to the simple statement cited above,[1] and still further enlarged in the Creed of Constantinople.[2] As nothing definite is here said about the manner of creation, there is nothing on which to remark in this distinction except the intention that nothing, no point of space and no point of time, should be exempted from the Divine All-Sovereignty. Further, the expressions relating to the Trinity are neither peculiar to the Gallican Confession nor do they first appear in this period; the same expressions occur in the Augsburg Confession, where the Trinity is said to be Creator and Preserver; and they originate in the creed *Quicunque vult,* where *omnipotens* and *dominus* are predicated of the three Persons, which clearly means the same thing. Since the doctrine of the Trinity is neither presupposed in every Christian religious experience nor contained in it, these definitions do not belong to our present discussion.

But there is unmistakably a gradation in these expressions, so that the original expression in the Roman symbol and the Gallican Confession form the extremes. While in the former there is no separation, in the latter it is so complete that the doctrine of preservation is not treated at all in connexion with the creation, but is merged later in the government of the world. The Bohemian and Scots Confessions are therefore nearest to the former, the Augsburg and Swiss Confessions to the latter. Moreover, all belong under our formulation, though they do not all go back to the stimulated religious self-consciousness as definitely as the expression in the Bohemian Confession; for they describe attributes of God as little as attributes of the world, and concerning God state only ideas of relation and operation. For it is only by describing God as the sole original activity that the relation of absolute dependence can be expressed.

2. From this situation it follows[3] that we of the Evangelical Church not only have a very wide field for a more diversified exposition of this article of doctrine, but are also called upon to make use of it. For, by returning to the first source, we are free not only to

[1] *εἰς θεὸν πατέρα παντοκράτορα ποιητὴν οὐρανοῦ καὶ γῆς.*

[2] *ὁρατῶν τε πάντων καὶ ἀοράτων.*

[3] Cf. § 27, 2.

adhere more closely to the oldest and simplest expression, and develop it without any such distinction as far as the purpose of Dogmatics requires it, but also in the formulation of the distinction between the two topics in the Evangelical Church everything must rank as an opinion men are free to hold which, equally with the rather broad and vague statements of the different Confessions, can be traced back to the simple expression of primitive feeling. If we consider that the attention of the Reformers was not directed to this doctrine because of its remoteness from what at first was matter of dispute in the early days of our Church, then (especially as these doctrines are exposed to so many foreign influences, which ought to be resisted) it is our duty to inquire whether traces of such influences are not to be found in the credal formulas themselves. Even if that is not the case, it is our duty to discover whether they satisfy our present need and whether, perhaps, the further development of the evangelical spirit, and the many revolutions in the province of philosophy as well as of the natural sciences, do not necessitate other definitions ; in which case we need have no scruples in completely abandoning the credal expression.

3. Now in this respect the standard adopted for our treatment appears to be not only appropriate but adequate. For although the aim of Dogmatics does undoubtedly compel us to develop the simple expression to such a point that the language of popular religious teaching on this fundamental relation of the world to God can be regulated and guarded, it is clearly appropriate at the present time to consider the separation of Creation from Preservation. But the danger threatens us of losing ourselves on alien ground, and passing from the more peculiarly religious province into the speculative, and such a danger will be best averted if every individual proposition, no matter how we may have arrived at it, is constantly traced back to that simple expression which most truly interprets the immediate religious self-consciousness. But, if each of these doctrines completely coincided with that original expression, so that both ideas were contained in each later doctrine just as much as in the original one—the doctrine of Preservation in that of Creation and *vice versa*—then one or other doctrine would be superfluous. We should then have either to present the whole content of the fundamental feeling twice over, or else so to arrange the two that only when taken together did they make explicit the undeveloped content of the original expression. This latter method is evidently to be preferred.

§ 38. *The content of the original expression can be evolved out of either of the two doctrines, provided that in both of them, as in the original expression, God is regarded as the sole Determinant.*

Calvin, *Inst.* i. 16. 1 : In hoc praecipue nos a profanis hominibus differre convenit, ut non minus in perpetuo mundi statu quam in prima ejus origine praesentia divinae virtutis nobis eluceat.—Nemesius, *d. nat. hom.*, p. 164, Ed. Ant. : Ἐι γὰρ λέγοι τὶς, ὅτι κατὰ τὴν ἐξ ἀρχῆς γένεσιν εἱρμῷ προβαίνει τὸ πρᾶγμα, τοῦτο ἂν εἴη λέγων, ὅτι τῇ κτίσει συνυπάρχει πάντως ἡ πρόνοια. τὸ γὰρ εἱρμῷ προβαίνειν τὸ κτισθέν, δηλοῖ τῇ κτίσει συγκαταβεβλῆσθαι τὴν πρόνοιαν· καὶ οὕτως οὐδὲν ἂν ἄλλο λέγοι, ἢ τὸν αὐτὸν εἶναι ποιητὴν ἅμα καὶ προνοητὴν τῶν ὄντων.

1. If, with the statements of the Confessions, which uniformly speak of all things, not of an All, we refer the idea of creation primarily to particular things, what from this point of view we conceive of as their origin will really be simply the preservation of species, which is conditioned by the renewal or re-emergence of individual things.[1] Since the underlying self-consciousness here represents the whole of finite being, the concept of species suggests itself as naturally as that of the individual life, for in our self-consciousness we always posit ourselves as men ; and thus the statement that the re-emergent things exist through God, will correspond to the content of this self-consciousness just as adequately as the statement that individual things arise through God.

Now, with our increased knowledge of the world, we may indeed conceive the heavenly bodies and all the life developing upon them as particular things which have not all necessarily come into existence simultaneously ; yet their successive origination must obviously be also conceived as the active continuance of formative forces which must be resident in finite existence. And thus, however far our consciousness extends, we find nothing the origin of which cannot be brought under the concept of Preservation, so that the doctrine of Creation is completely absorbed in the doctrine of Preservation. In the same way, if we regard individual things as created, and follow this a step further, we find that the preservation of these same things is equivalent to that alternation of changes and movements in which their being perdures. But as these always form more or less coherent series, there is always something new implied either in the beginning of each series of activities or in the effects produced by a subject—something which was not formerly contained in that particular thing. This is, therefore, a new beginning and can be regarded as a creation, and the more properly

[1] So also Nemesius, p. 163 : πῶς οὖν ἕκαστον ἐκ τοῦ οἰκείου σπέρματος φύεται καὶ οὐκ ἐξ ἄλλου προνοίας ἀπούσης ;

so regarded the more such a beginning appears to be an important link in development: nevertheless 'more' and 'less' here do not give us ground for a definite distinction. But as every individual activity forms in itself a fresh series, and its beginning is a new origin, so, as far as our consciousness extends, all that we are accustomed to regard as object of the divine preservation falls under the conception of creation. Thus the concept of creation if taken in its whole range makes the concept of preservation superfluous, just as we have already seen happens inversely; for what does not wholly fall under one of the two is not given for the other.

Popular religious teaching cannot be blamed for clinging to this freedom and regarding the same event alternatively as either new creation or preservation in accordance with natural law. And devotion will scarcely consent to recognize the precedence of either, as if the one more perfectly, or in a loftier style than the other, corresponded to the absolute feeling of dependence.

2. This equivalence, however, is certainly dependent on our conceiving of the divine origination on the one side, and the dependence of the finite being on the other as equally complete, whether we imagine a thing to be created by God or sustained by Him. If we think of the creation of the world as a single divine act and including the whole system of nature, then this conception may be a complete expression of the feeling of absolute dependence, so long as we do not conceive of that act as having ceased, and consequently imagine on the one side, in God, an alternation of activity and rest relatively to the world, and on the other side, in the world, an alternation between a determination of the whole through God and a determination of all single individuals through each other. In the same way if we regard Preservation as a continuous divine activity exerted on the whole course of the world, covering the first beginning no less than each subsequent state, then this is a complete expression of the self-consciousness in question, provided we do not think the origin of the world is conditioned by something else before and after that activity. For, otherwise, in every situation only some elements would be dependent on the divine activity, while the rest, though ever so small a part, would be conditioned by what had previously existed. And thus the divine activity, whose object should be the whole world, would be always mingled with passiveness.

The same results follow in another way if we conceive of the divine creative activity, not indeed as momentary, yet as recurring only at particular points and certain times. For even though the sustaining activity extended between these points so that divine activity never alternated at any point with inactivity, yet creative activity would then come in distinguishably from sustaining activity, and each in limiting the other would exclude it ; and thus the world would certainly remain entirely dependent on God but irregularly, and on divine activities which mutually restrict each other. And the position is not altered if we think of the sustaining activity as unmixed with passivity but suppose either that, following on a pure creative act, it has to overcome an opposition which develops therefrom, or suppose that the creative activity enters at individual points as another activity. The tendency, however, to such perverted formulas, which in no way express the pure feeling of dependence but misrepresent it in every way, is nearly always unmistakably present. This naturally has its roots, not in Christian piety, but in a confused world-view which in ordinary life is only too common—a view which only uses dependence on God as an explanation of the course of the world where the causal nexus is concealed, and thus makes use of it mostly where something severed from what went before as well as separated from its context, appears either as a beginning or in isolation.

§ 39. *The doctrine of Creation is to be elucidated pre-eminently with a view to the exclusion of every alien element, lest from the way in which the question of Origin is answered elsewhere anything steal into our province which stands in contradiction to the pure expression of the feeling of absolute dependence. But the doctrine of Preservation is pre-eminently to be elucidated so as to bring out this fundamental feeling itself in the fullest way.*

1. Our self-consciousness, in its universality, as both these doctrines relate to it, can only represent finite being in general so far as it is a continuous being ; for we only know ourselves in this manner but have no consciousness of a beginning of being. Hence as we have seen, though not impossible, it would be extremely difficult to develop the same material principally or exclusively under the form of the doctrine of Creation. Such an attempt would be just as arbitrary as it would be inappropriate for the purpose of Dogmatics, in view of the fact that in popular religious teaching the doctrine of Preservation has a far greater importance. In general the question of the origin of all finite

being is raised not in the interest of piety but in that of curiosity, hence it can only be answered by such means as curiosity offers. Piety can never show more than an indirect interest in it ; *i.e.* it recognizes no answer to it which brings the religious man into contradiction with his fundamental feeling. And this is the position given the doctrine, both when it occurs in the New Testament and in all regular Confessions of Faith. Whereas the Old Testament basis of it lies in the beginnings of a history-book which as such chiefly satisfies the desire for knowledge.

2. In the doctrine of Creation, then, we have pre-eminently to prevent anything alien from slipping in from the field of knowledge. But the opposite danger is also certainly to be kept in view, namely, the development of our self-consciousness must not be so conceived as to set the man who desires knowledge in contradiction with the principles of research he follows in the sphere of nature or of history. But as the self-consciousness we have here to consider itself implies that we are placed in a nature-system, any doctrine of Preservation which could immediately follow from this would find no motive in the working out of this self-consciousness for wishing to overthrow that assumption. And this mistake will be the less likely to occur if the treatment of the doctrine of Creation already specified has gone before.

3. If the immediate higher self-consciousness which is to be represented in both doctrines be one and the same, then the aim of Christian Dogmatics is twofold. On the one hand, to bring together the various presentations current within our Church in the different spheres of religious teaching, to show their true content, and to make them clear and coherent ; on the other hand, to set up safeguards in order to ensure that nothing should insinuate itself which—though in any given context the fact might not be noticed—might contradict what really belongs here. Both doctrines taken together will then exhaust the dogmatic presentation of the fundamental feeling of absolute dependence, if in the one we seek more particularly to secure the necessary precautions, and if in the other we have predominantly in view its positive development.

First Doctrine : Creation

§ 40. *The religious consciousness which is here our basis contradicts every representation of the origin of the world which excludes anything whatever from origination by God, or which places*

God under those conditions and antitheses which have arisen in and through the world.

Acts 17[24], Rom. 1[19, 20], Heb. 11[3].

1. The New Testament passages quoted above lead us to reject any more definite conception of the Creation. The expression ῥήματι is merely the negative of any closer definition, so as to exclude all idea of instrument or means. It is quite consistent with it and equally correct to say that the world itself, since it came into existence through the spoken word, is the word of God.[1] Thus we may be satisfied to put forward this negative character as a standard of criticism for that which has, as it seems to us, wrongly intruded itself as a more exact definition of this conception in Dogmatics. For as our immediate self-consciousness represents finite being only in the identity of origination and continuance, we find in that self-consciousness neither motive nor guidance for a treatment of origination taken by itself, and therefore we can take no particular interest in it.

The further elaboration of the doctrine of Creation in Dogmatics comes down to us from times when material even for natural science was taken from the Scriptures and when the elements of all higher knowledge lay hidden in Theology. Hence the complete separation of these two involves our handing over this subject to natural science, which, carrying its researches backward into time, may lead us back to the forces and masses that formed the world, or even further still. On this assumption we may patiently await the result, since every scientific endeavour which works with the ideas 'God' and 'world' must, without being dependent on Christian doctrine or becoming so, be limited by the very same determinations, if these two ideas are not to cease to be two.

2. As the New Testament passages give no material for a further development of the doctrine of Creation, and dogmaticians have always referred back to the Scriptures even when confusing their problem with that of philosophy, we must, in the first place, pass in review the Mosaic narrative and the Old Testament passages, which really in a sense are wholly dependent on it.

The Mosaic account was undeniably received by the Reformers as a genuinely historical narrative.[2] Luther's statements, how-

[1] 'What is the whole creation else than a word of God, said and spoken by God? . . . thus it is for God no harder to create than for us to speak.'—Luther in *Genesis*, i. § 51.

[2] Luther in *Genesis*, i. 3, § 43: 'Moses is writing a history and narrates things that happened.'—Calvin, *Instit.* i. 14. 3: Moses vulgi ruditati se accom-

ever, are chiefly directed against the allegorical interpretation, and Calvin's view really excludes any use of the narrative for the development of a genuine theory. It is an advantage in every way that nothing on the subject has become a part of Confessions of Faith, especially as (if we do not force ourselves to look upon the second account in Genesis as a recapitulating continuation of the first) the difference between the two is of such importance that we can hardly attribute to them a genuine historical character. If we further take into consideration that in the Old Testament passages referring to the Creation sometimes the same simplicity prevails as in the New Testament,[1] and that sometimes the Mosaic statements, although made fundamental, are very freely handled : [2] also that nowhere is a purely didactic use made of this account, and that Philo, who absolutely rejects the 'six days' in the literal sense, must certainly have had predecessors who did the same—in view of all this we may conclude pretty certainly that in that age the literal interpretation was never universally prevalent, but that there always survived a somewhat obscure but healthy feeling that the old record must not be treated as historical in our sense of the word. We have therefore no reason to maintain a stricter historical interpretation than the Hebrews themselves did in their best days.

Supposing, however, we were right in assuming that the Mosaic description was an historical account communicated in an extraordinary way, it would only follow that in this way we had attained to a scientific insight we could not otherwise have acquired. But the particular pieces of information would never be articles of faith in our sense of the phrase, for our feeling of absolute dependence does not gain thereby either a new content, a new form, or clearer definition. That is why it cannot be the task of Dogmatics to give an explanatory commentary or a criticism of such comments.

3. As regards the stated definitions themselves, it is quite clear that our feeling of absolute dependence could not refer to the universal condition of all finite being if anything in it (*i.e.* that being) were independent of God or ever had been. It is just as certain that if there could be anything in the whole of finite existence as such which entered into it at its origin independently of God, then because it must exist in us too, the feeling of absolute depend-

modans non alia Dei opera commemorat in historia creationis, nisi quae oculis nostris occurrunt.

[1] Isa. 45^{18}, Jer. 10^{12}.

[2] Ps. 33^{6-9}, Ps. 104, Job $33^{4f.}$

ence could have no truth even in relation to ourselves. But if, on the other hand, we think of God the Creator in any way as limited, and thus in His activity resembling that which should be absolutely dependent on Him, then the feeling expressing this dependence likewise could not be true (since equality and dependence neutralize each other), and thus the finite in that it resembled God could not be absolutely dependent upon Him. But except in one of these two forms, a contradiction between any theory of creation and the universal basis of our religious self-consciousness is not conceivable. With the Christian form of religious self-consciousness, which presupposes an experience, the doctrine of mere creation cannot be in contradiction, because it disregards continuity. Christian piety can, then, have no other interest in these researches than to avoid both these dangers. Whether this is easy, or if in avoiding one we only too easily fall into the other, must be seen from a closer consideration of the corollaries accepted by Dogmatics.

§ 41. *If the conception of Creation is to be further developed, the origin of the world must, indeed, be traced entirely to the divine activity, but not in such a way that this activity is thought of as resembling human activity; and the origin of the world must be represented as the event in time which conditions all change, but not so as to make the divine activity itself a temporal activity.*

Conf. Belg. xii.: Credimus Patrem per verbum hoc est filium suum coelum et terram ceterasque creaturas omnes quandoque ipsi visum fuit, ex nihilo creasse.—Joh. Dam., *d. orth. f.* ii. 5: . . . *ἐκ τοῦ μὴ ὄντος εἰς τὸ εἶναι παραγαγὼν τὰ σύμπαντα.*—Luther on *Genesis*, ii. 2, § 7: 'And God is in short outside all means and circumstances of time.'—*Ibid.*: 'Everything which God has willed to create He created at that moment when He spake, though certainly everything does not at once appear before our eyes. . . . I am indeed something new . . . but . . . for God I have been born and preserved even from the beginning of the world, and this word when He said, "Let us make man," created me as well.'—Hilar., *d. f. Tr.* xii. 40: Nam etsi habeat dispensationem sui firmamenti solidatio—sed coeli terrae ceterorumque elementorum creatio ne levi saltem momento operationis discernitur.—Anselm, *Monol.* 9: Nullo namque pacto fieri potest aliquid rationabiliter ab aliquo, nisi in facientis ratione praecedat aliquod rei faciendae quasi exemplum, sive ut aptius dicitur forma . . . quare cum ea quae facta sunt, clarum sit nihil fuisse antequam fierent, quantum ad hoc quia non erant quod nunc sunt, nec erat ex quo fierent, non tamen nihil erant quantum ad rationem facientis.—Phot., *Bibl.*, p. 302, Bekk.: *ὅτι ὁ Ὠριγένης ἔλεγε συναΐδιον εἶναι τῷ . . . θεῷ τὸ πᾶν. Ἐι γὰρ, ἔφασκε, οὐκ ἔστι δημιουργὸς ἄνευ δημιουργημάτων . . . οὐδὲ παντοκράτωρ ἄνευ τῶν κρατουμένων . . . ἀνάγκη ἐξ ἀρχῆς αὐτὰ ὑπὸ τοῦ θεοῦ γεγενῆσθαι, καὶ μὴ εἶναι χρόνον, ὅτε οὐκ ἦν ταῦτα. εἰ γὰρ ἦν χρόνος, ὅτε οὐκ ἦν τὰ ποιήματα . . . καὶ ἀλλοιοῦσθαι καὶ μεταβάλλειν τὸν ἄτρεπτον καὶ ἀναλλοίωτον συμβήσεται θεόν· εἰ γὰρ ὕστερον πεποίηκε τὸ πᾶν, δῆλον ὅτι ἀπὸ τοῦ μὴ ποιεῖν εἰς τὸ ποιεῖν μετέβαλε.*—Hilar., *d. f. Tr.* xii. 39: Cum enim praepararetur coelum aderat Deo. Numquid coeli praeparatio Deo est temporalis ? ut repens cogitationis motus subito in mentem tamquam antea torpidam . . . subrepserit, humanoque modo fabricandi coeli impensam et instrumenta quaesierit ? . . . Quae enim futura sunt, licet in eo quod creanda sunt adhuc fient, Deo tamen, cui in creandis rebus nihil novum ac repens est, iam facta sunt : dum et temporum dispensatio est ut creentur, et iam in divinae virtutis praesciente efficientia sint creata.—Augustin., *d. civ. D.* xi. 4. 2 : Qui autem a Deo factum fatentur, non tamen eum volunt temporis habere sed suae creationis initium, ut modo quodam via intelligibili semper sit factus : dicunt quidem aliquid, etc.—*Ibid.* xii. 15: Sed cum cogito cuius rei dominus semper fuerit, si semper creatura non fuit, affirmare aliquid pertimesco.—*Ibid.* 17: Una eademque sempiterna et immutabili voluntate res, quas condidit, et ut prius non essent egit, et ut posterius essent, quando esse coeperunt.—*Ibid.* xi. 6: Procul dubio non est mundus factus in tempore sed cum tempore.—Idem, *de Genes. c. Man.* i. 2 : Non ergo possumus dicere fuisse aliquod tempus quando Deus nondum aliquid fecerat.

1. The expression 'out of nothing' excludes the idea that before the origin of the world anything existed outside God, which as 'matter' could enter into the formation of the world. And undoubtedly the admission of 'matter' as existing independently of the divine activity would destroy the feeling of absolute dependence, and the actual world would be represented as a mixture of that which existed through God and that which existed independently of God. But since this phrase undeniably recalls Aristotle's category ἐξ οὗ and is formed on it, it reminds us on the one hand of human methods in construction which give form to an already existing matter, and on the other hand of the processes of nature in the composition of bodies out of many elements. The expression is harmless if everything that is a part of the processes of nature is strictly separated from the first beginning of things, and creation is thus raised above mere formation.

Yet from Hilary and Anselm we can see how easily, behind the denial of matter, may lie the idea of the pre-existence of form before things, though of course in God and not outside God. This position, too, appears to be quite harmless in itself, but as the two terms of the antithesis, matter and form, are not in the same relation to God, He is drawn away from an attitude of neutrality to the antithesis and placed in some degree under it. Hence the existence of forms in God prior to the existence of things but already related to it may naturally be called a 'preparation.' But in this way the other rule is violated, and we must regard as valid Luther's contention that if there are two divine activities which, like preparation and creation, can be conceived of only in a definite time-sequence, then God is no longer outside all contact with time. Anselm in his own way has expressed this time-relationship most bluntly and frankly. Hilary would have done away with it, but he only succeeded in eliminating it with regard to things now happening separately in time and not in respect of the original creation. For it cannot be said of the original creation that it was created by the activity of foreknowledge prior to its actual existence.

Here it can only be remarked in passing that the phrase 'out of nothing' is also used frequently to differentiate the creation of the world from the generation of the Son.[1] If it were generally understood that the latter is eternal and the former temporal, or if we could come to a general agreement as to the difference between generation and creation, there would be no necessity to draw any further distinction. But even so the expression is not essential for this purpose, for even if we do not at all identify the 'Word' and the 'Son,' the phrase 'to be created through the "Word"'[2] sufficiently obviates any confusion of this kind; even if the difference between creation and generation is not emphasized.

2. If, as suggested above, we strictly isolate the first creation, so that all things not absolutely primitive are regarded as part of the developing processes of nature and thus brought under the conception of preservation, then the question whether the creation occupied time, is answered in the negative. The distinction between a first and second creation, or an indirect and direct creation, always comes back in general to the evolving of the complex from the simple[3] and of the organic from the elementary.[4] But to acknowledge another creation here is either again entirely to abolish the difference between creation and preservation or to assume different kinds of matter devoid of inherent forces, which is surely meaningless. But even if in the case of creation we think

[1] Fecisti enim coelum et terram non de te, nam esset aequale unigenito tuo—et aliud praeter te non erat unde faceres ea, et ideo de nihilo fecisti coelum et terram.—Augustin., *Conf.* xii. 7.

[2] 'All things are so made through God's word that they may more rightly be said to be born than made or renewed, for no instrument or means comes in.'—Luth., Th. v. p. 1102.

[3] *Τῇ μὲν πρώτῃ ἡμέρᾳ ἐποίησεν ὁ θεὸς ὅσα ἐποίησεν ἐκ μὴ ὄντων. ταῖς δὲ ἄλλαις οὐκ ἐκ μὴ ὄντων, ἀλλ' ἐξ ὧν ἐποίησε τῇ πρώτῃ ἡμέρᾳ μετέβαλεν ὡς ἠθέλησε.*—Hippolyt. in *Genesis*.

[4] *Τὰ μὲν οὐκ ἐκ προϋποκειμένης ὕλης, οἷον οὐρανὸν* (where *οὐρανός* is the Aristotelian fifth substance) *γῆν ἀέρα πῦρ ὕδωρ· τὰ δὲ ἐκ τούτων, οἷον ζῶα φυτά*, etc.—Joh. Damasc. ii. 25.

first of matter (though we might equally well think of forces), then, from that point, living mobile being must have existed and undergone a continuous development. Otherwise the creation of bare matter would only have been a preparation, that is an external material corresponding to the previously mentioned inner formal one. We must refer these definitions back to a time when men delighted in such abstractions because there was then no question of a dynamic aspect of nature.

Another point with respect to the relation of the creation to time which does not lie in our purview is the question whether there was time before the world existed or whether time began with the world. If we take the world in its widest sense, we cannot admit the first, since a time before the world could only have referred to God, and He would then be placed in time. The *Confessio Belgica* with its ' quando ipsi visum fuit ' clearly falls into this error, and in opposition to it we must return to Augustine's formula.

Finally, the controversy over the temporal or eternal creation of the world (which can be resolved into the question whether it is possible or necessary to conceive of God as existing apart from created things) has no bearing on the content of the feeling of absolute dependence, and it is therefore a matter of indifference how it is decided. But in so far as the idea of a creation in time must be related to that of a beginning of divine activity *ad extra* or a beginning of divine sovereignty as Origen suggested, God would be brought within the region of change and subjected to time. Thus the antithesis between Him and finite beings would be lessened, and the purity of the feeling of absolute dependence endangered.

Augustine is hardly more satisfactory when, in order to avoid this position, he declares that a single act of the Divine Will is sufficient to account for the earlier non-existence and the later existence of the world. For if a similar action of the Divine Will is required to explain the prior non-existence of the world, then we must suppose that, apart from this Divine Will, the world would have come into existence earlier, and consequently that there was a possibility of its coming into existence independently of the Divine Will. But if we regard the one Divine Will as ineffectual prior to the existence of the world, neither preventing nor producing anything, then the transition from non-activity to activity remains, even though it be differently expressed as a transition from willing to doing ; [1] while, on the other hand, it is impossible to see how

[1] Addamus eum ab aeterno id voluisse. Quicquid enim vult, id voluit

the idea that God does not exist without something absolutely dependent on Him could weaken or confuse the religious self-consciousness. Just so the tracing of the Word through which God created the world (a subject not to be considered here) back to the Word which was with God from eternity, can never be made clearly intelligible[1] if there is not an eternal creation through the eternal Word.

Postscript.—We can also attach to this the definition that God created the world through a *free* decree. Now it is self-evident that He on Whom everything is absolutely dependent is absolutely free. But if we suppose that the free decision implies a prior deliberation followed by choice, or interpret freedom as meaning that God might equally well have not created the world (because we think that there must have been this possibility, otherwise God was compelled to create), we have then assumed an antithesis between freedom and necessity, and, by attributing this kind of freedom to God, have placed Him within the realm of contradictions.

First Appendix. The Angels

§ 42. *This conception is indigenous to the Old Testament and has passed over into the New. It contains in itself nothing impossible and does not conflict with the basis of the religious consciousness in general. But at the same time it never enters into the sphere of Christian doctrine proper. It can, therefore, continue to have its place in Christian language without laying on us the duty of arriving at any conclusion with regard to its truth.*

1. The narratives of Abraham, Lot, Jacob, of the call of Moses and Gideon and the prophecy of Samson, bear the stamp very clearly of what we are accustomed to call 'myth.' Indeed, in many of them God Himself and the Angels of the Lord are so interchanged that the whole can be thought of as a Theophany in which the appearance perceived by the senses need not be that of a being independent and different from God. In this indefinite form the idea is older than these narratives, perhaps even older than the narrated events. That they are not exclusively Hebraic in the narrower sense seems clear from many other traces, such as the history of Balaam. Poetical representations of many kinds in the Psalms

ab aeterno. Jam quod voluerat ab aeterno id aliquando tandem factum est. 'Thus He now worked and was active that the world should come into being.' —Morus, *Comment.*, t. i. § 292.

[1] Cf. Luther, *W. A.*, i. pp. 23–28, and iii. pp. 36–40.

and the Prophets lead to the same conclusion ; anything can be called an angel that is a bearer of a divine message. So that sometimes definite individual beings are to be conceived under this term and sometimes not. Of the former we have scarcely any other explanation to give than that in general different peoples have imagined many kinds of spiritual beings in different forms because of a consciousness of the power of spirit over matter ; and the less this problem is solved the more that consciousness gives rise to a tendency to suppose there is more spirit than that manifested in the human race and different from that in the living animal, whose powers and mechanical instincts with their own power over matter, must themselves as matter be brought within our power.

Now we, to whom the majority of the heavenly bodies are known, satisfy this longing by the familiar supposition that most or all of these are filled with animated beings of varying grades. Previously there was no alternative but to people either the earth or the heavens with hidden and spiritual beings. The Jewish people seem to have decidedly adhered to the latter method, especially after the highest Being came to be thought of also as the King of the people, who therefore must have servants around Him to send as He chose to every part of His kingdom and to allow them to share in every branch of administration. This is certainly the most developed conception of the angels. Consequently we must distinguish them clearly from our conception of spiritual life developed on other planets according to their nature and in association with an organism, since the Biblical idea cannot be connected with this, but is something quite different.[1] We ought rather to think of them as spiritual beings, not belonging to any definite heavenly body, who could embody themselves temporarily, according to their tasks, in the manner in which they have appeared from time to time in our world. And obviously we know far too little of the interstellar spaces, as also of the possible relations between spirit and body, to deny outright the truth of such a notion. Indeed, if we regard the appearance of such beings as something miraculous, this is not so much because we must necessarily hold that such a temporary incursion of alien beings into the order of our lives would interrupt the course of nature, but much more because (in Christianity generally and also to a great extent in the Old Testament) their appearance is associated with special points of development and revelation. In the New Testament angels appear at the

[1] Cf. Reinh., *Dogm.*, § 50.

Annunciation of Christ and of His forerunner and at Christ's Birth in narratives of a more or less poetical character which lie outside the proper field of the Gospel tradition. This is true also in some measure of the strengthening angel in Gethsemane, with respect to whom at any rate no witness is quoted. In the case of the Resurrection and the Ascension, as well as the conversion of Cornelius and the liberation of Peter, it is possible to doubt whether angels or men are meant. In the account of Philip, the expressions 'angel of the Lord' and 'spirit' alternate as they do in the Old Testament. But after this angels disappear altogether even from the Apostolic history.

2. Everywhere, however, in our Holy Scriptures the angels are assumed; but nowhere is anything taught respecting them. Apart from the usual prophetic and poetical language in descriptions of the Last Day,[1] Christ Himself refers to them only in His warning against despising little ones [2] and in connexion with Peter's useless defence of Him.[3] If we want to take this as definite teaching we must also put forward the doctrine that children (and perhaps every individual) have special angels, that the angels behold the face of God, and that they can be employed in legions.[4] The same applies to the Apostolic passages if we refer to angels all the obscure and ambiguous expressions about thrones and principalities.[5] Even in the Epistle to the Hebrews [6] the angels are not so much subjects of dogmatic teaching as mediums for such teaching. The writer maintains that Christ is more exalted than all the angels, as they are mentioned in the Old Testament, in the Prophets, and the Psalms; to the angelic appearances in the New Testament there is no reference. Christ and the Apostles might have said all these things without having had any real conviction of the existence of such beings or any desire to communicate it, just as everyone adopts popular ideas and makes use of them in discussing other things, as, for example, we might talk of ghosts or fairies, although these ideas had no definite sort of relation to our actual convictions. We do not mean to suggest what is usually understood by 'accommodation,' which is often taken to mean adapting oneself to prevailing ideas whilst holding opposite convictions.

The Confessions of the Protestant Church have accepted these conceptions only incidentally, and the statements show clearly enough that they place no value on any teaching about angels.[7]

[1] Matt. 16²⁷ and 25³¹. [2] Matt. 18¹⁰. [3] Matt. 26⁵³.
[4] John 1⁵¹ is plainly figurative. [5] Col. 1¹⁶. [6] Heb. 1⁴ᶠᶠ..
[7] Apol. Conf. Art. ix.: Praeterea et hoc *largimur* quod angeli orent pro nobis. *Art. Smalc.*: Etsi angeli in coelo pro nobis orent, etc.

This does not in the least mean that the Reformers were unfamiliar with the subject or doubted the literal truth of the angelic appearances in the Biblical narratives: their Church hymns prove the contrary, but in the sphere of piety they attached no great value to the matter.

§ 43. *The only tenet which can be established as a doctrine concerning angels is this: that the question whether the angels exist or not ought to have no influence upon our conduct, and that revelations of their existence are now no longer to be expected.*

1. It is not without considerable hesitation that the confidence of Christians in the protection of angels can be encouraged. For in the first place, that they avert the power of evil spirits [1] could hardly be told to any but children without detriment, because against all that is usually ascribed to the devil, we should use the spiritual armour recommended by the Bible, and not rely on angelic protection.[2] It is not less serious to teach an external protection through angels.[3] For we must teach that God has no need of angels for our protection, unless we assume a continual activity on the part of angels, and thus do away with the entire interdependence of nature. But it is said that it affords more consolation if God makes use of angels than if our preservation is effected by natural means, so that God, in view of our weakness, employs angels and then reveals the fact to us. On the one hand, this theory could not be carried through without very limited and almost childish conceptions of God, and on the other hand, it can only feed our vanity if we accept the idea that a whole species of higher beings exists only for our service. Wisely, therefore, in our Confessions—although strictly in opposition to the saints of the Roman Church—the intercessions of the angels have taken the place of their active influence. We cannot, however, take the Biblical passage on which this is founded as a convincing proof.[4]

That this conception is losing its influence among Christians follows naturally from the fact that it belongs to a time when our knowledge of the forces of nature was very limited, and our power over them at its lowest stage. In every such situation our reflections now instinctively take another direction, so that in active life we do not easily turn to angels. The argument of Luther [5]

[1] Luth., *Catech. Min.*: Tuus sanctus angelus sit mecum ne diabolus quidquam in me possit.

[2] Eph. $6^{11ff.}$, 1 Pet. $5^{8.9}$. [3] Cf. Calvin, *Instit.* i. xiv. 6–11. [4] Zech. 1^{12}.

[5] In *Genesis*, ii. § 19: 'The angels must be our protectors and guard us,

has, moreover, as regards the angels, tended to repress the levity so easily elicited by the supernatural. But the confidence he wishes to strengthen will be the same even if we do not think of the angels, but expect the divine protection in the usual way. Since the Church has itself declared against the veneration of angels, we can rightly say it would be the worst form of veneration if, in deference to their unknown service to us, we believed we might omit any of the care recommended us for ourselves and others.

2. But more closely considered, nothing can be concluded from all the angelic appearances of which we have knowledge, either for present or future times, partly because these appearances occurred in that primitive period when the interdependence of man with nature was not yet settled and he himself was undeveloped; and, as even to many a philosopher at that time the notion of an education through higher beings was not unfamiliar, these warning and prophetic appearances might be an echo of that connexion of ideas. At a later time we find angels almost exclusively at great points of development when other wonderful events are wont to happen. Moreover, when the earlier teachers of the Church [1] assert that the intercourse between men and angels, which for so long a period had been interrupted, was only restored through Christ, this, too, must be understood in the same way, for this restoration did not extend beyond the Apostolic times.

Since they are so entirely outside our province, there is no reason for more accurate inquiry into the creation of angels either in itself or in relation to the Mosaic creation story, nor again into their general nature, manner of life, and activities.[2] On the contrary, for the actual province of Dogmatics the subject remains wholly problematic, and none but a private and liturgical use of this conception is to be recognized. The private use of the conception will always confine itself to visualizing the higher protection so far as that does not make use of conscious human activities. In the liturgical use the thought which has been specially in view is that God must be represented as surrounded by pure and innocent spirits.[3]

but only so far as we remain in our path. Christ points to this explanation when He confronts the devil with the command from Deut. 6[16]. For thereby He shows that man's appointed path is not to fly in the air. Hence, when we are in our calling or office and have a command from God or from the men who have the right to direct our calling, then we must believe that the protection of the dear angels cannot fail us.

[1] Cf. Chrysost. on Col. 1[20].

[2] Cf. Reinhard, *Dogm.*, §§ 53, 54.

[3] Cf. Heb. 12[22].

Second Appendix: The Devil

§ 44. *The idea of the Devil, as developed among us, is so unstable that we cannot expect anyone to be convinced of its truth; but, besides, our Church has never made doctrinal use of the idea.*

1. The chief points in this idea are as follows: spiritual beings of a high degree of perfection, who lived in close relation with God, voluntarily changed from this state to a state of antagonism and rebellion against God.

Now we cannot ask anyone to accept this unless we are able to help him over a great number of difficulties. First, as to the so-called fall of the good angels: the more perfect these good angels are supposed to have been, the less possible it is to find any motive but those presupposing a fall already, *e.g.* arrogance and envy; [1] furthermore, if after the Fall the natural powers of the devil remained undiminished,[2] it is impossible to conceive how persistent evil could exist side by side with superlative insight. For such insight must, in the first place, have shown every conflict with God to be an entirely useless undertaking. It can only be thought to afford a momentary satisfaction even to one lacking true understanding, whereas an intelligent being, to undertake such a conflict and persevere in it, must of necessity will to be and remain unblessed. Now in speaking of such a man we say he is 'possessed,' because no explanation of his attitude can be derived from the subject himself. Is it not, then, still more impossible to find an explanation in the more perfect condition of the angels—by whom would *they* be possessed? Again, if the devil at the time of his fall lost the finest and the purest intelligence (and it is indeed the worst possible derangement to become the bitterest and most obdurate enemy of God after being His friend), then it is inconceivable, on the one hand, how through one error of the will the intelligence could be for ever lost, unless the error was already due to a lack of intelligence; and on the other hand, how could the devil, after such a loss of intelligence, be so dangerous an enemy? For nothing is easier than to contend with senseless wickedness. It is just as difficult to explain the relation of the fallen angels to other

[1] So rightly Luther (Hall. ed.), Th. i. p. 36. In Bernard, too, the idea is to be found that Lucifer perceived in God that man was to be raised above the angelic nature; hence that *arrogant* spirit had *envied* man such blessedness, and thus had fallen. Such ideas have their own value. But I should not care to compel anyone to yield to them.

[2] Cf. Luther, *ibid.* pp. 261, 262.

angels. For if they were all alike, and in that case no special personal motive could be felt by one group, how is it to be explained that the one group sinned and the other did not? It is certainly no less difficult if we assume that,[1] prior to the fall of one group, all the angels may have been in a partially unstable state of innocence, but that one group because of one deed have been for ever judged and condemned while the other group, because of their resistance, have been for ever confirmed and established, so that henceforth they cannot fall. Lastly, with regard to the condition of the fallen angels after the Fall, it is difficult to see how the two following ideas can be held consistently: The fallen angels, already oppressed by great ills and expecting still greater, at the same time out of hatred to God and to relieve their feeling of distress, engage in active opposition to God, while yet they are unable to effect anything except by God's will and permission,[2] and thus would find far greater alleviation for their distress as well as satisfaction for their hatred of God in absolute inactivity.

Finally, can the devil and his angels be thought of as a kingdom, and thus working unanimously although only outwardly and mostly in human affairs? Now, with the limitations already outlined and generally acknowledged, such a kingdom is inconceivable unless the overlord is omniscient and therefore knows in advance what God will permit; and besides not only does the evil in one man mostly hinder the same evil in another, but in each man one evil hinders another.

2. There are two ways, in particular, in which a doctrinal use might be made of this conception. The evil in man may be traced back to the prior evil in Satan and explained by it; and the devil may be represented as active in the punishment of sin. Our Confessions, however, are too cautious to base anything concerning this doctrine on so hazardous an idea. As regards the former, they only group the devil with the wicked by making him their leader,[3] in which case the existence of evil in man is in no way explained by its existence in Satan, and the latter requires just as much elucidation as the former. In other passages, moreover, if evil is traced back to the temptation of Satan,[4] the purpose in some

[1] Cf. Luther, *ibid.* p. 202.

[2] Mosh., *Th. dogm.*, t. i. p. 417 sq.; Calv., *Instit.* i. 14, 16.

[3] Aug., *Conf.* 19: Causa peccati est voluntas diaboli et malorum quae . . . avertit se a Deo.

[4] *Conf. Belg.* xiv.: verbis diaboli aurem praebens.—*Conf. Helv.* viii.: instinctu serpentis et sua culpa.—*Sol. decl.* i.: seductione Satanae iustitia concreata amissa est.

of them is less to provide an explanation than a modification of the opinion that the devil was instrumental in putting quite another creature in the place of the original man. But, indeed, the fact that man allowed himself to be tempted presupposes aberration and evil, so that the explanation is seen to be no explanation at all. If, again, here and there the power and might of the devil is included under the punishment of sin, on the one hand we find that this does not have any special bearing on the deliverance of man from sin and its punishment, and we might as well speak simply of the influence of evil apart from a personal overlord of evil; on the other hand, if the power of the devil (and his greatest power lies in tempting to sin) were the result of sin, then when he accomplished his greatest act of temptation he must have been powerless—which is plainly inconsistent. Elsewhere, however, punishment too is represented as something that the devil and sinful men have in common.[1] And again, the fairly frequent idea that the devil is the instrument of God in the punishment of the wicked, is inconsistent with his antagonism to the divine purpose.

§ 45. *In the New Testament Scriptures the Devil is, indeed, frequently mentioned, but neither Christ nor the Apostles set up a new doctrine concerning him, and still less do they associate the idea in any way with the plan of salvation; hence the only thing we can establish on the subject for the system of Christian doctrine is this: whatever is said about the Devil is subject to the condition that belief in him must by no means be put forward as a condition of faith in God or in Christ. Furthermore, there can be no question of the Devil having any influence within the Kingdom of God.*

1. There is not a single passage in the New Testament where Christ or His Apostles definitely and indisputably refer to the devil with the intention either of teaching anything new or peculiarly their own, or of correcting and supplementing current beliefs. They make use of the conception in its current popular form. If, nevertheless, we wished to formulate a Christian doctrine of the devil we should be obliged to assume that this conception as known to Christ and His disciples corresponded perfectly with the truth and could not be improved. This position must certainly be taken up by anyone who is unwilling to admit that Christ made use of what

[1] *Conf. Aug.* xvii.: impios autem homines et diabolos condemnabit ut sine fine crucientur.

we usually call accommodation. Such a complete development of the idea is the more improbable because its chief characteristics have no basis even in the Old Testament, their origin being wholly apocryphal. It is apparent from the incidental way in which the subject occurs that neither Christ nor His disciples desired either to give support to the idea or vouch for its truth. For Christ seems to introduce it for no particular reason into parables, maxims, and short instructions dealing with quite other subjects. In the parable of the Sower, the expressions [1] are of doubtful meaning, and the hostility of man to the divine message would be just as relevant as the hostility of the devil. If it were only a question of his relation to the human soul and his influence on it, then the uncertainty would be removed and we could draw up a doctrine about him. But, at best, he is represented as a quite unknown cause of rapid transitions from one state of feeling to another of an opposite kind. It is equally impossible to base a doctrine on the parable of the Tares in the Field. The Sower is like the Son of Man Who sows openly by teaching: and the Sower of Tares does the same, but by night, *i.e.* not openly. Thus here, too, we are brought to see the real meaning of the name 'the Slanderer.' The Apostles, at least, did not understand the parable to teach doctrinally that it was the devil who sowed tares in the field tilled by Christ; for when speaking of false brethren and unworthy members of the community, they never quote the devil as the cause of the evil, but at most they deliver such men over to the devil. If we remember that 'his seed' is explained as 'children of the evil one,' [2] we are reminded of an important passage [3] where Christ tells the hostile Jews that 'they are of their father the devil.' Obviously, according to the Hebrew idiom, these expressions are used only of the relations of likeness and affinity. Nobody can propose to take the expression literally, as if they could be descended from the devil in the same sense as they gloried in descending from Abraham, or in the sense in which Christ, Whose words they were mocking, had originally asserted that God was His Father. Thus we cannot take this passage literally and assume the real existence of the devil without either placing the devil on an equality with God, as the Manichæans did, or else applying the phrase 'Son of God' to Christ merely in the wider sense in which the Jews could really be termed 'sons of the devil.' There is certainly here a reference to a story

[1] πονηρός in Matt. 13^{19}, διάβολος in Luke.
[2] υἱοὶ τοῦ πονηροῦ Matt. 13^{38}.
[3] John 8^{44}.

about the devil, but only as to something well known, and this description, like the other, only stands here as related to the central statement that 'they were not of God.'[1]

The expression that 'Satan had desired to have the disciples that he might sift them'[2] bears the stamp of a proverb, and does not imply that the devil is to be regarded as the overlord of the wicked. The phrase, as a whole, is derived from Job, and in both passages Satan is pictured as bargaining with God. So that here what is being uttered is only a warning borrowed from a truly Biblical idea, and there is no intention either to teach anything with regard to Satan or to confirm that older belief.

The phrase 'to be overreached by Satan'[3] is a similar proverbial expression. Here certainly it is used in connexion with the fact that one had been delivered over to Satan; but apart from this instance, it is applicable to any case in which something done from a good motive proves to be detrimental to the good. Only, we must not think here of Satan as simply bringing evil to light, but as the one who fights against good. The 'roaring lion' of Peter[4] obviously hovers between these two meanings, for 'devouring,' points to the deadly enemy, but 'adversary' to the accuser. So that these three passages should be taken together, supplementing each other perfectly and forming a useful adaptation of a varying Biblical tradition. If we compare the relevant passages, we shall find that the expression 'Prince of this world,'[5] used frequently by Christ, admits equally well of a different interpretation. At any rate, if Christ's disciples did refer this saying to the devil, he is passed over without any specifically Christian doctrine being opposed to the popular tradition. For some New Testament writings refer the 'binding of Satan' to an earlier time,[6] and others, though admittedly of doubtful interpretation, assume a still continuing conflict with him.[7] Thus if Christ had intended to formulate a doctrine in the above-quoted passages He certainly would have failed in His intention.

The story of the Temptation is equally unsuited for the purpose. Even if we must accept it as literal fact (and there is much to be said against this), it does not give us material to construct a complete idea of the devil or to apply it in any further way. In the two

[1] John 8^{47}. [2] Luke 22^{31}. [3] 2 Cor. 2^{11}. [4] 1 Pet. 5^{8}.

[5] John 12^{31}: *ὁ ἄρχων τοῦ κόσμου τούτου ἐκβληθήσεται.*—John 14^{30}: *ἔρχεται ὁ τοῦ κόσμου ἄρχων, καὶ οὐκ ἔχει ἐν ἐμοὶ οὐδέν.*—John 16^{11}: *ὁ ἄρχων τοῦ κόσμου τούτου κέκριται.*

[6] 2 Pet. 2^{4}, Jude 6. [7] 2 Cor. 12^{7}, Eph. $6^{11.12}$.

passages where Christ is specially led to mention the devil,[1] the question is of so-called 'possession,' and therefore concerns the natural explanation of this phenomenon, which has nothing to do with faith. Though the first passage may be obscure, still it is closely connected with the casting out of demons. The same is true of the saying concerning the 'divided kingdom of Satan,' and the highly figurative representation of the return of an evicted spirit, which is a continuation of the same story, is not intended in any way to throw doubt on the certainty of salvation; it bears on the same realm of phenomena as 'possession' and indicates primarily the difference between the real and permanent healings of Christ and the merely apparent and transitory healings of the Jewish exorcists. In these cases and in others which may have happened without being recorded there was no occasion to examine critically the current ideas, nor is there any ground for regarding their use as indicating an intention to sanction them as divine teaching. If we consider that John in his Epistle [2] sees the relation between the devil and the sinner (doer of evil) exactly as Christ saw it in the above-quoted discussions with the Jews, we must give a similar explanation of the fact that John attributes the betrayal of Judas to the devil, as Christ never does. The few remaining Apostolic passages [3] cannot be used doctrinally any more than those already cited. For if Christ and the Apostles had ever desired to combine Christian piety with the fear of the devil, and, at the same time, had wished to establish a particular doctrine drawn from and corresponding to this element of the religious consciousness, they would have had to allow proper space for the idea when treating didactically of the origin and propagation of evil in mankind generally, when dealing with the manner in which sin remains in believers, and when discussing the necessity of redemption. It is just at this latter point that the question arises whether the Son of God was not necessary in some way because of the power the devil had over man. But of this there is not the slightest trace,[4] nor do we find any mention of the devil,[5] even when sin is being discussed, and we should most expect it. Such a complete silence in every essentially didactic passage ought to have been seriously considered.

[1] Luke 10^{18}, Matt. 12^{43}, Luke 11^{24}.
[2] 1 John 3^{8}.
[3] 2 Cor. 4^{4} 11^{14}, 2 Thess. 2^{9}.
[4] The passage Heb. $2^{14, 15}$ has little relevance here, for it is not said of the devil that he has power over men, but only over death, so that we must think here chiefly of the angel of death; and men are not said to be in slavish fear of the devil but of death.
[5] Cf. Matt. 15^{19}, Rom. 5^{12-19} $7^{7ff.}$, Jas. 1^{12}.

2. But even if we could regard some or, indeed, all of the above-quoted passages of Scripture as referring to the devil, there is still no reason for our accepting this notion as a permanent element in Christian doctrine and defining it accordingly so accurately that everything attributed to the devil could be conceived as a consistent whole. For Christ and His disciples did not hold this idea as one derived from the sacred writings of the Old Testament, or in any way acquired through Divine revelation ; it was drawn from the common life of the period just as it is still present more or less in all our minds in spite of our utter ignorance as to the existence of such a being. Since that from which we are to be redeemed remains the same (as does also the manner of our redemption) whether there be a devil or no, the question as to his existence is not one for Christian Theology but for Cosmology, in the widest sense of that word. It is exactly similar to questions as to the nature of the firmament and the heavenly bodies. In Christian Dogmatics we have nothing either to affirm or deny on such subjects ; and similarly we are just as little concerned to dispute the conception of the devil as to establish it. The Biblical usage merely shows that among the Jewish people the idea was really a fusion of two or three quite different elements. The first element is that of the servant of God who, while searching out the evil, has his rank and function among the other angels and cannot be regarded as expelled from the presence of God. Another element is that of the original source of evil in Oriental dualism, the conception being modified in such a way that the Jews alone were able to assimilate it. Now this function to some extent suggests joy in evil, and thus easily enough through some such fictitious story as the apostasy, the former could become the latter, or rather the name of the former pass over to the latter. It was obviously from these two elements that the acute mind of Calvin composed his formulas,[1] though they will not harmonize in one consistent view.

The third element, the angel of death, though not quite so certain, is also a combination of native and foreign ideas ; this angel, too, can be represented as having his kingdom in the underworld. On the other hand, the spirits active in the possessed are always represented differently, and are only indirectly brought into connexion with the devil. The conception was probably developed

[1] *Instit.* i. 14, 17 : Quamvis voluntate et conatu semper Deo aversetur tamen nisi annuente et volente Deo nihil facere potest.—Legimus illum se sistere coram Deo nec pergere audere ad facinus, nisi impetrata facultate . . . 18, Deus illi fideles cruciandos tradit, impios gubernandos.

through the assimilation of these various elements ; but apart from this it has obtained a strong hold by reason of the manifold enigmas presented to introspection by sudden changes of feeling—so strong, indeed, that we might almost say that it suggests itself to nearly everyone who has not the gift for self-analysis of the more accurate kind. For all too frequently we find that evil emotions arise in us in a strange and abrupt manner, having no connexion with our ruling tendencies, but up to a certain point gaining strength irresistibly, so that we feel obliged to look upon them as not belonging to us but alien, while at the same time we are unable to indicate any external cause. And as good, for the most part unexpected, its origin not being easily perceived, was attributed to the ministry of angels, in the same way the origin of wickedness and evil, not being discoverable, has been explained as due to the craft and influence of the devil and of evil spirits. Thus the idea is always recurring, especially when we reach the limits of our observations in regard to evil. But since in this matter the Scriptures always refer us to our own inner life, we ought to carry our observations further ; and then more and more it would cease to be possible to consider things as the work of the devil, and the conception would thus gradually become obsolete. The same holds good of the interlocking and co-operation of evil,[1] which, at important junctures, when it is a question of antagonism to some sudden development of good, seems to reveal it as a kingdom and a power. But the more the good establishes itself as a whole in history, the less often will such antagonisms appear, and the more disintegrated will they be, so that here too the devil will no more be thought of.

On the other hand, anyone seeking to put forward, as a part of Christian doctrine, belief in a permanent influence of the devil either in the Kingdom of God itself or in a permanent kingdom of Satan opposed to the Kingdom of God, will not only be in direct contradiction to many of the above-quoted passages of Scripture, but will also be making very dangerous assertions. For in the first case at every difficult point he makes harder the endeavour, which cannot be sufficiently encouraged for the sake of inward blessedness, to explain all the phenomena (even the strangest) of the individual soul by its own peculiar qualities and by the influences of common life. And at the same time he gravely strengthens the already strong inclination of men to deny their own guilt. It would be bad enough if anyone neglected due care for himself and others because of his

[1] Cf. § 43, 1.

trust in the protection of angels; but it would certainly be more dangerous if at will, in place of severe self-examination, he attributed his growing wickedness to the influence of Satan—a purely arbitrary proceeding, since no definite marks and limits can be given and the merest caprice has free scope. If, then, the influence of Satan in the strictest sense can only be directly inward, and must therefore be magical, a firm belief in any such doctrine must destroy the joyful consciousness of a sure inheritance in the Kingdom of God; for everything wrought by the Spirit of God must then be at the mercy of the antagonistic influences of the devil, and all confidence in the guidance of one's own mind be abolished. Even if we only believed in such influences as existing outside the Christian Church, it would hinder the true Christian treatment of the individuals to whom the Gospel is to be preached. Moreover, belief in a lasting kingdom of Satan, which still implies that individual men are regarded as his instruments, is bound not only to impair joy of heart and to endanger steadfastness in conduct, but also to destroy Christian love. But those who actually go so far as to maintain that living faith in Christ is in some way conditioned by belief in the devil ought to be on their guard lest, by so doing, they depreciate Christ and unduly exalt themselves. For the ultimate meaning is that salvation by Christ would be less necessary if there were no devil; and so, on the one hand, salvation appears to be only a help against an external enemy, while, on the other hand, man would be well able to help himself if there were no devil and evil had its seat solely in human nature.

Postscript.—So long as it is not a question of connected doctrine but of particular applications of this or that feature of a vague notion, we cannot deprive any Christian of the right, not only (within the limits defined above) to set forth elements of his own religious self-consciousness in terms of this kind, but also to make use of this idea in religious teaching—as indeed everything mentioned in the New Testament Scriptures proper may legitimately be given a place in our religious teaching as well. The idea may be so used if we find it suitable, or perhaps apparently indispensable, in order to make clear the positive godlessness of evil in itself, or to emphasize the fact that it is only in a higher protection that we can find help against an evil the source of whose power our will and intelligence seem unable to reach. So long as in this way the idea finds support in the living tradition of religious language, there will occasionally be a liturgical use of it which must, however, conform in every respect to the scriptural type, since deviation from that would only introduce more confusion, and this confusion would be increased the more, on the one hand, the susceptibility of people to the idea diminishes in course of time and, on the other hand, the liturgical expressions tend to assume a scientific character or to acquire confessional authority. The poetic use is therefore the freest and the least harmful. For in poetry personification is quite in place, and no disadvantage is to be feared from an emphatic use of this idea in pious moods. It would therefore be inexpedient and in many ways unjustifiable to wish to banish the conception of the devil from our treasury of song.

Second Doctrine: Preservation (Conservation)

§ 46. *The religious self-consciousness, by means of which we place all that affects or influences us in absolute dependence on God, coincides entirely with the view that all such things are conditioned and determined by the interdependence of Nature.*

1. It is not in the least meant that the pious self-consciousness is realized with every stimulation of the sensuous consciousness, any more than every perception causes us actually to visualize the interrelatedness of nature. But whenever objective consciousness reaches this degree of clarity we assume afresh the interdependence of nature as universal and as determining everything which has not led to our consciousness of it; and in the same way we recognize in the moments when the pious self-consciousness is present that those in which it is lacking are really imperfect states, and we postulate the feeling of absolute dependence as valid for everything without exception, because we apply it to our own existence in so far as we are a part of the world.

But neither is our proposition meant to fall short of the conception of preservation, although in accordance with the nature of self-consciousness it is limited to what affects us; and, indeed, only the movements and changes of things stimulate us directly, not the things themselves or their inner being. For every impulse directed towards perception and knowledge which yet has the qualities, essence, and being of things as its object, begins with a stimulation of self-consciousness which thus accompanies the process of apprehending; and, consequently, the being and nature of things belongs to that which affects us. Within this range our proposition admits no distinction; in each and every situation we ought to be conscious of, and sympathetically experience, absolute dependence on God just as we conceive each and every thing as completely conditioned by the interdependence of nature.

But we find the opposite idea to this very widely spread. Namely, the idea that these two views do not coincide, but that each excludes the other as its contradictory. It is said that the more clearly we conceive anything to be entirely conditioned by the interdependence of nature, the less can we arrive at the feeling of its absolute dependence upon God; and, conversely, the more vivid this latter feeling is the more indefinitely must we leave its interrelatedness with nature an open question. But it is obvious that, from our standpoint and in consistency with what we have already said, we cannot admit such a contradiction between the two ideas. For otherwise (since everything would present itself to us as always in the system of nature), as our knowledge of the world grew perfect, the development of the pious self-consciousness in ordinary life would cease; which is quite contrary to our presupposition that piety is of the essence of human nature. And on the other hand, conversely, the love of religion would be opposed to all love of research and all widening of our knowledge of nature; which would entirely contradict the principle that the observation of creation leads to the consciousness of God. And besides, prior to the completion of both tendencies the most competent naturalist would have to be the least religious of men, and *vice versa*. Now, as the human soul is just as necessarily predisposed towards a knowledge of the world as towards a consciousness of God, it can only be a false wisdom which would put religion aside, and a misconceived religion for love of which the progress of knowledge is to be arrested.

The only apparent ground for this assertion is the fact that, as a rule, the more strongly the objective consciousness predominates at any given moment, the more at that identical moment the consciousness of self is repressed and *vice versa*, because in the one case, through absorption in ourselves, we lose consciousness of the object affecting us, just as in the other case we are entirely merged in the object. But this in no way prevents the one activity, after having satisfied itself, from stimulating and passing over into the other. We are clearly quite wrong if we allege, as a general experience, that the incomprehensible as such is more conducive to the awakening of the religious feeling than that which is understood. The favourite example is the great natural phenomena, produced by elementary forces; but in point of fact the religious feeling is not destroyed even by the completest confidence with which we accept this or that hypothetical explanation of these phenomena. The reason why these manifestations so readily arouse religious feeling lies rather in the immensity of their operations both in the promotion and destruction of human life and works of skill, and thus in the awakening of the consciousness of the limitation of our activity by universal forces. But this precisely is the most complete recognition of the universal interrelatedness of nature, and thus it turns out in fact to be the other way round, a support for our thesis. It is certainly, however, an expedient often adopted by human indolence to attribute what is not understood to the supernatural immediately; but this does not at all belong to the tendency to piety. Since the Supreme Being here takes the place of the system of nature, we find ourselves tending rather to knowledge; besides, in that case not everything but only the incomprehensible would be placed in absolute dependence upon God. Starting from this men have imagined evil and destructive supernatural powers in the same way as they have gone back to a highest good Power; which makes it immediately evident that this kind of linking up (with the supernatural) has not arisen in the interests of religion, for such a setting of one over against the other would inevitably destroy the unity and completeness of the relation of dependence.

As furthermore we regard everything stimulating us as an object of the pious consciousness, it follows that not even the least and most unimportant thing should be excluded from the relation of absolute dependence. But here it should be remarked that frequently, on the one hand, an undue value is placed on expressly tracing back the least detail to this relation; while on the other hand, with no greater justice, we often oppose such a relation. The first mistake appears in the view that, because the greatest events often arise from small, the smallest detail must be expressly ordained by God. For it appears to be only an empty, and by no means trustworthy, play of the fantasy, when we so often hear people describing great events as arising from small causes, and thereby drawing away our attention from the universal relatedness in which the true causes really lie hidden. A clear judgment can only be formed on the principle of the similarity of cause and effect in the domain of history or of nature, and it is only under definite conditions that individual changes with their causes can be severed from the universal interrelatedness and taken separately. But as soon as the pious feeling combines with such a view, thought has no choice but to recur to the universal interdependence of nature; otherwise an isolated and separate activity would be ascribed in too human fashion to God. The second point, *i.e.* that the application of absolute dependence to the smallest matters is felt to be objectionable, has its origin in the fear that religion might be drawn into blasphemy, if, say, our free choices in little things were to be traced back to divine appointment: for instance, the point which foot shall be put forward first, or chance in matters of no serious importance such as winning or losing in sports and contests. Still, the incongruity here does not lie in the object, but in our way of thinking about it: that is, in the isolation of single events, because in cases of the first kind the apparent free choice is sometimes only an individual instance of a general situation, from which many similar events follow, and sometimes it is the expression of a more general law by which many similar events are controlled; while in cases of the second kind, the issue can always be regarded as submission to a universal will. Neither of these can be regarded as insignificant, and thus no reason can be found against treating both as subsumed under absolute dependence on God.

2. If now we examine our proposition purely in itself, it must be directly evident in its wider scope to everyone who accepts it as a general principle of experience that the feeling of absolute dependence can be aroused through stimulations of our sensuous self-consciousness. For that feeling is most complete when we identify ourselves in our self-consciousness with the whole world and feel ourselves in the same way as not less dependent. This identification can only succeed in so far as in thought we unite everything that in appearance is scattered and isolated, and by means of this unifying association conceive of everything as one. For the most complete and universal interdependence of nature is posited in this 'All-One' of finite being, and if we also feel ourselves to be absolutely dependent, then there will be a complete coincidence of the two ideas—namely, the unqualified conviction that everything is grounded and established in the universality of the nature-system, and the inner certainty of the absolute dependence of all finite being on God. From this follows, on the one hand, the possibility of pious self-consciousness in every moment of the objective consciousness, and on the other the possibility of com-

plete world-consciousness in every moment of pious self-consciousness. For with regard to the latter, where a pious feeling is actually existent, there the interdependence of nature is always posited; and therefore the effort to extend the idea of the latter and perfect it in a world-representation will not be detrimental to the former, but can be effected just in so far as the tendency towards knowledge is predominant. And as regards the former, wherever there is an objective idea, there is always a stimulated self-consciousness; and from this the pious self-consciousness can develop without prejudice to the objective idea (with its world-conception, which is more or less clearly co-posited), in proportion as the tendency in each towards feeling is dominant. Now if we conceive both tendencies as fully developed in a given man, then each would with perfect ease call forth the other, so that every thought, as part of the whole world-conception, would become in him the purest religious feeling, and every pious feeling, as evoked by a part of the world, would become a complete world-conception. On the contrary, if the one did not call forth the other, but in some way limited it, then the more completely the one developed, the more would it destroy the other. It has been always acknowledged by the strictest dogmaticians [1] that divine preservation, as the absolute dependence of all events and changes on God, and natural causation, as the complete determination of all events by the universal nexus, are one and the same thing simply from different points of view, the one being neither separated from the other nor limited by it. If anyone should detect in this an appearance of Pantheism, he ought to bear in mind that so long as philosophy does not put forward a generally accepted formula to express the relation of God and the world, even in the province of Dogmatics, directly we begin to speak not of the origin of the world but of its co-existence with God and its relatedness to God, we cannot avoid an oscillation between formulas, on the one hand, which approach to the identification of the two, and formulas, on the other, which go near to putting them in opposition to one another. Moreover, in order not to confuse ourselves in this way, we ought to observe

[1] Quenstedt, *Syst. theol.*, p. 761: . . . ita ut idem effectus non a solo Deo nec a sola creatura, sed unâ eâdemque efficientiâ totali simul a Deo et creatura producatur . . . actum dico (*sc.* concursum Dei) non praevium actioni causae secundae nec subsequentem . . . sed talis est actus, qui intime in ipsa actione creaturae includitur, imo eadem actio creaturae est.—*Ibid.* p. 782: Non est re ipsa alia actio influxus Dei, alia operatio creaturae, sed una et indivisibilis actio utrumque respiciens et ab utraque pendens, a Deo ut causa universali, a creatura ut particulari.

more carefully the difference between a universal and an individual cause. For in the totality of finite being only a particular and partial causality is given to each individual, since each is dependent not on one other but on all the others; the universal causality attaches only to that on which the totality of this partial causality is itself dependent.

Postscript.—In Dogmatics the analytical method originating with the Scholastics has led to a division of our simple proposition in a number of different ways into many elements and sections, and it will not make much difference which of these divisions we select in order to show its relation to our statement. Some have divided the conception of preservation, which is expressed in our proposition as referring both to the whole and the parts, into the following: the *general*, which is related to the whole world as a unity; the *special*, which is concerned with species; and the *most special*, which is concerned with individuals (*generalis, specialis et specialissima*). This classification does not appear to be made in the interest of religion (from which here everything should start), for the simple reason that it leads to a question which is purely one for natural science, *i.e.* whether there is anything in the world which cannot be brought under the idea of a species. But supposing this question must be answered in the affirmative and the division be made complete, nevertheless universal preservation must include everything, and the division thus becomes quite superfluous to us, since our fundamental feeling rests solely on the finiteness of being as such. But a further purpose of this division may be surmised, if we take into account the addition usually made to the third member of it—namely, that God sustains individual things in their existence and their powers as long as He wills. For in that case the species, as reproductions of individual things, are in a sense immortal, but the individual is mortal; and the wish arose to establish a difference between the preservation of what endures and of what is mortal.

For those, however, who accept a beginning and an end of the world there is absolutely no reason to differentiate between the world and individual things. But in any case the proposition must cover equally the beginning and the end; and we know fairly certainly of our earth that there have been species on it which are no longer extant and that the present species have not always existed; so that our proposition must be stretched to embrace these also. It really affirms nothing except that the temporality or the duration of the finite is to be conceived solely in absolute dependence upon God. But since the duration of individual as well as of universal things is simply an expression for the degree of their power as each coexists with all the rest, it follows that the addition taken in itself contains nothing which our statement had not expressed already. But the way in which the addition is framed might easily give rise to the idea that the sustaining will of God began or ended at some particular time, and in anticipation of this it must be said that God, in sustaining as in creating, must remain apart from all means and occasions of time.

Another similar division is to discriminate between the work of God as *preserving* and as *co-operating* ; but the distinction is not made in the same way by all teachers of doctrine, for some connect the expression 'preservation' only with matter and form, and 'co-operation' with powers and actions ; others again connect preservation with the existence and powers of things, and co-operation only with activity. The fact, however, that the expression 'co-operation' contains a hidden meaning should not be overlooked, as if there were in the finite an activity in and for itself and thus independent of the sustaining divine activity. This tendency must be entirely avoided and not merely covered over by indefiniteness.[1] If, however, such a distinction ought not to be drawn, and if the powers of things are something as little separated from the divine sustaining activity as their being itself (the latter we only divide into matter and form by an abstraction which has no place here), then the difference between preservation and co-operation rests also on a similar abstraction. For being posited for itself can only exist where there is also power, just as power always exists only in activity ; thus a preservation which did not include the placing of all the activities of any finite being in absolute dependence on God would be just as empty as creation without preservation. And in the same way, if we conceived co-operation without conceiving that the existence of a thing in its whole duration was dependent on God, then this thing might be independent of God even at its first moment of existence, and this would be equivalent to conceiving preservation in such a way that it did not include creation and positing it without creation. It should be added here that even theologians who have treated the subject quite correctly on

[1] *E.g.* Morus, i. p. 306 : limites non definiuntur quousque operatur sol, agricola, et ubi incipiat Deus . . . adjuvando et limitando efficit Deus, ut fiat consilium suum.

the whole have allowed themselves to be led into describing co-operation as something more immediate than preservation,[1] so that deeds, as distinct from the preservation of powers, proceed from a divine activity. The result of this would be, if we took it seriously, to reduce the preservation of power to nothing, for in the system of nature power is always dependent on the activity of the rest of things. Thus we can only say that, in the region of absolute dependence on God, everything is equally direct and equally indirect, some in one relation and some in another.

Some combine the idea of divine *government* immediately with these two ideas. But if by that is meant the fulfilment of divine decrees[2] or the guidance of all things to divine ends, and if it be taken as signifying anything else than that everything can happen and has happened only as God originally willed and always wills, by means of the powers distributed and preserved in the world—this is already included in our proposition, and we cannot consider it here. For here we are concerned in general with the description of the feeling of absolute dependence, and must set completely aside a view which is based upon the distinction between means and end without reference to the question whether this distinction can exist for God. On the one hand, for our Christian consciousness it could only be the Kingdom of God, established by means of redemption (*i.e.* something quite foreign to our present purpose), to which everything else is related as its goal: and on the other, if our self-consciousness is to represent finite existence in general, and end and means are related to one another as that which is posited for its own sake and that not posited for its own sake, or more exactly as what is willed by God and what is not willed by God, then we must take up into our religious self-consciousness an antithesis of which our present discussion knows nothing. The only thing then that this conception [divine government] could suggest to us at this point would be that so far as the divine preservation relates, as co-operation, to powers and activities taken separately, we require a counterpart to it to cover the passive state of finite things; but since these are just as essential parts for the attainment of the divine purpose, their absolute dependence is included in the conception of government. Even this is, however,

[1] Quenst., *l.c.*: Observandum quod Deus non solum vim agendi dat causis secundis et etiam conservat, sed quod immediate influit in actionem et effectum creaturae.

[2] Morus, i. p. 319: Gubernatio est opus Dei efficientis ut in mundo ipse suum semper adsequatur consilium.

superfluous so far as we are concerned. For since preservation has as its object the being of things, and in this, so far as they are centres of power, the antithesis of self-activity and susceptibility is included, the passive states are already subsumed under absolute dependence ; and particularly when they also belong to that which affects our self-consciousness, whether in the form of perception or of sympathy, they are included in our general proposition. But, in addition, the passive states of one thing are only the result of the active states of others ; while, on the other hand, the way in which the active states emerge successively and the strength which they display depends not only on each thing's peculiar mode of existence, but also on its concurrence with other things, hence on the influence of others and on its own passive states. From this we may think that perhaps we should differentiate better if we said that what proceeds from the intrinsic characteristics of each individual thing and what proceeds from its co-existence with all other things are both alike to be placed in absolute dependence upon God. But even this would be an abstraction without importance for our religious self-consciousness, for which the two are not distinguished from one another as stimulating objects ; and thus we should do better to include everything which stimulates our consciousness together in the idea of finite being which is only relatively individual and is conditioned in its individuality by the universal co-existence. And this is wholly identical with what our proposition denotes by the term interdependence of nature.

§ 47. *It can never be necessary in the interest of religion so to interpret a fact that its dependence on God absolutely excludes its being conditioned by the system of Nature.*

1. This proposition is so much a direct consequence of what went before that there would be no reason to make an express statement of it, but that ideas which have still a circulation in the Christian Church must be considered in their appropriate place in any Dogmatic. Now there is a general idea that the miracles which are interwoven with the beginnings of Christianity or at least in some form are reported in the Scriptures, should be regarded as events of the kind described : and yet if the idea itself is inadmissible, it cannot be applied to this or that particular fact. It is in this way that theologians from of old have generally treated the question. We have not to pass judgment here on its inherent possibility, but only on the relation of the theory to the feeling of

absolute dependence. If, then, this relation is what our proposition declares it to be, we must in our field try, as far as possible, to interpret every event with reference to the interdependence of nature and without detriment to that principle.

Now some have represented miracle in this sense as essential to the perfect manifestation of the divine omnipotence. But it is difficult to conceive, on the one side, how omnipotence is shown to be greater in the suspension of the interdependence of nature than in its original immutable course which was no less divinely ordered. For, indeed, the capacity to make a change in what has been ordained is only a merit in the ordainer, if a change is necessary, which again can only be the result of some imperfection in him or in his work. If such an interference be postulated as one of the privileges of the Supreme Being, it would first have to be assumed that there is something not ordained by Him which could offer Him resistance and thus invade Him and His work; and such an idea would entirely destroy our fundamental feeling. We must remember, on the other hand, that where such a conception of miracles is commonly found, namely, in conditions where there is least knowledge of nature, there, too, the fundamental feeling appears to be weakest and most ineffectual. But where a knowledge of nature is most widely spread, and therefore this conception seldom occurs, more is found of that reverence for God which is the expression of our fundamental feeling. It follows from this that the most perfect representation of omnipotence would be a view of the world which made no use of such an idea.

Other teachers [1] defend the conception in a more acute but scarcely more tenable way, by saying that God was partly in need of miracles that He might compensate for the effects of free causes in the course of nature, and partly that He might generally have reasons for remaining in direct contact with the world. The latter argument presupposes, for one thing, a wholly lifeless view of the divine preservation, and for another, an opposition in general between the mediate and immediate activities of God which cannot be conceived without bringing the Supreme Being within the sphere of limitation. The former sounds almost as if free causes were not themselves objects of divine preservation, and (since preservation includes in itself the idea of creation) had not come into being and been maintained in absolute dependence upon God. But if, on the contrary, they are in this condition there can be just

[1] Cf. Storr, *Dogm.*, § 25.

as little necessity for God to counteract their influences as to counteract the influences which a blind natural force exercises in the domain of another natural force. But none of us understands by 'the world' which is the object of the divine preservation a nature-mechanism alone, but rather the interaction of the nature-mechanism and of free agents, so that in the former the latter are taken into account just as in the latter the former is reckoned.

Moreover, the Biblical miracles, on account of which the whole theory has been devised, are much too isolated and too restricted in content for any theory to be based on them which should assign them the function of restoring in the nature-mechanism what free agents had altered. That one great miracle, the mission of Christ, has, of course, the aim of restoration, but it is the restoration of what free causes have altered in their own province, not in that of the nature-mechanism or in the course of things originally ordained by God. Nor does the interest of religion require that the free cause which performs the function of restoration in the sphere of phenomena should have a different relation to the order of nature from that of other free causes.

Two other reasons may be put forward why an absolute suspension of the interrelatedness of nature by miracles may be held to be in the interests of religion. And it cannot be denied that it is mostly for these reasons, even though they may never have been formulated as actual Church doctrine, that this conception of miracle has maintained its practical hold over many Christians. The first is that of answer to prayer; for prayer seems really to be heard only when because of it an event happens which would not otherwise have happened: thus there seems to be the suspension of an effect which, according to the interrelatedness of nature, should have followed. The other is that of regeneration, which, represented as a new creation, in part requires some such suspension and in part introduces a principle not comprised in the system of nature. Neither subject can be discussed in this place; but it may suffice to remark in relation to the first, which more concerns piety in general, that our statement places prayer, too, under divine preservation, so that prayer and its fulfilment or refusal are only part of the original divine plan, and consequently the idea that otherwise something else might have happened is wholly meaningless. With regard to the second we need only refer here to what was said above. If the revelation of God in Christ is not necessarily something absolutely supernatural, Christian piety cannot be held bound in advance to regard as absolutely supernatural anything that goes along with this revelation or flows from it.

2. The more accurate definitions by which the acceptance of such miracles is brought into connexion with the propositions and concepts which indicate the complete dependence of the system of nature on God show very clearly how little that idea is demanded by our religious emotions. For the more they try definitely to fix an absolute miracle, the further off they are from making it the expression of a religious emotion, and, instead of genuine dogmatic material, something of quite a different character [1] comes in. Speaking generally, the question can most easily be considered if we start from the point that the event in which a miracle occurs is connected with all finite causes, and therefore every absolute miracle would destroy the whole system of nature. There are, therefore, two ways of looking at such a miracle—a positive way when we consider the whole future, and a negative way when we consider it as affecting in some sense the whole of the past. Since, that is, that which would have happened by reason of the totality of finite causes in accordance with the natural order does not happen, an effect has been hindered from happening, and certainly not through the influence of other normally counteracting finite causes given in the natural order, but in spite of the fact that all active causes are combining to produce that very effect. Everything, therefore, which had ever contributed to this will, to a certain degree, be annihilated, and instead of introducing a single supernatural power into the system of nature as we intended, we must completely abrogate the conception of nature.

From the positive point of view we must consider that some

[1] Mosheim, *op. cit.*, p. 462, calls the divine activity which works miracles 'gubernatio immediata' or 'inordinata,' and, by so doing, introduces an antithesis between miracle and the sustaining activity of God, to the advantage of the last-named in the latter formula, but to its disadvantage in the former. But religious feeling would equally refuse to interpose anything between that which is and the divine activity through which it is, and to impute something to the divine activity which is at the same time regarded as unordained. At the same time, the expression conflicts with the general explanation which he gives of 'gubernatio'—namely, that it stands for a 'directio virium alienarum,' if, that is to say, the miracle is not to be explained by means of the relevant natural forces.—Reinhard calls (*Dogm.*, p. 236) the same divine activity 'providentia miraculosa,' and explains it by 'cura divina, qua Deus aliquid efficit mutationibus a consuetudine naturae plane abhorrentibus.' If, as here, we look to find the antithesis in the divine care, then preservation would be an absence of care; if in the custom of nature, then the custom of nature is apparently something independent of the divine providence. Religious feeling would, necessarily, declare equally against both views.

event follows which is not to be explained by the totality of finite causes. But as this event now enters into the interrelatedness of nature as an active member, throughout the whole future everything will be different from what it would have been had this single miracle not occurred. Thus every miracle not only suspends the entire continuity of the original order for all future time, but every later miracle annuls all earlier ones, in so far as they have become part of the continuity of active causes. But now, in order to describe the origin of the effect, we have to allow for the entrance of a divine activity apart from natural causes.[1] Yet at whatever point we admit the entrance of this particular divine activity, which must always seem like magic, in each case there will always appear a number of possibilities according to which the same result could have been attained by natural causes if they had been opportunely directed towards this end. In this way we shall be driven to hold either that miracles have a purely epideictic tendency in view of which God purposely did not so order the system of nature that His whole will should be accomplished in it (a view against which we directed our earlier discussion of the relation between omnipotence and this conception of miracle), or if the totality of finite causes could not have been so directed, then what can be explained by the order of nature can never rightly evoke in us the feeling of the absolute dependence of all finite being.

Now, if others think it would be easier to establish this conception of miracles by first dividing the divine co-operation into ordinary and extraordinary (which, however, is only ostensibly different from the unordered), and then attributing the former to the natural and the latter to the supernatural, so that the negative aspect of a miracle would be the withdrawal of the ordinary co-operation,[2] but the positive aspect the entrance of the extraordinary, this means, on the one hand, that the ordinary co-operation is no longer ordinary if it can be withdrawn, and is not to be definitely

[1] The formula that in such a case God acts without intermediary causes is in contradiction to our fundamental feeling, if for no other reason than that it represents God as under constraint within the ordinary course of nature. At bottom, however, this use of terms which describes natural causes as intermediary causes, is itself infected by the radical error of conceiving the dependence on God of what happens as dependence on particular finite causes—a dependence of the same kind, only lying further back. And, in fact, Storr (*Dogm.*, p. 336), when seeking to show how God can act directly on the world, and change the course of nature without abrogating natural laws, seems to conceive Him in the manner of a finite free cause.

[2] Quenstedt, *l.c.*: Deo concursum suum subtrahente cessat creaturae actio.

distinguished from the extraordinary ; only that we call that which occurs more frequently the ordinary, and what seldom occurs, the extraordinary, a relation which might equally well be reversed. On the other hand, the miracle is effected in the first instance by finite causes, even if by means of extraordinary divine co-operation ; but since thereby something comes into existence which according to its natural character would not have come into existence, it follows that in this case either they are not causes, and the expression 'co-operation' is inaccurate, or they have become something different from what they were formerly. In that case, every such extraordinary co-operation is really a creation, on which afterwards the re-establishment of actual things in their original state must follow as a further creation cancelling the former one. Moreover, it should be recognized with regard to these explanations that the one corresponds more closely to the one class of Biblical miracle [1] and the other to the other class, and therefore the different characteristics of these events have had an important influence on the development of these different formulæ. If, however, anyone finds it difficult to accept this view, yet it must be admitted that although the older theologians on the whole [2] still maintain this conception of miracle, the younger ones [3] do not maintain its exclusive validity, but also admit the legitimacy of another hypothesis—namely, that God has prepared miracles in nature itself in some way incomprehensible to us ; and this, in the interests of religion itself, we must admit to be pure gain.

3. On the whole, therefore, as regards the miraculous, the general interests of science, more particularly of natural science, and the interests of religion seem to meet at the same point, *i.e.* that we should abandon the idea of the absolutely supernatural because no single instance of it can be known by us, and we are nowhere required to recognize it. Moreover, we should admit, in general, that since our knowledge of created nature is continually growing, we have not the least right to maintain that anything is impossible ; and also we should allow, in particular (by far the greater number

[1] Morus (*op. cit.*) describes it thus : aut enim mentio quidem fit adminiculi naturalis ; aut ne fit quidem mentio talis, sed praegresso verbo res facta est.

[2] Buddeus, *Thes. de atheism.*, p. 291 : Operatio, qua revera naturae leges, quibus totius huius universi ordo et conservatio innititur, suspenduntur. According to Thomas, p. 1, cap. cx. : ex hoc aliquid dicitur miraculum, quod sit praeter ordinem totius naturae creatae.

[3] Cf. Reinhard, *Dogmat.*, p. 238 : the above-quoted expression 'consuetudo naturae' is in this respect carefully chosen.—Morus treats the matter in the same sense but superficially in his *Commentary*, part i. p. 97 sq.

of New Testament miracles being of this kind), that we can neither define the limits of the reciprocal relations of the body and mind nor assert that they are, always and everywhere, entirely the same without the possibility of extension or deviation. In this way, everything—even the most wonderful thing that happens or has happened—is a problem for scientific research; but, at the same time, when it in any way stimulates the pious feeling, whether through its purpose or in some other way, that is not in the least prejudiced by the conceivable possibility of its being understood in the future. Moreover, we free ourselves entirely from a difficult and highly precarious task with which Dogmatics has so long laboured in vain,[1] *i.e.* the discovery of definite signs which shall enable us to distinguish between the false and diabolical miracle and the divine and true.

§ 48. *Excitations of self-consciousness expressing a repression of life are just as much to be placed in absolute dependence on God as those expressing an advancement of life.*

1. This statement deals more particularly with the contrast between the serene and the sad moments of life, but it follows so directly from our principal proposition,[2] or rather is so completely involved in it, that we should have had no reason for putting it specially forward if long experience had not taught us that imperfect piety has always found it difficult to harmonize the existence of sad and unhappy experiences with the God-consciousness, whether because it is overwhelmed by life's repressions or led astray by sceptical and unbelieving arguments. On this account almost every religious doctrine, and particularly the Christian doctrine of faith, must make it a special duty to show their compatibility. This has generally involved, however, a false complacency towards these imperfect emotions, partly by way of vindicating the Supreme Being with respect to the existence of such experiences and partly by admitting a variation in the absolute feeling of dependence in relation to them. It is sufficient here to enter a protest against both, as much against the counterfeit emotion itself as against the weak and obscure treatment of it, in order that the simple and complete apprehension of the fundamental feeling may not be endangered. Now if sad experiences only occurred separately, although frequently, and were such that we could trace no connexion between them, then they would hardly have been able to

[1] Cf. Gerhard, *loc. th. loc.* xxiii. § 271. [2] § 46.

produce such an effect ; but it is dependent on the fact that there are conditions which bring a persistent and regularly renewed consciousness of life's obstacles. These, then, are what we usually characterize by the term *evil*: and it is to be maintained that all evil, in the full meaning of that word, is just as much wholly dependent upon God as that which is in opposition to it, *i.e.* good. But clearly we must reckon moral evil under the term 'evil,' since where it exists it always shows itself to be an inexhaustible source of life's difficulties ; only here we have not to consider it as a human activity but as a state. Therefore, just as later we shall have to treat more fully the connexion of evil with moral evil and from a different standpoint, here, in the reverse order, moral evil is to be included under the term 'evil.' Thus it is to be considered now apart from ethics, and only as it appears and is given as a state affecting the self-consciousness as one of life's obstacles ; and after the present discussion it will not later be treated separately. There is, however, a further division of evil which we need only consider in order to make clear that, just as (we maintain) evil and good are alike rooted in universal dependence on God, from this point of view there is no difference between these two types or classes of evil. To the one belong those conditions which we call natural evil, in which human existence is partially negated. To the other, which we name social evil, belong those conditions in which human activity is in conflict with another activity and is partially overcome and depressed ; and here the influence of moral evil specially comes in. But clearly these two kinds of evil not only give rise to each other (since where there is diminution of being activity will more easily be depressed, and a depressed activity which is always decreasing reacts again on the whole being), but they also overlap in thought, for the being of man consists only in the totality of his activities, and *vice versa*. The difference consists then principally in this, that the one is much more determined by the total forces of nature, and the other by the collective conditions of human activity.

2. In order to solve our problem within the prescribed limits we do not at all require to enter deeply into teleological speculations or, in addition to evil itself, to consider what has resulted from it ; for it can never be proved that the results might not have been caused in some other way. It is just as unnecessary for us to work back from the idea of Preservation to that of Creation or beyond it, to show that evil was unavoidable. But remaining strictly within

our province, we have only to show that apparent oppositions come together under the universal dependence. And here two points arise with regard to both kinds of evil. First, the relation of the fluctuating and transitory to the permanent in all finite being. Individual beings belong to the transitory in the form primarily of a vital activity that takes a progressive development up to a certain climax, from thence gradually decreasing until death. Since, regarded as a whole, every relation which determines development arouses the consciousness of life as stimulated, and conversely what tends to bring death nearer is interpreted as an arrest of life, there is throughout the whole course a casual fluctuation between these two. Clearly then, on the one hand, it is the same entire relatedness of men with nature which determines both progress and arrest, so that the one cannot be apart from the other. It is just the same, again, in the sphere of social life, where, for example, a later formation of community life cannot grow and expand without the earlier formation being repressed and brought to decay; and thus there are here again two modes of life, progress and limitation, each conditioning the other. The second point is the relation of what is only relatively self-existent and the corresponding and mutual limitations of the finite. That is to say, there is no absolute isolation in the finite: each is only self-existent as it conditions another, and is in turn only conditioned in so far as it is self-existent. But another thing is only conditioned by me if I can in some way cause it to progress; but then this equally implies that I can be a hindrance. The whole relation can only be presented to consciousness in so far as both terms (in both forms, that of self-existence and that of conditionedness) are presented; and consequently both obstacles and progress are equally ordained by God. This is equally valid of personal feeling and of sympathetic and social feeling. So that without a very far-reaching misunderstanding, no one can find difficulty in the fact that even what appears to him an evil (be it his own, someone else's, or one common to many) exists as a consequence of absolute dependence, and therefore is to be regarded as ordained by God. Otherwise we should in general be neither willing nor able to think of the transitory and finite as existing through God—that is, we could not think any world at all as dependent on God; and in this way our fundamental proposition would be denied.

Now this misunderstanding is due, on one side, to the fact that we look at states themselves apart from their natural conditions;

and it is increased by the fact that we wrongly represent these influences which produce permanent life-repressions as if they were a separate self-contained province and thus could be isolated and eliminated—in short, that the world could exist apart from evil. The fact is rather that the very same activity or condition of a thing by which it enters on the one hand into human life as an evil, on the other hand is a cause of good, so that if we could remove the source of life's difficulties the conditions of life's progress too would disappear. This is true even of moral evil which only functions as evil in so far as it appears in external action: and it holds good not only accidentally because sin produces good effects sometimes in individuals and sometimes as a great historical lever, but as a general truth since sin only comes to be done by reason of that capacity of man to express his inner nature outwardly which is the source of all good. On the other hand, since in the same way it can be held as a general truth that in the universal system that which is the source of most of life's advancement, from some point of view has an aspect of evil, and that in virtue of the very characteristic which makes it helpful (as indeed all forces of nature and all social relations which originate in intelligence, with the single exception perhaps of intelligence itself, may be said to have this twofold aspect of good and evil), it is absolutely correct to say in another sense that evil as such is not ordained by God, because evil in isolation is never found, and the same is true of good, but each thing or event is ordained by God that it should be both.

There is an important point for us here—that it is an imperfection of self-consciousness when a limitation, as such, completely and exclusively engrosses a moment of experience, whether this imperfection be that of immediate self-consciousness or of that which accompanies the activities of the objective consciousness; and in the same way it is an erroneous view when its being the source of difficulties is regarded as the essence of any object that exists in absolute dependence on God. And even this imperfection is one which disappears with the increasing development of the good, like every evil vanishing into the good itself—that is, in the susceptibility of the sensuous consciousness in general for union with the God-consciousness.

3. The usual dogmatic definitions which try under the headings of preservation and co-operation to throw light on this subject, certainly appear to have the same solution in view but to reach it very inadequately. Thus, for this purpose they sometimes differ-

entiate a divine co-operation that is helpful from one that is not, and sometimes a merely material co-operation from one that is also formal. These terms seem to have been originally thought out with special reference to the antithesis between good and evil, and to the latter was assigned the co-operation which is not helpful or only material. But apart from the fact that co-operation and help are inseparable ideas, and no definite conception can be formed of a co-operation which is not helpful, we must observe that if co-operation with activity is in question there is no activity without form, so that there can be no co-operation with an activity which is not also a co-operation with the form of that activity, and a merely material co-operation would be nothing more than preservation without co-operation. The consequence of this would be that all activity so described would be placed outside the relation of absolute dependence. Hence, according to both these formulas, evil seems to be stronger and more powerful than good, since the latter can only be accomplished with the helpful or (in addition) formal co-operation, while the former needs neither of them. But, apart from this, I say that there can be no question in this place of treating evil as a purely inward disposition prior to all activity, because it could not then stimulate the self-consciousness of the individual, much less could it stimulate the self-consciousness of someone else. But, if we consider evil as active, then all sinful actions are performed not only by means of the material powers of men, but just like good actions, in a way appropriate to them ; so that there is no ground for making such a distinction.

Suppose now that all social evil was in some way bound up with moral evil, this distinction would no longer be applicable. But how about natural evil ? Since destructive events are precisely the strongest expressions of natural forces, they are thus less able to take place without helpful co-operation than other events, and just as little without formal co-operation, since no specific form can be ascribed to them. Thus if the intention is to maintain that in so far as co-operation is admitted, evil, too, comes within the absolute dependence on God, but that in so far as the co-operation is not helpful or only material, God cannot be the originator, this intention has, strictly speaking, not been fulfilled. Consequently, it appears to be a better expedient if we say that everything real without exception is the result of divine co-operation, so that this can suffer no diminution : but all evil, including moral evil as such, has its ground in a mere defect ; and, a mere defect being a partial *non-ens,* divine co-operation cannot be concerned with it. If then each finite thing is ordained simultaneously by God as an entity with its own dimensions, this does not mean that it exerts activities outside this limit ; on the contrary, the divine co-operation would be lacking to these, and consequently it could not resist external influences beyond this limit. But difficulties or obstacles do not arise from the circumstance that no opposition can be offered because divine assistance is lacking, but because an attack is made in a manner which is beyond the finite thing's power of resistance, whereas divine co-operation is available for the attack. Nothing remains but on the one hand to attribute the divine co-operation equally to everything that happens, and on the other to maintain that evil as such is not ordained by God, but only as related to the good and as one condition of it.

§ 49. *Whether or not that which arouses our self-consciousness and consequently influences us, is to be traced back to any part of the so-called nature-mechanism or to the activity of free causes—the one is as completely ordained by God as the other.*

1. The proposition is in itself only the expression of the undoubtedly generally admitted fact that we do not feel ourselves less absolutely dependent on God when anything happens to us through the actions of other men than in other cases. Also it is completely contained in the principal proposition of this Second Doctrine, and is only put forward in explanation in order to prevent a not infrequent misunderstanding, namely, that the consciousness of our free-will is in opposition to the feeling of absolute dependence. The question first of all is as to the effect of free actions, primarily on the lives of others but also on our own. But however much freedom resides in determination of will and resolution, action, emerging as it does under influences beyond itself, is always so conditioned that it only becomes what it is because it belongs to the very same universal system which is the essential indivisible subject of the feeling of absolute dependence ; and this would lose its significance in the whole province of history if we should think of free causes as excluded from this system. Indeed, what was put incidentally above must here be brought out in its full significance.[1] Just because free causes form a part of the general system, we must be able to assert the same of the moment of activity itself and of the accompanying self-consciousness. It

[1] See § 47, 1.

was in this sense that in our first elucidations of the fundamental feeling we explained how the relative feeling of freedom and the absolute feeling of dependence each involves and pervades the other, so that the latter cannot exist apart from the former.[1]

Let us consider now the moment of action, starting from the point that every other free agent in the same position would have acted differently, just as the same free agent would have acted differently in another position, and that this position, whatever it may be, is within the universal system. Then no one can doubt that the results of free activity take place in virtue of absolute dependence. What is certain, moreover, about the accompanying self-consciousness is that we are only capable of the feeling of absolute dependence as freely acting agents—that is to say, that we are conscious of our freedom as something which is received and is gradually developed in a universal system. Therefore in every religious experience of free self-activity the self-consciousness must contain both the feeling of absolute dependence and the relative feeling of freedom.

In our proposition, the expression 'free causes' clearly makes a difference between freedom and causality in general, and implies causes which are not free. And yet they are still causes. But in the customary conception of the universal nature-mechanism there is, strictly speaking, no causality apart from free causes. For by it we imagine a coherence and interaction of things which only react as such in so far as they have been acted upon; and in that case we can only think of each in its activity as a point of intersection: so that causality is only applicable to the first mover existing outside this sphere. That is to say that, according to this conception, free causes having been excluded, there is no causality in finite things, while outside there is only the free infinite cause, the divine causality which is presupposed as originally setting the whole sphere in motion by a first push. If we include in this mechanism all inferior life, animal and vegetable (since there can, in this conception, be no question of a universal life of the heavenly bodies), then free causes, by which we mean men, are the sole finite causality, and it only needs one step to leave the divine causality as the only one, *i.e.* to hold what we have already shown to be destructive of the feeling of absolute dependence, and with it all piety—that men should regard themselves too as simply part of this mechanism, and should treat consciousness of self-activity

[1] See § 4, 3.

as only an unavoidable illusion. Fortunately, few have ever been capable of this self-annihilating renunciation by which, after robbing the whole world of life, they sacrifice their own selves also to the completeness of their theory. By this method all causality of the finite is transformed into appearance, and consequently there is no ground for regarding individual finite being as existing for itself, and therefore no reason why a finite being should come to rest at one point rather than another in this universal flux of moving and being moved ; but all things are either an indivisible unity or else an innumerable multitude of points of transition, *i.e.* atoms.

Let us now attribute to ourselves free causality along with absolute dependence, and causality also to every living being as assuredly as we hold it to have being for itself ; and let us see complete absence of freedom only where a thing does not move itself and moves other things only in so far as it is moved ; in that case we should be able to regard the causality of living beings as simply a diminished freedom, and we should have to say that true causality only exists where there is life, and the complete absence of freedom is also a complete absence of causality, since the impulse which sets the lifeless thing in motion so that it moves other things always comes itself from what is living. In our proposition, then, the expression ' nature-mechanism ' is not used as our own, for we should be wrong to reduce anything which stimulates our self-consciousness and thus influences us to mere mechanism, to active points of transition. It lies, however, outside our province to inquire how far the sphere of true causality and therefore of life extends, and how in each particular case the true cause is to be discovered. But our self-consciousness, in so far as it is the consciousness of a finite being and we distinguish in it a partial consciousness of freedom and a partial feeling of dependence as belonging together, from the feeling of absolute dependence as including both, requires for every stimulation a finite causality in the sphere of the universal system of nature which, as a consequence of this, must be taken up into absolute dependence. For this feeling would not retain its uniform character if there were a sphere, *i.e.* that of natural causes, in which finite and divine causation met, and alongside it two others, that of mechanical or rather apparent causation where only divine causality reigned and finite causality was absent, and that of free causality where only finite cause reigned and divine causality was absent. At the same time we must observe, with reference to absolute dependence, that we assume no sharp antithesis between freedom and natural necessity in finite being, since anything which actually has a being for itself moves itself in some sense or other, even if it has no part in spiritual life ; but even in the most free cause its range is ordained by God.

2. In the dogmatic terminology which now prevails, this truth is expressed sometimes by the idea of preservation and sometimes by the idea of co-operation. The most usual form of the first kind is that God upholds each thing in its being, and therefore also free causes as such. In this statement we can find everything which we have ascertained, namely, that the activities of free beings are determined from within, without prejudice to the absolute dependence which is indicated by the expression preservation. Considered in itself, however, this formula may be open to the censure that it appears to obscure the essential difficulties in a superficial way rather than actually solve them.

In a similar way a distinction is drawn in the concept of co-operation between a co-operation after the manner of free cause and a co-operation after the manner of natural cause.[1] But this expression requires at least to be treated very cautiously if the differences of finite being are not to be placed within the Supreme Being and thus God Himself appear as the totality, a view which can scarcely be differentiated from that of Pantheism. The meaning can only be that God co-operates in every case with activities which are appropriate to the nature of the active thing, but only and always according to His own causality, which is entirely different from that which belongs to the sphere of reciprocal action.

Postscript to this Doctrine.—It seemed advisable to state these separate propositions, though it must be admitted that they were already implied in essence in the principal proposition of the doctrine, for two reasons. First, because it is easy here to put forward definitions which obscure the right relationship between creation and preservation. This is done when the miraculous is regarded as entirely supernatural, since in this way a secondary creative act comes in which partially suspends preservation and thus stands in opposition to it. The same result follows if we believe that evil was less ordained by God than other things, because, in that case, of the things equally created by Him, He would leave some in the lurch rather than others. And it occurs, finally, if

[1] Concursus ad modum causae liberae, *and* ad modum causae naturalis.

we oppose free causes to natural ones so strongly that the former in their activity appear to be less dependent on God ; for then they must derive their effectiveness partly from elsewhere while their existence itself they derive from God, and thus an inequality is introduced between creation and preservation.

Secondly, it was supremely important here to show the harmony between the interests of piety and science on the one hand and morality on the other. Indeed, morality must always be endangered or must endanger religion if the absolute dependence be so conceived that free self-determination cannot co-exist with it, or *vice versa*. Scientific knowledge, however, is twofold—that of natural science and that of history. Natural science is so hampered by the assumption of the absolutely supernatural within the course of nature that it would thereby be made entirely nugatory. History deals more particularly with the opposition between good and evil, and on account of the way in which they are clearly interwoven one with another, necessarily becomes fatalistic (that is to say, it must give up its relation to the idea of the good) if evil is either not ordained by God or less ordained by Him than its opposite. Our propositions, however, retain their purely dogmatic content and do not trench upon the ground of speculation, in spite of these connexions with it, because they are all implied in the principal proposition. Their common relation to it is not everywhere equally clear. It consists in this, that each in its own province puts forward a greatest and a least and, showing that the feeling of dependence holds good in an equivalent way for both limiting cases, establishes this equivalence as the rule for all religious expression. The antithesis between the ordinary and the miraculous goes back to the greatest and least in the sphere of nature from which both are to be explained ; the antithesis between good and evil goes back to the greatest and least in the harmony of universal reciprocal activity with the independent being of the individual ; the antithesis between freedom and mechanism goes back to the greatest and least in individualized life. It had, therefore, to be shown that if at any of these points the similarity of treatment failed, then the main proposition of the doctrine itself would fall to the ground, and neither the conditioned feeling of dependence nor the conditioned feeling of freedom could be combined with the absolute feeling of dependence. Beyond these there are no difficult cases to consider.

SECOND SECTION

The Divine Attributes which are related to the Religious Self-consciousness so far as it expresses the General Relationship between God and the World.

§ 50. *All attributes which we ascribe to God are to be taken as denoting not something special in God, but only something special in the manner in which the feeling of absolute dependence is to be related to Him.*

1. If an adequate expression of the absolute feeling of dependence here indicated has been given in the expositions of the preceding section, we cannot believe that the theory of the divine attributes originally issued from a dogmatic interest. But history teaches us concerning speculation that, ever since it took the divine essence as an object of thought,[1] it has always entered the same protest against all detailed description, and confined itself to representing God as the Original Being and the Absolute Good. And, indeed, it has frequently been recognized that even in these concepts (of which the first only is relevant here) there remains a certain inadequacy, in so far as they still contain an element of opposition or other analogy with finite being. This method of treatment, therefore, owes its origin first of all to religious poetry, particularly to hymns and other lyrics, and also to the more uncultured experience of common life which harmonizes with poetry and tries to vivify and establish the simple idea of the Supreme Being by the employment of expressions which we use about finite beings. Both methods proceed from religious interests, and have far more the

[1] As we can only deal here with Christian speculation it may be sufficient to refer to Dionys. Areop., *de myst. theol.* cc. iv. and v.: *Λέγομεν οὖν ὡς ἡ πάντων αἰτία καὶ ὑπὲρ πάντα οὖσα οὔτε ἀνούσιός ἐστιν οὔτε ἄζωος . . . οὔτε ποιότητα, ἢ ποσότητα ἢ ὄγκον ἔχει . . . οὔτε ψυχή ἐστιν οὔτε νοῦς . . . οὔτε λόγος ἐστιν, οὔτε νόησις . . . οὔτε ζῇ οὔτε ζωή ἐστιν . . . οὐδέ τι τῶν οὐκ ὄντων, οὐδέ τι τῶν ὄντων ἐστιν*, and to Augustin., *de Trin.* v. 1: ut sic intelligamus Deum, si possumus, quantum possumus sine qualitate bonum sine quantitate magnum, sine indigentia creatorem sine situ praesidentem sine habitu omnia continentem sine loco ubique totum sine tempore sempiternum, sine ulla sui mutatione mutabilia facientem. And Hilary, *de Trin.* ii. 7: Perfecta scientia est sic Deum scire, ut licet non ignorabilem tamen inenarrabilem scias. Cf. Anselm, *Proslog.* cc. xviii. and xxii.

aim of representing the immediate impression in its different forms than of establishing scientific knowledge. Therefore, just because both have been taken over from Judaism, it has been from the beginning the business of Christian Dogmatics to regulate these representations, so that the anthropomorphic element, to be found more or less in all of them, and the sensuous which is mixed in with many, may be rendered as harmless as possible, and that no retrogression towards polytheism should result. And in this direction the age of Scholasticism contributed much that was profound and excellent. But as afterwards Metaphysics came to be treated separately and apart from Christian Doctrine, in conformity with the nature of the subject, it was for long overlooked (as only too easily happens in such divisions of territory) that these representations of divine attributes are not of philosophical but of religious origin ; and they were taken over into that philosophical discipline which went by the name of Natural Theology. There, however, the more science developed a purely speculative character, the more these representations, which had not arisen on the soil of speculation were bound to be treated in a merely critical or sceptical way. Dogmatic Theology, on the other hand, tried more and more to systematize them, not, if it understood itself rightly, in order to arrive at the consciousness that they contained a complete knowledge of God, but only to assure itself that the God-consciousness which dwells in us in all its differentiations and as it realizes itself at the prompting of different elements of life, was included in them. As, however, the separation was not complete, and intercourse was always lively and manifold between the two disciplines, much has remained permanently under philosophical treatment which belonged only to the dogmatic, and *vice versa*. It is still therefore always necessary to premise that, without making any speculative demands but at the same time without bringing in any speculative aids, we keep ourselves altogether within the limits of purely dogmatic procedure, both with regard to the content of individual definitions and also as to method.

2. It is precisely in this connexion that our proposition denies in general the speculative character of the content of all the divine attributes to be affirmed in Christian doctrine, just for that reason and in so far as they are manifold. For if as such they present a knowledge of the Divine Being, each one of them must express something in God not expressed by the others ; and if the knowledge is appropriate to the object, then, as the knowledge is com-

posite, the object too must be composite.[1] Indeed, even if these attributes only asserted relations of the Divine to the world, God Himself, like the finite life, could only be understood in a multiplicity of functions; and as these are distinct one from another, and relatively opposed one to another, and at least partly exclusive one of another, God likewise would be placed in the sphere of contradiction. This does not fulfil the requirements of the speculative reason, and definitions of this kind could not pass for speculative propositions; and just as little could the interests of religion be satisfied if dogmatic definitions were interpreted in this way. For if differentiations were assumed in God, even the feeling of absolute dependence could not be treated as such and as always and everywhere the same. For, in that case, there must be differences having their source in something beyond the difference of the life-moments through which the feeling (of dependence) makes its appearance in the mind. So that while we attribute to these definitions only the meaning stated in our proposition, at the same time everyone retains the liberty, without prejudice to his assent to Christian Doctrine, to attach himself to any form of speculation so long as it allows an object to which the feeling of absolute dependence can relate itself.

3. But as concerns method, in the treatment of Dogmatics up to the present a double procedure is found to predominate. First, rules are put forward as to how one can arrive at right ideas of the divine attributes, and then further, certain rubrics are given under which the various conceptions of divine attributes are to be divided. Now since both aim at systematizing these ideas, the same general assumption has to be made. If the list of these attributes be regarded as a complete summary of definitions to be related to God Himself, then a complete knowledge of God must be derivable from conceptions, and an explanation in due theoretic form would take the place of that ineffability of the Divine Being which the Scriptures—so far as they mention divine attributes—recognize so clearly on every page that we need not quote passages. We have therefore to strive after that completeness alone which guards against letting any of the different moments of the religious self-

[1] Mosheim, *Theol. dogm.* i. p. 232: Si essentia Dei vere differet ab attributis, et si attributa realiter inter se differrent, Deus esset natura composita. Nevertheless many theologians come very near to admitting such differences in God; *e.g.* Endemann, *Instit.*, p. 51, who distinguishes ea attributa sine quibus Deus nequit esse Deus and determinationes internas Dei, quae salva eius essentia et actualitate abesse possunt, which he therefore calls analoga accidentium.

consciousness pass without asking what are the divine attributes corresponding to them. And with this procedure the classification emerges of its own accord, because in each division only the attributes belonging there can be subjects of exposition. All the more necessary is it to make clear at this point how little is lost for the real matter in hand when we set aside, as we do, the apparatus which has hitherto been employed.

Now we may remark concerning these methods that there are three accepted ways of arriving at the divine attributes—the way of removal of limits (*via eminentiæ*), the way of negation or denial (*via negationis*), and the way of causality (*via causalitatis*). Now it is self-evident that these are by no means homogeneous or coordinate. For in the first two a something apart from God must be posited as an attribute ; and this, after it has been freed from all limitations, is ascribed to Him, or else its negation is ascribed to Him ; while on the other hand causality stands in the closest connexion with the feeling of absolute dependence itself. And if the first two be viewed in their relation to each other, it is clear that negation by itself is no way to posit any attribute, unless something positive remains behind the negation. In that case the negation will consist simply in the fact that the limits of the positive are denied. But in the same manner the way of the removal of limits is a negation, for something is posited of God, but the limits which elsewhere would be co-posited are not posited of God. The identity of these two methods becomes quite obvious in the idea of Infinity, which is at the same time the general form of absence of limits, for what is posited as infinite is also freed from limitation ; but at the same time it shows quite generally (by the fact that it is a negation in which nothing is immediately posited but in which everything may be posited which can be thought of as either limited or unlimited), that by negation we can only posit an attribute in so far as something positive remains behind the negation. Both these methods then can only be applied either haphazard with reference to the question whether something, which as such could only be absolutely denied of God, can be conceived as unlimited and posited as a divine attribute ; or if this is to be avoided, the application of these methods must be preceded by a definition as to what kind of attribute-conceptions are rightly to be ascribed to God in an unlimited fashion, and what kind simply must be denied of Him. The third method, on the contrary, is certainly an independent one. And even if we do not wish to maintain that all divine attributes corresponding to any modification of our feeling of dependence can equally be derived immediately from the idea of causality, but rather here at the start must premise for one thing that to this conception the other methods must first be applied, *i.e.* that the finitude of causality must be denied and its productivity posited as unlimited; and again, that in so far as a plurality of attributes is developed out of the idea of the divine causality, this differentiation can correspond to nothing real in God; indeed, that neither in isolation nor taken together do the attributes express the Being of God in itself (for the essence of that which has been active can never be known simply from its activity alone)—yet this at least is certain, that all the divine attributes to be dealt with in Christian Dogmatics must somehow go back to the divine causality, since they are only meant to explain the feeling of absolute dependence.

Finally, with regard to the divisions of the divine attributes, their great diversity shows how little certainty attaches to the whole procedure and how little any division has been able to count on general agreement; but of some of them we can here give only brief indications. Some [1] put forward as chief division that into natural (also called metaphysical, which of course in the case of God must be the same thing) and the moral (which of course has a very objectionable sound, since it leads to the inference that the moral attributes do not belong to God in the same way).[2] Others first of all divide all divine attributes into active and inactive; but this is difficult to understand if God cannot be represented otherwise than as living, for in the living as such all is activity. The one class may indeed be described as inhering in God as determinations of the most perfect Substance, which include no activity *ad extra*; yet even the inactive attributes can be thought as possessing a purely inward activity; and in that case this division coincides with another, into absolute and relative attributes. Apart, however, from the fact that the presupposition of a creation in time implies either that the active attributes first came into being along with time or must previously have been inactive (and on this assumption the division is meaningless), the result is always a duality in God—a purely inner life in virtue of the inactive attributes, and a life related to the world in virtue of the active attri-

[1] Particular passages are not quoted, but the reader is referred to the doctrine of the divine attributes in Mosheim, Reinhard, and Schott.

[2] It would belong to the *locus* which some designate as *analogon accidentium.*

butes—and as in this way the two classes seem quite separated, still a third class of attributes might seem to be needed to combine them. Only if it be asked which are those inactive attributes, we find that there is really no inner life described by them ; in part they are simply formal, as unity, simplicity, eternity ; partly, like independence and unchangeability, they are merely negative ; and partly, as infinity and immeasurability, they are only the measure and quality of the active attributes. In addition, these divisions turn out not to be exhaustive, since often outside the division isolated attributes are added as inferences, *e.g.* blessedness, glory, majesty, or even that God is the Highest Good. Hence to avoid this kind of thing it at first sight seems commendable that some should from the outset divide the divine attributes into original and derived ; and although it is not easy to see how such a division could be made unless the attributes were themselves already given, it might be all the more genuinely dogmatic on that account. Yet, if it be generally conceded that the difference of the attributes is nothing real in God, each attribute is then only another expression for the whole Being of God, which remains always the same ; and consequently all are original, and the derived are not attributes at all in the same sense. But if the attributes so divided be developed from the religious self-consciousness, and the division in this sense be dogmatic, then again there would be no original attribute, but all would equally be very much derived. In fact, however, the division has not arisen from any such view, but from the view which holds that in another respect the Divine Essence alone may be regarded as original, and all the attributes derived. Such a derivation of the divine attributes from the Divine Essence would presuppose the latter as known, and would be a purely speculative proceeding. True, even the purely dogmatic presentation of the attributes can take no other form, except that here nothing can be taken as fundamental save that in the Divine Essence which explains the feeling of absolute dependence. But if the simple expression that 'everything depends upon God,' is further supplemented by the negative 'but He Himself upon nothing,' at once a fresh opening is given for a division into positive and negative attributes. And since here in the basis of division the relationship between the highest Essence and all other being is presupposed, it is evident that here absolute or inactive or natural or metaphysical attributes can only be considered as negative, and therefore, strictly taken, without definite content.

4. From this discussion it follows: (*a*) that the presupposition on which the idea is based that those attributes which express God's relation to the world have the appearance of mere additions and accidents, *i.e.* the presupposition of a separation between what God is, in and for Himself, and what He is in relation to the world, is also the source of the idea that the purely internal (*innerlichen*) attributes can only be conceived negatively; (*b*) that the rules laid down to secure the collection of all the divine attributes in one *locus* evoke conceptions which are quite foreign to the interests of religion, and result in a confusion of what it was intended to distinguish. We may hope, therefore, to solve our problem equally well without this apparatus and apart from any such collection if only we treat each individual part of our scheme as adequately as possible. Still, we too shall be able to make use of many of these formulas in our own way. For instance, since we have not to do as yet with the actual manifestation of religious self-consciousness in the form of pleasure and pain, but only with what lies uniformly at the root of these phenomena, *i.e.* with the inner creative disposition towards God-consciousness apart from the consideration whether it is hindered or encouraged, we may call those attributes which come up here 'original' in so far as the tendency itself is original, and we may call 'derived' those which will come to our notice in the Second Part. And in considering the manifestations of the religious self-consciousness, if we find that everything which would destroy His presence in us must specially be denied of God, and everything which favours His presence in us specially be affirmed of Him, we can say in our own way that thus divine attributes are formulated by the methods of removal of limits and negation; but those which arise from present observation, and there will be such, are reached by the method of causality. Still, this diverges fairly widely from the general usage of those formulæ, which rather betrays an analogy with speculation.

§ 51. *The Absolute Causality to which the feeling of absolute dependence points back can only be described in such a way that, on the one hand, it is distinguished from the content of the natural order and thus contrasted with it, and, on the other hand, equated with it in comprehension.*

1. We experience the feeling of absolute dependence as something which can fill a moment both in association with a feeling of partial and conditional dependence and also in association with a

partial and conditioned feeling of freedom; for self-consciousness always represents finite being as consisting in this mingling of conditioned dependence and conditioned freedom or of partial spontaneity and partial passivity. But whenever dependence or passivity is posited in a part of finite existence, then spontaneity and causality is posited in another part to which the former is related, and this condition of mutual relation of differently distributed causality and passivity constitutes the natural order. It necessarily follows that the ground of our feeling of absolute dependence, *i.e.* the divine causality, extends as widely as the order of nature and the finite causality contained in it; consequently the divine causality is posited as equal in compass to finite causality. And further, the feeling of absolute dependence stands in exactly the same relationship with the partial dependence-feeling as with the partial freedom-feeling, and so in that relationship the antithesis between these two last disappears; but finite causality is what it is only by means of its contrast with finite passivity, so it is to be inferred that the divine causality is contrasted with the finite. The divine causality as equivalent in compass to the sum-total of the natural order is expressed in the term, the divine *omnipotence*; this puts the whole of finite being under the divine causality. The divine causality as opposed to the finite and natural is expressed in the term, the divine *eternity*. That is, the interrelationship of partial causality and passivity makes the natural order a sphere of reciprocal action, and thus of change as such, in that all change and all alteration can be traced back to this antithesis. It is therefore just in the relationship in which the natural causality is set over against the divine, that the essence of the former is to be temporal; and consequently, so far as eternal is the opposite of temporal, the eternity of God will also be the expression of that antithesis.

In regard to what both terms according to general usage appear to imply as to something more than, and transcending, divine causality or the range of finite being—of this we shall speak in our further elucidation of both concepts. Here it is to be noted generally, that since these two ideas—omnipotence and eternity—are here related only to the divine causality, it may at once be proved in their case also that the individual attributes in their differences correspond to nothing real in God. It is always an inexactitude, which as such must be pointed out when we present these as two different attributes. For the divine causality is only equal in compass to the finite in so far as it is opposite to it in kind, since if it were like it in kind, as it is often represented as being in anthropomorphic ideas of God, it too would belong to the sphere of interaction and thus be a part of the totality of the natural order. In the same way, if the divine causality were not equal in compass to the finite, it could not be set over against it without at the same time disrupting the unity of the natural order ; because otherwise for some finite causality there would be a divine causality, but not for some other. Instead, therefore, of saying God is eternal and almighty, we should rather say He is almighty-eternal and eternal-almighty, or God is eternal omnipotence or almighty eternity. Still, in view of unavoidable comparisons with the more exact definitions of both attributes hitherto current, we must treat of each by itself.

2. It is however natural that, as people always started with a comparison of the divine causality with the finite, these two ideas should, in religious poetry as well as in religious speech, have been associated with two further ideas—the idea of eternity with that of omnipresence, and the idea of omnipotence with that of omniscience. If the two terms just dealt with completely corresponded with the two members of the relationship set forth in our proposition, we should not have to deal in the same manner with the two ideas just mentioned ; it would only be necessary to set forth precautionary rules to ensure that nothing should be included in the thought of them contrary to the two principal ideas and to our proposition. The situation, however, is not quite like that. The idea of eternity does, of course, express a contrast to the causality contained in the natural order, but primarily only as far as this is conditioned by time ; and actually it is conditioned just as much by space, and this no less in the case of the spiritual than of the corporeal. True, if we think of their equality in compass or comprehension, this itself implies that the finite causality everywhere in space is dependent upon the divine ; but the conception which expresses contrast is obscured by this relationship, and the complete expression of it is found only in eternity and omnipresence taken together.

Further, with regard to the conception of omniscience, it perhaps arose in the first place in the sphere of popular, poetical, and religious teaching, to indicate the relationship between God and that which goes on in man's inner life. In Dogmatics, however, it is always dealt with at this point, and taken in its widest application it belongs here; for we are accustomed to make an antithesis in the sphere of finite causality between living and 'dead' forces, and notwithstanding that in the doctrine of preservation even conscious finite causality is brought under the divine, the possibility is still not excluded (if once, rightly or wrongly, 'dead' forces are assumed) of conceiving the idea of omnipotence itself after the analogy of 'dead' forces. Since consciousness is the highest form of life known to us, this danger is averted by the idea of omniscience. Naturally, however, these additional attributes can just as little each for itself denote anything special and distinct in God as those set forth at the beginning; and as with reference to that pair it appeared that the most correct expression was to say that God, in His causality, was eternal omnipotence or the almighty-eternal, so this other pair of ideas also would best be included in a similar compound expression. But each of these two ideas also must in itself be an expression for the Divine Essence, because neither can betoken anything different in God; and thus omnipresence too, when ascribed to the divine causality, is itself eternity, and omniscience is itself omnipotence. But to express the identity of all these attributes in the briefest manner, still another usage may be chosen. If, that is, time and space everywhere represent externality, and we here always presuppose a something which, by extending itself in time and space, becomes an external object, in the same way the antithesis to time and space may be described as the absolutely inward. In the same way, if the term 'omniscience' well emphasizes the fact that omnipotence is not to be thought of as a 'dead' force, the same result would be reached by the expression 'Absolute Vitality.' And this pair, inwardness and vitality, would be just as exhaustive a mode of presentation, and one perhaps even more secure against all admixture of alien elements.

First Doctrine: God is Eternal

§ 52. *By the Eternity of God we understand the absolutely timeless causality of God, which conditions not only all that is temporal, but time itself as well.*

1. If the eternity of God be separated from His omnipotence, which is here confined to its special relation to eternity, it becomes only a so-called 'inactive' attribute; and thus is often described as infinity or immeasurability applied to time. To represent it

thus, however, would only encourage the representation of God apart from the manifestations of His power, an idea quite out of harmony with the religious consciousness and so quite empty for us. Such an idea would in any case include the antithesis of rest or idleness and activity, always suspect in relation to God, but in the sphere of Christian religion quite inapplicable. The religious consciousness, however (since we relate the world as such to God), becomes actual only as consciousness of His *eternal power*.[1] On the other hand, poetical representations express the eternity of God as an existence before all time; [2] but this cannot be taken up into didactic language without harm, for in this sphere a comparison of more or less can only be made between similars; but the divine causality, since time itself is conditioned by it,[3] must so much the more be thought of as utterly timeless.[4] This is achieved through expressions denoting the temporal, and therefore as it were pictorially, since the temporal oppositions of before and after, older and younger disappear in coincidence when applied to God.[5]

While, however, we relate the eternity of God to His omnipotence, and make it equal and identical therewith, it still does not by any means follow that the temporal existence of the world must reach back into infinity, so that no beginning of the world can be thought of.[6] For as what now arises in time is yet grounded in the omnipotence of God, and therefore willed and enacted by Him in an eternal, *i.e.* timeless, manner, the world also could be timelessly willed to emerge in the beginning of time. On the other hand, we need not be anxious lest, if the world is given no beginning or end, the difference between divine causality and causality within the natural order should be cancelled, and the world be as eternal as God. On the contrary, the eternity of God remains none the less unique, since the antithesis between the temporal and the

[1] Rom. 1[20]. [2] Ps. 90[2].

[3] Augustin., *de Gen. c. Man.* i. 3: Deus enim fecit et tempora . . . Quomodo enim erat tempus, quod Deus non fecerat, cum omnium temporum ipse sit fabricator.—The same meaning seems to be indicated by the phrase *ἄφθαρτος βασιλεὺς τῶν αἰώνων*, 1 Tim. 1[17].

[4] Aug., *Conf.* xi. 16: Nec tu tempore tempora praecedis, alioquin non omnia tempora praecederes; sed praecedis omnia celsitudine semper praesentis aeternitatis.—Boeth., p. 137: Interminabilis vitae tota simul et perfecta possessio. Aeternum necesse est et sui compos praesens sibi semper assistere, et infinitatem mobilis temporis habere praesentem.

[5] Augustin., *de Gen. ad litt.* viii. 48: Nullo temporum vel intervallo vel spatio incommutabili aeternitate et antiquior est omnibus, quia ipse est ante omnia, et novior omnibus, quia idem ipse post omnia. The same as 2 Pet. 3[8], in another form.

[6] Cf. Joh. Damasc., *c. Man.* vi.: *οὐ γὰρ πρότερον μὴ θέλων ὕστερον ἠθέλησεν, ἀλλ' ἀεὶ ἤθελεν ἐν τῷ ὑπ' αὐτοῦ ὡρισμένῳ καιρῷ γίνεσθαι τὴν κτίσιν.*

eternal is not in the least diminished by the infinite duration of time.[1]

2. But, of course, this relationship is much obscured by all explanations of the eternity of God which either equate it with apparent eternity,[2] *i.e.* endless time, or even merely compare it therewith.[3] Even the common formula to the effect that the eternity of God is the attribute in virtue of which He has neither begun nor will cease to exist, is of this kind. For since here only the terminal points of temporal duration are negated, while between them the existence of God is made equivalent to a temporal one, the intrinsically temporal character and the measurability of the Divine Being, and therefore also His activity through time, are not denied but rather indirectly affirmed. We must therefore reject as inadequate all those explanations which abrogate for God only the limits of time and not time itself, and would form eternity from time by the removal of limits, while in fact these are opposites. Even if poetical passages cannot describe eternity except by pictures of unending time,[4] the New Testament itself teaches us how for didactic purposes these must be supplemented.[5] While therefore it must be admitted of some theologians that, with Socinus, only for other dogmatic reasons, they have here rejected the perfectly scriptural statements of Augustine and Boethius, in the case of others that rejection can only be explained as due to the fear that if eternity be taken as timelessness nothing really is affirmed at all. But this can only happen if eternity is placed among the inactive attributes, while yet it is also thought that each such attribute by itself alone expresses the Essence of the Divine Being. On the other hand, it disappears if, as we demand, this conception is combined with that of omnipotence. For, in that a divine activity is posited, something may be posited, unknown indeed and perhaps not clearly conceivable, but by no means simply nothing. Indeed, finite being offers us some real help in

[1] Augustin., *de mus.* vi. 29: tempora fabricantur et ordinantur aeternitatem imitantia.—Idem, *de Gen. c. Man.* i. 4: Non enim coaevum Deo mundum istum dicimus, quia non ejus aeternitatis est hic mundus, cuius aeternitatis est Deus.

[2] Socin., *Praelectt.* cap. viii. : Nec vero in mundi creatione tempus primum extitit . . . quamobrem ipsius quoque Dei respectu aliquid praeteritum aliquid vero praesens, aliquid etiam futurum est. Mosheim, *Theol. dogm.* i. p. 254: Aeternitas est duratio infinita. Cf. Cudw., *Syst. intell.*, p. 780.—Reinh., p. 104: Aeternitas est existentiae divinae infinita continuatio, which assumes an inadmissible distinction between substance and existence in God.

[3] Eckermann, *Dogm.* i. p. 123, calls it a necessity, because he compares it with the immortality of the soul and the indestructibility of force.

[4] Job 36^{26}, Ps. 102^{28}

[5] Cf. 2 Pet. 3^{8} with Ps. 90^{2}.

conceiving the idea of eternity, since to a great degree time is merely an adjunct to finite being in so far as it is caused, and to a less degree in so far as it is cause. But in so far as finite being produces time-series with their content, thus remaining the same and identical with itself (as, *e.g.*, the Ego, as the enduring ground of all changing spiritual states, especially of resolves, each of which again as a moment of the Ego produces a concrete time-series), then, as the enduring causal ground relatively to the changing caused, it is posited as timeless. And with some such kind of analogy we must rest content.

Postscript: The Unchangeability of God

If the idea of eternity is thus conceived, there is no reason to introduce unchangeability as a separate attribute : it is already contained in the idea of eternity. For if God, in His relation to the world, conditioning its absolute dependence, is completely timeless, there is in His being no manifold of parts following one upon another. It appears to be different if, setting out from a distinction between substance and existence in God, eternity is presented merely as one aspect of unchangeability.[1] But for us it comes to the same thing, since the other aspect is an inactive attribute which expresses nothing actually present in the religious consciousness. We may do better, therefore, to take the principle, that God is unchangeable, merely as a cautionary rule to ensure that no religious emotion shall be so interpreted, and no statement [2] about God so understood, as to make it necessary to assume an alteration in God of any kind.

Second Doctrine: God is Omnipresent

§ 53. *By the Omnipresence of God we understand the absolutely spaceless causality of God, which conditions not only all that is spatial, but space itself as well.*

1. This proposition is quite similar in verbal form to the foregoing ; and the idea of omnipresence, indeed, is only taken up here because the contrast between the divine causality and the finite in the term eternity has been predominantly referred to time. It

[1] Cf. Reinhard, *Dogm.*, p. 105. If we regard unchangeableness in relation to the essence of God, it is simplicity; if in relation to His existence, it is eternity. But previously he had treated simplicity as a separate attribute, and eternity was unendingness contemplated as belonging to God's existence.

[2] Ex. 32^{14}, Jer. 26^{13} 42^{10}.

seems unnecessary then to do more than to carry over in the same form everything belonging to the former proposition, changing time into space. In religious poetry from of old, indeed, this conception has been more splendidly and more widely honoured than that of eternity.[1] Indeed, it must be said in general that far more religious moments evoke the idea of omnipresence, and therefore it is a more living idea and has a more general currency. The relation of God and time expressed in the conception of eternity, on the other hand, pervades the religious life to a lesser degree, and is marked by a colder tone in consequence. This is probably due to the fact that the majority of religious people are bound up in their consciousness with the present. The equivalence of divine causality with the whole content of the finite enables every act to excite the religious consciousness, every act, that is, in which we take up into ourselves a part of the natural order or identify ourselves with such a part, every moment of our self-consciousness as it extends over the whole world. And thus, whenever a person either moves or is moved, he is also drawn to a conscious apprehension of the power of the Highest directly near to him in all finite causality. It is natural, then, that we are far more prone to transfer ourselves in thought to the farthest point of space, which after all comes immediately to our apprehension, than to go back to the remotest time. And yet from our standpoint this difference appears unjustifiable, however natural it may be ; and it is incumbent on Dogmatics as a scientific discipline to see whether it can remove the discrepancy arising from the immediate juxtaposition in this way of the two ideas. At the same time it must take care lest the greater vividness of the conception now to be dealt with should be associated with a large admixture of the sensuous, and should be affected by it.

Now, just as the divine causality as eternity may easily appear to have lost its invariableness if the non-existence of the finite causality be asserted prior to its existence, in the same way a like result easily appears to hold in connexion with space. For we have to admit that finite causality is greater and less at different points in space ; least, *i.e.* where the space is occupied with so-called 'dead' forces, and greater where there is a greater development of life, and greatest where clear human consciousness is active, and so upwards. Now as against this it must be said, first of all, that, of course, no distinction in the almighty presence of God is hereby

[1] Ps. 139, and elsewhere in the Psalter.

posited, but only in the receptivity of the finite being to the causal activity of which the divine presence is related.[1] For thus the receptivity of man is greater for it than that of any other earthly being, but amongst men it is greatest in the religious. Yet even this only becomes plain when it is remembered that, according to the statement given in our proposition, the divine omnipresence ought to be thought of as completely spaceless,[2] and consequently not as greater or smaller at different places.

2. It is, however, difficult successfully to avoid all such definitions as put something spatial into the divine omnipresence, if we try to carry over the poetical and popular descriptions (which almost always set forth the space-conditioning causality of God by the figure of unlimited space itself), into the dogmatic sphere. It is no less difficult if we begin by looking on the divine omnipresence, without relation to the divine causality as an inactive attribute. In relation to the first, we may not without advantage employ the description of the divine causality, as current in Greek theology, by the expressions *ἀδιαστασία* and *συνουσία*—both, of course, related to God's almighty presence. For the negation of all remoteness expresses the contrast with finite causality, which—as well in the case of the spiritual as in that of the corporeal—becomes weakened by distance from its place of origin or central point, so that each force, as it is no longer present where it no longer works, is also less as such where it effects less. This difference it is which is denied, and thus an everywhere uniform self-identity of the divine causality is affirmed. The relation to space, however, which lurks in the expression 'not *outside* one another,' and thus also in '*everywhere* uniform self-identity,' applies only to the finite as that which is effected, but not to God. The same is to be noted of the term *συνουσία*, which can only lay down that finite causality is nowhere without the divine, but not also that the divine with the finite is in space. For not only is the *συνουσία ἐνεργετικὴ* related to finite causality, but also the *ὑποστατικὴ* in so far as it lays down the divine omnipresence as the maintenance of things in their being

[1] Joh. Damasc., *de fid. orth.* i. 13: *αὐτὸς μὲν γὰρ διὰ πάντων ἀμιγῶς διήκει, καὶ πᾶσι μεταδίδωσι τῆς ἑαυτοῦ ἐνεργείας κατὰ τὴν ἑκάστου ἐπιτηδειότητα καὶ δεκτικὴν δύναμιν.*

[2] Augustin., *de div. quaest.* xx.: Deus non alicubi est, quod enim alicubi est, continetur loco; et tamen quia est, et in loco non est, in illo sunt potius omnia quam ipse alicubi. Nec tamen ita in illo, ut ipse sit locus.—Idem, *Ep.* 187, 11: Et in eo ipso quod dicitur Deus ubique diffusus carnali resistendum est cogitationi . . . ne quasi spatiosa magnitudine opinemur Deum per cuncta diffundi, sicut aër aut lux.

and in their powers. Any other explanation would find it difficult to avoid the suspicion of a mixture of the divine being with the finite, and therefore a semblance of pantheism. This semblance belongs also very strongly to the definition that God is everywhere not *circumscriptivè* but *repletivè*. For when there is space-filling, we cannot get away from the analogy with expansive forces, and then the notion of an infinite extension to be predicated of God lies too near; and even the improvement which is introduced when we say that this is not to be understood corporeally (as though the existence of a finite in space were hindered by the divine space-filling), but in a divine way, is seldom interpreted with proper caution.[1] And if the expression used be that God includes all places in Himself,[2] this easily suggests the opposite, namely, that God is that which universally includes all things even spatially; and if this omnipresence be thought of as inactive instead of active, nothing almost remains except that God is that which is in itself empty. So, too, the kindred expression, that God Himself is the place of all things, ought on this very account to be used only with the greatest caution.[3] Hence in this matter there remains a fundamental improvement, one which removes the spatial element altogether, namely, the formula that God is in Himself;[4] but, of course, along with this it must be asserted that the effects of His causal being-in-Himself are everywhere. The same result is reached indirectly and, as it were, pictorially by the abrogation of spatial contrasts.[5] As far as other matters are concerned, the distinction between the divine omnipresence as an inactive and as an active attribute almost inevitably destroys the essential self-identity of the divine causality, and thus only produces confusion. If, for example, one distinguishes between the omnipresence of God so far as related to Himself and omnipresence in relation to the creatures,[6] and in

[1] This is to be commended in Joh. Damas., *l.c.*: *Ἔστι δὲ καὶ νοητὸς τόπος, ἔνθα νοεῖται καὶ ἔστιν ἡ νοητὴ καὶ ἀσώματος φύσις, ἔνθαπερ πάρεστι καὶ ἐνεργεῖ . . . ὁ μὲν οὖν θεὸς . . . λέγεται καὶ ἐν τόπῳ εἶναι, καὶ λέγεται τόπος θεοῦ, ἔνθα ἔκδηλος ἡ ἐνέργεια αὐτοῦ γίνεται.*

[2] Hilar., *d. f. Trin.* i. 6: Nullus sine Deo, neque ullus non in Deo locus est.

[3] Theoph., *ad Aut.* ii.: *Θεὸς γὰρ οὐ χωρεῖται, ἀλλ' αὐτός ἐστι τόπος τῶν ὅλων.*

[4] Augustin., *Ep.* 187, 14: Nullo contentus loco, sed in se ipse ubique totus.

[5] Augustin., *de Gen. ad litt.* viii. 48: incommutabili excellentique potentia et interior omni re quia in ipso sunt omnia, et exterior omni re, quia ipse est super omnia.—Hilar., *l.c.*: ut in his cunctis originibus creaturarum Deus intra extraque et supereminens et internus, id est circumfusus et infusus in omnia nosceretur, cum . . . exteriora sua insidens ipse, rursum exterior interna concluderet atque ita totus ipse intra extraque se continens neque infinitus abesset a cunctis, neque cuncta ei, qui infinitus est, non inessent.

[6] radicaliter et relative. Cf. Gerh., *loc. th.* t. iii. p. 136.

addition accepts a creation in time, then before creation there would only be the first kind of omnipresence and the other would be then added. Or if one makes the world finite in space, and thus, of course, at the limit supposes an always empty space outside, then again the first kind of omnipresence stretches further than the other, and it very easily comes to be said that in and for Himself God is outside the world, but, in relation to the creatures He is present only *in* the world—which introduces a similar inequality. Here, too, the Socinians have gone furthest,[1] but principally in order to avoid the appearance of pantheism,[2] which they thought could only be achieved in this way; for they could not quite free themselves from spatiality in thinking of the being and activity of God. And this becomes most clearly apparent when in defence of this view it is alleged that it is a perfection in finite things if their power extends further than their essence. As opposed to this, the everywhere-ness of God must, of course, be related equally to His essence and His power.

Postscript: The Immensity of God

It follows clearly that we shall not need to treat further of this term as the designation of a special divine attribute. Its use is bound up with the greatest difficulties.[3] Partly it is equated with the infinity of God, and in part it is derived therefrom; since of course infinity regarded as substance yields immensity, but regarded as existence eternity. But just as when taken so time is not done away in eternity, but only its limits; so too with immensity, it is not space but its limits that are abrogated;[4] and we should then in this way have only an omnipresence separated from omnipotence, and consequently conceived as inactive but always spatial. But if immensity is thought of as infinity itself, this again is frequently presented as the attribute of all God's attributes. In that case we should have no reason whatever to speak of it here, nor indeed would it ever come up for discussion; for in virtue of its negative content it could be no true attribute, not even of the attributes, but only a reservation with regard to

[1] Smalcius, *refut. Franc.*, p. 4: Essentia et praesentia Dei in locis omnibus nulla datur, nec enim frustra in coelis Deus esse dicitur.

[2] Thom. Pisecius, *respon. ad rat. Camp.*: Virtutem Dei infinitam permeare omnia scripturae testantur, non essentiam, cujus infinitate concessa universa orbis machina, quam cernimus, corpus quoddam divinum esset.

[3] Cf. Gerh., *loc. T.* iii. p. 122, and Reinhard, *Dogm.*, pp. 101–104.

[4] See Mosheim, *Theol. dogm.* i. p. 247: Quando infinitas cum respectu loci seu spatii consideratur dicitur *immensitas*.

them. It would then have to repudiate for all the attributes every analogy with the finite, and would be the general anti-anthropomorphic and anti-somatomorphic formula. As such it has guided us even here and will do so also in the future, without our finding it right on that account to erect it into an attribute. For since here we have to do only with the causality of God, the conception of the infinity of God is useful only as warding off analogy with finite causality. But all finite causality is measurable in time and space; consequently we have made the Divine infinite in the most proper sense, since we made it absolutely timeless and non-spatial. And the term immensity is easily brought round to equivalence with this proper meaning of infinity, if one only says *immeasurability*; because all measure may be resolved into time and space determinations. Immensity is usually defined by laying down, on the one hand, a being everywhere, and, on the other, a warning that this is not to be taken to imply extension. But once the activity of God has been separated from the being of God, and only the latter regarded, there of course remains for this immensity only a negation with no positive substratum which could have emerged from religious emotion. Whereas, on the contrary, it is self-evident that the contrast between the feeling of absolute dependence and the feeling of either partial dependence or partial freedom (both being equally spatial and temporal) includes in itself the implication that the causality which evokes the former feeling cannot be temporal and spatial.

Third Doctrine: God is Omnipotent

§ 54. *In the conception of the divine Omnipotence two ideas are contained: first, that the entire system of Nature, comprehending all times and spaces, is founded upon divine causality, which as eternal and omnipresent is in contrast to all finite causality; and second, that the divine causality, as affirmed in our feeling of absolute dependence, is completely presented in the totality of finite being, and consequently everything for which there is a causality in God happens and becomes real.*

1. Since the natural order is naught but the twofold mutually determined sum of the finite causing and the finite caused, the first part of our proposition first of all implies that each finite given as such, in virtue of its foundation in the divine omnipotence, effects everything which the causality implanted in it makes it capable of

effecting in the sphere of universal causality. It is, however, equally implied that every effect within the natural order is also, in virtue of its being ordained by the divine causality, the pure result of all the causes within the natural order, according to the measure in which it stands in relation with each of them. As now everything that we can regard as a separate thing for itself within the totality of finite being must be 'cause' as well as effect, there is never anything of any kind which can begin to be an object of the divine causality, though previously—hence somehow independent of God and opposed to Him—in existence. Rather on such a view (whether it be that the activity of the divine omnipotence as such begins in this way, or that by such opposition its activity is interrupted, whether seldom or often matters not), the foundation feeling of religion would thereby be destroyed. If this is not the immediate result, it at once appears when we extend our self-consciousness to cover the whole of finite being and so represent that object also; for then there would no longer be absolute dependence but only partial dependence.

Further, since divine omnipotence can only be conceived as eternal and omnipresent, it is inadmissible to suppose that at any time anything should begin to be through omnipotence; on the contrary, through omnipotence everything is already posited which comes into existence through finite causes, in time and space. Similarly, because a thing can be recognized as having happened through finite causation, it is not on this account the less posited through the divine omnipotence, nor is that which cannot be traced to finite causation the more on that account to be referred to divine omnipotence. Thus the divine omnipotence can never in any way enter as a supplement (so to speak) to the natural causes in their sphere; for then it must like them work temporally and spatially; and at one time working so, and then again not so, it would not be self-identical and so would be neither eternal nor omnipresent. Rather everything is and becomes altogether by means of the natural order, so that each takes place through all and all wholly through the divine omnipotence, so that all indivisibly exists through One.

2. The second part of our proposition rests upon the fact that in our sphere we only come to the idea of the divine omnipotence through the conception of the feeling of absolute dependence, and we lack any point of connexion for making demands upon the

divine causality which extend beyond the natural order embraced by this feeling. As against this it seems as though it might be said that what we call 'all' consists of the actual and the potential, and omnipotence must therefore embrace both of these; but that if it presents itself completely and exhaustively in the totality of finite being, then it includes only the actual but not also the potential. But how little the difference between actual and potential can exist for God will appear very clearly, if we only notice in what cases we ourselves chiefly apply it. We conceive, in the first place, much to be possible in a thing by virtue of the general conception of the species to which it belongs, which is not actual, however, because excluded by its special character; whilst in the case of other individuals of the same species other determinations, possible in virtue of the idea of the species, remain excluded for the same reason. Here, however, something appears to us as possible only because we find that the particularity of the individual is a problem we are never fully in a position to solve. But with regard to God such a distinction between the general and the individual is not applicable; in Him the species exists originally as the sum-total of its individual existences, and these in turn are given and established together with their place in the species, so that what does not hereby become actual, is also, so far as He is concerned, not potential. In the same way, we say that much is possible by virtue of the nature of a thing (when we take together its determinations by its species and as an individual being), which yet does not become actual because it is hindered by the position of the thing in the sphere of general interaction. We rightly make this distinction and attribute truth, as in the former case, to that which is thought of in this way as being possible, because it is only by this indirect method that we pass from the unfruitful sphere of abstractions and put together a view of the conditioned development of individual existence. On the other hand, if we could have taken into account for each point the influence of the whole system of interaction, we should then have had to say that what was not actual was also not possible within the system of nature. In God, however, the one is not separated from the other, that which exists for itself having one ground and the system of interaction another, but both these are grounded with and through each other, so that in relation to Him only that is possible which has its foundation in both equally. But every case which has any validity for us, may be reduced under one of these heads. The idea of a potentiality outside the sum of the actual[1] has no validity even for our minds; for not only does the religious self-consciousness not lead us to such a point, but, in addition, however we arrived at it, we should then have to accept a self-limitation of the divine omnipotence which can never be given in experience. Nor can we conceive any ground for such a self-limitation, unless that which is thought of as potential could enter into existence, not as an increase, but only in some way or other as a diminution of the actual, whereby the whole assumption is destroyed.[2]

3. Since in relation to God no distinction between the potential and the actual can be allowed, it is easy to pass judgment on the popular explanation of God's omnipotence, which has often been adopted even in scientific discussions, namely, that it is the attribute in virtue of which God is able to effect all that is possible, or all which contains no contradiction in itself. If, of course, contradiction is taken *realiter* and that is called contradictory which can find no place in the whole of existence, this is perfectly correct; for all the compossible is certainly produced by the divine omnipotence. Objection might still be made to the one point of saying that, in virtue of omnipotence, God *can* effect, not *does* effect, everything; for thereby a distinction is made between 'can' and 'will,' and the explanation comes near to another, namely, that omnipotence is the attribute by which God can do what He will. There is, however, as little distinction between 'can' and 'will' in God, as between the actual and the possible.[3] For whichever is greater than the other, the will or the ability, there is always a limitation, which can only be done away with if both be made equal in range. Moreover the very separation of each in itself, as though, that is, ability were a different condition from will, is an imperfection. For should I think of an ability without will, the will must proceed from an individual impulse, and so also always from a caused impulse; and should I think of a will without

[1] Statements such as that of Basil, *hom. I. in hexaëm.*: τὸν τοῦ παντὸς τούτου δημιουργὸν οὐχ ἑνὶ κόσμῳ σύμμετρον ἔχειν τὴν ποιητικὴν δύναμιν, ἀλλ' εἰς τὸ ἀπειροπλάσιον ὑπερβαίνουσαν, we must explain by the limits of contemporary knowledge of the universe, in contrast to which we have already arrived at the ἀπειροπλάσιον.

[2] Abelard rightly says, *Introd.* iii. 5: Potest, quod convenit, non convenit quod praetermittit, ergo id tantum facere potest, quod quandoque facit. Cf. August., *Enchirid.* 24: Neque enim ob aliud veraciter vocatur omnipotens, nisi quoniam quicquid vult potest.

[3] Joh. Damasc., *d. fid. orth.* i. 8, calls God indeed δύναμιν οὐδενὶ μέτρῳ γνωριζομένην, μόνῳ τῷ οἰκείῳ βουλήματι μετρουμένην. But this is only meant to bring out one side, for he says, i. 13: πάντα μὲν ὅσα θέλει δύναται, οὐχ ὅσα δὲ δύναται θέλει.

ability, the ability cannot be grounded in the inner power, but must be given from without. And if, since in God there is no willing through individual impulses, and no ability given from without, waxing and waning, the two in God cannot be separated even in thought, so also, since 'can' and 'will' together are necessarily doing, neither willing and doing are to be separated, nor 'can' and 'do,' but the entire omnipotence is, undivided and unabbreviated, the omnipotence that does and effects all. But it is useless to say anything further on this view on account of its inevitable separation between 'can' and 'will.'[1]

4. With the misunderstanding just exposed there are connected many distinctions within the divine omnipotence, as well as divisions of it, given currency especially by the scholastics, which can be ruled out without loss. To these belongs, in the first place, the contrast between a mediate and immediate, or absolute and ordered, exercise of the divine omnipotence, *i.e.* between cases when it acts without or with intermediary causes. Now when individual effects are referred some only to the former and some only to the latter, the distinction is false. For everything which happens in time and space has its determinations in the totality of that which is outside it in space and before it in time, however much they may be hidden, and so far come under the ordered power; and if some, to the exclusion of others, be referred back to the immediate power, the whole order of nature would be abrogated. If, however, we think not of the individual but of the world itself as the effect of the divine omnipotence, we have no choice but to recur to its immediate exercise. Hence in so far as we can apply the idea of creation in detail, we apply at the same time and equally the idea of the absolute exercise of omnipotence; but in so far as we use the idea (rightly understood) of concurrence or preservation,[2] in this aspect of it, everything is referred to the ordered exercise of power which establishes the dependence of each individual on the totality of existence eternally, and for the maintenance of the general interaction makes use of the forces of individual things. There is no point, however, which we can relate only to the absolute (which by way of stricter contrast we ought to call not 'unordered' but 'ordering') exercise of omnipotence and not to the ordered exercise and conversely.

[1] This is true of all such formulæ as Deus absoluta sua potentiâ multa potest, quae non vult nec forte unquam volet; or Nunquam tot et tanta efficit Deus, quia semper plura et majora efficere possit (cf. Gerh., *loc. theol.* i. pp. 132 f.).

[2] Cf. § 38. 1 and § 45, *Postscript*.

The case is similar with the distinction almost everywhere drawn between the divine will as absolute and as conditioned. It is clear that on this view ability is still made greater than will, because in the former no such distinction is drawn; and there arises a gradation, so that of what God can do some things He wills absolutely, some under conditions, and still others not at all. But it is by no means the case that God wills some things absolutely and others conditionally; just as with regard to every event there is something of which one can say, if this were not then that event would not be; so with regard to every individual thing—the fact that it exists and that it exists in this way—we can say that God wills it conditionally, because everything is conditioned by something else. But that whereby something else is conditioned is itself conditioned by the divine will; indeed in such a way that the divine will upon which the conditioning rests, and the divine will upon which the conditioned rests is not different in each case, but one only and the same; it is the divine will embracing the whole framework of mutually conditioning finite being: and this naturally is the absolute will, because nothing conditions it. In this way everything individual would be willed by God conditionally, but the whole willed absolutely as a unity. On the other hand, if for once we take an individual out of the order, and relate it *so* to the divine will, we shall have to say that each individual existing for itself, so far as we regard it not as conditioned by, but as co-conditioning the whole, is so fully willed by God as what it is, that everything else must be so, and cannot be otherwise than as follows from its action; which is as much as to say that it is absolutely willed by God. In this respect, therefore, it can be said that every individual, so far as it must be affected by the rest, is also only conditionally willed by God; but, of course, not as though on that account it were any the less willed, or any the less came to reality. Everything, however, so far as it is itself effective, and in various ways conditions other things, is absolutely willed by God.

But the whole idea of the divine omnipotence appears most endangered, when an active and an inactive, and a free and a necessary, divine will are set one over against the other. The *necessary* will would be related to what God wills in virtue of His essence, the *free* to that which, so far as His essence is concerned, He could just as well not will; [1] where it is assumed that it does

[1] Gerh., *loc. th.* iii. p. 203: *Ex necessitate naturae* vult quae de se ipso vult,

not belong to His essence to reveal Himself. Thus by means of the necessary will God wills Himself, and by means of the free will He wills what is other than Himself. But a 'self-willing' of God is always a most awkward formula, and almost inevitably raises the hair-splitting question whether, just as the world exists by reason of His free will, so also God exists because, by reason of His necessary will, He wills Himself, or whether He wills Himself because He is. Or, to express it rather differently, whether this self-willing is more in the way of self-preservation, or more in the way of self-approval, or (if both are taken together) after the manner of self-love.[1] Now since self-preservation can scarcely be thought of as a real will unless there is something to be striven for or averted,[2] and self-approval almost necessarily implies a divided consciousness, it is easily seen that this self-willing can mean nothing but the very existence of God posited under the form of will. But this, which is in God purely inward and related solely to Himself, can never come into our religious self-consciousness. In any case, therefore, this necessary will of God, as in no way belonging here, would fall under speculative theology. Moreover, it seems that this contrast cannot be applied to God at all, and what has been brought under the contrasted heads respectively is not really separable. For where such a contrast exists the necessary must be unfree, and the free be grounded in no necessity, and so arbitrary. Each, however, is an imperfection; and consequently this contrast has its place solely in that existence in which each being is co-determined by the rest. We must therefore think of nothing in God as necessary without at the same time positing it as free, nor as free unless at the same time it is necessary. Just as little, however, can we think of God's willing Himself, and God's willing the world, as separated the one from the other. For if He wills Himself, He wills Himself as Creator and Sustainer, so that in willing Himself, willing the world is already included; and if He wills the world, in it He wills His eternal and ever-present omnipotence, wherein willing Himself is included; that is to say, the necessary will is included in the free, and the free in the necessary. Obviously, too,

nulla re sive extra se sive intra se permotus. *Libere* vult, quae de creaturis vult, quae *poterat* et velle et nolle.

[1] Wegscheider, *Institt.*, § 67: Voluntas necessaria, *i.e.* actus voluntatis quae e scientia necessaria promanare dicitur, amor nimirum quo Deus . . . se ipsum complectatur necesse est.

[2] Many, of course, still describe the divine will in this way, *e.g.* Mosheim, *Th. dogm.*, p. 277: actus appetendi quae bona sunt et aversandi quae mala sunt.

there is nothing in the way in which God comes into our religious self-consciousness which corresponds to this contrast, and it lacks dogmatic content.

And finally as to the contrast between the *active* and *inactive* divine will: it first of all contradicts the generally recognized proposition that the divine will extends no further than divine ability.[1] For how should a true and real will be inactive unless it lacked the ability? But it is to be noted that the one all-embracing divine will is identical with the eternal omnipotence; and if then, as eternal, it is timeless, the content of no definite time can quite correspond with it, and so from this point of view the divine will is always inactive. But it is also always active, because there is no fraction of time which does not pass in fulfilment of it, and what seems to resist or repress the divine will is always simply co-operating in its temporal fulfilment.[2] If, then, we hold this fast and distinguish between will and command, it is quite unnecessary to deal with the idea of a precedent and a consequent will, expressions which again suggest the appearance of a change in the will of God.

Postscript: The Independence of God

If the feeling of absolute dependence comprises a reference to divine omnipotence, it is no longer necessary to bring out the independence of God as a special attribute. For if one remains at all true to the derivation of the word, it is, as the opposite of that dependence in which we find ourselves, simply a negative attribute and, as it were, a shadow-picture of omnipotence, and only states that God has no foundation or cause of His being outside Himself, which coincides with the scholastic '*aseitas*,' virtually 'existence-from-self.' If, now, this be changed into a formula of quite similar content, namely, that in relation to God there can be no question of a ground, one sees at once how this is already completely contained in our two main conceptions, eternity and omnipotence. But, of course, the term independence is dealt with in very different ways. Some include in the idea that God is Lord over all.[3] But

[1] Cf. Gerh., *loc. th.* i. p. 154: Praeter voluntatem non indiget aliqua potentia.

[2] On this are also based the formulæ of Augustine, to which we must always come back, *Enchirid.* 26: Omnipotentis voluntas semper invicta est—nec nisi volens quicquam facit, et omnia quaecunque vult facit. 27: dum tamen credere non cogamur aliquid omnipotentem Deum voluisse fieri, factumque non esse.

[3] Reinhard's *Dogm.*, p. 106: Independentia est illud attributum, quo nemini quicquam debet, et ipse solus est omnium rerum dominus.—Joh. Damasc., *de orth. fid.* i. 19, can scarcely have regarded αὐτεξούσιος (which, for

Lordship is connected with independence only on the presupposition that the independent is at the same time in need of something, for otherwise one can be completely independent without having even the slightest Lordship. Thus if the divine attributes are to be separated at all, this combination is not practicable. Then if 'indebted to no one' has only a moral sense, and denies the applicability of the conception of obligation in relation to God, the conception is thereby divided, and there is, according to the usual procedure, a physical and a moral independence. About the latter we have nothing to say here; and since 'to be Lord over all' can be only an expression of omnipotence (if, that is, we leave out in advance the moral consideration which here too enters, that God as Lord cannot be obligated, *i.e.* can stand under no law), we have nothing left but the above-mentioned 'existence-from-self' of God—a speculative formula which, in the dogmatic sphere, we can only convert into the rule that there is nothing in God for which a determining cause is to be posited outside God. But this is so clearly defined in our first explanation,[1] that it is unnecessary to bring it up specially here.

Fourth Doctrine: God is Omniscient

§ 55. *By the divine Omniscience is to be understood the absolute spirituality of the divine Omnipotence.*

1. This explanation is quite in keeping with the manner in which we arrived at this conception above.[2] And yet even here it is to be premised that everywhere it is chiefly intended much more to bring out the truth that the divine causality should be thought of as absolutely living than that a similarity should be definitely established between God and that which we designate as spirit in the existence presented to us. The former is essential if the feeling of absolute dependence, or piety, is to be true and real; for a lifeless and blind necessity would not really be something with which we could stand in relation; and such a necessity, conceived as equal to the whole of finite causality yet contrasted with it, would really mean positing the latter alone, and thus declaring an absolute dependence unreal, because as self-caused beings we are not absolutely dependent on finite causality. But to define the similarity

the most part, corresponds to *independent*) as forming one predicate together with αὐτοκρατής and ἀνενδεής.

[1] Cf. § 4, 4.

[2] § 51, 2.

between God and the spiritual in a finite sense is certainly a problem only to be solved by endless approximation; for owing to the intermixture of receptivity and passivity in some degree to be found (even if unrecognized) in every available term, we inevitably co-posit something which must then be got rid of again by the use of some other term. If then here (where we are considering the feeling of absolute dependence only in its essence, and so have to do with the divine causality also only in its essence), Spirituality be denoted by the function of knowing, our first rule must be to exclude from the spirituality of the Divine Essence everything which necessarily contains in itself receptivity or passivity. Therefore just as the divine will must not be thought of as a faculty of desire, so the divine omniscience must not be considered as a perceiving or experiencing, a thinking together or a viewing together. Now since we are acquainted with no other kind of knowledge than that in which spontaneity and receptivity pervade each other, only in different degrees, we distinguish, according as one of the two predominates, between the knowledge which is chiefly constructed from within and that which is chiefly derived from without; and still more, since the greater part of our thinking presupposes existence as its object, and is related only slightly to our productive activity, we distinguish between the purposive activity of thought upon which production follows, and the observing activity which relates to something already present. But this last distinction is completely inapplicable to God, for there are no objects of observation for Him other than those which exist through His will, but the divine knowledge is exclusively a knowledge of the willed and produced, not a knowledge for which an object could be given from any other source.[1] Indeed, since there is for Him no succession, it can never be said that in Him the purposive thought-activity precedes the will-activity.[2] In consequence of the above, there can be in God no distinction between resolving and the execution of the resolve (where in our case purposive ideas remain wholly or in part ideal), since otherwise the divine omnipotence would not perfectly express itself in the finite.[3] Just as little can any activities more analogous with the corporeal or any kind of matter[4] be added to the divine

[1] This is Calvin's meaning, *Instit.* iii. 23. 6: Quum nec alia ratione quae futura sunt praevideat, nisi quia ut fierent decrevit; where only the idea of seeing *beforehand* is awkward. Erigena puts it better, *de praedest.*, p. 121: Ea ergo videt quae facere voluit, neque alia videt, nisi ea quae fecit.

[2] Idem, *ibid.* p. 125: Non in eo praecedit visio operationem, quoniam coaeterna est visioni operatio.

[3] Cf. § 53, 2.

[4] Cf. Anselm, *Monol.* cap. xi.

thinking, so as to make its object real. Hence the divine thinking is the same as the divine will, and omnipotence and omniscience are one and the same. And since in God there is no duality between thought and word (nay, even the term 'word' can only mean the activity of the thought outwards), this precisely is the point expressed in all formulæ which exhibit the divine Word as creating and preserving; and it is quite correct to say, as has been said in multifarious ways, that everything exists by reason of God's speaking or thinking it.[1]

Since then this divine knowledge is recognized as the very productivity of God, the creative as well as the preservative, it follows at once that it is entirely the same divine knowledge which constitutes the divine omniscience and the divine wisdom.[2] If the two are separated, something out of our existence is transferred to God, which even if we make it infinite can still be for Him only an imperfection. Since it is the least part in the existence which surrounds us that proceeds from our own activity, a knowledge of things independent of our influence upon them certainly is for us a good and a perfection. But if in thought we shut off the sphere of our formative production by itself, for all that it is so limited, then it will always indicate an imperfection if the later cognition by the artist of the whole of his works contains something besides what was in his purposive idea, whether it be that the original image or the formative activity was imperfect, or that the sphere was not so completely shut off but that some foreign influence could have told upon his works. But now the world as the whole content of the divine formation and production is so self-enclosed that there is nothing external which could gain an influence upon it. Thus every distinction in content between wisdom and omniscience must presuppose an imperfection in God. But even as to form, a distinction between the two can hardly be granted; for neither can the one have a more inner and the other a more outward origin, nor can the one be more and the other less bound up with the divine will. If omniscience is simply the absolute livingness of the divine will, this must be just as true of the divine

[1] Hilar. in *Ps. cxviii. sgm 4:* Ergo omne ex quo vel in quo mundi totius corpus creatum est, originem sumit ex dicto, et subsistere in id, quod est ex verbo Dei, coepit.—Anselm, *Monol.* cap. xii.: Quicquid fecit, per suam intimam locutionem fecit, sive singula singulis verbis, sive potius uno verbo simul omnia dicendo.

[2] Augustin., *de div. qu. ad Simpl.* ii. 2. 3: Quamquam et in ipsis hominibus solet discerni a sapientiâ scientia . . . in Deo autem nimirum non sunt haec duo sed unum.

wisdom, if wisdom be a comprehensive name for the divine purposes.

Hence it can only be from a special point of view that wisdom is regarded as a special attribute, and in this respect there will be something to say about it elsewhere. But it also follows, that finite existence must merge as completely in the divine knowledge as in the divine omnipotence, and that in finite existence the divine knowledge is exhibited as completely as the divine omnipotence; so that when both are held one against another, there is nothing left in the divine knowledge to which there is no correlative in existence, or which stands in a different relationship to existence, so that the latter would always have to be presupposed in order that the former might be posited. Or, to put it briefly, God knows all that is; and all that God knows is, and these two are not twofold but single; for His knowledge and His almighty will are one and the same.

2. It is in the light of what has already been said that the further, and for the most part later, definitions concerning divine omniscience must be judged. Of these it may, of course, be said in general that they transfer to God human activities, so conceived as still to include imperfection, and in such a way that by illimitation the imperfection is by no means done away. The first case where this holds good is when, in God's knowledge of existence, perception, memory, and prescience are distinguished, and then the divine omniscience, as the absolutely perfect cognition of things, is made up compositely of these three.[1] For as the same thing which now is present directly after is past, as it was previously future, in God all these three kinds of knowledge must either be simultaneous even for the same object, in which case the distinctions would be quite blurred by their simultaneity; or, if they remain distinct and outside one another, they must follow one upon another even in God, according as the thing known passes out of the future into the past. And then this means that in the case of the divine knowledge the rule that in God there is no change is broken.[2] If

[1] So Reinhard, *Dogm.*, § 25: Omniscientia divina est attributum, quo omnium rerum cognitionem habet longe perfectissimam. But this very superlative contains in it an analogy, and thus ascribes to the divine knowledge a similarity with that of finite beings, thus making it temporal. From this we get praescientia, visio, and reminiscentia.

[2] Augustin., *l.c.*: Quid est enim praescientia, nisi scientia futurorum? Quid autem futurum est Deo, qui omnia supergreditur tempora? Si enim scientia Dei res ipsas habet, non sunt ei futurae sed praesentes, ac per hoc non jam praescientia sed tantum scientia dici potest. Si autem sicut in ordine temporalium creaturarum, ita et apud eum nondum sunt, quae futura sunt,

then we say (as indeed already by combining opposites we have often sought to present the divine as raised above all opposition) that the perfect knowledge of a thing's existence for itself is the same as the knowledge of the inner law of its development, and the perfect knowledge of a thing's place in the sphere of universal interaction is one with the knowledge of the influence of all other things on it, but that both these perfect kinds of knowledge form in God one and the same timeless knowledge, determining the existence of the object, while with us both are incomplete and so temporally distinct, because our knowledge does not determine the existence of a thing, but is determined by it—then we have at least an indication as to how to avoid as far as possible too great a humanizing of the divine knowledge.[1]

Nor is a better scheme achieved by the division into *free* or intuitive knowledge and *necessary* knowledge or pure thought;[2] for as the first member comprehends in itself those three modes of thought already noticed, the other would comprehend that divine knowledge which would have God Himself and all that is possible for its object.[3] It must strike everyone as peculiar as well as most unfortunate that under one name there should be comprised God's knowledge of Himself, and His knowledge of that which is merely possible. For whether one thinks of the merely possible as including only that which never becomes real, or whether one also includes that which comes to reality, in abstraction from its reality, God always remains that which is truest and most original, but the simply possible that which is most shadow-like and ineffectual; so that such a combination almost assumes that God knows even Himself only through an abstract shadow-like presentation.[4]

sed ea praevenit sciendo, bis ergo ea sentit, uno quidem modo secundum futurorum praescientiam, altero vero secundum praesentium scientiam. Aliquid ergo temporaliter accedit scientiae Dei quod absurdissimum et falsissimum est.

[1] Augustin., *l.c.*: Cum enim demsero de humana scientia mutabilitatem et transitus quosdam a cogitatione in cogitationem, cum . . . de parte in partem crebris recordationibus transilimus . . . et reliquero solam vivacitatem certae atque inconcussae veritatis una atque aeterna contemplatione cuncta lustrantis, immo non reliquero, non enim habet hoc humana scientia, sed pro viribus cogitavero: insinuatur mihi utcumque scientia Dei; quod tamen nomen, ex eo quod sciendo aliquid non latet hominem potuit esse rei utrique commune.

[2] Scientia libera or visionis and scientia necessaria or simplicis intelligentiae.

[3] Gerhard, *loc. th.* i. p. 148 note.

[4] This is only very slightly modified by such a remark as that of Thomas (in Gerh., *l.c.*): Deus se ipsum videt in se ipso, quia se ipsum videt per essentiam suam: alia a se videt non in ipsis sed in se ipso, in quantum essentia sua continet similitudinem aliorum ab ipso. Here the question is rather of the actual, and the meaning really is that God knows about finite

Thus we should have to admit besides a divine self-consciousness partaking of the nature of intuitive knowledge and resembling it; the latter would be the living consciousness of God in His reality, but the former an inactive and, as it were, passive element of the Divine Essence. Only, since all are at one in asserting that God's essence and God's attributes (and so also the active attributes) are one and the same, this distinction comes to nothing, as also does this aspect of pure thought in God. Next, the one description appears to be formed very much on the analogy of the fact that with us the indefinite idea of what is simply possible must have an immediate sense-impression added to it, if it is to pass over into the consciousness of an object as real. If now in all cases perceptual knowledge is richer in content than pure thought (since the former has a real existence corresponding to it and the latter has not), and if none the less finite existence is dependent on divine thought, the question inevitably arises why God, who must will to have the absolute maximum of cognition in Himself, knows with intuitive knowledge only *some* of what is possible, *i.e.* that which at any time becomes real, and not *all*. And if we do not wish to fall back upon simple arbitrariness, which in thought is always an imperfection, and so a self-diminution of God, there can hardly be any other answer to this question than that some of what is possible lacks the possibility of existing along with the rest. But that, the existence of which conflicts with the existence of all else, is also contradictory to itself. Thus there is no divine knowledge of it even on the traditional explanation of the divine omniscience, for the self-contradictory is neither a thing nor cognizable. But if we look at the matter from the point of view of the other description, that intuitive knowledge is free, while the other is necessary, then (since the free is something other than the necessary), God thereby is brought under this antithesis, and the necessity whereby anything not free exists in Him is not anything in Him (otherwise it would be His freedom itself), but something outside and above Him—which conflicts with the conception of the Supreme Being.

From the foregoing it is now very easy to conclude what is to be held regarding the so-called *mediate knowledge* of God,[1] by means of which He would know just what would have resulted had something happened which did not happen. It rests altogether upon

being in the same way that He knows about Himself without reference to the possible.

[1] Scientia media also futuribilium, or de futuro conditionato.

the assumption of a possible outside the real, which we have already put aside. As soon, then, as we express it so, namely, that God knows what would have resulted if at any point the impossible had become real, this knowledge, as a whole, dissolves into nothing, because what rests solely upon the becoming real of the impossible is itself impossible. However, even apart from this it would follow that if anywhere even for God anything is possible outside the real, then infinitely much is possible at every point, and as each point is co-determinant for all the rest, a different world arises for each case from each point. The infinitely many times infinitely many worlds which thus, infinitely often, are formed (amid which the real world is lost as something infinitely small), are thus the object of this mediate knowledge—an object which still multiplies itself to infinity, if one considers that the necessary knowledge of God already of itself contains an infinite number of worlds originally different from the real world, for each of which again there obtains a mediate knowledge just as full as that which relates to the real world. So, measured thus, even the works of the divine omnipotence appear in the divine omniscience as something infinitely small in comparison with what omnipotence does not bring to reality, and consequently there is in God eternally and imperishably a mass of rejected thoughts ; and, if we accept this mediate knowledge, the imperfection of a human artist, who, because his formative capacity is fluctuating and uncertain, thinks out the individual parts of his work in various ways other than as he afterwards fashions them, will, freed from all limitations and made infinite, be transferred to God. Looked at by itself, this whole apparatus of rejected thoughts is simply a knowledge of nothing ; and it can only have a meaning if we could suppose that God also decides and produces by choice and deliberation, a view which from of old every form of teaching in any degree consistent has repudiated.[1] Hence it would have been far safer, if one does start from what is human, to transfer to God, illimited and perfect, the certainty of the perfect artist, who in a state of inspired discovery thinks of nothing else, to whom nothing else offers itelf, save what he actually produces. This also agrees very well with the story of the Creation, which knows nothing of any intervening deliberation and deciding choice, but keeps contemplation entirely to the end,

[1] Joh. Damasc., *d. f. orth.* ii. 22 : χρὴ δὲ γινώσκειν, ὅτι ἐπὶ θεοῦ βούλησιν μὲν λέγομεν, προαίρεσιν δὲ κυρίως οὐ λέγομεν· οὐ γὰρ βουλεύεται θεός· ἀγνοίας γάρ ἐστι τὸ βουλεύεσθαι· περὶ γὰρ τοῦ γινωσκομένου οὐδεὶς βουλεύεται.

where it appears simply as absolute approval, without ascribing to God any contemplation of what He did not make or any comparison of the real world with those possible worlds. If, however, the edifying and tranquillizing effect of the conception of such a mediate knowledge of God be alleged,[1] what that really amounts to is this, that, if we lift ourselves up to the religious consciousness in our pain over disappointed expectations, we should think that our wishes were also among God's thoughts, but amongst the rejected. But (we may take it) true religious submission makes no such demand as that God should have had our foolish thoughts as His own, but is content with seeing from the result that our plans were not contained in that original or rather eternal sanction.

The name 'mediate knowledge' does, however, call for special consideration, since its reference can only be to the naming of the other two kinds of knowledge. Should it be a mediate between the necessary and the free, then God would be (as it were) more tied up in thinking that which from a given point is possible than in thinking the real, in spite of the fact that the last presents the greatest degree of 'tied-up-ness,' namely, the whole of the natural order. Or if the free knowledge of God is at the same time the productive, the mediate would present a transition from productivity to the idle, ineffective activity of pure thought. Thus the mediate, as a diminishing production, would be, as it were, the divine preservation and co-operation restraining itself in all directions, as in us the ever-stimulating idea of the real shades off into that of the probable, still lively-coloured and affecting us through hope and fear, and then loses itself in indifferent shadow-pictures of the merely possible. But we may reasonably hesitate to transfer such things from ourselves to God. If, however, this knowledge is the mean between perceptual and pure thought, it affords a passage from the former to the latter, which is inconceivable without a diminution of living power. And so, even from this point of view, we reach the final result, that the possible as distinct from the real cannot be an object of the divine knowledge.

3. If one adds to this the fact that unquestionably there exists at least a strong appearance as though, on the one side, a dual self-consciousness—an original and a reflected—were attributed to God, and as though, on the other, the piece-by-piece character of His knowledge were being assumed, it follows that till now the theory of these divine attributes has transferred to the Supreme

[1] Reinhard, *Dogm.*, p. 112.

Being all the imperfections of our consciousness. The appearance of a dual consciousness issues from the fact that the whole of God's knowledge about Himself (which is similar to His knowledge of all that is possible, as it remains wholly separate from the Divine activity) can only be thought of as objective and indeed on the lines of our most abstract knowledge ; yet as such it cannot be the only knowledge He possesses, but has necessarily beside it an original knowledge. This, indeed, does not come out immediately in the language of the Schools, but mediately, and as presupposed wherever emotional excitations attributed to God in popular preaching and religious poetry are treated dogmatically—which means that there is all too easily suggested such a sensibility on the part of the Supreme Being as destroys the basal relationship of absolute dependence. But such excitation of itself always implies the second imperfection we have to prove—the piece-by-piece quality of knowledge in God. For it is only the influence of a definite moment (which we feel is making such a demand upon us that in relation to it something must happen) that evokes an emotion in us. And so for a right theory on this point there is nothing left but the formula that God is related to the object in an eternal and omnipresent way, as in us the evocation of the emotion is related to the momentary impression. Then there will no longer be any cause either to introduce in the divine self-consciousness the above-mentioned contrast between original and reflected, or even to make a contrast between the latter and the objective, to avoid which the above formula [1] was chosen. The second point, namely, the piece-by-piece character of the divine knowledge, still lurks curiously in the treatment of the question whether even the trivial is an object of the divine knowledge. For this question could simply not have been raised if a start had been made from the formula that God knows each in the whole, as also the whole in each—a formula which utterly abolishes the contrast between great and small, and which alone is correct because already given in the idea of a settled natural order. This, however, follows of itself on the customary method of illimitation, for in fact we consider even a human consciousness more perfect the more there is present to it in each individual moment.

And this leads us to consider still further, in the light of this divine attribute, a subject which might really be regarded as already done with,[2] namely, whether the divine knowledge about

[1] Page 217, l. 29. [2] § 49.

the free actions of men can co-exist with their freedom. Most thinkers, indeed, perhaps even the Socinians, would have felt ashamed to answer the question in the negative, or even to raise it, if they had reflected that in that case not only could there have been no further question of an eternal decree of God regarding salvation, but that history in general would become something which God only gradually experienced, and consequently the idea of providence must be wholly given up.[1] If, then, the temptation to answer the question in the negative, and the need to raise it is grounded in the interests of human freedom, it must be considered that one's own foreknowledge of free actions and the foreknowledge of others must destroy freedom still more than divine foreknowledge does. And yet we deem those people least free who cannot in general know their actions beforehand, *i.e.* those who are not conscious of any definite course of action. But in such cases this special foreknowledge is lacking only because foreknowledge is lacking of the special relevant outer conditions and inner conditions produced from without. In the same way we estimate the intimacy of relationship between two persons by the foreknowledge one has of the actions of the other, without supposing that in either case the one or the other's freedom has thereby been endangered. So even divine foreknowledge cannot endanger freedom.

Appendix to the Second Section: Some other Divine Attributes

§ 56. *Among the divine attributes usually mentioned, the Unity, Infinity, and Simplicity of God especially might conveniently come in here, as having no relation to the antithesis in the excitations of the religious consciousness; only they could not be regarded as divine attributes in the same sense as those already dealt with.*

1. The attributes mentioned here are not related (as are those to be dealt with in the Second Part of this Dogmatic) to the ease or difficulty with which the consciousness of God develops in us at different moments; and so far they would belong here, if they

[1] The Socinian principle when fully applied really seems to imply this. We may find directly contrasted formulæ in Augustine, *de civ. Dei* v. 9: Non est consequens ut si Deo *certus* est causarum omnium ordo, ideo nihil sit in nostrae voluntatis arbitrio; and in Socin., *Praelect.* cap. viii.: Namque non entium nullae sunt qualitates. Atqui ea quae nec fuerunt nec sunt, nec *certo* futura sunt, nullo modo sunt, itaque ea Deo praesentia esse nequeunt. Eiusmodi autem sunt voluntariae hominum actiones, quae nondum revera extiterunt.

had any dogmatic content. But this they lack because, unlike the other four, they do not issue from the relationship between the feeling of absolute dependence and the sensibly stimulated self-consciousness, nor are they statements about it. But even the three attributes here appended stand in close relationship with the four former ones, in so far at least as they negate, if only in a pictorial way, the similarity of divine and finite causality; but not even such a place can be given them in Dogmatics. There arises then only the question whether to turn these expressions out of our province, and send them back to the speculative doctrine of God, or whether there is really some meaning to be gained from them for Dogmatics. This, however, must be examined in each instance by itself, since we cannot maintain in advance that in this respect they are in the same case.

And first as to the *Unity* of God—strictly taken it can never be an attribute of a thing that it only exists in a definite number. It is not an attribute of the hand to be dual; but it is the attribute of a man to have two hands, and of a monkey to have four. In the same way it could be an attribute of the world to be ruled by One God only, but not of God to be One only. And so if a divine attribute is here in question, we must turn away from mere number; and in that case what we have first to insist upon is the general expression that God has no equal,[1] which, of course, our language can more distinctly express by 'uniqueness.' And inasmuch as many similars are always of the same kind or species, the individual beings representing the existence of the species and the species the essence of the individuals, it might be said that the unity or uniqueness of God is that attribute in virtue of which there is no distinction of essence and existence. Now this as such could belong only to speculative theology. But if, on the other hand, we abstract from what in strictness must be understood by an attribute, and if we consider that the excitations of the religious consciousness are individual moments, while that upon which in those excitations we feel ourselves absolutely dependent is not objectively given, then this term 'unity' expresses the fact that all those excitations are meant and comprehended as indications of One, and not of many. And, indeed, if we go back to the earlier explanation of the original meaning of the expression, 'God,' [2] what is stated in the expression

[1] Mosheim, *Th. dogm.* i. p. 241: Quando ergo dicimus Deum esse unum, negamus Deum habere socium.

[2] Cf. § 4, 4.

'unity of God' is that this homogeneity (*Zusammengehörigkeit*) of the religious excitations is given with the same certainty as these excitations themselves. Since now it is only on the assumption of this homogeneity that concepts of divine attributes can be developed from observation of the content of religious moments, this expression, the 'unity of God,' is not so much a single attribute as the principle of monotheism,[1] lying from the first at the foundation of all inquiry into the divine attributes, and can no more be proved than the existence of God itself. In fact an attempt to discuss this unity further or to prove it will scarcely be able altogether to escape making a distinction between the idea of God and the idea of the Supreme Being. Moreover, these attempts always occur in controversy with Polytheism[2] and, indeed, proceed from the assumption that the same idea underlies both. This assumption, however, we have already discarded.

The term *Infinity* is likewise too negative to be a proper attribute-conception; and indeed it has been dealt with in very different ways. The customary explanation,[3] 'negation of limits,' is most indefinite. For if one had already a description of the Supreme Being, there could be no question at all of any possibility of conceiving this as limited. But if this description is first formed by means of the term 'infinite' itself, we can see that all we have is a precautionary rule for the formation of ideas of divine attributes, the rule, *i.e.*, that attributes which cannot be conceived as without limits ought not to be ascribed to God; and thus indirectly infinity becomes an attribute of all the divine attributes. Hence every discussion leads over to other attributes which partake of infinity.[4] Only it is a sign that even this rule is not being properly applied to the formation of the divine attributes, if instead of taking omnipotence as the infinity of the divine productivity and omniscience as the infinity of the divine thought, one distinguishes rather between an infinity of substance and an infinity of existence; and so a distinction which has to do with the finite only is made fundamental in the description of the Divine Being. For infinite does not really mean that which has no end, but that which is in con-

[1] It is rightly taken so in Rufinus, *Expos. symb.*: Deum non numero unum dicimus sed universitate.

[2] Lactant., i. 3: Virtutis perfecta natura non potest esse nisi in eo, in quo totum est . . . Deus vero si perfectus est . . . non potest esse nisi unus ut in eo sint omnia.

[3] Mosheim, *l.c.*, p. 299: Infinitas itaque sic absoluta nihil aliud est, quam absentia finium in Deo.

[4] Cf. Mosheim, *ibid.*, and Reinhard, *Dogm.*, § 33, 3.

trast to the finite, *i.e.* to that which is co-determined by other things. Interpreted thus the term stands in the closest connexion with the monotheistic basic rule stated above, and, under the form of a cautionary predicate, expresses the difference of the divine causality from all finitude. For already we have often seen how this formula only produces confusion if it is treated as a means of transferring to God by illimitation attributes which essentially are only attached to the finite.

The idea of *Simplicity* too is constantly treated as a negative—although regarded literally it is not so—either as simply negating matter of God or as excluding all idea of parts or of composition.[1] As regards the former, it is pretty clear that, if God and the world are to be kept distinct, in whatever way, all matter must belong to the world. But simplicity strictly taken excludes not only materiality but also participation in everything by which we characterize the finite spirit as such; and the finite spirit can in no way be called simple in the strictest sense of the word,[2] but must belong solely to the world, just as much as matter does. For the relative separation of function itself conflicts with simplicity,[3] and each temporal moment of spiritual manifestation[4] is just as really a result of the mutual inherence of the relatively opposed as in the case of matter, which we declare to be composite in this sense only in so far as we can develop oppositions within it. As therefore infinity on the one hand is an attribute of all the divine attributes, so simplicity, as here expounded in general and in each particular case, is the unseparated and inseparable mutual inherence of all divine attributes and activities. And as on the other hand infinity ensures that nothing shall be ascribed to God which can be thought of only as limited, so simplicity ensures that nothing shall be adopted which belongs essentially to the sphere of contrast and opposition.

Postscript to this Section.—The whole circle of divine attributes here dealt with thoroughly illustrates the characteristic feature of this First Part of Dogmatic, namely, that of being derived from the

[1] The former in Reinhard, *Dogm.*, § 33, 2. The latter in Mosheim, *Th. Dogm.* i. p. 243.

[2] What the older writers called μονοειδές and ἀμερές.

[3] The Socinians consequently were not wrong when they maintained that there is always a synthesis where there is either a connexion or union of the diverse (see Vorst., *Parasceve*, p. 50). But they were wrong to separate the being of God from the will of God.

[4] Augustin., *Tract.* xix. 9 *in Joan.*: Non est Deus mutabilis spiritus . . . Nam ubi invenis aliter et aliter, ibi facta est quaedam mors.

religious self-consciousness as it is presupposed in every Christian religious life-moment. This is clear for the following reasons among others. In view of the teleological character of Christianity we can conceive no completely developed moment of religious experience which does not either itself pass over into some activity or in a definite way influence activities already going on and combine with them. Every such moment must be capable of description just as well under the form of this section as under that of the first or third. So if one individual attribute of these, or all of them together, were to condition a definite religious moment, out of it it would have to be possible to derive either a sentiment or a so-called duty towards God, or at least a course of action in general or in relation to others demanded by this God-consciousness. This, however, is not the case; and no proposition in the Christian Doctrine of Morals can be based solely on the attributes dealt with here, either individually or taken together, but there are always others that go along with them. Hence even these attributes, however completely viewed together and related to each other, can in no way suffice as a description of the Divine Being. But it must be clearly understood here in advance, that whatever additional divine attributes may emerge later, those described here will always have to be thought of as inhering in the others; so that an activity which does not admit of being conceived under the form of eternal omnipotence ought not to be posited as divine.

THIRD SECTION

The Constitution of the World which is indicated in the Religious Self-Consciousness, so far as it expresses the General Relationship between God and the World.

§ 57. *The universality of the feeling of absolute dependence includes in itself the belief in an original perfection of the World.*

1. By the *perfection* of the world nothing is to be understood here except what we must name so in the interests of the religious self-consciousness, namely, that the totality of finite existence, as it influences us (including also those human influences upon the rest of existence resulting from our place in the same), works together in such a way as to make possible the continuity of the religious self-consciousness. For since the religious self-consciousness can only fill a moment when combined with an excitation of the sensuous self-consciousness, and every such excitation is an impression of the world, the demand that the God-consciousness should be able to unite itself [1] with every sensuous determination of the self-consciousness would be in vain unless all the world-impressions (and this is only another way of saying the relation of all other finite being to the being of men) concurred in making the direction of the spirit to God-consciousness compossible with them. The same also holds good from the other side of the relationship, namely, from the determinability of the given through our spontaneity, because this also is always accompanied by a self-consciousness capable of such excitation. Inasmuch, however, as we have laid down that the feeling of absolute dependence does not diminish, still less cease, if we extend our self-consciousness to a consciousness of the whole world [2] (that is, so far as we represent in it finite existence in general), this implies that all different gradations of existence are comprehended in this feeling, and consequently no closer definition of it could destroy that co-existence of the God-consciousness with the consciousness of the world, nor the fact

[1] See § 5, 5, pp. 24 f.

[2] Cf. § 8, 2, pp. 35 f.

of the former being excited by the latter. It must be premised, however, that the term *original* does not refer to any definite condition of the world or of men nor of the God-consciousness in men, all of which are a developed perfection admitting of a more and less; the question is rather of self-identical perfection prior to all temporal development and based on the inner relations of the relevant finite existence. Such perfection is affirmed in the above sense, *i.e.* it is laid down that all finite being, so far as it co-determines our self-consciousness, is traceable back to the eternal omnipotent causality, and all the impressions of the world we receive, as well as the particular way (consequent on human nature) in which the predisposition towards God-consciousness becomes realized, include the possibility that the God-consciousness should combine with each impression of the world in the unity of a moment. This is implied in the certainty which is directly bound up with the God-consciousness. For were the God-consciousness not grounded thus inwardly, it would be something accidental, and so uncertain and arbitrary. From this it also follows that this belief naturally and necessarily belongs together with belief in the eternal omnipresent and living omnipotence, since both are related in exactly the same way to our basic assumption. For, as the former belief expresses the fact that in all excitations of the religious consciousness, the consciousness of God, as united with consciousness of the world, is related to One, so the latter belief asserts that in every such excitation the world-consciousness as united with the God-consciousness is related to All. And just as in belief in the eternal omnipotence it is implied that the world is the complete revelation of it, so in belief in the original perfection of the world it is implied that through the feeling of absolute dependence the divine omnipotence in all its livingness reveals itself everywhere in the world, as eternal omnipresent and omniscient, without any distinction of more or less, without even a contrast in respect of dependence between one part and another.

2. Inasmuch as the selected terms are to be taken in this sense, it at once follows that here any content of an actual life-moment mediated through a definite world-impression must be disregarded, since we have to do only with the original, ever-identical and enduring, inner demands of the lower and higher self-consciousness, and with the constitution of all given existence, as the perpetually effective cause of the world-impressions co-determining the predisposition to God-consciousness. And so we shall not directly

deal at all here with any temporal condition of the world and of mankind in particular, whether past, present, or yet to come; but only with those relationships which uniformly underlie the whole temporal development and throughout it remain the same. As to what in the sphere of experience we call perfection or imperfection, the former is simply that which by means of the original perfection has already come to pass, the latter that which has not yet come to pass by the same means; both taken together, however, are the perfection which is coming to pass. Hence we can say that for each given moment the original perfection is in that which underlies it as pure finite causality; but the definitive perfection is in the totality of all the effects thereof, the development being thought of as included in the moment. But now what underlies each moment as finite causality is nothing but the totality of all enduring forms of existence and all contrasted functions of the same; and consequently the original perfection is the coherence of all these in virtue of which they are equal in compass to the divine causality, and on account of the contrast evoke the consciousness of it.

The original expression of this belief, though in another form, is the divine approval of the world [1] which, in relation to the act of creation as such, has for its object no temporal condition arising out of an earlier one, but only the origin of finite existence, but this, of course, as the source of the whole temporal development. Hence, just as this divine approval cannot be abrogated by anything temporal, so no more can the truth of our proposition be prejudiced by the differing content of the temporal moments, though they appear now as accomplished perfection, and now as lessening imperfection. On the other hand, what is usually dealt with in Dogmatics under this phrase is historical moments—for instance, a paradisical condition of the world and a condition of moral perfection of man, both of which lasted for a period of time; but it is clear that such a doctrine could not be given the same place as that advanced here. For an actual condition, one therefore in any case subject to change, cannot be related in the same way to the divine omnipotence, as that in finite existence which lies at the base of all succeeding conditions, and least of all one which has altogether disappeared; for then the divine omnipotence itself could not have remained the same. Whereas if we on our part were to take up into the idea of original perfection something which, on closer scrutiny, revealed itself as changeable, it would be

[1] Gen. 1[31].

only an oversight resting on an incorrect subsumption which could be corrected as soon as discovered without making any change in the doctrine. But even if the course of our presentation had not led us to it, this idea of a historically given real perfection, posited as original, is at all events to be found in Dogmatics; and we must therefore inquire whether, in fact, there is any place at all for such a doctrine, or whether it always rests simply on a misunderstanding.

§ 58. *The belief described is to be set forth in two doctrines, of which one deals with the perfection of the rest of the world in relation to man, the other with the perfection of man himself.*

1. The belief described is nothing but a statement of the common factor in the religious excitations, only related to the finite co-determining them (although this too is taken in its generality), *i.e.* to the world-impressions which we receive; hence this division follows naturally. For the God-consciousness could not be excited by these world-impressions if they were of a nature discordant with it, or if man were not so constituted that these impressions reached, as it were, the region of his higher self-consciousness, or again, unless there existed in him that relation of the lower and the higher self-consciousness to each other which occasions the whole process of the excitation of the God-consciousness. Accordingly, these two conditions come to be considered each in itself. It could of course be said that man himself, with his constitution, is an integral part of the world, and that it is only in virtue of this constitution that he is precisely the part he is; and hence that the original perfection of man is already included in the original perfection of the world. This is quite correct; and in a purely scientific inquiry, where what was in question was a view of finite existence in itself, such a division would only be permissible in so far as other divisions were made, and the idea of the perfection of the world analysed into the perfection of all its different parts, and their relations to one another. It is different in the dogmatic sphere, where the original object is not the objective consciousness at all but self-consciousness, especially in so far as in self-consciousness man contrasts himself with the world, and stands in the relationship of interaction to the rest of existence.

2. For the same reason there can even here be no question of the original perfection of the world in itself and in relation to the idea of finite existence, but only in relation to man. But if in

addition it were maintained that there is no other perfection of the world—this being regarded purely teleologically, in the usual sense of that word—such a position would call for a more precise explanation, in order to avoid the appearance of representing man as the central-point of all finite existence, in relation to which alone everything had a perfection. This explanation would not be hard to give, for, assuming an organic construction of the whole, all is just as much for each as each for all ; hence it is true even of the most remote thing (since, after all, its condition corresponds to the totality of its mediate and immediate relationships) not only that it stands in relationship with man, but also, on a complete view, that precisely this relationship might be an expression of the peculiarity of its nature. But we need not go into such explanations, for we have not to advance any exhaustive doctrine of the perfection of the world (which would be a task for cosmology) ; the belief to be set forth here will not go beyond the sphere of religious excitations, which is only touched by the relationships of the world to man. But, in going back to the common ground of these relationships, we at the same time lay it down that no still future development of them can ever involve what would abrogate this belief. As regards the perfection of man, it would not be in keeping to add that it also is only to be interpreted in relation to the world. Man's original perfection is primarily meant rather in relation to God, *i.e.* to the presence in him of the God-consciousness, and his endowments relatively to the world belong here only in so far as they awaken the God-consciousness. The whole tone of the proposition, however, certainly does imply that all those endowments, in virtue of which man is this specific part of the world, belong here—a proposition which, in the sphere of Christian morals, has regulative importance averting a crowd of misunderstandings.

3. This of itself makes clear how natural it is that the doctrine of the peculiar original perfection of man should have been much more fully elaborated in Dogmatic than that of the perfection of the world in relation to man. If, however, the latter be entirely lacking, this certainly is no advantage to the former ; and not only so, but the treatment of developed perfection, whether under the heading of Divine Providence or otherwise, often takes a wrong line, because a right idea of original perfection has not been taken as basis. But the less urgent and therefore also the less elaborate inquiry ought reasonably to precede the more important and more complex as an introduction.

First Doctrine: The Original Perfection of the World

§ 59. *Every moment in which we confront externally given existence involves the implication that the world offers to the human spirit an abundance of stimuli to develop those conditions in which the God-consciousness can realize itself, and at the same time that in manifold degrees the world lends itself to being used by the human spirit as an instrument and means of expression.*

1. It has been taken for granted above (§ 5, 3) that the God-consciousness may develop in every state of consciousness which has risen above animal confusion, so that in it there is expressed the contrast between the self and the 'given,' and the contrast between self-consciousness and objective consciousness, inasmuch as the two elements in the antithesis confront each other simultaneously. The same holds good also of the contrast between passive and active. But while in the sphere we are dealing with the God-consciousness, owing to the teleological character of Christian piety,[1] can unite with the passive only as it is related to self-activity, the interposition of the passive none the less is necessary to mark out clearly the moments of self-activity, because clarity of consciousness only arises through a successive contrast of distinct moments. Passive states, however, can only arise through operative influences, and hence the original perfection of the world in relation to men consists primarily in this, that in it is temporally grounded the excitation of passive states which are to pass into active states (these we name *incentives*), or, in other words, that they sufficiently determine the receptivity of man to the awakening and shaping of his self-activity. If now we take man first of all purely on his inner side, as a self-active being in whom God-consciousness is possible—that is, as spirit; then, from this point of view, his bodily side, which is not the man himself, belongs originally to this material world into which the spirit enters. Only gradually does it become for the spirit instrument and means of expression—as later, mediately through it, all other things likewise become instrument and means of expression—but first of all and primarily it mediates the stimulating influences of the world upon the spirit. Thus the whole of this aspect of the original perfection of the world can be summarily expressed by saying that in it there is given for the spirit

[1] See § 9, 1 and § 11.

such an organism as the human body in living connexion with all else—an organism which brings the spirit into contact with the rest of existence.

Clarity of consciousness, however, is also conditioned by the contrasted distinction of self-consciousness and objective consciousness, and this is closely connected with the fact that different kinds of influences can be related to the same self-consciousness, so that the self-consciousness can be regarded as an entity existing independently of every particular influence (upon this all experience and eventually all science depend, though here we are only interested in the latter for the sake of the former). Hence we may summarily express this aspect of the original perfection of the world by the concept of its knowability. The two aspects are essentially bound up together, for without an organism such as ours there would be no interrelation between finite spirit and corporeal existence, however suitably adapted to such interrelation the latter might be. And without such an ordered distinction of existence the human organism would be a meaningless phenomenon. So, then, the two together are one : the knowability of existence is the ideal side of the original perfection of the world, and the natural subsistence of the human organism is the real side of the same perfection as directly related to human receptivity.

2. We must now put the same series in the reverse order. For if all self-activity in men were determined by the influences of the (external) world it would be merely reaction, and every feeling of freedom, even partial freedom, would be illusory. But if the receptivity is at least living and individual, so that the same influence is not the same thing for all, still more, if irrespective of influence, we can attribute to the spirit an original self-activity that is not simply immanent in the individual spiritual personality (which indeed might be the root of that consciousness of species which is so distinctively human), then to the perfection of the world there belongs also such a receptivity for the influences of the spiritual self-activity of man as is, considered in itself, unlimited. This receptivity must naturally begin at the human organism regarded as a constitutive part of the world ; but from this it broadens out more and more until it reaches those constitutive elements of the world which are of such a nature that they are subject to no other influences except that of being known—which brings us to the borders of the preceding section. Though we sum up this receptivity of the world under the two terms,

instrument and means of expression, we do not in the least mean to indicate a division, as if one thing could only be one and another the other. Rather the organism is itself both, the most immediate instrument and the most immediate means of expression; and so every thing, if it is the one, is always the other also. Nevertheless, these are the two relations through which the self-consciousness accompanying states of self-activity becomes a means of awakening the God-consciousness. For it is only in connexion with his organs that man realizes sovereignty over the world,[1] of which he can only be conscious as something based upon the divine omnipotence; and it is only inasmuch as the simple activity of spirit is expressed through the medium of space and time that it awakens, as a copy thereof, the consciousness of the divine causality.[2]

3. That these two chief moments of the original perfection of the world essentially go together is self-evident. For the first moment would be simply an imperfection—that is, an arrangement leading to nothing—apart from the second; the knowability of the world would be empty if it did not include in itself the expression of its being known; and the human organism would be lost among the more imperfect kinds of existence as similar to them, even though it were supposed to include the inner life of the spirit, if there did not proceed from it a new power of organization into which everything else could be taken up. On the other hand, the receptivity of the rest of existence to the influence of the spirit would be empty and meaningless unless the spirit could be filled by it. But now both these together embrace completely the relations of the world to the spirit as the seat of God-consciousness, since in the existence presented to it the human spirit can find no means other than this for developing this consciousness. And indeed in this relation to the passive states which arise through the influence of the world, taken in itself, the human spirit has precisely the same means of development whether these states as life-moments are pleasant or unpleasant, elevating or depressing; and the same holds good of its acquired instruments and gathered means of expression in so far as, being external, they are capable of reacting upon men in various ways and of exciting passive states. For the relation of either to man's self-activity is not thereby altered, nor is the God-consciousness as such more tardily aroused by the unpleasant than by the pleasant.

Postscript.—Two doctrines must be distinguished from the

[1] Gen. 1[28]. [2] Gen. 1[26].

proposition here laid down: on the one hand, that known as the doctrine of the Best World; and on the other, the assertion that there was a perfection of the world which can be called original, though not in the sense used above, but in the sense that prior to its present condition it endured for a period of time and afterwards became changed into its present imperfect condition.

The doctrine of the Best World originally belongs, especially since Leibniz, to the so-called natural or rational theology, and thus did not arise as a statement about the religious consciousness but as a product of speculation. Hence there would have been no mention of it here if various theologians [1] had not taken it over in the same form into Christian Dogmatics. The doctrine is concerned not only with what lies at the basis of temporal existence but with temporal existence itself, in which it is impossible to separate between the historical (*i.e.* the activity of the human spirit) and the natural (*i.e.* the activity of physical forces); and it maintains that, notwithstanding all the mists and imperfections of the world, no greater amount of being and of well-being could have been attained. It is true, our two doctrines also imply the position that, since the entire course of time can only be an unbroken activity of the whole original perfection, the final result must be an absolute satisfaction, and similarly each moment, taken in the whole, satisfactory as an approximation. But this conviction, issuing as it does solely from the religious consciousness, has no need to be introduced into speculative theology exactly as it has been taken up into Christian Dogmatics. So far as the latter is concerned we must stop at the affirmation that the world is *good*, and can make no use of the formula that it is *the best*; and this because the former assertion signifies far more than the latter.[2] The latter expression is connected with the idea (which we have already rejected) of many worlds all originally equally possible with the one which actually came into existence, and also it seeks to represent the entire course of time in the actual world as the result of mediate divine knowledge (the idea of which we have also rejected), so that the whole productive activity of God is assumed to be selective and therefore secondary.

The second doctrine is to be found in the tradition of most peoples—the fable of a Golden Age previous to actual history. The essential element in it is always the belief that the world was then of such a character as to assure satisfaction to man apart from

[1] See, among others, Michaelis, *Th. Dogm.*, § 55. [2] Cf. § 54, 2.

any need on his part to develop self-activity. Something similar —but with the addition that, if this state had endured, man would not have died—has been found in the brief Old Testament indications of the life of Paradise,[1] which do not, however, indicate an age but only a relatively short period in the life of the first man. Thus, first of all, we should have to settle the conflict over interpretation which has been waged so long, whether actual history is meant to be recorded there, and hence whether there is a question of a temporal condition or not. If the narrative is historical it would as such have no place here, except in so far as such a temporal condition (it may be held) presupposes as its ground another original perfection which has been transformed into the one just described, from which such a temporal process could no longer follow; or else, it may be argued, the original perfection described here underlay the narrative, but now is no longer to be assumed. The latter view has never been maintained, and would be contradicted by the fact that the historical process nowhere presents anything but functions of the original perfection as above described. But the former view must be considered. Now, if it necessarily implies that the original perfection of the world has not remained the same, it fails to maintain the unity of the whole world-order in its relation to the Creation and the continuity of the divine Preservation. But apart from this undeniable and fundamental error, it follows further that God approved that initial state even with respect to that part which was capable of deterioration and was in fact to deteriorate. Moreover, it seems contradictory that those fundamental conditions under which the Redeemer was actually ordained to come into the world and establish the invincible Kingdom of God should be less perfect than those under which the first man came into the world, since far greater things were to come to pass in the former case than in the latter. If now we examine this alleged primordial state of the world, we shall find that it is in contradiction with the divine commission to man; for man could only attain to dominion over the earth by the development of his powers, and the constitution of the world, which occasioned this development and which implies a receptivity for the influence of those developed powers, must be contemporaneous with the divine command. Lastly, if history is essential to the fashioning of the world by man, then from this point of view the narrative belongs solely to pre-history, and its real content is simply

[1] Gen. $2^{8f.}$.

that an adaptation of nature for the existence of the human organism preceded all development of human powers, and that on our planet the very significant detrimental differences in this adaptation could only come to light with the dissemination and further development of the human race. And if perhaps it may be concluded also from the narrative that there were at one time no hostile contacts in the animal kingdom [1] and nothing at all injurious or useless to mankind,[2] it does not by any means follow that this applied also outside the place where man originally lived, nor even that later this place lost its peculiar advantages.

If, however, the result of exegetical inquiry should be that no actual history is recounted in this passage, and if the story therefore is to be regarded as a kind of poetry, it would come up for consideration here in so far as it either contained a direct utterance of the religious consciousness or was occasioned by it. Its statements about the origin of sin do not concern us. Even the connexion between sin and evil and sin and death, on which it evidently proceeds, does not in and for itself need to be discussed here ; only, with reference to the doctrine of the perfection of the world set forth above, the following observations should be made. Even if we accepted absolutely the idea that apart from sin there would have been neither evil nor death, it would by no means follow from this that the earth must originally have been adapted to an enduring condition of sinlessness ; evil and death may none the less have been preordained as certainly as God foreknew sin. And other points must be considered. If we think away the gradual decay of organic powers, the possibility that the organism may be destroyed by external forces of nature, and disappearance through death, what we are thinking of is no longer beings of our kind, while yet real human history would only begin when all these things were present. Again, care for the preservation of life and the avoidance of what would disturb it, which is conditioned by mortality, is among the most powerful motives of human development, so that through mortality and the evils which are associated with it more human activities due to our relations with the external world have been developed than could be expected without mortality, and (assuming that the totality of human life increases rather than diminishes) the death of individuals does not lessen the fitness of the world for man's dominion over it, nor is it thereby hindered

[1] Gen. 2^{19} does not go quite so far.
[2] *Ibid.* ver. 16 ; that is, if the tree (ver. 17) was not in itself harmful.

in the development of its wealth of means of stimulation. Finally, enduring sinlessness would have stood out far more strongly and conspicuously if man, unimpeded in the development and use of his powers, bore evil, and, combining God-consciousness with love of his race, overcame the impulse to cling to his own life and accepted death. In view of all this, no reason can well remain for doubting that the original perfection of the world relatively to man was at the beginning no other than what we have here described, and that neither the Old Testament story [1] nor the relevant indications in the writings of the New Testament [2] compel us to hold that man was created immortal, or that, with alteration in his nature, the whole arrangement of the earth relatively to him was altered as well.

Second Doctrine: The Original Perfection of Man

§ 60. *The predisposition to God-consciousness, as an inner impulse, includes the consciousness of a faculty of attaining, by means of the human organism, to those states of self-consciousness in which the God-consciousness can realize itself; and the impulse inseparable therefrom to express the God-consciousness includes in like manner the connexion of the race-consciousness with the personal consciousness; and both together form man's original perfection.*

1. If the God-consciousness in the form of the feeling of absolute dependence [3] can only become actual in connexion with a sensible determination of self-consciousness, the tendency towards God-consciousness would be altogether nugatory if the condition necessary for it in human life could not be evoked; and we should be no more able to think of it as actual than in the case of the beasts, because the confused state of man's consciousness would not exhibit the conditions under which alone that feeling could emerge. Religious experience, however, consists precisely in this, that we are aware of this tendency to God-consciousness as a living impulse; but such an impulse can only proceed from the true inner nature of the being which it goes to constitute. Hence, at least in so far as we are religious men, we reckon the whole range

[1] Gen. 2^{17}.

[2] Rom. 5^{12}, based on Gen. 2^{17}, just as little excludes the possibility that Adam may have been created mortal; and 1 Cor. 15^{56} actually indicates death as such as existing before the advent of sin.

[3] Cf. § 5, 1–3.

of those states with which the God-consciousness can unite as belonging to this true inner nature. And as it would be an absolute imperfection of human nature—that is to say, a complete absence of inner coherence—if the tendency were indeed present latently, but could not emerge, so it is an essential element in the perfection of human nature that those states which condition the appearance of the God-consciousness are able to fill the clear and waking life of man onwards from the time when the spiritual functions are developed. And as we consider it an imperfect state of religious life in the individual if many moments of clear sensibly-determined self-consciousness occur without the God-consciousness being combined with them, so we account it part of the original perfection of man that in our clear and waking life a continuous God-consciousness as such is possible ; and on the contrary, we should have to regard it as an essential imperfection if the emergence of the feeling of absolute dependence, though not abrogating any feeling of partial dependence or freedom, were confined as such to separate and scattered moments.

The God-consciousness, moreover, combines not only with those sensible excitations of self-consciousness which express life-enhancements or life-hindrances immediately arising out of the impression of the world, but also with those which accompany the cognitive activities, and finally with those which are connected with every kind of outwardly directed action. Hence all these mental life-functions and the relative disposition of the organism belong together to the original perfection of man, though only in so far as the demand which we make for God-consciousness is conditioned by them, and in such a way that the first place always belongs to it. Thus, first of all, there is the physical basis of spiritual life, *i.e.* the fact that the spirit, become soul in the human body, acts also on the rest of the world in innumerable ways, and asserts its nature, just as the other living forces assert their nature relatively to it, so that life-feeling in general takes shape as the consciousness of interaction ; from which it follows that to the original perfection of man this also belongs, that opposite life-moments, hindrances and furtherances, have one and the same bearing on the excitation of the God-consciousness. Next, there is the intellectual basis of spiritual life, *i.e.* the fact that the spirit by means of sense-impressions can obtain that knowledge of existence which is one element in its own nature, as also knowledge of what we ourselves by our activity can produce in and from existence, and can express this knowledge with actual consciousness in the most varied degrees of general and particular ideas, and that thereby it arrives at the accompanying consciousness of a natural order in connexion with which the God-consciousness develops. Upon the agreement of these ideas and judgments with the being and relations of things depends all the influence of man on external nature which is more than simply instinctive, and also the connexion between knowledge and practical life. But though the knowledge of God, in this sphere, is bound up pre-eminently and fundamentally with the idea of a natural order, the excitation of the God-consciousness is not at all imperilled though certain ideas should not agree with the actual being of the object presented ; as indeed the comprehensive interconnexion of all being would not be mirrored in our idea if we did not assume that so long as the whole of existence is not reflected in our thought every act of thought contains an element of error.

2. With regard to the impulse to express the God-consciousness externally : there is, of course, no 'inner' which does not become also an 'outer,' and thus there are expressions of the God-consciousness, in which no relation to the race-consciousness can be directly shown. But the question here is of those expressions which aim at fellowship and on which all such fellowship is based. Now the fellowship without which there can for us be no living and vigorous piety is conditioned by these external expressions ; it therefore is conditioned also by the inner union of the race-consciousness and the personal self-consciousness, for as this is the general source of all recognition of others as being of like nature with ourselves, it is also the only source of the presupposition and the ground of the fact that the 'inner' is known and grasped along with and by means of the 'outer' ; hence we may justly regard the two thus interrelated as belonging to the original perfection of man. This inclusion of the race-consciousness in the personal self-consciousness and the communicability of the 'inner' through the 'outer,' which is connected with it, is the fundamental condition or basis of social life, for all human fellowship rests solely upon it ; and even in this wider connexion it belongs here, for, in every other kind of fellowship also, whatever its object, a man's acts, because accompanied by a sensible excitation of self-consciousness, may contain at the same time a communication of his God-consciousness. Nay more, the free and mobile outward life of man must be able in its whole range to serve this external expression and communication of the God-consciousness (though not in the case of each individual

taken singly, but only in combination with others), for otherwise there would be a sensuously stimulated self-consciousness with which the God-consciousness could unite inwardly, but in conjunction with which it could not express itself outwardly; and thus the range of externalization and communication would be more narrowly limited than that of the inner excitation. Such a discrepancy we should have to call an original imperfection.

3. The statements in our proposition then include all the conditions necessary for the continuous existence of the God-consciousness in every human individual, and also for its communication from one to the other in proportion to the different levels of human fellowship, including also the perfection with which it can be communicated from the Redeemer and through Him to the redeemed: hence the requirements of this section are fulfilled. In the knowledge of the elements of this original perfection as present in every one we find a justification for the original demand that the God-consciousness should exist continuously and universally; and human nature, repeating itself identically through heredity in every human being, is seen to be sufficient for its realization.[1] We found ourselves obliged to treat the two chief points as one whole complete in itself, which is a fresh justification, in the sphere of the God-consciousness, of a scientific method of treatment which everywhere aims at totality and is impossible on any other terms; it is justified both for Dogmatics proper, where we have to reduce the whole of religious affections to *loci communes*, and for religious Ethics, where we have to distinguish those types of conduct which show the influence of the God-consciousness on our purposes; also for Practical Theology in general, which is concerned with the description and distinction of the different forms of fellowship in God-consciousness. This is natural, for the whole procedure of Dogmatics—in which, if we take the word in a rather wider sense than usual, the last-mentioned discipline also is included—rests on what we have here exhibited as the original perfection of man.

§ 61. *Fulness of experience in the sphere of faith is due to the individual development, in virtue of this original perfection of human nature, of each human life brought into existence by procreation. But how, on the same presuppositions, the first men developed, history gives no account, and the hints we*

[1] Omnes homines in primo homine sine vitio conditi (Ambrose, *de vocat. Gent.* i. 3).

have on that subject cannot form a religious doctrine in our sense of the word.

1. To understand the fundamental aspects of human life as set forth in the above description of man's original perfection, *i.e.* so that everything is related to the God-consciousness, is undoubtedly a matter of faith ; for it depends entirely on the certainty which accompanies religious experiences, by virtue of which alone all other states of life attain certainty through sharing in those experiences. If, on the contrary, we suppose a man to have religious experiences, but unaccompanied by certainty, so that he can equally well regard them as deceptive or veridical, he will not arrive at the idea of original perfection given above, but will co-ordinate the God-consciousness with other elements of life, or will possibly even take original perfection to consist solely in the possibility of freeing himself from the God-consciousness as a product of human imperfection ; and thus what one experiences as a furtherance another will experience as a hindrance. Now matters of fact in the development of man are never questions of faith but of history, and statements concerning matter of fact, whether general or particular, are not propositions of faith but historical statements, even when, viewed directly, their subject-matter is the state of the God-consciousness in an individual or a community. In this respect there can be no distinction between the first men and ourselves. Everything we know of the actual conditions of the first men and of their course of development, including the manner in which the indwelling tendency to God-consciousness became operative in them without the stimulating influence of tradition, all this is in no sense faith but history—unless we are prepared to alter completely the usage of the word and, say, call history which is mingled with uncertainties, 'faith.' Otherwise 'faith' would consist simply in historical knowledge, and would be held and disseminated by historical statements and portrayals. That even in their case we should regard as an advance only those conditions which express an increased value of the God-consciousness, is certainly a matter of faith, but of the very same faith as is expressed in the conception of original perfection given above. There could only be specific doctrines of faith concerning the first men in so far as their unique manner of coming into being and of temporal existence might modify the application of our conception to them. Even then we should, of course, always have to maintain that the applica-

tion of our conception is limited to the sphere of procreation, and could leave aside the question what in their case took its place, except in so far as the relation thence arising between them and us altered our God-consciousness in its combination with our race-consciousness. The question arises, then, whether their history has come down to us in such a form that we are compelled to lay down such propositions.

2. Now it is clear that the Old Testament narrative,[1] on which alone we have to depend, is far from putting forward a history of this kind. For even if the question whether this narrative is meant to be taken historically were answered entirely in the affirmative, the particular points which it presents simply take for granted most of what we chiefly want to know about the first men. Especially, for one thing, speech, and the form of consciousness determined by it, the acquisition of which by men after birth is the surest proof that in their case the state of animal-like confusion is already disappearing, is here everywhere assumed ; and in the same way, the God-consciousness appears as already present, and we learn nothing of the mode of its development. Even what is recounted of the converse of God with man, instead of helping the solution of the other problems, is itself a new and still more difficult one. For we learn nothing more exact of the way in which God made Himself intelligible to men, except that bodily form is quite plainly ascribed to Him. But it is equally difficult to see how an idea of God already existing could have been referred to such a phenomenon as its object, or how on occasion of such a phenomenon a true God-consciousness could have arisen. And indeed, even with regard to external conditions, the description of the life of Paradise is only helpful in a negative way, for though the question how man could have supported life from the beginning raises no particular difficulty, no information is given about how the first men spent the time, or of the result in the expansion both of the objective consciousness and of self-consciousness. Even what is said about the naming of the animals[2] leaves us quite uncertain whether the designation had any regard to the relation of the kinds of animals to their species and of the species to the larger classes, and if so, to what extent. The moral situation is equally undefined, for their innocent lack of modesty, as well as their initial obedience to the divine command, admits of the most diverse interpretations. Since, then, besides all this, no measure of time is given, and conse-

[1] Gen. 1^{26} ff. 2^{7}–3^{24}.

[2] Gen. 2^{19}.

quently all materials for forming a historical picture are wanting, we can only say that everything we are told about the first men before the Fall is adequately elucidated by the conception of original perfection which we have proposed.

3. If the narrative is regarded not as history but simply as an ancient attempt to make good the lack of a historical account of the beginnings of the human race, the particular points in it will have inner truth for us in so far as they agree with the conception which we have laid down. But all attempts to form a historical picture of the first beginnings of human existence are bound to fail, because, as we have no experience of an absolute beginning, we have no analogy by which we could make the absolute beginning of rational consciousness intelligible. We have no clear idea even of the consciousness of the child in the first period of life. Yet we cannot miss the fact that in the case of the child the arising of consciousness out of unconsciousness coincides with the detachment and separation of its life from community with the life of the mother, and forthwith the environing spirit, already developed, influences the spirit which is just arriving at conscious thought; the first man, on the other hand, can only be described as one to whom this means of development was wholly lacking. The formula which accords best with this analogy and with our experience of the conditions of any as yet largely undeveloped human society is that the first men are to be regarded as good-natured grown-up children;[1] but this is really quite inappropriate and gives us no clear view, for we cannot think of their spiritual development any more than that of the child as proceeding purely from within outwards, and the bodily sustenance of adult primitive man required from the outset activities which we can only conceive as acquired by memory, association, and repetition. If it be suggested that the first man was more like an animal and guided only by instinct, we cannot understand the passage from this condition to one of consciousness and thought without the assistance of a life which was already intelligent, since it would be the beginning of a new kind of existence wholly unconnected with what went before. Attempts have been made to avoid this difficulty by means of two ideas, the grounds of which, at least to some extent, are to be found in the Old Testament narrative. One is the proposition, familiar in many dogmatic systems, that the necessary capacities were from the first present in man by creation, and were capable of extension

[1] Cf. de Wette, *Sittenlehre*, § 38, and *Theol. Zeitschrift*, ii. pp. 84–88.

from what was necessary for the preservation of life further and higher to the genuinely spiritual level. But this really only means that the first condition of man cannot be conceived as different from the later conditions which are determined by previous conditions ; that is to say, an absolutely first condition cannot be conceived at all. Also, if we are unwilling to fall back on instinct, it is unthinkable that there should be a consciousness of these created capacities before they are applied, and again it is inconceivable that, in a genuinely human situation, there should be an impulse which would set them in motion without consciousness of them. Certainly those theologians [1] do not lessen the difficulty (rather they simply return to the starting-point and give a description of the problem more than a solution) who are ready to make assertions about an actual condition of the first man, but at the same time represent the personal perfections which they ascribe to him as mere potentialities, excluding everything which requires previous exercise. The other expedient is as follows : it is supposed that those things which secure for a human being, when born, fellowship with those who are already grown and developed, the newly created man obtained through a revealing and educative fellowship with God or the angels. But if we examine this more closely it leads us back, by one way or another, to the first idea. For if this educative revelation were a purely inward influence, this would be immediately connected with creation itself and indistinguishable from it, and the true and proper life of man would, on this view, begin in much the same way as on the view that there were abilities implanted at creation. If, on the other hand, the fellowship in question is external and mediated through human language, then of course the grown-up child, with this environment, can through speech learn also to think by innate human reason ; but if it is to be set in motion in definite activities demanded by self-preservation, either those higher Beings too must lead a completely human life so as to bring the imitative impulse into play, or else we must assume that the understanding is sufficiently developed to apprehend the teaching and precept which would exert an educative influence.

4. If, then, we are unable to form an intelligible idea of the first states of development of primitive man, and if we cannot point to anything compelling us to modify the application of our conception to them in any special way, there is no reason why we should lay

[1] Reinhard, *Dogm.*, §§ 70, 73.

down any special doctrines concerning the first men. All that follows is that we can only exhibit the validity of our conception within the context of earlier and later generations, where human existence begins in the manner with which we are familiar and depends for its development upon human tradition. In this connexion, our certainty of the original perfection of human nature, as set out by us, furnishes ground for the assumption that the first men themselves, when their influence on a second generation began, stood at some quite definite point in the line of development (though a point which we may be unable further to define), and consequently they were in a position to influence the development of the God-consciousness in the next generation; that is to say, self-communicating piety is as old as the self-propagating human race. This assumption is implied in the consciousness that piety is a universal element of human life.

If, then, following the Mosaic account of the creation, which views all organic beings 'after their kind,'[1] we take the expression of the divine will given there with respect to man[2] not as referring exclusively to the first men in their unique position, but to them only in so far as they were the first instances of the human species, and if we ask whether the designation, 'image of God' (which indisputably denotes the superiority of human nature over the other creatures described), is in harmony with the conception we have set forth, we can only answer 'yes' with great caution. For even though we can describe the living presence of the God-consciousness as a being of God within us, which seems to be something much greater than a resemblance to God, yet this living presence of the God-consciousness is something different. And since this activity of the God-consciousness occurs in us only in connexion with our physical and bodily organism, if we would argue regressively from the likeness or image of God, as it is and has been described here, to God Himself, then we should have to accept one of two alternatives: either the whole world is related to God in the same way as our whole organism is related to the highest spiritual power in us, in which case it would be difficult to see how God could fail to be identical with the world; or else there is something in God which at least corresponds to our psychical organization, which is largely constituted by the so-called lower psychical forces; and in this way the idea of God would acquire a strong and really defiling admixture of humanity, and attributes

[1] Gen. 1[11. 21. 24]. [2] Gen. 1[26].

would have to be ascribed to God which can mean nothing when taken as divine,[1] or else attributes would have to be ascribed to men which could not be thought of as human.[2] Here, then, is another instance of the truth that Biblical expressions, especially when they do not occur in a purely didactic context, can seldom be adopted in the terminology of Dogmatics without more ado. Hence it is not surprising that many of our theologians, taking what immediately follows it as the explanation of the divine words regarding 'the image of God,' have, like the Socinians, connected the divine image with man's formative and governing relation to external nature rather than with his own inner being.

The other common phrase, 'original righteousness,' which is not quite so scriptural, gives rise to other difficulties. These difficulties arise not only because righteousness in the ordinary sense is concerned only with more extended social relations, such as a first human pair could not possibly have ; it is, in fact, concerned primarily with the sphere of law proper which, starting from a state of simple family life, could only reach development in later generations. But the difficulties in question arise even more because we are accustomed to include righteousness under the general idea of virtue ; yet a basal disposition is never called virtue, but only one which arises through spontaneity. Here, however, it is a question of just such a basal disposition, or of one present in man by creation, from which a development should start such as can relate itself to divine demands ; and it is a conformity to these demands, achieved by an active attitude to them, which is so frequently called 'righteousness' in the Old Testament Scriptures : thus giving rise to a very undesirable double meaning of the word. In this way we should be led back, only too easily, to the idea of created capacities, a result which could only be avoided by a most definite explanation that in this connexion the word 'righteousness' has a totally different meaning—a meaning which certainly can be traced back to the usage of common life, inasmuch as we call a thing 'just' (right) when it corresponds to its definition. If now we consider the divine decree ordaining the whole development of the human race by means of redemption, and the fact that this was included in the idea of human nature from the beginning, though unknown to mankind itself, then it will be precisely those attributes

[1] So Quenstedt, *Syst. Theol.*, p. 843, reckons as part of the original perfection *conformitas appetitus sensitivi cum Dei castitate.*

[2] *Ibid.* p. 844 : In corpore primi hominis eluxit imago Dei . . . per impassibilitatem.

laid down in the proposition given above on which this capacity for redemption depends.

5. In view of these considerations, it will be felt as very natural that our symbolical documents and, in agreement with them, later teachers of doctrine have wavered in their use of these expressions, sometimes designating by them those original excellences of human nature which lie at the root of all later development [1] and sometimes asserting a definitely perfect condition of the first man, thus laying down doctrines about the first man [2]—this condition being regarded sometimes more as present by creation and sometimes as in part acquired. Now if we interpret the first class of passages quoted in such a way that 'nature' in the second of them is called 'good' and 'holy' because the perfections asserted in the first passage develop out of it (as indeed the first passage itself represents them as still in the future), then our proposition makes clear how and why this development takes place. For even the uniform *temperamentum* of the bodily functions can only indicate, on the one hand, the uniformly easy control of the soul over them in every direction; and on the other hand, of course, there must here be reckoned the resistance, equally adequate on all sides, which the organism offers to external influences, thus always maintaining itself in its original relation. This latter point is not definitely included in our formula, because the power of the God-consciousness does not immediately depend upon it; rather it shows itself to be so indifferent to the favourable or unfavourable relations of bodily life to external nature that it has often been maintained that piety flourishes best in sickness and poverty. In fact, this sufficiency of the organism, and everything pertaining exclusively to the natural side of man [3] in his conflict with other

[1] *Apolog. Conf.* i. (p. 20. Ed. Lücke) inclines in this direction: Justitia originalis habitura erat non solum aequale temperamentum qualitatum corporis, sed etiam haec dona, notitiam Dei certiorem timorem Dei fiduciam Dei, aut certe rectitudinem et vim ista efficiendi; though even this shows some confusion. And *Solid. Decl.*, p. 643: In Adamo et Heva *natura* initio pura bona et sancta creata est.

[2] Here belongs *Solid. Decl.*, p. 640, in so far as it calls original sin a privatio concreatae in Paradiso justitiae originalis seu imaginis Dei, ad quam homo initio in veritate sanctitate atque justitia creatus fuerat; and *Conf. Belg.* xiv.: Credimus Deum ex limo terrae hominem ad imaginem suam bonum scilicet iustum et sanctum creasse, qui proprio arbitrio suam voluntatem ad Dei voluntatem componere et conformem reddere posset. Less clearly, *Conf. Helv.*: Fuit homo ab initio a Deo conditus ad imaginem Dei in iustitia et sanctitate veritatis, bonus et rectus.

[3] Cf. Luther in *Genes.* i. § 187: 'To this inner perfection was later added the most beautiful and admirable strength and glory of the body and all its members.'

natural forces, would be better dealt with under the heading of the Perfection of the World in relation to mankind, on the same principle as that which led us to discuss human mortality not in the form of the question whether it conflicted with man's proper perfection but rather as the question whether the perfection of the world in relation to man was diminished by it. With regard especially to the obedience of the lower powers of the soul to the higher (a point which is always reckoned an essential part of original righteousness) the question only arises here, where we are altogether disregarding the actual condition of the first pair as individuals, in so far as there resides in the lower functions a receptivity for the impulses of the higher ; and this not only in the state of quiescence but during their proper life-process. And this point is, of course, brought out in our proposition, since the activities in which the influence of the God-consciousness takes effect determine all its communications. But when Augustine understands by the expression ' desire '[1] simply the proper life-process of these functions, and at the same time holds that it cannot be thought of as co-existing with original righteousness, he seems to be at least as much open to blame as the Pelagians, if they considered the opposition between the lower and higher faculties as man's original condition, and included all acquired perfection under the concept of the removal of that opposition. For Augustine's opinion presupposes also an original contradiction between the spirit in man and that which is necessary for his animal life.

But this leads us over to the other point of view—namely, the representation of original righteousness or the divine image as an actual condition of the first man. Now if, on this view, the statement that man was created by God good, righteous, and holy, means no more than that, in opposition to the Pelagian doctrine, the first real state of man could not have been one of sin, we may unreservedly assent. For sin must have been preceded by knowledge and recognition of the divine will, and in that case it must have been preceded by free activity which was not sinful. But if what is meant is a real power exercised by the higher faculties over the lower, then (even if we do not conjoin with this the position of Augustine referred to above), the greater this power is taken to be, it is from this point of view impossible to conceive of anything but

[1] *Concupiscentia.* The relevant passages are too many to give in detail, but the use of the word is so varied that it would be hard to decide whether, and if so how far, his doctrine goes beyond the proper bounds.

a growing intensification of that power in the same regard. This is probably the real reason why the Roman Church has explained man's original state of sinlessness, not by the original perfection of human nature, but rather by an extraordinary divine influence—an explanation which clearly implies a Pelagian conception of human nature as such.[1] It may not be quite so harmful in its consequences, but it confuses the idea of original perfection none the less, when our dogmatic theologians maintain that the first pair, in their original condition, were partakers of the Holy Spirit.[2] Thus the attempt to define more closely the primitive condition of the first man seems to lead nowhere, whether he be considered as completely corresponding with what we can recognize in later times as a progressive development of original perfection, or whether he be considered as completely corresponding to what appears to us a retrogressive state. The Pelagians, starting from the second of these presuppositions, gain a double advantage—they admit no original perfection which has been lost, and a progressive development can take place from the point of departure which they accept ; but they incur a double disadvantage—that the good for them is not original, and that the Redeemer appears only as an individual member in the development. The doctrine of the Church, on the other hand, gains a double superiority—it postulates the good as immediately produced by God, and, since with the loss of this condition the development is broken and a new point of departure is needed, the Redeemer can come in as the turning-point ; but it incurs a double disadvantage—the good which was already actual in the phenomenal world has been lost, in spite of the sustaining divine omnipotence, and the sole purpose for which we are tempted to form a picture of the original state of the first man, *i.e.* in order to have a starting-point for the genetic conception of all that follows, is not attained. Hence we may take it as more to the purpose not to define anything more accurately as regards the condition of the first man, but simply to elicit the ever self-identical original perfection of nature from the higher self-consciousness viewed universally. But if we are to see everything that can develop out of such original perfection all together in a single human instance, it is not to be sought in Adam, in whom it must have again been lost, but in Christ, in whom it has brought gain to all.

[1] Frenum extraordinarium. See Bellarmin., *de Gratia pr. hom*, cap. v.

[2] Melanchth., *loc.*, p. 112 : Adam et Eva erant electi, et tamen revera amiserunt Spiritum Sanctum in lapsu.

SECOND PART OF THE SYSTEM OF DOCTRINE

SECOND PART

Explication of the facts of the religious self-consciousness, as they are determined by the antithesis.

INTRODUCTION

§ 62. *The God-consciousness described in the foregoing occurs as the actual content of a moment of experience only under the general form of self-consciousness,* i.e. *the antithesis of pleasure and pain.*

NOTE.—Cf. § 5.

1. The disposition to the God-consciousness can be represented as a continuous impartation of that consciousness, but only in a degree that is infinitely small ; with the consequence that the transition to a definite and perceptible magnitude is always dependent on some other fact of consciousness. Now, were such a transition to take place in our self-consciousness apart from the form of the antithesis, *i.e.* neither as an advancement nor as an arrestment of the God-consciousness, it would need to be a transition that was continuous and uniform. This is conceivable if, independently of any other fact of consciousness, the God-consciousness were to rise noticeably above the infinitely small degree just referred to. The condition of the God-consciousness in such a case would be one of constant repression, dull uniformity, any emergence of vitality above a very low average being found only among the other facts of consciousness. A constant uniformity in the God-consciousness, however, is conceivable also in a state of existence where an absolute facility existed of evoking it in its absolute strength from every other fact of consciousness. The condition of the God-consciousness in this case would be that of a blessed uniformity of constant predominance. Clearly, however, our religious consciousness is not such that more and less do not apply to it ; on the contrary, it oscillates between these extremes, sharing, as it does, the variations of our temporal life. True, this more and less, simply as such, may seem to be of the nature of a fluctuating difference rather than of an antithesis. Still, contrariety

of movement creates an antithesis ; for a movement from less to more indicates that the disposition to the God-consciousness is developing with increasing freedom, while one from more to less is an arrestment of it and indicates that other impulses are more powerful.

But now in this as in other provinces of experience (as there is no such state as absolute blessedness or as complete abeyance of the God-consciousness) pleasure and pain are by no means to be regarded as so separate from each other that one of them might in some circumstances actually exist without the other. If, then, the determining power of the God-consciousness is felt to be limited, pain is bound up with it, *i.e.* is present even in the highest pleasure. Whereas, if the consciousness that this power is arrested excites pain, the God-consciousness is nevertheless willed as such a power, and is thereby in and for itself an object of pleasure.

2. If, however, our proposition is to be understood as implying that what emerges in actual consciousness, under whichever form of the antithesis, as God-consciousness is always what has already been described, namely, the feeling of absolute dependence, and that no modification of the God-consciousness can be instanced where this feeling might either be absent or have added to it anything except what is related to and constitutes the antithesis in question ; and if there is taken along with this our former assertion [1] that in the Christian consciousness (the same has always held good, however, of religion moulded by any other form of belief) the feeling of absolute dependence never purely by itself fills a moment of religious experience—then each of the two statements is explained by the other in this way, namely, that what was described in our First Part (taken along with what in other forms of religion develops otherwise out of the fact that, as often as the indwelling God-consciousness really seeks to emerge, it appears either as advanced or arrested in its functioning) likewise constitutes the God-consciousness in its entire range, and that this fact must govern our conception of the whole content of every moment of religious experience, occur where it may. This assertion is challenged mainly on the ground that in our use of the idea of absolute dependence we have annulled every distinction between human freedom and subordinate forms of finite being,[2] while yet the God-consciousness surely (if one's own acceptance of the divine will and one's love to God form part of the God-consciousness) has

[1] § 29. [2] § 49.

a content which relates exclusively to human freedom and presupposes it. These elements, it is held, consequently cannot be derived from the feeling of absolute dependence, and just as little from the antithesis mentioned if it refers solely to that feeling. To dispose of this objection in all its aspects, and thereby to substantiate our assertion with respect at least to all monotheistic forms of faith, lies outside our present task.

One point, however, common to all forms of faith in so far as they all participate in the antithesis, may be adduced here. This, namely, that absolute facility in the development of the God-consciousness from any given stimulus and in every situation, which is proposed as the end, is equivalent to constant communion with God, while every retrograde movement is a turning away from God. Now if, religion being admittedly an essential element of life, only communion and not turning away can be willed, the latter can be received into consciousness only if it is what was originally in harmony with the divine will. In Christianity this proviso is enunciated in the most general and fruitful way by the postulation of redemption as the work and dispensation of God, and hence also of faith in redemption as conformity to the divine will.

3. Everything related to the Redeemer in the religious consciousness of the Christian is peculiar to the distinctively Christian articulation of the antithesis under discussion. No proposition, as we have already said, describing the feeling of absolute dependence apart from this antithesis, can be a description of a religious moment in its entire content, for in every such moment that feeling occurs only as a relative turning away from God or turning towards Him. From these two statements we must go on to assert that no proposition merely describing the condition of the individual life with reference to this antithesis is a description of the entire content of a religious moment, since in every such moment the condition described must needs manifest itself in the emergence of the feeling of absolute dependence. In the actual life of the Christian, therefore, the two are always found in combination: there is no general God-consciousness which has not bound up with it a relation to Christ, and no relationship with the Redeemer which has no bearing on the general God-consciousness. The propositions of the first part, which lay less direct stress on what is distinctively Christian, are on that account often treated as Natural Theology of an original and universally valid kind, and as such are overrated by those who are themselves less permeated by the distinctive

element in Christianity. Others, again, underrate these propositions as attainable even apart from Christianity, and will only allow those propositions which express a relation to the Redeemer to rank as specifically Christian. Both parties are in error. For the former propositions are in no sense the reflection of a meagre and purely monotheistic God-consciousness, but are abstracted from one which has issued from fellowship with the Redeemer. Similarly, propositions expressing a relation to Christ are genuinely Christian propositions only in so far as they recognize no other criterion for relationship with the Redeemer than the measure in which the continuity of the God-consciousness is produced thereby; so that a relationship with Christ, which resulted in the God-consciousness losing its prominence or being, as it were, superseded (because Christ alone and not God had a place in self-consciousness), might indeed be a most intimate one, but strictly speaking it would not belong to the sphere of religion at all.

§ 63. *While in general the manner in which the God-consciousness takes shape in and with the stimulated self-consciousness can be traced only to the action of the individual, the distinctive feature of Christian piety lies in the fact that whatever alienation from God there is in the phases of our experience, we are conscious of it as an action originating in ourselves, which we call Sin; but whatever fellowship with God there is, we are conscious of it as resting upon a communication from the Redeemer, which we call Grace.*

1. Let us suppose an æsthetic form of faith.[1] It will reduce both these arrestments and continued developments of the God-consciousness, as indeed every other change in man's experience, to passive states, and represent them consequently as the effects of external influences in such a manner that they will appear simply to be appointed events, while the ideas of merit and guilt will really not apply to them at all. Accordingly, we may say that the controversy regarding freedom, as it is usually urged in this sphere, is just the controversy as to whether our passive states are to be regarded as subordinate to our active states or *vice versa*; and that freedom in the latter sense is the universal premiss of all teleological forms of faith, which alone, by starting as they do from the ascendency of spontaneous activity in man, are able to find guilt in all arrestments of the disposition to the God-consciousness,

[1] § 9.

and merit in every progression of it. More precise determinations, however, of the 'how' of either are not to be found in the common nature of these forms of faith; this only is self-evident, namely, that if both arrestment of the impulse to the God-consciousness and quickened development of it are to be equally the act of one and the same individual, and consequently opposites are to be explained by the same cause, then, in relation to the doer, the two must cease to be opposed.

2. In Christian piety as described here there is no such initial difficulty to be surmounted. The description given here, however, is identical with the general exposition put forward above.[1] For if the feeling of absolute dependence, which was previously in bondage, has been set free only by redemption, the facility with which we are able to graft the God-consciousness on the various sensuous excitations of our self-consciousness also springs solely from the facts of redemption, and is therefore a communicated facility. And if the bondage of the feeling of absolute dependence did not betoken its real absence (for absence would imply the impossibility of such an act as is here designated sin), then in every portion of life that could be regarded as a whole in itself, the God-consciousness too was present in degree even if only as something infinitely small, and thus whenever such a portion of life came to an end there took place an act having relation to the God-consciousness. Not, however, an act involving the evocation of the God-consciousness as a co-determinant of the moment, *i.e.* not a turning to God (from which an experience of communion with God always arises of itself), but a turning away from God,[2] so that with the acceptance of such a redemption there is always conjoined a backward look to sin as prior to it. Now the fact that here communion with God rests on an act extraneous to it by no means prevents our bringing Christianity under the general category of teleological forms of faith. For, on the one hand, communication and action are not mutually exclusive, for corporate acts, *e.g.*, have their origin for the most part in a single person, and yet are acts also on the part of the rest; while, on the other hand, appropriation of redemption is always represented as action, as a laying hold of Christ, or the like.[3]

[1] § 11, 2 and 3.

[2] Cf. Rom. 3^{23}. *Conf. Aug.* xix.: Voluntas . . . avertit se a Deo.

[3] *Augsb. Conf.* xx.: 'He therefore desires that we should *embrace* the promise of God by faith.' Melanchthon, *Loci Comm. Theol.* De Vocabulo Fidei: 'Si fides non est fiducia intuens Christum . . . non applicamus nobis eius beneficium.' De Fide: 'Pia mens . . . intelligit hanc misericordiam fide id est fiducia apprehendendam esse.'

In the case, however, of a religious consciousness contrariwise regarding its derangements as coming from elsewhere, but communion with God (into which these do not enter) as proceeding from the individual's own spiritual vitality, the term redemption could be applied (and even that in a very subordinate sense) only to that which sealed up the external sources of the derangements. Redemption through Jesus, however, has never been thought of in this way. And the further we carry the way of looking at things just indicated, then the more the lack of communion with God is taken to be merely fortuitous, the less definitely are sin and grace as such (and as earlier and later) differentiated from each other, and the more does the conception of redemption recede into the distance, till all three disappear together. This disappearance actually occurs when it is assumed that the unity of the sensuous and the higher self-consciousness is the natural basic condition of the individual—a condition in which the absence of the God-consciousness in any particular moment remains merely accidental, something which at once cancels itself out in corporate life, inasmuch as all do not suffer from the same accident at once. This, taken strictly, is the non-Christian view which recognizes no need of redemption ; for in Christianity these two, sin and grace, are valid ideas only on the basis of redemption and on the assumption that it has been appropriated.

3. Moreover, the proposition cannot be taken as implying that in the immediate Christian self-consciousness sin and grace are to be referred to separate moments and to be kept absolutely apart from each other as mutually incompatible. On the contrary, as the energy of the God-consciousness is never at its absolutely highest any more than the engrafting of the God-consciousness on the excitations of the sensuous self-consciousness is ever absolutely constant, there is involved in this circumstance a limiting deficiency of the God-consciousness, which is certainly sinful. Just as little, however, in a truly Christian consciousness can the connexion with redemption be utterly null, for in that case the Christian consciousness would, until the connexion was re-established, be, contrary to what is assumed, non-Christian. And as this connexion proceeds originally from the Redeemer, so His communicated action is implied throughout. Here, accordingly, while the elements we are discussing are antithetic they are only such as in the religious life of the Christian are conjoined in every moment, though always in varied measure.

§ 64. *For the purpose of our exposition, it is necessary to separate the two subjects, so as to treat first of Sin and then of Grace; and of each in accordance with all the three forms of dogmatic propositions.*

1. In our exposition all doctrines properly so called must be extracted from the Christian religious self-consciousness, *i.e.* the inward experience of Christian people. Since, however, it is the case that every Christian is conscious both of sin and of grace as always combined with each other and never dissociated, we may well be asked what warrant we have for separating them, seeing that if either be described by itself alone what results will not be the description of a Christian consciousness. A description of the sense of sin as the exclusive content even of merely detached portions of life would only amount to a historical sketch, the accuracy of which would require some sort of proof, but could find no verification in the Christian consciousness itself; such a description would therefore be no doctrine of the faith. Similarly the description of an inherently absolute and continuous efficacy of the God-consciousness would only be an anticipation; no one could point to such a state as actually brought about in him by redemption; so that this again would be no doctrine of the faith. Granting both positions (on the understanding that in each case one of the two elements is absolutely excluded), the separation of the two is nevertheless necessary to our exposition; only we must recognize that it is not met with in any Christian consciousness, but is an arbitrary expedient adopted here with a view simply to greater clarity of thought. For although our dogmatic propositions as a whole represent only the doctrine held to be valid in the Evangelical Church of our time, yet the Christian self-consciousness which they are meant to articulate with the utmost precision is not really confined to any definite period, but is the universal, the always and everywhere self-identical element in the Christian Church—so far, that is to say, as dogmatic propositions do not relate to the *differentiæ* of the Christian communions, as they do not wherever the antithesis of sin and grace is in question. We must accordingly describe the Christian consciousness with reference to its content, composed of these antithetic elements, in such a way that even the first moment of the genesis of the Christian consciousness and everything that in later moments represents the first, may be comprised in our description. Now, in the case of those who are not

born in Christianity but come to accept it, it is obvious that their appropriation of redemption, and therefore of grace, must be preceded by a recognition of their need of redemption ; and this emerges only in connexion with the consciousness of sin. In such persons, accordingly, there is a consciousness of sin anterior to the consciousness of grace ; and since everything sinful in their later life is connected with the sin that was present prior to grace, they have in every moment of their later life the consciousness of sin as of something present in them before grace was there. Nay, this consciousness must be shared without exception even by those who are born within Christendom, were it only in virtue of their corporate feeling, the formula that sin is anterior to grace being simply the expression of the human race's need for redemption and of its relation to Christ. Hence to vindicate our proposition we do not even need to decide whether or not each individual born in Christendom was at first outside of grace for a time, and, like those not so born, attained to grace only after passing through a state characterized exclusively by the consciousness of sin.

2. In pursuance, then, of this course of separating the consciousness of sin and the consciousness of grace in our exposition, we shall first describe by itself that element of the Christian self-consciousness which is more and more to disappear through the action of the other, and which, arising out of man's common condition anterior to the entrance of redemption, likewise represents that condition. Thereafter we shall describe by itself that element which is ever to be less and less limited by the other, and which, arising out of redemption, likewise represents the total efficacy thereof. The separation of these two elements common to all Christian states of mind into which the antithesis has developed is an obvious possibility for the simple reason that otherwise there can scarcely be a full perception of the two implied relations. It is more difficult, however, to show that, and how, the separation can be managed in the other two types of dogmatic propositions without disadvantage to their content. Thus, if, to begin with, we were to speak of the world by itself and not in relation to man, then, first, whether the antithesis in question had unfolded itself in man or not, whatever in the world influences man would always be the same, and there could accordingly be no special relationship between the world and either member of the antithesis. But again, such change as has been wrought in the world by human activity is always as regards the world simply the work of the

whole man, and there least of all differences relating to the God-consciousness would have to be taken into account. But what we have to deal with in this connexion is always simply states of the world in relation to man, and there it is evident that the world will be a different thing to a man according as he apprehends it from the standpoint of a God-consciousness completely paralysed or of one absolutely paramount. It will accordingly be possible to distinguish in the Christian life itself between what in our conception of the world is to be placed to the account of sin, and what to the account of grace. The like holds good also of the results of man's action upon the world as far as these are realities to himself and come within his consciousness. For the more significance he attaches to the antithesis, the more apparent will be to him the homogeneous and self-coherent character of what has proceeded from him because of sin and without the prompting of the God-consciousness, and on the other hand of what, as resulting from the operation of redemption, must bear the impress thereof. Finally, as regards the divine attributes, it is of course evident that statements concerning God cannot issue from a condition of alienation from God, but are only possible when a man is in some sense turned again towards Him ; for all statements concerning God presuppose a turning towards Him. But not even where sin is viewed from the standpoint of a paramount God-consciousness can we conceive of divine attributes that have to do with sin apart from its disappearance as a result of redemption. For since all divine attributes are activities, attributes of the kind in question must be activities making for the maintenance and confirmation of sin ; but to admit such attributes would be to run counter to Christian piety. Similarly, should we assume a divine agency as the source of the God-consciousness but not as developing out of sin and limited by sin, it too could only be formulated in terms of concepts of the divine attributes from which the distinctively Christian character had completely vanished ; so that within the range of this particular type of concept that character would never appear at all. Surely, however, it is natural for Christian piety, seeing as it certainly does in redemption a divine measure, to make statements concerning God that relate to the God-consciousness ; and in fact it will be these very statements which set forth the trend and aim of the divine causality, as reflected in our feeling of absolute dependence in general, so that it is only in combination with them that the ideas underlying our First Part attain to perfect precision and vivid clearness. In order to discover these statements it is certainly quite unnecessary to separate the two members of our antithesis from each other ; yet a correct, and, in view of what has already been said, perhaps a preferable, way of describing the divine activity by means of which the God-consciousness attains to supremacy, will be to ask, first, what divine attributes are to be discerned in the state of sin—though, of course, only in as far as there is therein an expectation of and preparation for redemption ; and then, secondly, to what attributes the growing dominion of the God-consciousness points back, as it comes to be formed out of the state of sin through redemption. Even were these attributes mere abstractions (as would obviously be less true of the latter than of the former), yet, when viewed in combination—just as it is the fusion of the two elements that constitutes the reality of the Christian life—they would yield a truly living representation ; and if we then view them in combination with the divine attributes set forth in our First Part, the exposition of our God-consciousness under this form will be complete.

3. This Second Part of Dogmatics might accordingly be arranged in two ways. Thus we might take the three forms of dogmatic proposition as our primary division, and then under each of them treat first of what relates to sin, and secondly of what relates to grace. Or, again, we might set forth these two elements of our self-consciousness as the main heads, and treat first of sin under all the three forms of proposition, and next of grace in the same way. The latter scheme seems preferable inasmuch as the main division will then be formed by what is found already divided in the immediate Christian self-consciousness. This part of our work will therefore have two aspects, in one of which we shall deal with the consciousness of sin under all the three dogmatic forms, in the other with grace on similar lines.

FIRST ASPECT OF THE ANTITHESIS

EXPLICATION OF THE CONSCIOUSNESS OF SIN

§ 65. *The propositions to be enunciated here must all harmonize with those of the same type in our First Part; but they must also have regard to the propositions of the Second Aspect, which explicate the consciousness of grace, these last being meanwhile held in reserve.*

1. Any attempt to consider the fact of sin purely by itself is at once confronted by an apparent antinomy. Thus were we from our point of view to regard every arrestment of the God-consciousness that takes place merely as the act of man, then, as being a turning away from God, it would be in contradiction with the disposition to the God-consciousness which is present in man as a vital impulse, and is here assumed as such. Equal difficulty would appear to lie in the necessity of the actual existence of sin being consistent with divine omnipotence, since man's turning from God must like all else be ordained by God; for of course man even in the state of sin is involved in the natural order, and it is only in virtue of his position within that order—with the entire range of which the divine causality is co-extensive—that sin can develop in him at all. Again, if there are divine attributes related to sin, indeed, but not in the way of giving it persistence and confirmation, how should even that, which from its very nature ought not to continue, have come into being in association with all that owes its being to the eternally omniscient divine omnipotence? Finally, if sin exists only where there is a powerlessness of the God-consciousness, and if it develops in man in consequence of impressions received from the totality of finite existence, how could this fail to abrogate what we laid down as the original perfection of man and the perfection of the world in relation to him?

2. Although this antinomy can be only apparent (the two sets of propositions alike having their source in our immediate self-consciousness, which as the truth of our being cannot be in contradiction with itself), yet it follows from this relationship that we

are here face to face with a large number of difficulties. For if we are too readily disposed to exclude sin from the range of our absolute dependence on God, we inevitably verge upon Manichæism ; while if we seek to reconcile it with the original perfection of man, we shall hardly avoid Pelagianism. It may, in fact, be said that in the development of the Church's doctrine there has been an almost constant wavering between these antagonistic positions. Nevertheless, though this wavering cannot now be brought to rest, and though no formula can be found which would not be felt by some to lean more towards the latter extreme, and by others towards the former, yet in a general way, at least, the second part of our proposition is as well adapted to smooth out the difficulties as the first part of necessity raises them. Thus since in our statements about sin we are to keep in view those still to be made about grace, we may regard sin on the one hand as simply that which would not be unless redemption was to be ; or on the other as that which, as it is to disappear, can disappear only through redemption. In the first case we obviate any seemingly inevitable risk of approximating to Manichæism ; in the second we can scarcely, except by wantonness, fall into Pelagianism. If, however, the danger indicated is not perpetually to recur in consequence of our having to refer to the terms recognized by the Church, we must claim the right to interpret these terms in such a way as most adequately to secure ourselves against the danger, or else, should they not lend themselves to this, to replace them by others. In order to attain at least to an approximate solution of our problem we must have recourse to one or other of these alternatives under all the three forms.

FIRST SECTION

Sin as a State of Man

§ 66. *We have the consciousness of sin whenever the God-consciousness which forms part of an inner state, or is in some way added to it, determines our self-consciousness as pain; and therefore we conceive of sin as a positive antagonism of the flesh against the spirit.*

1. Without running counter to our method we cannot at the outset give an objective elucidation of sin, but must revert to the personal self-consciousness which attests an inner state as sin—a procedure all the less open to objection because sin cannot emerge in the life of the Christian apart from such a consciousness. To lack this consciousness would simply be an additional sin, of which, as such, we could not fail subsequently to become conscious. If, then, it is our primary object to ascertain the characteristic element in the consciousness of sinfulness, we ought not, within the sphere of Christian piety, to look for it except in relationship to the God-consciousness, and accordingly the only course open to us is to reckon everything as sin that has arrested the free development of the God-consciousness. Now, if in any particular moment under examination God has formed part of our self-consciousness, but this God-consciousness has not been able to permeate the other active elements therein, thus determining the moment, then sin and the consciousness of sin are simultaneous, and the sensuous self-consciousness by reason of its having been gratified is affected with pleasure, but the higher, owing to the impotence of the God-consciousness, with pain. If, on the other hand, God has not formed part of the moment at all, if, that is to say, the occurrence of the moment excludes the God-consciousness, showing that the God-consciousness cannot make the moment its own, which also means that it cannot be supposed to accord and acquiesce in it, then the consciousness of sin follows on the sin itself. Supposing, however, that the God-consciousness has determined the moment, and that pleasure is present in the higher self-consciousness, still every attendant feeling of effort implies a consciousness of sin—in some

degree, consequently, annulling that pleasure—since we thereby are made aware that if the sensuous elements which have been overcome had been reinforced from without, the God-consciousness would have been unable to determine the moment. In this sense, therefore—but only because there exists a living seed of sin ever ready to burst forth—there is such a thing as an abiding consciousness of sin, now preceding the sin itself as a warning presentiment, now accompanying it as an inward reproof, or following it as penitence. That no God-consciousness, however, should ever be directed at all upon a moment such as that described could only happen if in the person acting there were no relationship between the moment and the class of actions under discussion (in which case he would be in a state of innocence), or if the God-consciousness were no longer active within him (which would be the state of hardening).

2. If we conceive now a state in which the flesh, *i.e.* the totality of the so-called lower powers of the soul, were susceptible only to impulses proceeding from the quarter of the God-consciousness, and were never an independent motive principle, a conflict between the two would not be possible, but we should again have conceived a sinless state. In every moment in this self-consciousness the two powers would be perfectly at one, every moment beginning in the spirit and ending in the spirit, and the flesh serving only as a living intermediary, a healthy organ, and never exhibiting anything not initiated and directed by the spirit, whether as an act of its own or as an intrusive extraneous element in an act proceeding from the spirit. As long, however, as spirit and flesh have not in this sense become one, they co-exist as two powers at issue with each other,[1] and in so far as the spirit presses towards the perfect unity indicated, this state can be characterized only as an incapacity of the spirit. The possibility of this we left aside when treating of the original perfection of man,[2] except that there those relationships, and no others, had to be brought out which contain in themselves the principles of progressive development. Since, however, the consciousness of sin never exists in the soul of the Christian without the consciousness of the power of redemption,[3] the former is never actually found without its complementary half which we are to describe later, and, if taken by itself alone, represents only that state of a hopeless incapacity in the spirit, which prevails outside the sphere of redemption.

[1] Gal. 5^{17}, Rom. 7^{18-23}. [2] § 60. [3] Rom. 7^{25} 8^{2}.

This explanation of sin as an arrestment of the determinative power of the spirit, due to the independence of the sensuous functions, is certainly reconcilable with those explanations which describe sin as a turning away from the Creator,[1] though less so with those which interpret sin as a violation of the divine law.[2] But it cannot be of any great consequence to insist on a reconciliation with the latter, for in the sense in which God and the eternal law might be distinguished—as if one could turn away from the latter as from a single and perhaps arbitrary act of God without turning away from Himself—law is not an originally Christian term and must therefore be merged in a higher. We should certainly require to widen it in a very indefinite and arbitrary way if we had to bring under it all that may count as sin not only in deeds, but in thoughts and words. Our explanation, however, unifies this division in the most natural way. For if a thought or word viewed otherwise than as an act did form the content of a moment, it could only incorrectly be called a sin. An interpretation more Christian in its origin, and at the same time directly in keeping with our own, is that which says that sin consists in our desiring what Christ contemns and *vice versa*.[3]

§ 67. *We are conscious of sin as the power and work of a time when the disposition to the God-consciousness had not yet actively emerged in us.*

1. It is in reality already implied, in the relation of this proposition to all that has been said above, that in the period to which the consciousness of sin points back, sin was not present in us in the same way as we are now conscious of it. For in this latter form it can be present only simultaneously with and as related to the God-consciousness. If our God-consciousness is not yet developed, there can be in us no resistance to it, but merely an independent activity of the flesh which, though in time it will quite naturally come to act as a resistance to the spirit, cannot at that stage be regarded as sin in the proper sense, but rather as the germ of sin. This interpretation we apply generally to individual persons in their earliest stages of development, and in exactly the same way to whole peoples and eras. Nevertheless, the proposition is not to be understood as implying that all sin, whatever its content, is to be relegated to that prior time; it refers only to the state of sin in general.

[1] *Conf. Aug.* xix. : Voluntas . . . quae avertit se a Deo.
[2] For others of this type cf. Gerhard, *Loc. Th.* t. v. pp. 2 ff.
[3] Aug., *de vera relig.* 31 : Non enim ullum peccatum committi potest, nisi aut dum appetuntur ea quae ille contemsit, aut fugiuntur quae ille sustinuit.

The functions of the lower life which may come into conflict with the spirit are not all developed prior to the God-consciousness, but as they do develop without having the God-consciousness directed upon them in their initial stages, the same result follows.

2. Resistance, as an activity by which an opposed activity is to be neutralized, has naturally its degrees of more and less, and is thus an intensive phenomenon conditioned by time, and when present in anything that has life advances by repetition in time to proficiency. Now our proposition goes back to the universal experience that in each individual the flesh manifests itself as a reality before the spirit comes to be such, the result being, that, as soon as the spirit enters the sphere of consciousness (and it is involved in the original perfection of man that the independent activity of the flesh cannot of itself prevent the ingress of the spirit), resistance takes place, *i.e.* we become conscious also of sin as the God-consciousness awakes within us. The activity of the spirit, however, not merely in general, as present in the distinctive form of human life, but also in particular, in its effort to win dominion over the flesh, is likewise an intensive phenomenon, and, as a living force, attains by repetition in time to proficiency. Thus the strength which the spirit gradually acquires is the work and power of the period subsequent to the awaking of the God-consciousness, though of course in association with the previously given spiritual forces to the promptings of which that awaking was due ; while the strength of the resistance made by the flesh and manifested in the consciousness of sin, is due to the advantage gained by the flesh during the prior time,[1] though again, of course, in association with the corporate life upon which the amount of that advantage depends. Now if the whole situation subsequent to the awaking of the God-consciousness could be conceived as a progressive ascendancy of the spirit over the flesh, self-consciousness could hardly have such a phase as the consciousness of sin ; and accordingly this phase will be more and more attenuated as that conception becomes dominant, and *vice versa*. We actually find, however, that our development is always an irregular one, and also that the spirit is obstructed in its action by the flesh—the circumstance, indeed, to which our consciousness of sin is due. This irregularity is twofold. In the first place, the development of the spirit proceeds intermittently through widely separated moments of exceptional illumination and stimulation ; and thus if, after such a

[1] Gen. 8²¹.

moment, the activity of the spirit should seem less than it was during the moment, or if the stimulation did not from the outset correspond with the illumination, we become conscious of our state as one of sin, since in the actual experience of the moment the flesh overrides the effort of the spirit.[1] Secondly, we are conscious of the spirit as one, while the flesh is a manifold, and a manifold composed of diverse elements, so that the spirit cannot stand in a uniform relation to it. Since, however, the spirit's demand is always the same, the spirit itself, wherever it is less able to work effectively, appears as a baffled and defeated force, and the subject therefore as in a state of sin. The more thoroughly we trace back the state of our spiritual life to a conscious beginning, to a general 'taking command of one's self'—so to call it[2]—which is represented in every decision of the will, then, whenever the act does not correspond with that decision, the more conscious we are of a domination of the flesh, and we cannot do otherwise than trace this back to a time prior to that beginning.

§ 68. *Although sin, as a result of the unequal development of insight and will-power, can be conceived in such a way that its existence does not invalidate the idea of the original perfection of man, still we are bound to regard it as a derangement of our nature.*

1. This proposition would seem to bring the entire life of the spirit under the two contrasted categories of intellect and will, but it is far from being intended here to make light of the third element in our experience, namely, our immediate self-consciousness, which in fact forms the starting-point in every part of our exposition. Indeed, it is precisely the relationship of that self-consciousness to the other two factors that serves as the measure of the disparity in their development. Let us figure to ourselves the above-mentioned 'taking command of one's self' in its most general form; it is simply the discernment of the absolute superiority of those states of mind which combine with the God-consciousness without obstructing it. That discernment cannot emerge without the individual's appropriating it, and this takes place only through an act of self-consciousness in which the said discernment, as giving approval and recognition, becomes a command. Now the fact that this excitation of the self-consciousness follows upon the discernment more rapidly than it is able to determine our volitions, constitutes just that inequality along with which sin and the con-

[1] Rom. 7^{18}. [2] Rom. 7^{22}.

sciousness of sin are given. It is true that there are two ways in which at the very start we might conceive of this disparity as being removed, and in either case there would be no consciousness of sin. Thus if a man were to attain gradually to a discernment of the relationship of his various inner states to the God-consciousness, but only in the same measure as his recognition thereof could set the will in operation, then for him no consciousness of sin could arise, as indeed he could never imagine a more divine life than that which he actually exhibits at every moment. Similarly, if the antithesis were actually present in its full extent and clearly realized, but the will were uniformly powerful enough to resist every impulse of the flesh, then again a person having this experience could never come to be conscious of sin as his own condition. Neither of these cases, however, occurs in our experience ; in fact we can see quite well why they cannot. Thus—to begin with the second case—the antithesis presents itself to our understanding in the manner of a general pattern or formula which in any particular instance is, so to speak, recognized from afar ; and it is in this way too that the immature begin to receive the said discernment from their elders soon after their own earliest experiences of excitation. But the impulse that the commanding recognition is to give to the will must —just because the flesh has to do with the particular only, and knows nothing of the general—in every given instance be a special one ; and here the flesh has habit on its side as the real law in its members,[1] whereas it is only gradually that the earlier happier moments come to the succour of the spirit. If, however, we turn to the first case, then, while we might perhaps regard this (though, as a matter of fact, we never do find perfect equipoise, but always advance and retreat) as a possibility in a single individual, it could not be so in a communal life. For all would not take the same path, and consequently each would necessarily see in the case of others, and then recognize in his own, something for which at the moment he had not the requisite will-power. Accordingly, since without this disparity—as a counterpart to which we might also imagine a lagging of the intelligence behind the will, though this would be in appearance only—there could arise no consciousness of sin, the latter is to be understood simply as issuing from the former ; indeed, it would be impossible for any one to specify any other mode of attaining to that consciousness. It is along the same lines that we can understand what is unquestionably the most pernicious

[1] Rom. 7^{23}.

element of all, namely, how the resistance of the flesh reacts upon the intelligence, so that for one thing the intelligence seeks to palliate the inner states thus produced, on the pretext of their being compatible with the God-consciousness ;[1] and for another the God-consciousness, being seized upon when but in germ by the power of the flesh, is altered and disintegrated to such a degree that every state comes to be compatible with some aspect of it, and thus the moral antithesis itself is lost.[2] If on this view idolatry may rightly enough be thought to have the same origin as sin, no less rightly will all anthropopathic ideas of God which attenuate the antithesis or base it on distinctions of human law be regarded as survivals of idolatry.

2. Nevertheless, we are not entitled to say that sin, on the view taken of it here, would conflict with the original perfection of man, and thus annul it. On the contrary, we must rather insist upon the fact that sin in general exists only in so far as there is a consciousness of it ; and this again is always conditioned by a good which must have preceded it and must have been just a result of that original perfection. The 'bad conscience' which we may have within us is there, for one thing, only because of our seeing the possibility of what is better—a conviction which must accordingly have come to us in a different way ; and for another, because of the mere fact of our *having* a conscience, *i.e.* an inward demand for harmony with the God-consciousness. Hence if in an individual, at a time of life when the God-consciousness could have been developed, or among a people still at an early stage of development, the notion of that 'better' has not been evolved in similar fashion, we regard their imperfection and the power of the flesh in them not as sin, but as grossness and ignorance. Sin, accordingly, manifests itself only in connexion with and by means of already existent good, and what it obstructs is future good. Similarly, if the consciousness of sin comes about through the experience that the God-consciousness operates less effectively upon a sensuous disposition than upon any other, even in that case, too, it issues from a comparison with a previously existent good. And in point of fact that is confirmed by what forms a counterpart to the foregoing, namely, that a trace of the consciousness of sin lurks even in the most exalted moments of religious experience, just because the God-consciousness does not permeate our whole being uniformly ; and this residuum is carried onwards to the time

[1] Rom. 2^{15}. [2] Rom. $1^{18,25}$.

following, since a moment of that kind cannot leave behind it effects that will be homogeneous at every point. Thus the state of sin over its entire range actually presupposes the original perfection of man, and is indeed dependent upon it; and, accordingly, just as the latter conception expresses the unity of our development, so sin in turn represents its intermittent and disjointed character, though without in any way abrogating the unity itself.

3. Now if, after having thus found ourselves able to interpret sin in its relation to the original perfection of man, we could likewise become perfectly certain of its inevitability, we should have no choice but to acquiesce in the latter. The most natural thing would then be to say that the consciousness which we characterize as the consciousness of sin, taken in its widest compass and even including the God-consciousness, vitiated as that may be and in its distinctive nature subverted by disruption, is nothing but that consciousness of good still lacking to us which arises within us, as a result of individual acts and inner states. But this view, in nullifying as it does not only the reality of sin but also the need of redemption, leaves so little room anywhere for the peculiar work of a Redeemer that it can scarcely be regarded as a Christian view at all. As a matter of fact, the certainty with which we are aware of the good realized within us in some exceptional moment is at the same time a conviction that we might evade every moment in which the same degree of will-power is not demonstrably present; while again, every retrograde movement is a derangement of one originally provided for in our nature; and thus the experience of an abatement in will-power and the consciousness that sin can be avoided, as also the conception of sin as a derangement of our nature, are so far one and the same. In order to affirm, however, that it is possible to obviate entirely the active resistance of the flesh, we require to have an assured belief in a development of power of the God-consciousness that has proceeded continuously from its earliest manifestation to a state of absolute strength, *i.e.* a condition of human perfection evolved without sin. This certainty is therefore at once the basis of the full consciousness of sin as a derangement of our nature, and of faith in the possibility of redemption by the communication of the spiritual power so attested. For since even our most perfect inner states still retain traces of sin (this is the testimony of the universal consciousness of mankind), then *he* alone to whom we do not ascribe that common consciousness of sin, and in so far only as we are justified in not so ascribing it (such justifica-

tion being asserted in the above formula itself), can exercise redeeming activity.[1] It is of course true that the consciousness of sin comes from the law,[2] but as the law in the very multitude of its precepts is but an imperfect representation of the good, and even in the unity of an all-embracing maxim does not show how it can be obeyed, the knowledge of sin that arises out of it is ever in some respects incomplete and in some uncertain; and it is only from the absolute sinlessness and the perfect spiritual power of the Redeemer that we gain the full knowledge of sin. And our belief that sin is a derangement of human nature rests solely upon the possibility that, on the assumption of the original perfection described above, the God-consciousness could have developed progressively from the first man to the purity and holiness which it manifests in the Redeemer.

§ 69. *We are conscious of sin partly as having its source in ourselves, partly as having its source outside our own being.*

1. The relation of the various dispositions and activities of sense—a relation varying in a special way with every single person—to the higher activity of the soul is based upon what we may provisionally call an innate difference in these dispositions, which serves in part to constitute the peculiar personality of the individual. Such differences, however, we observe being handed on within the same stock, and thus also coalescing when new families are formed from various stocks, while we find them also established among larger human masses as the distinctive characteristics of tribes and peoples. Hence in virtue of this dependence of the specific constitution of the individual life upon a larger common type, as also of the later generations upon the earlier, the sin of the individual has its source in something beyond and prior to his own existence. Hence it is just the same even if such differences are held not to be innate, but to be due to education alone, since the type of education itself is determined by proclivities and experiences which precede in time the life of the learner. On the other hand, as the swift movement of a sensuous excitation towards its object without ranging itself with the higher self-consciousness is unquestionably the act of the individual, every single sin of the individual must necessarily have its source in himself.

From the one point of view we distinguish between our good nature—for many impulses even of sense do not seek to pass

[1] Rom. 7²⁴ 8².   [2] Rom. 7⁷.

beyond what the spirit itself demands of them—and our evil nature, and we are conscious of each of these as something got and received by us conjointly with others. From the other, we recognize our evil nature as being also our own sin, since, instead of having overcome it by our action, we voluntarily perpetuate it from one moment to another.

2. The fact that one person is more disposed to reflection, his external activity being either on the whole feeble, or, if vigorous, yet crude and ignorant, and that another gives himself to external activities, and, generally speaking, thinks but little, or thinks in a dull and confused way—this, too, we place among the innate differences. True, by the social life around him the former will be drawn into the sphere of activity; while, as regards the latter, the results of reflection that are accepted in his community will somehow be lodged also in his mind; but the original idiosyncrasies will continue to operate; and in the case of the former, dawning piety will combine more easily with his thought, though his modes of action will remain carnal; while, in the case of the latter, it will be the intelligence that proves refractory; and thus sin will take a different form in each. Now, in whatever degree such diversity is connected with the disposition natural to each, and in each prior to all action, in the same degree the sin of each, as regards its particular form, will be rooted in something beyond his own life. On the other hand, in so far as every moment (be its content an idea or an action in the narrower sense) owes its occurrence solely to voluntary action—even a moment which, though the God-consciousness has already become active, does not contain that consciousness—the sin of each, as regards its reality, uniformly has its source in himself.

3. It is true also of the development of the sensuous life, which takes place in all men before that of the spiritual, that it does not depend upon the individual alone. The coming of the Ego into this world as a result of conception and birth cannot be regarded by our immediate self-consciousness as our own act—though speculation has sometimes sought to represent this as the primary apostasy, and as due to ourselves. In truth, however, just as the coming of the Ego is, with respect to each later generation, due to the action of the one before it, so the sinful self-assertiveness of sense, proceeding as it does from its earlier development, has a more remote source than the individual's own life. But once the God-consciousness has emerged as a definite and effective agency, and

as capable of growth, then every moment in which it does not manifest itself as such, and with a certain increment of power, even if infinitesimal, in comparison with earlier moments of the same kind, is an arrest upon the higher activity—an arrest originating in the doer himself—and is a veritable sin.

Postscript.—It is this twofold relation, found universally though in varying proportion in all consciousness of sin, that forms the essential and ultimate ground of the fact that the explication of the Christian consciousness of sin in the teaching of the Church falls into the two doctrines of 'original sin'[1] and 'actual sin.'[2] And in fact the true significance of that division emerges clearly from the foregoing exposition. Thus under the one head the state of sin is considered as something received, something we bring with us, prior to any act of our own, yet something in which our own guilt is latent; under the other, it is set forth as becoming apparent in the sinful acts which are due to the individual himself, but in which the received element brought with us is revealed. The traditional terminology, however, is in every aspect unsatisfactory. Thus, in the second expression (actual sin), the term 'sin' is, in accordance with common usage, predicated of the real act, but the adjective suggests the misleading idea that original sin is nothing real, or at least that alongside of actual sin there is a type of sin that is merely in seeming or that lies outside the sphere of action. In the first term again, 'original' (*Erb*) correctly expresses the connexion of the later generations with the earlier, as well as with the process by which the race is preserved; but the word 'sin' is misleading, being used here apparently in the same sense as in the other expression; in which case an earlier source would be predicated only of some actual sins and not of others. Such, however, cannot be the true purport of the expression, since original sin indicates that inherent quality of the acting subject which is a part condition of all his actual sins and is anterior to all action on his part.[3] Hence we might well wish for an alteration in these inexact designations, which besides are not found in Scripture; but such alteration will have to be introduced with great caution—a process to which the following treatment is meant to contribute; and if we would avoid breaking the historical continuity of doctrine, and causing fresh misconstructions and misunderstandings, we shall have to carry out the change by means of gradual adjustments.

[1] Peccatum originis. [2] Peccatum actuale.

[3] Peccatum enim originis non est aliquod delictum quod actu perpetratur :

First Doctrine: Original Sin

§ 70. *The sinfulness that is present in an individual prior to any action of his own, and has its ground outside his own being, is in every case a complete incapacity for good, which can be removed only by the influence of Redemption.*

Conf. Aug. 2: Docent quod—omnes homines secundum naturam propagati nascuntur . . . sine metu Dei sine fiducia erga Deum et cum concupiscentiâ, quodque hic morbus seu vitium originis vere sit peccatum damnans et afferens nunc quoque aeternam mortem his qui non renascuntur per baptismum et spiritum sanctum.—*Apol. Conf.* I: hic locus testatur nos non solum actus sed potentiam seu dona efficiendi timorem et fiduciam erga Deum adimere propagatis secundum carnalem natüram . . . ut cum nominamus concupiscentiam non tantum actus seu fructus intelligamus sed perpetuam naturae inclinationem.—*Conf. Gall.* ix.: Affirmamus quicquid mens humana habet lucis mox fieri tenebras cum de quaerendo Deo agitur, adeo ut sua intelligentia et ratione nullo modo possit ad eum accedere. Item . . . nullam prorsus habet ad bonum appetendum libertatem, nisi quam ex gratia et Dei dono acceperit.—*Expos. Simpl.* viii.: Peccatum autem intelligimus esse nativam illam hominis corruptionem . . . qua concupiscentiis pravis immersi . . . nil boni ex nobis ipsis facere imo ne cogitare quidem possumus.—ix.: proinde nullum est ad bonum homini liberum arbitrium nondum renato.—*Conf. Angl.* x.: Ea est hominis conditio, ut sese naturalibus suis viribus ad fidem convertere et praeparare non possit. Quare absque gratia Dei quae in Christo est ad facienda quae Deo grata sunt nihil valemus.—*Repetit. Conf.*: Et haec depravatio est carere iam luce Dei seu praesentiâ Dei quae in nobis fuisset, et est aversio voluntatis nostrae a Deo . . . et hominem non esse templum Dei sed miseram massam sine Deo et sine iustitia.

1. This idea of a sinfulness present from the first in every human being is in perfect accord with what has been set forth above. For if, even in the life of the man who has been received into fellowship with the redeemed, there is in the strict and precise sense no moment in which the consciousness of sin, as something present and operative, would not form an essential part of his self-consciousness were this latter clearly and fully realized,[1] then a sinfulness which is not completely overcome even by the power of redemption must for that very reason be regarded as in itself literally infinite. And if the disposition to the God-consciousness is thereby obscured and vitiated,[2] then man, just because his God-consciousness, though the best thing in him, is thus polluted and untrustworthy, must be wholly incapable not only of developing, but even of consciously aspiring to, such inner states as would harmonize with the proper

sed intime inhaeret infixum ipsi naturae substantiae et essentiae hominis (*Epitom.*, Art. I, p. 577, Ed. Rech.).

[1] § 62, I; § 64, I and 2. [2] § 8, 2.

aim and object of the said disposition. Hence, as Christian piety traces everything at all connected with the God-consciousness either to sin or to grace,[1] everything in our inner states that is not sin must be attributed to our share in redemption, and this redemption must be regarded as the only thing that can remove the incapacity referred to.

2. We admit then unreservedly this incapacity for good—good being understood here solely as that which is determined by the God-consciousness—between the limiting points of willing and doing,[2] within which all self-activity proper must fall. Yet we must not magnify our congenital sinfulness to such an extent as would involve the denial of man's capacity to appropriate redemption, for that capacity is the very least that can be predicated of that disposition to the God-consciousness which is inherent in man's original perfection.[3] In the light of such a denial nothing would remain of those higher gifts which constitute the prerogative of human nature, and in which everything that distinguishes man from brute must have some share ; these gifts would in fact be so utterly extinct that we should have literally to say that man has been born without human nature—an assertion that contradicts itself as soon as it is made. Again, were we to affirm that the capacity for redemption has been lost,[4] we should come into conflict with our very belief in redemption. The capacity to appropriate the grace offered to us is the indispensable condition of all the operations of that grace, so that, without it, no improvement of man would be possible ; or else to render such improvement possible, we should have to make another assumption—namely, such a new creation of man, he remaining absolutely passive, as alone could produce the capacity in question. But in that case this creative act might equally be applied to the whole process, and man's complete sanctification effected in the same way, so that

[1] § 62. [2] Phil. 2^{13}, cf. 4^{13}.

[3] Cf. *Conf. Belg.* xiv., the two statements : Adeo ut ipsi (homini) tantum exigua illorum (donorum omnium quae a Deo acceperat) vestigia remanserint : and, Nulla enim intelligentia nec voluntas conformis est divinae, nisi quam Christus in illis fuerat operatus.

[4] *Solid. declar.* ii. p. 656 : ita ut in hominis natura post lapsum ante regenerationem ne scintillula quidem spiritualium virium reliqua manserit aut restet, quibus ille ex se ad gratiam Dei praeparare se, aut oblatam gratiam apprehendere aut eius gratiae capax esse possit. This, however, as may be readily discerned, is cancelled (so far at least as it conflicts with our statement) by what follows (p. 771) : Hoc Dei verbum etiam nondum ad Deum conversus externis auribus audire aut legere potest. In eiusmodi enim externis rebus homo adhuc aliquo modo liberum arbitrium habet, ut . . . verbum Dei audire vel non audire possit.

redemption would become superfluous. For these reasons the incapacity spoken of is only to be referred to our personal activity in the narrower and proper sense, and not to our receptivity; and if anyone chooses to speak of vital inward receiving as the beginning of co-operation, we should not admit unconditionally that original sin debars man from all initiative and co-operation in spiritual things.[1] In fact, however, the work of this vital receptivity is not really initiation; there must be first of all a drawing-near of what is to be received, and similarly the said working is, strictly, not a co-operation at all, but a yielding of the self to the operation of grace. Our statement, moreover, has in its favour all the invitations of the Redeemer, which in reality were appeals to this receptivity; and no less the universal practice of the heralds of God's kingdom, who invariably called upon men to receive the grace of God. In fact, even if we start from the assumption of a constantly increasing deterioration of mankind, we must nevertheless acknowledge with Augustine that some element of the original good must still survive in human nature.[2]

3. Even within the sphere of voluntary action, however, thinkers have always taken care to confine the incapacity in question to what Christian piety regards as alone good in the strictest sense. This again takes for granted that there is a distinction of praiseworthy and blameworthy which is quite independent of a man's relationship to redemption; in fact, just as the unredeemed may have in themselves that which is commendable, so the redeemed are conscious of having acquired it without the aid of grace. Now this whole phase of life may very appropriately be described as 'civil righteousness'—the expression taken in a broad sense. For, to begin with, all that lies nearest to what is determined and effected by the God-consciousness has a communal reference, and evidence that might be brought forward against this will always be merely apparent; while, again, the mind of the civil community cannot apply the standard of the God-consciousness to the human actions and inward states that bear upon the communal interest, but can at most demand a spirit of patriotism in its highest purity and perfection. This spirit, however, while capable of evoking the most

[1] *Solid. declar.*, p. 643: Repudiantur . . . qui docent . . . hominem ex naturali nativitate adhuc aliquid boni . . . reliquum habere, capacitatem videlicet . . . in rebus spiritualibus aliquid inchoandi operandi aut cooperandi.

[2] *Enchirid.* xii.: Quamdiu itaque natura corrumpitur inest ei bonum quo privetur . . . quocirca bonum consumere corruptio non potest nisi consumendo naturam.

consummate self-renunciation in the individual, is merely the self-love of the nation or the country as a composite person, and may be conjoined with animosity and injustice of all kinds towards those who are outside the group, unless the reverse is dictated by the group's own selfish interest or love of honour—and these, again, are but self-love. Hence the very best elements of this side of life, so far as they subsist independently of the power of the God-consciousness, can rank only as the mind, wisdom, and righteousness of the flesh. Still, far too much is conceded, and an important aspect of Christian piety greatly obscured, when the incapacity is restricted to the so-called works of the First Table of the Decalogue on the ground that it is these alone which man cannot perform apart from redemption, and that the works of the Second Table are identical with that civil righteousness of which man is capable even without the aid of God's Spirit. The truth is rather that the latter works, in any sense in which the Christian can regard them as fulfilling the divine law,[1] are in no sense external or carnal; they are truly spiritual works, and are possible only in virtue of an efficacious and purified God-consciousness, so that in this respect no distinction can be drawn between duties towards God and duties towards our neighbour.[2]

§ 71. *Original sin, however, is at the same time so really the personal guilt of every individual who shares in it that it is best represented as the corporate act and the corporate guilt of the human race, and that the recognition of it as such is likewise recognition of the universal need of redemption.*

Conf. Aug. ii.: Quodque hic morbus seu vitium originis vere sit peccatum damnans et afferens nunc quoque aeternam mortem his qui non renascuntur.—*Apol. Conf.* i.: Quodsi has tantas vires habet humana natura . . . quorsum opus erit gratiâ Christi? *Ibid.* ii.: Quia igitur . . . omnes sunt sub peccato . . . ideo data est promissio iustificationis propter Christum.—*Conf. Basil.* viii.: Atque haec lues, quam originalem vocant, genus totum sic pervasit, ut nulla ope nisi divina per Christum curari potuerit.—*Conf. Gall.* xi.: Credimus hoc vitium vere esse peccatum, quod omnes et singulos homines, ne parvulis quidem exceptis adhuc in utero matris delitescentibus, aeternae mortis reos coram Deo peragat.—*Conf. Belg.* xv.: Credimus quod peccatum originis ita foedum et execrabile est coram Deo, ut ad generis humani condemnationem

---

[1] Matt. 22:37-39, supplemented by John 13:34 and Col. 3:23.

[2] We must accordingly adhere to the quite general statement in Melanchthon, *Loc. theol.* (*De lib. arb.*): Non potest voluntas exuere nascentem nobiscum pravitatem, nec potest legi Dei satisfacere.—(*De pecc.*): Peccatum originis est in natis ex virili semine amissio lucis in mente et aversio voluntatis a Deo et contumacia cordis ne possint *vere* obedire legi Dei.

sufficiat.—*Art. Smalc.*: Si enim ista (*sc.* hominem posse naturalibus viribus mandata Dei servare) approbantur, Christus frustra mortuus est, cum nullum peccatum aut damnum sit in homine pro quo mori eum oportuerit.—*Conf. Bohem.* iv.: Necessum esse ut omnes norint infirmitatem suam, quodque se ipsos modo nullo servare possint, neque quicquam habere praeter Christum, cuius fiducia sese redimant ac liberent.—*Epitom. Artic.*, p. 575: Affirmamus quod hanc naturae corruptionem ab ipsa natura nemo nisi solus Deus separare queat.—Reiicimus . . . dogma quo asseritur peccatum originale tantummodo reatum et debitum esse ex alieno delicto . . . in nos derivatum.—*Solid. Decl.*, p. 639: Et propter hanc corruptionem . . . natura aut persona hominis lege Dei accusatur et condemnatur . . . nisi beneficio meriti Christi ab his malis liberemur.—Melanchth., *Loc.*, p. 94: Propter quam corruptionem nati sunt rei.

1. In not a few of these symbolical passages, and in many theologians the doctrine of original sin appears to imply that the sinfulness innate in all men, just in so far as received from an external source, is yet in every case the individual's own guilt; a guilt indeed which involves eternal punishment as its due, so that the greatest possible accumulation of actual sins could add nothing to the penal desert which attaches to everyone on account of this so-called disease. Nor can we regard it as other than natural that the doctrine in this form has been repudiated by many who, to avoid recognizing as guilt anything that lies wholly outside a man's own action, prefer to describe original sin as an evil.

The doctrine, however, is given this incredible turn and acquires its repellent and offensive tone only when, alike against the nature of things, and in opposition to a true and generally recognized principle,[1] original sin is divorced from actual sin. Yet this is not to be understood in the sense that original sin is not guilt until it breaks forth in actual sins, for the mere circumstance that there has been no opportunity for and no outward incentive to sin cannot enhance the spiritual status of man; it is to be understood rather as implying that in the individual original sin is the sufficient ground of all actual sins, so that only something else outside of him, and not anything new within him, is needed for the generation of actual sin. Original sin is purely a thing received only in the degree in which the individual is not yet spontaneously active, and it ceases to be such in the degree in which that activity is developed. Up to that point, and in that measure, it is rightly termed *originated*,[2] as having its cause outside the individual. None the less,

[1] Melanchth., *Loc.*, p. 110: Itaque semper cum malo originali simul sunt actualia peccata.
[2] Peccatum originis originatum.

as every predisposition in man attains by exercise to proficiency and thereupon grows, so, by the exercise due to the voluntary action of the individual, is there growth in congenital sinfulness. But this growing increment, similar in character to what was originally inherited, namely, a persistent inward ground of sinful actions, though on the one side a result of actual sin, is yet in this respect, as an intensified sinfulness, always anterior to the actual sins emanating from it, and is therefore original sin, though no longer merely 'originated' but individually committed; it is, in fact, like the sin of our first parents which is usually designated by the term *originating original sin,*[1] since it brings forth and increases sin in oneself and others. Since, then, this later sinfulness which has issued from the individual's own action is one and the same with that which was congenital in origin, it follows that, just as the supervening sinfulness has arisen within him from voluntary acts based upon the original sinfulness, so the latter, which in fact falls more and more into the background in comparison with the former, and which always forms his starting-point, does not continue in him, and therefore would not have arisen through him, apart from his will. We are thus justified in calling it the guilt of the individual. From this point of view it may doubtless be said that the foregoing can hold good of human beings only in so far as they themselves have acted, but not in the same sense of children or the unborn. Here certainly there is a distinction not to be overlooked. Since, however, it is an accepted fact that actual sin proceeds unfailingly from original sin, then wherever human life exists, actual sin has its root within, and the link in virtue of which original sin is guilt exists also in the immature, even though as yet it has not manifested itself in time. So that of them it may be said that they will be sinners because of what is already within them. That they are not such in the same sense and degree as those in whom actual sin has become permanent has probably never been seriously questioned, more especially as the reference here is exclusively to guilt. But this difference does not touch congenital sinfulness, and so far as the confessional passages which refer to children are chiefly bent on bringing this out, we can altogether adopt them as our own.

2. Now if the sinfulness which is prior to all action operates in every individual through the sin and sinfulness of others, and if, again, it is transmitted by the voluntary actions of every individual to others and implanted within them, it must be something

[1] Peccatum originis originans.

genuinely common to all. Whether, in fact, we regard it as guilt and deed or rather as a spirit and a state, it is in either case common to all; not something that pertains severally to each individual and exists in relation to him by himself, but in each the work of all, and in all the work of each; and only in this corporate character, indeed, can it be properly and fully understood. Hence the doctrinal statements that deal with it are not to be regarded as utterances of the individual consciousness, which fall to be treated rather under the doctrine of actual sin, but are utterances of the corporate consciousness. This solidarity means an interdependence of all places and all times in the respect we have in view. The distinctive form of original sin in the individual, as regards its quality, is only a constituent part of the form it takes in the circle to which he immediately belongs, so that, though inexplicable when taken by itself, it points to the other parts as complementary to it. And this relationship runs through all gradations of community—families, clans, tribes, peoples, and races—so that the form of sinfulness in each of these points to that present in the others as its complement; and the aggregate power of the flesh in its conflict with the spirit (it being the source of everything in human action which is incompatible with the God-consciousness), is intelligible only by reference to the totality of those sharing a common life, and never fully in any one part; and whatever of that power appears in the single unit, whether personal or composite, is not to be attributed to, or explained by, that unit alone. The like holds good also of time. What appears as the congenital sinfulness of one generation is conditioned by the sinfulness of the previous one, and in turn conditions that of the later; and only in the whole series of forms thus assumed, as all connected with the progressive development of man, do we find the whole aspect of things denoted by the term, 'original sin.' Moreover, the interconnexion of places and that of times condition each other and indicate dependence on each other. And every man will readily testify that it is only in relation to the totality of things that either the idea of the sinfulness of individuals or his sense of sharing it becomes to him certain and adequate. It is precisely in virtue of this connexion, in fact, that the individual is the representative of the whole race in this regard, for the sinfulness of each points to the sinfulness of all alike in space and time, and also goes to condition that totality both around him and after him.

In this view, moreover, the various expressions used to denote original sin—all of which have a relative truth—most readily find their mutual reconciliation. Thus it can be called guilt [1] with perfect accuracy only when it is regarded simply as meaning the totality of the whole race, since it cannot in similar fashion be the guilt of the individual, so far at least as it has been engendered in him. It is called corruption of one's nature [2] as contrasted with the original perfection, inasmuch as the latter in its true development has to some extent been subverted by original sin; original defect,[3] inasmuch as it is the source of all individual perversions of the relation between the spirit and the several functions of our sensuous life; original disease,[4] inasmuch as on its account an element of death is lodged in every action of the spiritual life; original evil, inasmuch as in the individual it is a persistently operative cause of impediments to life which is independent of his own action. How difficult it is to describe original sin—I will not say wholly, but even partially—as punishment [5] need hardly be emphasized, not only because punishment is always something inflicted while sin can never be inflicted, so that punishment in the person who suffers it must always be that which is not sin; but also because in every sin for which original sin is supposed to be the penalty original sin itself is always presupposed, and thus in the last resort the punishment would precede the sin.

3. Were the phase of consciousness denoted by the concept of original sinfulness thus far developed not a corporate feeling, but one personal to the individual, it would not have necessarily bound up with it the consciousness of a universal need of redemption; for each individual would think himself thrown primarily on his own particular group for the increase of his spiritual strength. Hence the denial of the corporate character of original sin and a lower estimate of the redemption wrought by Christ usually go hand in hand. Nor would the connexion of the two things be stronger if the original sinfulness could exist in us without our being conscious of it, since the consciousness of sin would either not emerge in us at all, or would do so only in consequence of each actual sin as it occurred, and be referred to that alone. In such case the individual would primarily be thrown upon his own resources, falling back from his

[1] Reatus.

[2] Corruptio naturae. Another interpretation of this phrase will be referred to later.

[3] Vitium originis.

[4] Morbus originis. On *morbus* and *vitium*, cf. Cicero, *Tusculanae disputationes*, iv. 13, Ern.

[5] *Apol. Conf.* i.: Defectus iustitiae originalis et concupiscentia sunt poenae.

weaker moments to his assumed stronger moments. This, however, is possible only where the God-consciousness has not evolved at all, or where the disposition towards it has not been aroused by communication—only in a sphere, that is to say, outside Christianity and Christian teaching. It is only when the God-consciousness has been attained that we acknowledge its pre-eminence among the elements of consciousness and strive for its supremacy ; and when this takes place, the antagonism of the flesh, as a permanent factor determinative of the actuality of individual sins, must also become a fact of consciousness. Of this antagonism we only gain a clear understanding when we regard it as belonging to our consciousness as universalized to represent that of the human race ; hence we must either abandon all our struggle for the supremacy of the God-consciousness or else recognize our need of a succour lying outside the sphere of that universalized self-consciousness ; which means that for us there will either be a surrender to the absolute futility of any such struggle, or a presentiment of such succour. We can now see the appropriateness of linking the first consciousness of sin, due to the accession of the God-consciousness, with the first presentiment of redemption. And how the two have been conjoined in the Protestant Church from the outset is made clear by the passages cited. Equally clear is the connexion between the conviction that powers beyond the existing corporate human consciousness cannot be set in motion on our behalf and in our midst, and the resolve to do one's best (*with* that consciousness but *without* redemption properly so called) to overcome, even if only partially, the antagonism of the flesh.

4. This inherent connexion between the consciousness of a universal original sinfulness and the sense of our need of a redemption is broken and set awry—not without serious detriment to genuine Christian piety—when the idea that original sin ought to be punished is thrust between the two. If punishment be taken to mean, not the intensification of sin itself—which in a teleological form of faith could be regarded only as further guilt and sin, so that here the connexion specified would not be inherent—but the evil that issues from sin or is ordained as its concomitant, then the sense of our need of redemption as mediated solely by a consciousness of penal desert will not be so pure as that described above. This is quite clearly the case where penal desert is affirmed solely in view of the punishment itself, and where it is supposed that the fear of punishment will evoke or at least deepen the felt need of redemption

from sin ; for in that case the removal of the state of sin is desired, not with a view to freeing the God-consciousness from obstruction and widening its scope, but in order to secure particular states of the sensuous consciousness and avert their opposites. One's motive for not willing the antagonism of the flesh, and for willing redemption, would then be merely the sensuous consequences of each, and here accordingly piety in the real sense fades out. Again, it might be thought that the matter to be considered is not so much punishment itself as one's deserving to be punished, and that the feeling to be stimulated is not so much fear of punishment as the dread of deserving it. But here, too, the relation to the sensuous is made the standard for the spiritual, the assumption in this case being that if a given individual is not in himself concerned to make the God-consciousness supreme, he may be induced to do so by the consideration that otherwise he will appear as one unworthy of sensuous well-being. And this view is as great a danger to Christian piety as the other. It is on these grounds that we have not adopted this idea here. From the symbolical passages cited, however, we can see how essential it is for them to deduce the need of redemption from the consciousness of sinfulness, but also how easy it is for us, without breaking that connexion, to set aside the irrelevant idea of the penal desert of original sin. The latter idea will be discussed in its proper place.

§ 72. *While the idea that we have thus developed cannot be applied in precisely the same way to the first human pair, we have no reason for explaining universal sinfulness as due to an alteration in human nature brought about in their person by the first sin.*

1. This proposition, which is merely precautionary and is not meant to settle anything regarding the way in which sin originated in the first human pair, really assumes that, agreeably to our earlier explanation,[1] we are not required to formulate any doctrine, properly so called, upon the subject. While we can universalize our self-consciousness to represent the consciousness of the whole human race, and thus bring it into connexion with the God-consciousness, yet just because of what in our first parents was definitely and precisely related to the fact that they were not born but created, we cannot include them in that community of consciousness, their consciousness being, so far, the opposite of ours. It is true that if

[1] Cf. § 15.

the point at issue were their sin during the further course of their life, the diversity would gradually disappear, but it is otherwise with a sinfulness which we assume to be prior to all action. Hence, since we can have no experience in common with our first parents in this regard, and have therefore no testimony of consciousness on the matter to set forth, we have likewise no relevant doctrine to formulate.[1] If, however, we had any knowledge from another source (whether speculative or more historical) as to the relation between sinfulness in them and their nature as created beings, it would of course be necessary to inquire how such knowledge was related to our doctrinal statements; and, so far as such knowledge was not purely historical, but interwoven with our own presuppositions and theories, precautions could then be taken, as is done here, to prevent the Christian from unwittingly framing doctrines incompatible with his faith. After all, our consciousness of sin and its connexion with the longing for redemption will always remain absolutely the same whatever may have been the circumstances of the first pair, unless it be maintained that so long as the begetting and training of children was their task they had not yet sinned; for in that case a still larger area would be excluded from the sphere of our universalized self-consciousness, since the elements of original sinfulness might then have come together only by degrees. If, however, it is assumed that they had already sinned at that stage, their earliest offspring might, like ourselves, have a sinfulness existing prior to all action of their own, and derived from a source outside their own being. And this will sufficiently serve our purpose here, even though we thereby gain no clear idea of how that sinfulness passed, and still passes, from the first pair to their posterity. And, after all, no special importance is attached to this point in our symbolical books, which, while tracing the loss of innocence in all later human beings to the rise of sin in the earliest,[2] yet in some cases do not enter upon further explanations as to the nature and mode of this influence, and in others actually renounce the problem.[3]

2. On the other hand, the question how sin originated in our first parents after their God-consciousness had developed is, though not a question arising directly out of the interests of Christian piety, nevertheless a most natural one. Obviously we cannot answer it

[1] Cf. § 60, 1.

[2] *Conf. Aug.* ii.; *Apol. Conf.* i.; *Conf. Helv.* viii.; *Conf. Belg.* xv.; *Art. Smalc.* i.

[3] *Conf. Gall.* x.: Nec putamus necesse esse inquirere, quinam possit hoc peccatum ab uno ad alterum propagari.

in their case with the same assurance as we answer it in our own by propositions elaborated here. To begin with, we cannot frame any clear idea of how in them the sensuous functions gained power before the spiritual; for the first pair must from the outside have stood upon a level similar to that on which, in those who are born, the spirit already is a power. If, then, we are to regard the God-consciousness as evolving in them from within or by means of a communion with God which we cannot adequately figure to ourselves, no reason can be given why it should have developed more potently and rapidly as an inactive consciousness, but more tardily and feebly as impulse to action. And the less so because, in the case of such a development from within, we have no grounds whatever for assuming an unequal growth of intelligence and will such as we might find where the two factors received unequal stimulus—the one by communicated ideas, the other from customs already prevalent. Nor can we imagine any one-sided tendency—except that of sex—inherent in the first pair in this or any other respect, since otherwise the profusion of diverse characters which experience now reveals could not have developed from them as being an epitome of human nature. Since, then, in the nature of things, analogy fails us here, all turns upon the endeavour to elucidate the genesis of sin in the first pair apart from an already existent sinfulness. But whether we take the narrative of the first sin literally or ascribe to it a universal significance, the attempt seems doomed to failure. The prevalent interpretations are that man sinned through the seductions of Satan [1] and by a misuse of his own free will.[2] In the present instance these two factors cannot well be separated completely, for sin is always a misuse of free will. On the other hand, the more we ascribe to the action of Satan, the more nearly the temptation approximates to magic or mere compulsion, and the human act and therefore also the sin are correspondingly less. But again, the less the temptation of Satan, the less is it possible to explain the facts apart from a sinfulness already present, since misuse of free will by itself is no explanation, but forces us to assume something else as prompting it. Then if we fall back directly upon the suggestions of Satan, these again could not have taken effect unless there was something already present in the soul which implied a certain readiness to pass into sensuous appetite; and any such

[1] *Conf. Belg.* xiv.: verbis et imposturis diaboli aurem praebens. Cf. Gerh., *Loc. Th.*, t. iv. p. 294 sq.

[2] Augustin., *Enchirid.* 30: Homo libero arbitrio male utens et se perdidit et ipsum.

inclination toward sin must therefore have been present in the first pair before their first sin, else they would not have been liable to temptation. Nor does it avail to break up the first sin into a number of elements with a view to finding some infinitesimal part as its germ;[1] for when what we have to deal with is a definite act, we must seek for something that will explain the act as a whole. And this we can never find as long as we assume an inner state in which there was no spontaneous activity of the flesh, and the God-consciousness alone held sway; for in that case no sinful appetite could ever have arisen in the pair themselves, nor could Satan have made them believe that God had forbidden something out of jealousy, but their trust in God must already have been extinguished. But if such trust had died out, they must already have lost the image of God,[2] and sinfulness must already have been present, whether in the form of pride[3] or otherwise. Our last resource would then be to explain the first sin as due to such a misuse of freedom as had no ground whatever in the first man's inward being, *i.e.* to say that he chose the evil without a motive. But either this must have taken place prior to his having had any exercise in the good at all, since even the briefest exercise would have induced a facility which, in the absence of conflicting motives, would necessarily have proved operative, in which case his sin must have been his first free act—the least admissible of all positions; or else there was an impossibility that repetition of actions should produce any facility in the first pair, and this again would imply that no confirmation in good and no increase in the power of the God-consciousness was possible for them[4]—an idea that conflicts with every view of man's original perfection.

This difficulty of representing to ourselves the emergence of the first sin without assuming a foundation for it in a prior sinfulness is immensely aggravated if we consider the circumstances in which the Mosaic narrative exhibits the first pair. For one thing, it is

[1] Luther, on Gen. 3³, finds the beginning of sin in the fact that Eve tampers with God's word, and adds to God's command the word 'perhaps'; as if that would have been a sin unless the emergent wanton appetite had not lain behind it. Others, like Lyra, insist rather upon the sensuous pleasure itself, and regard the act of looking at the tree as the beginning of the sin; but here a like criticism applies.

[2] Non est anima ad imaginem Dei, in qua Deus non semper est (Ambros. *Hexaëm.* vi. 18).

[3] Augustin., *d. Gen. c. Man.* ii. 22: Videmus his verbis per superbiam peccatum esse persuasum.

[4] Origen. in *Matth.* x. 11: Πάλιν τε αὖ οὐκ ἄν, ἀστείας καὶ ἀμεταβλήτου φύσεως ὢν ἀπὸ τοῦ καλοῦ ἀπέστρεφεν ἄν, μετὰ τὸ χρηματίσαι δίκαιος ἐκ τῆς δικαιοσύνης αὐτοῦ, ἐπὶ τὸ ποιῆσαι ἀδικίαν.

almost impossible to conceive of temptation, or of the abuse of free will, amid such simplicity of life, and where the natural wants were so easily satisfied; since in such a condition of things no single object could have offered an exceptionally strong allurement. And again, it is quite impossible to imagine a direct intercourse with God without an intensified love to God and an increased knowledge of Him which must have preserved our first parents from the influence of foolish illusions. This has indeed been recognized from early times.[1] And, indeed, in view of the ease with which sin might have been avoided, the more literally we accept the narrative, the greater is the propensity to sin which must be assumed as already present. Indirectly this appears to be assumed even by those who assert that God did not will to confirm man in good prior to his voluntary obedience.[2] For, as such confirmation in good must have been a special work of God, and not something effected by the exercise of powers lodged in human nature, this fact, while presupposing the above-mentioned incapacity to acquire facility through exercise, also presupposes that, without such special divine aid, the spiritual energy in man might quite as readily at any moment have proved too weak to meet a sensuous impulse.

3. With this is connected the fact that, apart from the vitiating power exercised even in our condition of innate sinfulness by actual sin in strengthening inclination by habit, nothing of a peculiar or novel nature took place in our first parents as a result of the first sin; [3] and that what is represented in our symbolical books as such a result must be assumed to have preceded the sin. The understanding must have been involved in an utterly heathen darkness before it could have credited a falsehood to the effect that God grudged man the knowledge of good, and the will must have lacked the energy to resist even the weakest enticement if the mere sight of the forbidden fruit could exert such power over it. In fact, Adam must have been sundered from God before his first sin; for, when Eve handed him the fruit he ate it without even recalling the divine interdict; and this presupposes a like corruption of his nature; for surely incorrupt nature could not have indulged appetite in express

[1] Augustin., *de corr. et grat.* xii.: Adam et terrente nullo et insuper contra Dei terrentis imperium libero usus arbitrio non stetit in tanta non peccandi facilitate.

[2] See Gerhard, *Loc. Th.*, t. iv. p. 302.

[3] *Conf. Helv.* ix.: Post lapsum intellectus obscuratus est, voluntas vero ex libera facta est serva.—*Conf. Belg.* xiv.: Homo se ipsum verbis diaboli aurem praebens . . . a Deo, qui vera ipsius erat vita, penitus avulsit totamque naturam suam corrupit.

disobedience to the divine command. Nor can it fairly be maintained that this reasoning hangs entirely on a literal interpretation of the Mosaic narrative, for, whatever idea we may have of the first sin, we must always assume the priority of some sinful element; and if we seek to understand that sin genetically, we must follow a method akin to that adopted here. If, however, human nature in the first pair was the same before the first sin as it appears subsequently alike in them and in their posterity, we cannot say that human nature was changed as a result of the first sin, and the statement of our symbolical books to that effect is one we must depart from. No one can be asked to believe that in a single individual the nature of the species could be changed and yet that individual remain the same; for the terms 'individual' and 'species' lose their meaning unless everything met with in the individual, whether successively or simultaneously, can be understood from and explained by the nature of the species. If an individual belonging to a certain species manifests some attribute incompatible with the definition of the species, then either the definition of the species has been wrong from the start and needs to be corrected, or we were misled as to the identity of the individual. Still less is it possible to suppose that such an alteration of nature should have resulted from an act of the alleged individual as such, since the individual can act only *in accordance with* the nature of his species, but never can act *upon* that nature. Hence we cannot well hold to the idea under discussion without conceding a share in the matter to the devil; and if we do this, we find an equal difficulty in avoiding the Manichæan heresy.[1] For if it is quite certain that an alteration in a determinate nature cannot be effected by that nature itself, the actual alteration can be apportioned between the man and the devil only in this way, that the element of action is ascribed to the latter, and mere passivity, or receptivity, to the former. But in that case, it must be further admitted that, if the individuals are to remain the same, it is a mere confusion of speech to describe the outcome as merely an alteration of their nature, and that it is more correct to say that the human nature which God originally created was destroyed by the devil through the first sin, when the nature acquired is the work of the devil in the same degree as was the first sin, because the nature created by God so remained purely passive as to allow itself to be completely permeated by the alteration wrought by the devil. To the view that of course in that case the counter-change to be wrought

[1] Cf. § 22.

by redemption is once more a subversion of preceding nature, little objection can be taken by those who maintain that the present nature of man is incapable even of appropriating redemption.[1] These things, however—alike the passivity of man in the event by which his nature was subverted, and the power ascribed to Satan of subverting the work of God and putting his own work in its place, so as to bring an entire world of human beings under its partial control—are quite unmistakable approaches to Manichæism. And what is said on the other side in order to nullify this adjunct of the Flacian teaching [2] seems to have very little foundation indeed. For, on the one hand, bare possibility is nothing except as there is a transition to actuality, and if man now cannot act otherwise than sinfully and perversely, and such self-determination to evil is the work of Satan, the still remaining work of God, so far as it is actuated by the work of Satan, now subsists only as an instrument of Satan, and is therefore only seemingly the same as it was. On the other hand, if the original work of God consisted not merely in man's ability to think, speak, and act, but also in the free will that sets these capacities in operation, then if free will is lost, the work of God no longer has any existence. To this difficulty of avoiding on the ordinary line of thought everything of a Manichæan character is probably due the hypothesis which, while admitting a change in human nature in consequence of the first sin, still regards it as operating rather in a bodily way.[3] In order to keep clear of the idea that the change, namely, the loss of the power of the God-consciousness, was not prior to the sin, it is not said to have been preceded by any express interdict of God ; but in that case it is not blameworthy in the first pair to have been unwilling to acknowledge the authority of obscure sentiments : and the resolve to suppress these, whatever the occasion of it, could not be reckoned sinful. And thus the spiritual vitiation of man following upon the eating of the forbidden fruit, and brought about by the effect thereof upon the body, would have taken place without sin at all, and universal sinfulness would be attributable to evil—a conclusion which, conflicting as it does with the essence of a teleological type of faith, cannot be regarded as Christian, especially as the administration of

[1] *Solid. Decl.* ii., p. 656.

[2] *Solid. Decl.*, p. 648 : Asserimus id ipsum esse Dei opus, quod homo aliquid cogitare loqui agere operari potest . . . quod vero cogitationes verba facta eius prava sunt . . . hoc originaliter et principaliter est opus Satanae.

[3] Reinhard, *Dogm.*, §§ 75–80.

a material antidote at the right time would have rendered redemption superfluous.

We must accordingly adhere to the position that the idea of a change in human nature entailed by the first sin of the first pair has no place among the propositions which rank as utterances of our Christian consciousness. The less we found cause at a previous stage [1] to ascribe a high degree of religious morality and religious enlightenment to the first pair before their first sin, and the less we are able to explain the first sin as proceeding from a perfectly sinless condition, the more decisively does every reason disappear for admitting that a change in human nature was then produced. The grounds of our renouncing that idea will be all the stronger because it cannot be clearly presented to the mind, and on the one hand merely begets the Manichæan heresy, while on the other it drives many Christians, from mere dread thereof, into the Pelagian heresy, in that they will rather deny the universal incapacity of all men apart from redemption for good than derive that incapacity from such a change. The untenable character of the theory of a change, moreover, becomes specially evident when we go back to the rigid formulæ in which the older dogmaticians gave unqualified expression to the confessional view.[2] Thus the very first statement, namely, 'the person corrupts the nature,' brings out clearly the fact that, in the act in question, if the nature corrupted in consequence of it was good, the person cannot have been good, for good cannot corrupt good; but if the nature was already bad, its corruption had not been brought about by the action of the person. Similarly on the other alternative: if the person no longer was good (since in corrupting the nature it acted wrongly), while the nature was good still, since it required to be corrupted, then all wrong action on the part of all later individuals must be explicable apart from the hypothesis that their nature had to be corrupted beforehand. In that case all corruption would fall under the third formula, namely, that persons corrupt themselves and one another; which manifestly is an adequate description of all the sin that ever appears amongst men. Here, however, the nature is kept out of the matter altogether; whereas, if it is assumed that the nature had already been corrupted, there can be no talk of its corrupting the

[1] Cf. § 61.

[2] Quenstedt, *Syst. Theol.*, p. 913: Tribus autem modis fit peccatum quando persona corrumpit naturam, ut factum ab Adamo et Eva, quando natura corrumpit personam, ut fit in propagatione peccati originis, quando persona corrumpit personam, ut fit in peccatis actualibus.

person, since the person must necessarily have within itself the corruption of the nature. Finally, if the second formula, namely, 'the nature corrupts the person,' is meant to refer to the propagation of original sinfulness, then, while it is true that individuals can only be as their nature is, they are nevertheless such from the first; and the form of expression is faulty, since they must have been uncorrupt before they could be corrupted. This, in turn, gives rise to fresh doubts about the first formula, for it is inconceivable that the individual person should do more to the nature than the nature to it. Were we to admit, however, and to admit as universally true that the nature corrupts the individual, then since the nature has no existence save in the totality of individuals, a fourth formula would emerge, namely, that the nature corrupts itself; a statement by the use of which hardly anyone could indicate the thoughts he really had in his mind.

4. If, accordingly, no change in human nature took place in the person of the first pair as a result of their first sin, and what is alleged to have developed from that sin must be assumed to have been in existence before it; and if this does not apply merely to the case of some particular first sin, but a like situation emerges (whatever the nature of that sin may have been) in the case of every individual; then the universal sinfulness that precedes every actual sin in the offspring is to be regarded not so much as derived from the first sin of our first parents, but rather as identical with what in them likewise preceded the first sin, so that in committing their first sin they were simply the first-born of sinfulness. It is true that our confessional books adopt the derivation in question,[1] but in such matters we are the less obliged to follow them because our consciousness of universal sinfulness, as set forth above,[2] is something inward and immediate, while that derivation of it gives a purely external account on which the inward in no way depends, and by which it cannot in any way be reinforced. But it is solely on that inward experience that our consciousness of the need of redemption depends; hence the derivation referred to is in no sense an element of our faith. And as even the confessional books for the most part do not engage in any detailed discussion as to the nature and manner of that derivation,[3] we could not but feel

[1] *Conf. Aug.* ii.; *Apol. Conf.* i.; *Conf. Helv.* viii.; *Conf. Belg.* xv.; *Art. Smalc.* i., etc.

[2] § 70.

[3] The *Conf. Gall.* x. says explicitly: Nec putamus necesse esse inquirere quinam possit hoc peccatum ab uno ad alterum propagari. Similarly Calvin,

a difficulty if the derivation occurred in Scripture in conjunction with statements of faith properly so called. But the classical passage usually cited in its support [1] shows nothing of the kind. The apostle refers to the origin of sin only with a view to elucidating the doctrine of the restoration of life through Christ, and the point of comparison is simply that each originates in and emanates from one. It is true that the apostle sets forth sin as dependent upon its first occurrence, and thus as something continuous, so that the whole continuous process of sin was introduced along with Adam's sin, and if Adam had been able to refrain from sin, we too could have refrained. Then if we take also the previous statement, namely, that death passed upon all men for that all sinned themselves, and observe how Paul, while he certainly distinguishes between the sin of Adam and that of those who had not sinned after the likeness of Adam's transgression, yet, though including all in one condemnation, describes Adam's contribution thereto as a small thing in comparison with what Christ had done for the removal of sin ; we see that all this signally agrees with the idea that corporate sin is the corporate act of the human race, originating in the first human beings, and can be taken away only by the activity of Christ, which likewise extends to all mankind. In similar fashion Paul contrasts Adam and Christ in another reference ; [2] just as again he testifies that sin arises in us, and that our mind can be defiled, in the same way as in the case of Eve ; [3] whence it follows that in going back to the first man for an explanation of sinfulness, we gain nothing of special importance, and that in the passages cited the sole concern was to give due weight to the relation between the earlier and the later dispensation.

We can thus readily dispense with all those artificial theories which for the most part tend only to lay stress upon the divine justice in imputing Adam's sin to, and exacting its penalty from, his posterity. To have done with them is all the more satisfactory because they (*e.g.* those which assert that all mankind, as embraced in Adam's being,[4] participated in his sin) rest upon a particular

Instit. ii. 1, 7 : Neque in substantia carnis aut animae causam habet contagio : sed quia a Deo ita fuit ordinatum, ut quae primo homini dona contulerat, ille tam sibi quam suis haberet simul et perderet. From which we see clearly that Calvin's main concern is to repudiate explanations which might have links of connexion with non-Christian views.

[1] Rom. 5^{12-21}. [2] 1 Cor. 15^{21-22}. [3] 2 Cor. 11^{3}.

[4] Ambros., in *Rom.* v. : Manifestum in Adam omnes peccasse quasi in massa.—Ex eo igitur cuncti peccatores quia ex ipso omnes sumus.—Hieron., in *Hosea* vi. 7 : Et ibi in paradiso omnes praevaricati sunt in me in similitudinem praevaricationis Adam.

theory of the origin of individual souls, while, within our limits, we have neither grounds nor materials for propounding any such theory. Or else (*e.g.* those which most arbitrarily interpret God's command as a covenant made in the person of Adam with the entire human race, the legal consequences of violating which fall also on his posterity) they bring man's relation to God and God's imputation of sin under the category of a merely external legal relationship, a view which has had a most detrimental effect upon interpretation of the work of redemption. This view is carried to its extremest point when people assume what has often been asserted and is widely current, though quite arbitrary and wholly groundless, that, had our first parents only withstood their first temptation successfully, no second would have been imposed upon them, and they, and we as well, would have remained for ever exempt from all temptation. The truth is rather that the temptation given in the Mosaic narrative is a most trifling one, representing the simplest and most primitive conditions; and it is in the nature of things that the more variously the powers of man came to be drawn upon, and the more complicated his circumstances became, the more dangerous must his temptations have been; while again, it seems the very acme of inconsistency to say that the Redeemer could be tempted in His earthly life, but that, if Adam and Eve had been victors in their first conflict, they would have become proof against all temptation. And indeed it is glaringly and intrinsically incompatible with all that we can learn of the divine ways, to suppose that to such an extent God should have made the destiny of the whole human race contingent upon a single moment, the fortunes of which rested with two inexperienced individuals, who, moreover, never dreamt of its having any such importance.

5. If then, on the one hand, we discard the view that a change took place in human nature itself, but, on the other, still maintain that an incapacity for good is the universal state of men, it follows that this incapacity was present in human nature before the first sin, and that accordingly what is now innate sinfulness was something native also to the first pair. This we admit; yet it must be so construed as to be compatible with the equally inherent original perfection of man, and in such a way that the state of the first human pair is understood to have been throughout analogous to our own, as described above.[1] In no sense, therefore, are we substituting for the idea of a longer or shorter state of perfectly active piety, the idea

[1] Cf. §§ 60, 61, 68.

that the first free act after the awakening of the God-consciousness was sin—a conception already negatived by what has been said above.[1] The truth is rather that the awakening of the God-consciousness implies also the initiation of the good, which in turn could not remain without consequences [2] that proved operative even after the first sin. In that case, however, there must have come for our first parents a time when their sensuous nature on one side or another would gain such strength that it could win the mastery as easily as lose it. For, while we cannot be expected to form a vivid idea of the first man in his necessary diversity from us, yet there are two points in which he resembles us, and to which in him, too, we can fasten the rise of sin. Thus there was in the first pair, if not the idiosyncrasies of personal constitution, yet the idiosyncrasies of sex; and, again, while we cannot conceive of the will lagging behind the intelligence precisely as it does in ourselves, yet they were subject (in their simple life possibly in a less degree) to changes of mood amid which such shortcoming of will-power showed itself intermittently on various sides. In the light of all this, the origin of sin and the consciousness of it become quite intelligible.

Now, while the first appearance of sin in the first pair, due to that original sinfulness, not only was in itself a single and trivial event, but in particular was without any transforming influence upon human nature, yet the growth of sin in consequence of the increase of the human race by ordinary generation had its origin in the first emergence of sin, and therefore in the original sinfulness itself. And in its relation to redemption this is to be understood in the sense that without the entrance into all mankind of an element free from that sinfulness, nothing could be expected but that the disposition to the God-consciousness inherent in human nature should be constantly vitiated in its action, and everything that was developing spiritually in man ever dragged downwards under the dominion of the flesh. Finally, as regards the Mosaic narrative: in accordance with the limits which we have assigned to Dogmatics, that science cannot be expected to determine how the said record is to be interpreted, and whether it purports to be history or allegory. Without encroaching upon the work of exegesis or criticism, however, we can

[1] Cf. § 67, 2.

[2] Hugo of St. Victor, *Opp.* iii. 181: Paradisus est locus inchoantium et in melius proficientium, et ideo ibi solum bonum esse debuit, quia creatura a malo initianda non fuit, non tamen summum. This implies, of course, that as soon as sin appeared, the state of Paradise must have come to an end altogether.

use the story, as the early theologians did,[1] in illustration of the universal process of the rise of sin as something always and everywhere the same, and it is in this illustrative quality that, for us, the universal significance of the narrative resides. There we find in Eve, on the one hand, a clear representation of the independent activity and revolt of the sensuous element that develops so readily upon any external incentive by way of opposition to a divine command, and likewise a clear view of how there comes to be conjoined therewith an all too easily effected vitiation of the already developed God-consciousness. On the other hand, in Adam we see how easily sin is assimilated by imitation even without any overpowering activity of sense, and how this presupposes some degree of forgetfulness of God, traceable possibly to mere lack of thought. If, moreover, we bring the story into connexion with the ideas of original perfection and original sinfulness as formulated here, by connecting the earlier state with the later, it sets before us in general how outside the sphere of redemption the good develops only alongside what is bad, and how this good includes that knowledge of the distinction between good and evil which is essential to the development of man. It is plainly indicated in the story that that knowledge was not bestowed prior to the sin, and this can easily be extended into the view that man could only have remained without sin as long as he remained without that knowledge.

6. If, accordingly, for the contrast between an original nature and a changed nature we substitute the idea of a human nature universally and without exception—apart from redemption—the same; and if, for the contrast between an original righteousness that filled up a period of the first human lives and a sinfulness that emerged in time (an event along with which and in consequence of which that righteousness disappeared), we substitute a timeless original sinfulness always and everywhere inhering in human nature and co-existing with the original perfection given along with it—though in such a way that from the concomitance and development of the two there could issue no active righteousness properly so called, but at best a vacillation between vitiated spiritual efforts and increasing and fully matured sin; if, finally, for the antithesis between an original guilt and a transmitted guilt we substitute the simple idea of an absolutely common guilt identical for all; then the confessional formulæ in which this doctrine in its relation to the succeeding one is most

[1] Augustin., *de Gen. c. Man.* ii. 21: Etiam nunc in unoquoque nostrum nil aliud agitur, cum ad peccatum delabitur, quam tunc actum est in illis tribus, serpente, muliere, et viro.

succinctly expressed may be qualified and supplemented as follows. In the first place, we certainly admit a universal imputation of the first sin, an imputation resting upon the belief that to whatever human individual had fallen the lot of being the first, he, too, would have committed the sin. So, too, had the actually first man been one of those born later, he would have added his quota to the deterioration above described, and therefore bears the guilt thereof as does any other. Further, in the doctrine of the Church the first sin of the first man, and that only, is called 'originating original sin,' and the sinful constitution of all other men 'originated original sin'—the bent and inward disposition thus bearing the name of 'sin' equally with the act itself; but we transfer this to the relation between each earlier generation and the one immediately succeeding it, and maintain that the actual sin of the earlier is always the originating original sin for the later, while the sinfulness of the later generation since it produces the actual sins thereof, is also original sin, while yet as dependent upon the sin of the earlier it is originated, and thus is originated original sin as well. Finally, we make good another defect by applying the distinction of 'originating' and 'originated' also to actual sin in its relation to original sin. On the one hand, we use this distinction to set forth the interrelationship of all who are living at one time, the actual sin of those who play a more vigorous and stimulating rôle being the originating, that of the more passive the originated; on the other hand, the collective sin of each generation is in turn originating with respect to the sinfulness of the succeeding one, just as that collective sin itself is rooted in the original sin originated by the earlier. In this compact group of ideas sin in general, and original sin in particular, are seen to be the corporate action and the corporate guilt of the whole human race.

Second Doctrine: Actual Sin

§ 73. *In all men, original sin is always issuing in actual sin.*

Melanchthon, *Loc. Th.*, p. 123: Semper cum peccato originali sunt peccata actualia. Augustine *c. Julian.*: Lex ista quae est in membris . . . manet in carne mortali . . . quia operatur desideria contra quae dimicant fideles.—*Conf. Gall.* xi.: Dicimus praeterea hanc perversitatem semper edere fructus aliquos malitiae et rebellionis, adeo ut etiam qui sanctitate excellunt quamvis ei resistant, multis tamen infirmitatibus et delictis sint contaminati quamdiu in hoc mundo versantur.

1. This proposition is to be taken in its most universal sense; it is only as we exclude Him from the context of universal sinfulness

that we acquit even Christ of actual sin. Taken thus universally, however, it is an expression of our Christian consciousness. The more definitely and vividly anyone sets the Redeemer before him, the more he realizes that he is at no moment free from sin. He knows this, however, not simply from his own personal idiosyncrasy, but in a universal way, *e.g.*, inasmuch as he is a constituent portion of humanity as a whole ; *i.e.* he knows it through his consciousness as enlarged to a racial consciousness, and thus knows it true of others as well as of himself. And this consciousness goes back to that of universal sinfulness ; it is, in fact, simply the latter from another point of view. For the disposition to sin, of which our apprehension is at once inward and timeless, would not be a reality at all unless it were constantly manifesting itself ; and conversely, that which does manifest itself would merely be something adhering to us from without and therefore no sin, unless it formed part of the manifestation and temporal process of original sin. And just as all that is involved in original sin must manifest itself somewhere in the measure in which it is variously distributed among men, so it necessarily has a part in every act (*Bewegung*) of every man in whom it is present and makes some element thereof to be sin in manifestation. Thus throughout the entire range of sinful humanity there is not a single perfectly good action, *i.e.* one that purely expresses the power of the God-consciousness ; nor is there one perfectly pure moment, *i.e.* one in which something does not exist in secret antagonism to the God-consciousness.

2. It would not at all harmonize with this universal consciousness, however, were we to restrict actual sin to those cases in which our sinfulness breaks forth externally in actions perceptible by others as well as by ourselves. Such outbreakings of sin always depend upon external conditions—conditions quite different from those that have brought about this or that definite sinful state. Just as those last, the external solicitations, can evoke only such inner movements as are already prepared for in the personality of the individual, so the sinfulness of one's condition cannot depend upon the occurrence of circumstances favourable or unfavourable to its outward manifestation. In point of fact, the sinfulness of a man's condition is not in itself really aggravated by its finding external expression, for actual sin in the precise sense is present even where the sinful element shows itself only internally, and enters into a moment of consciousness merely as a thought or a

desire.[1] Just as love, as an inward affection, is the fulfilling of the law, since it infallibly manifests itself in outward act on every given opportunity, so, for the same reason, evil desire, though working only within, is already actual sin. And this is a principle which, if we take the term ' desire ' in its widest sense, applies to all actual sin, with the exception perhaps of those cases in which the activity of the God-consciousness seems to be obstructed only by slothfulness ; although these cases, too, may well be traced to a desire that only awaits its opportunity. Any explanation of actual sin, whether more or less general, will be valid only in so far as it teaches that actual sin springs from an underlying sinfulness, and as it can easily be united with the consciousness of the need of redemption.[2]

While we regard the original sinfulness from which all actual sin proceeds as the corporate act and the corporate guilt of the human race—distributed among individuals in respect of place and time not equally and uniformly, but unequally—yet this means no more than that in one individual one type of sin is specially predominant and another less so, while in another individual the case is reversed, according as in each case, conformably with his personal temperament, a weaker enticement only is needed for one kind of sin than for another. It must certainly not be taken to mean that, apart from redemption, any given individual is so well secured by his personality against any of the various forms of sin that he could not possibly fall into it. On the contrary, our consciousness testifies in each of us that neither he nor any other, if thrown upon his own resources, has within him a perfect security against any form of evil ; for every observant person discovers in himself so many anticipations and, so to say, germs of all evil that, if only the incentive that must always be added to the original sinfulness in order to produce actual sin could become strong enough, any kind of evil, if not habitually yet in particular cases, might emerge as actual sin.[3]

[1] Actio pugnans cum lege Dei (Melanchthon, *l.c.*) might also denote such a movement, as yet entirely inward.

[2] Hence, the Christian consciousness can least of all be satisfied with theories like that of Reinhard (*Dogmatik*, § 75) : Peccatum est quaevis aberratio a modo tenendae verae felicitatis.

[3] Calvin, *Inst.* ii. 3.3 : Omnibus ejusmodi portentis obnoxia est unaquaeque anima.

§ 74. *There is no difference of worth between men in regard to sin, apart from the fact that it does not in all stand in the same relationship to redemption.*

1. In harmony with what has been said above, all actual sins must rank as equal not only in respect of their nature and character, but also of their origin; for every such sin is a manifestation of the universal sinfulness, and represents a victory, though but momentary or partial, of flesh over spirit. The determining power of the God-consciousness, which in sin is obstructed, may of course be greater or less. Now if it is greater, then on the one hand the spiritual life in which it is found as such must be stronger, and in such a life, by reason of that strength, sin is increasingly in process of disappearing, and is therefore less. On the other hand, however, we may affirm that if the spiritual strength is greater, the resistance of the flesh that overcomes it must be stronger, and therefore the sin greater. Since, therefore, from different points of view we get opposite results as to the one and the same case of sin, we must either regard all sins as equal, because from opposite points of view each is at once greater and less; or we must first combine the two points of view, whereupon we find that the determination of the sinful quality of single moments becomes feasible only by reference to the condition of the acting subject as a whole, *i.e.* his state as one in which sinfulness is on the increase or on the wane—which, within the sphere of the Christian consciousness, means by reference to the individual's state of grace, precisely as our proposition affirms. Apart from this, however, and each moment being taken by itself, it remains true that what gives a moment the character of sin is the self-centred activity of the flesh, whereas the content of the sin does not enable us to differentiate; for all activities of the flesh are good when subservient to the spirit, and all are evil when severed from it. The same result follows when we note that the amount of sin is greater, the slighter the outward solicitations which need to be overcome. For these, too, are not the same for everyone; to a more experienced subject a particular solicitation may be insignificant which to others is strong and urgent. Doubtless, therefore, there are greater and lesser sins, though for us they are so only with respect to the efficacy of redemption; and, accordingly, Church teaching has rightly excluded from this sphere the doctrine of the equality of all sins.[1] Taken by itself, however, the

[1] *Conf. et Expos. simpl.* viii.: Fatemur etiam peccata non esse aequalia, licet ex eodem corruptionis et incredulitatis fonte exoriantur. Melanchth.,

doctrine might possibly be defended. Hence most of the ordinary classifications of sin, disregarding as they do the relationship to redemption, assert a distinction among sins as concerns their form and appearance, but do not assert a difference in their proper quality as sins.

2. Surveying the diversities of actual sin with a view to arranging them in distinct groups, we encounter at the outset the two principal forms which are associated with the two main elements of original sinfulness;[1] thus actual sin may be either more *an expression of appetite* or more a positive obscuration, i.e. *a vitiation, of the God-consciousness.* We cannot wholly separate the two, for the one ever evokes the other; thus when in any social group, some definite form of appetite breaks out predominantly, it is presently followed by a transformation of the God-consciousness as a means of cloaking the discordance. So Paul[2] explains how each of the two aggravates the other; and if we imagine the two at their climax—the superstitious frenzy that heaps up all the products of idolatrous error, and the passionate frenzy of unbridled lust—and if each of them inevitably seems equally deserving of condemnation, it is clear that they must have been equal in their original action and reaction upon each other.

As regards the division into outward and inward sins, what was said above[3] with a view to setting aside this distinction might be open at most to the following objection. The external accomplishment of an act of sin occupies a divisible portion of time, and for the most part can be resolved into a succession of moments. Now just as it is obvious that, if a reaction of the God-consciousness takes place during that time, a different quality emerges, so the sinful quality of an action—other things being equal—is the more aggravated the longer the interval in which no such reaction supervenes. What follows from this, however, is simply that there are some sinful acts that point to a greater power of sin than others; but in no sense does it follow that anyone is incapable of committing acts of the same sinful quality, though not of the same kind as these. On the other hand, it remains true that in every individual there are inward stirrings, sinful or akin to sin, which never take shape as outward sins because at bottom and even inwardly they are the workings of others' thoughts and excitations rather than his own,

Loc. Th. p. 126: Ac stoicae illae disputationes execrandae sunt, quas servant aliqui disputantes omnia peccata aequalia esse.

[1] *Apol. Conf.* i. (from Hugo of St. Victor): Originale peccatum est ignorantia in mente et concupiscentia in carne.

[2] Rom. 1^{21-28}.

[3] In section 2 of the foregoing paragraph.

and thus belong to the communal life rather than to the individual himself. But there will be no one whose life exhibits these only, and when we discount them the distinction between outward and inward sins is seen to be fortuitous rather than essential.

Again, when a distinction is drawn between intentional and unintentional sins, it is customary to regard the former as in general the greater. But this is wrong. Unintentional sins, so far as they are really actions and not mere consequences,[1] are sins either of ignorance or of impetuosity. But if the ignorance is due to a defective estimate of the ethical significance of our actions generally, or the impetuosity due to a passionate tendency of one kind or another ; and if, on the other hand, a transient incapacity during an instant peculiarly unfavourable to one's resisting a sensuous impulse can be thought of as a completely isolated moment having no subsequent results ; then intentional sins of the latter type will be lesser than unintentional sins of the former type. If, accordingly, sometimes the one class may be greater, and sometimes the other, the two, considered in themselves, are equal.

The most important division of sins in the present reference is unquestionably that of mortal and venial sins ; yet as these terms do not themselves involve a rigorous antithesis, it is difficult to say what the distinction really means. Some thinkers ascribe to them the very sense which is indicated in our proposition as constituting the only tenable distinction ; [2] in which case we should have to discuss only how far the idea of punishment must have a place in the definition or not. Certainly, such interpretations make it quite clear that otherwise the distinction rests solely on the relationship of the acting subject to redemption. But this agreement seems once more to vanish when it is likewise asserted that even those who have been brought within the scope of redemption can commit mortal sins, but that the redemptive link is thereby severed [3]—

[1] In the latter case they would not be sins at all, and in view of this some qualification must be applied to the principle found in Melanchth., *Loc. Th.*, p. 117: Nihil est peccatum nisi sit voluntarium. Haec sententia de civilibus delictis tradita est . . . sed non transferendum est hoc dictum ad doctrinam Evangelii de peccato.

[2] Melanchth., *op. cit.*, p. 332 : Haec mala in renatis sunt . . . sed quia persona accepta est . . . fiunt huic personae haec mala venialia peccata ; and p. 123 : actualia peccata quae in non renatis omnia sunt mortalia. The most definite statement of this view is found in Baumgarten, *Theol. Str.* ii. 484 : Since, however, we do not admit this, namely, that *mortalia* and *venialia* are to be distinguished by a *discrimen objectivum*, but rather take the relationship of the person concerned to the reconciliation brought by Christ as the ground of distinction, etc.

[3] Melanchth., *op. cit.*, p. 124 : Necesse est autem discernere peccata quae

a view the possibility of accepting which cannot be discussed here.

As, however, the possibility of restoring the redemptive tie must not be excluded, we are brought back, on the one hand, to the older definition, according to which only those non-venial sins are absolutely mortal in the interval between which and death no restoration of the redemptive link takes place;[1] while, on the other, we must now make a distinction amongst venial sins themselves, since even mortal sins under certain conditions become venial; and thus the intrinsic distinction is lost. If to this we add the fact that the sin against the Holy Spirit is thought by many to be a sin which renders impossible any restoration of the link with redemption, then, instead of a simple antithesis we get the following gradation. Sins in themselves venial are those of the forgiven which can hardly be avoided in the present life,[2] and always carry their remission with them;[3] moreover, all the sins of the unforgiven become venial should the unforgiven be converted, as also all intentional sins of the redeemed, should they return to grace. Mortal sins again, strictly so called,[4] are those of the two last-named groups should the connexion with redemption not be respectively effected or restored; while the only absolutely mortal sin—assuming that the exegesis is correct—is that against the Holy Spirit. Obviously, however, the difference between sins in themselves venial (requiring as they do repentance and prayer for pardon) and the mortal sins of the forgiven (which become venial if by repentance the forgiven again attain to the temporarily lost state of grace), is the less pronounced the shorter the interval between the lapse and the recovery. Indeed, in the light of the qualification 'against conscience,' this difference might be traced back to that between intentional and unintentional sins. Since, however, even in the state of grace the power of the will always lags behind the intelligence even though the knowledge of the sinfulness of one's ordinary states becomes deeper,

in renatis in hac vita manent ab illis peccatis, propter quae amittuntur gratia et fides.

[1] Augustine, *de Corr. et Grat.* 35: Ego autem id esse dico peccatum ad mortem, fidem quae per dilectionem operatur deserere usque ad mortem.

[2] Augustine, *de Spir. et Litt.* 48: non impediunt a vita aeterna iustum quaedum peccata venialia, sine quibus haec vita non ducitur.

[3] Baumgarten, *loc. cit.*: For, although we say that they are called *venialia* because they always carry remission with them . . .

[4] Melanchthon, *loc. cit.*: Est igitur actuale mortale in labente post reconciliationem actio interior vel exterior pugnans cum lege Dei facta contra conscientiam. p. 276: nec potest stare cum malo proposito contra conscientiam fides.

it follows that intentional sins will occur which, being as they are associated with progress, cannot bring about a complete lapse from grace. Ignoring this aspect of progress, some rashly contend that the regenerate can no longer sin knowingly—'knowing' implying at all events the lowest degree of 'intentional'; whereas all we are entitled to say (on the analogy of what was said regarding the relationship of the individual man to his nature) is that he cannot by a single act (an act, moreover, not exempt from the influence of divine grace) wholly dispossess himself of this state of grace. In the last resort, accordingly, there is no essential distinction except that which is based upon the relations of the acting subject to redemption. As regards the sin against the Holy Spirit, that no doubt would form a species by itself; but as long as the interpretation of the passages upon which the conception rests [1] is in dispute, Dogmatics must leave the ascertainment of the facts to the exegetes—just as it must leave to the pastoral office the handling of the case where a man believes himself guilty of the sin, and cannot presume to decide either what the sin is or in whom it is found. In general, however, it must repudiate the suggestion that there may be a sin which, though repented of in view of redemption, yet cannot be forgiven, as setting a limit to the universality of redemption.

3. A like result follows from a closer study of those gradations of human states relatively to sin which, taken directly from passages of Scripture, or indirectly from popular exposition, have passed into Dogmatics. Thus the state of *freedom*,[2] in contrast to that of *bondage*, is taken to be that in which (conceived in its ideal form) only sin in itself venial is to be found, this being due to a link with redemption so stable and vital that unintentional sins in such a life always are less grave than any intentional sin. The very term 'bondage,' however, as applied to the state in which sin is predominant implies that the man, by reason of his inward recognition of the God-consciousness, is not fulfilling the demands of the flesh with entire acquiescence. But if we reflect that freedom, as a consequence of the link with redemption, can grow only out of a state of bondage, we can see how freedom, in its gradual development through exercise, will still continue to exhibit traces of bondage. From the state of bondage, again, it is customary to distinguish as still worse the states of self-assurance, hypocrisy, and hardening. But if there should supervene a state worse than bondage, the inward recognition just referred to must needs have been utterly

[1] Matt. 12^{31}, Luke 12^{10}.

[2] Rom. 6^{18-22} 8^{2}.

stifled. Yet, since even in the state of freedom it momentarily falls silent, when sins of impetuosity are done, such silence could only serve to introduce an altogether distinct state if it could be regarded as continuous, and the inner voice as irretrievably extinguished; and this is in fact the sense of the term *hardening*[1]—a state which manifests itself most distinctly in a conscious and fixed will not to give effect to the God-consciousness. This condition, however, can never be more than approximated to, for the disposition to the God-consciousness is a constituent element of human nature,[2] so that, even in such a vitiation of that consciousness as ascribes human vices to the gods, the soul is never wholly without a dim sense of the presence of something incompatible with the God-consciousness. But were we to assume that that consciousness is dead beyond recall,[3] and thus that the hardened soul is altogether impervious to grace, we should be placing a particularistic limitation on the sphere of redemption. The consciousness of the divine law, accordingly, cannot be wholly wanting except when the God-consciousness has not developed, *i.e.* at a period prior to the state of bondage. If in the individual soul the development is obstructed by the power of the sensuous, this may be a state of brutishness; but that, too, would belong to the state of bondage, for the obstructive element is identical with that which impedes the efficacy of what has already developed. The states of *self-assurance* and *hypocrisy*,[4] lying between the two extremes of freedom and hardening, do not stand in markedly different relations to these extremes, nor are they at all mutually exclusive; they really belong to the state of bondage, and are compatible with all its various degrees, except the bondage present to a minor extent in the state of freedom. Here too, then, we ultimately have only the antithesis of freedom and bondage, and these in turn simply reflect the two diverse relations to redemption.

4. The distinction amongst sins which our proposition sets forth as the only essential one, if we also take account of the relationship of actual sin to original sinfulness, can be most definitely expressed

[1] Reinhard's explanation in *Dogm.* § 88, 'Conditio hominis qui diutius peccando tandem desiit propositis ad virtutem incitamentis moveri,' requires to be brought closer to the standpoint of religion, but even so would come to the same thing.

[2] Augustine, *de Spir. et Litt.* 48: Nam remanserat utique id, quod anima hominis nisi rationalis esse non potest; ita ibi etiam lex Dei non ex omni parte deleta per iniustitiam.

[3] This is certainly not implied either in Heb. 3^{8-13} (taken in relation to Ex. 17^{7}) or in 2 Cor. 3^{14}.

[4] Cf., amongst others, Reinhard, *loc. cit.*

as follows. The actual sin of those who have been brought into permanent connexion with the power of redemption is no longer 'originating' in themselves, or, through their ill-doing, in others. It has been vanquished by the energy of the God-consciousness implanted in them personally and spontaneously, so that where it still shows itself it is seen to be on the wane, and has no further contaminating power. Hence the sins of the regenerate are such as do not obstruct the spiritual life either in themselves or in the community. On the other hand, the sins of the unregenerate are always 'originating,' not only in the individuals themselves, since every sin adds to the force of habit and thus to the vitiation of the God-consciousness, but also beyond themselves, since like instigates like, and the vitiated God-consciousness spreads and establishes itself by communication to others. Thus whatever element of spiritual life may exist in a society still outside the sphere of redemption, and may seek to expand and rise from lower stages to higher, whether in political life or in science and art, has its progress constantly thwarted by such sin, and dragged back into the whirlpool, so that the sin may be truly said to be detrimental to the spiritual life of the community, or in other words to rob the community of spiritual life. If we incline to abrogate this antithesis, and assume merely a difference between a larger freedom in some and a lesser freedom in others without reference to a definite point of demarcation at which a bondage characterized by a mere presentiment of freedom passes into a freedom merely showing traces of bondage, we shall thereby be abandoning the attitude of at least the stricter type of Christianity, and our position, in virtue of its Pelagian tendency, would at last merge in naturalism, for once that antithesis has been surrendered, redemption would come to have no distinctive inner effect whatever. Such effect, however, is so palpably present everywhere in Holy Scripture as an ultimate fact of consciousness, that it is unnecessary to go back to particular expressions and formulæ, such as 'being buried in the death of Christ,' or 'the new creature,' or in the contrast between the carnal and the spiritual man. If, however, we thought of describing the latter contrast as one between a state in which sin still persists and a state in which everything is sin, we should thereby warp the facts, since there is no hard-and-fast distinction between the two; and, besides, it would be unduly harsh to stigmatize as sin everything noble and beautiful that has developed in heathenism. Here we can only seek to supply what is defective in that statement of the antithesis. We say then, in harmony with what was argued above, that in all good works of the regenerate there remains some form of venial sin, but it is, so to speak, merely the shadow of sin, that is—if we consider the inward state as a whole—the not-willed but actually repudiated after-effect of the force of habit, which can only be overcome by degrees. On the other hand, in the sins of the natural man, which as such are not yet forgiven, there is always the now deeper and now fainter shadow of the good, namely, an acquiescent presentiment or imagining of a state free from inward conflict ; only a shadow, it is true, because these imaginings never take practical shape or become permanently effective. So, too, in heathenism the communal life, principally because of the vitiated God-consciousness with which it was necessarily bound up, was never able to produce anything higher. Similarly in the unenlightened man who has only an outward connexion with Christianity we may indeed trace many a Christian feature, which nevertheless is not in him a thing of living power, but merely the reflection of what is present as a reality in others.

SECOND SECTION

THE CONSTITUTION OF THE WORLD IN RELATION TO SIN

§ 75. *Once sin is present in man, he finds also in the world, as his sphere, persistent causes of hindrance to his life,* i.e. *evils. This section, accordingly, will deal with the Doctrine of Evil.*

1. It is clear that in a system of doctrine the world cannot come under discussion at all except as it is related to man. Even though, in consequence of sin, the world were to suffer a change outside the human relation, new elements being introduced or the old modified, this could have no place whatever in Dogmatics. Only incidentally, therefore, and only because the idea of such a change is frequently brought into religious teaching, do we need to state that this is a wholly untenable idea, deduced from certain Mosaic passages [1] on quite insufficient grounds. Even in its relation to man, in fact, the world can only assume different characteristics in the manner indicated in our proposition—partly by its appearing different to him, and partly because the results of sin dissolve the original harmony between the world and man. Thus the conception of the original perfection of the world,[2] if brought into relation to the original perfection of man, does not imply that the world is the domain of evil. No doubt there must always have been a relative opposition, making itself felt with varying intensity, between the existent as externally given and the corporeal life of human individuals, otherwise human beings could not have been mortal; [3] but as long as every moment of human activity might have been a product of the original perfection of man, every moment being determined by the God-consciousness, and all the sensuous and bodily aspects of life being brought into in exclusive relation to it, that opposition could never have been construed by the corporate consciousness as an obstruction to life, since it could not in any sense act as an inhibition of the God-consciousness, but at most would give a different form to its effects. This holds good even of natural death and the bodily afflictions that precede it in the shape of disease and debility; for what can no longer serve the guiding

[1] Gen. $3^{14. 16-18}$. [2] Cf. § 59. [3] On this, cf. § 59.

and determining higher consciousness, is not willed. Hence it is not by death, but, as Scripture says, by the fear of death, that we are subject to bondage.[1] If, however, the predominant factor is not the God-consciousness but the flesh, every impression made by the world upon us and involving an obstruction of our bodily and temporal life must be reckoned as an evil, and the more so, the more definitely the moment of experience terminates solely in the flesh apart from the higher consciousness; the reason being that there is then a repression of the only principle which could in such a case restore the harmony. Since, then, the relative opposition between the external world and the temporal life of man is an inevitable and universal fact, sin involves evil of the first type indicated above; the world, that is, appears otherwise to man than it would have appeared had he had no sin. As regards the second type, which must primarily have its source in human activity akin to sin, it is obvious that an activity that was purely and simply an expression of man's original perfection could never turn out to be a hindrance to the spiritual life. For, even if such activity, through the error and against the intention of the agent, were to turn out a hindrance, though only to the life of sense, then, since along with this would necessarily go an incentive to correct the error, it would not be regarded as an evil. Just as little again could the action of one person prove a hindrance to another's life, since, in virtue of the God-consciousness that was supreme in all, each could not but acquiesce in the other's every action. But if that supremacy is done away, there emerges opposition between the individual beings, and what is a furtherance to one will often for that very reason become a hindrance to another. So that here, too, evil arises only with sin, but, given sin, it arises inevitably.

2. Now, anything that gives rise to obstructions in human life so far as it is independent of human action, we call *natural* evil; while what in bringing about such obstructions is really due to human action, we call *social* evil. The latter term is preferable to 'moral' evil; for if we say 'moral' we suggest that the bad also as such (*das Böse*) is subsumed under the concept of evil.[2] It is true that social evils too presuppose sin; what in one person issues from sin becomes an evil for another, and probably for himself as well; but precisely on that account it seems the more necessary to insist, even by our use of terms, on the essential difference in the reference involved in the two. The above division may not look

[1] Heb. 2^{15}.

[2] Cf. § 48, 1.

quite satisfactory, since, *e.g.*, disease may in many cases be a natural, and in other cases a social, evil (this ambiguity being inherent in general terms) ; indeed, we must often regard as one and the same evil what should be ascribed partly to the one source and partly to the other, and it would perhaps, therefore, be more accurate to say that all evils arise from the two elements together or from one of the two. Still, the main fact remains unaltered, namely, the different way in which the two kinds of evil stand related to sin. Both kinds, however, when viewed from the standpoint of the original perfection of the world,[1] are evils only because they either diminish the wealth of stimuli which further men's development or make the world less tractable to human effort. Of the former class are the evils of scarcity and want, of the latter those of oppression and antagonism ; and everything that from our point of view may be regarded as evil, together with all the deadening and derangement of our spiritual powers in consequence of sin, must be traceable to these two types.

3. As summarizing the foregoing, our proposition implies, first, that without sin there would be nothing in the world that could properly be considered an evil, but that whatever is directly bound up with the transitoriness of human life would be apprehended as at most an unavoidable imperfection, and the operations of natural forces which impede the efforts of men as but incentives to bring these forces more fully under human control. Secondly, it is implied that the measure in which sin is present is the measure in which evil is present, so that, just as the human race is the proper sphere of sin, and sin the corporate act of the race, so the whole world in its relation to man is the proper sphere of evil, and evil the corporate suffering of the race. Finally, the proposition signifies that, apart from such evil, there is no other consequence of sin that bears upon the relationship of the world to man, and that our religious consciousness makes no claim to substantiate the theory of some sort of magical effect which sin at its first appearance must have produced upon the world as a whole.

§ 76. *All evil is to be regarded as the punishment of sin, but only social evil as directly such, and natural evil as only indirectly.*

1. It would be altogether contrary to this proposition to admit only such a connexion between evil and sin, as implied that evil was the original and sin the derivative, *i.e.* that it was the obstruc-

[1] Cf. § 59.

tions to man's sensuous life that first evoked in him the bad, and repressed his God-consciousness. Such things are often enough said in particular cases, and the morally bad derived from natural imperfection, physical or psychical. Were it really so, however, the Christian consciousness would necessarily be in conflict with itself; for to see an obstruction of life in any moment of experience in which there was a disturbance merely of the sensuous consciousness would of itself argue an impotence in the God-consciousness, and therefore sin. The said theory, therefore, can hold good only of an individual case as such, certain evils favouring the development of certain forms of sin, but only because these evils themselves have had their source in sin. To advance the view as universally and exclusively true, however, would imply that the ultimate ground of sin lies wholly outside human activity, in an original ordainment of evil independent of such activity; and this would mean that sin was not the collective act of the human race, but in the first instance the work of external nature, where evil was supposed to have its basis, and ultimately a divine appointment. This view, however, would not only take us beyond distinctly Christian ground—since redemption would then be essentially an emancipation from evil—but it would carry us out of the sphere of the teleological, *i.e.* the distinctively ethical religions, into that of æsthetic or of nature-religion, where the guiding hope would be merely that a joyous emergence of the God-consciousness might possibly take place once we had become prosperous and happy.

In opposition to all this we record our consciousness that in the admitted connexion between sin and evil, sin is ultimately always the primary and original element, and evil the derivative and secondary. For the term 'punishment' implies, first, an evil actually existing in relation to some preceding badness (*Böse*). This does not indeed exhaust the connotation of the term, and when we use it in its true sense we really refer the said connexion to an originator, and ascribe it to a free action on his part; and it is either in an improper sense, or because we actually refer the connexion to the divine causality, that we apply the term punishment to an evil that, instead of being inflicted upon a wrong-doer, rather befalls him. Our formulated statement is accordingly the expression of our religious consciousness in so far as we refer that connexion to the absolutely living and active divine causality as described above, and do not seek to involve that causality in any particular way in the antithesis of free and necessitated. And for that very reason this consciousness, of which probably no one can divest himself, is essentially different from the partly one-sided and partly perverted mode of it found in Judaism, and still more in heathenism ; for, when that ordained connexion between sin and evil is divorced from the universal world-order and the system of nature, and is represented as something individual and unequal in its incidence, or is referred to some superinduced change in the Supreme Being, we have a view which rests upon a vitiated God-consciousness, and thus itself is of the nature of sin.

2. In distinguishing here between social evils and natural evils we are proceeding upon the fact that the former alone are dependent upon sin directly. It might no doubt be argued that the expressions 'due to human activity' and 'due to sin' do not mean the same thing, since the root of evil is often not sin so much as error. Nevertheless, when we try to conceive of an error absolutely free from guilt, we find that the range of such errors is much narrower than is usually supposed, so that, strictly speaking, we have to fall back, not upon free human action at all, but upon merely passive states which in reality belong to our natural imperfection. Evils which could be explained in this way, because not due to sin, would in fact fall into the category not of social but of natural evils.

The connexion of the latter group with sin, again, is only an indirect one ; for death and pain, or at least analogous natural maladjustments of the individual life to its environment, are found where no sin exists. Natural evils, therefore, objectively considered, do not arise from sin ; but as man, were he without sin, would not feel what are merely hindrances of sensuous functions as evils, the very fact that he does so feel them is due to sin, and hence that type of evil, subjectively considered, is a penalty of sin. That even the most serious maladjustments of this kind, considered purely by themselves and from the standpoint of man's natural perfection, are not punishments, but incentives rather to the development of the spirit, is taught by Christ Himself with reference to the man born blind ;[1] for what He says there regarding His own special miraculous power is susceptible of universal application. Even if we probe still more deeply, and assert that the obstructions to our life, taken purely by themselves and before they become evils through sin, are nevertheless rooted in the same evil as sin was said above to be,[2] in the temporal frame and the spatial individualization of existence, upon which the beginnings of all sin depend ; yet,

[1] John 9³. [2] § 69.

even as thus connected in their common origin, sin would for us still be first and evil second, as certainly as man is primarily an acting subject, and his activity not wholly dependent upon his passive states.

3. As the value of the Mosaic narrative must be estimated in view of the fact that there can be no proper history of the first man, and as a state of being which offered him abundant enjoyment without effort on his part can be no genuine representation of the original perfection of the world, it is possible that the true significance of that symbolic narrative may be seen in its relation to the contrasted states. Thus the fact that, when man after the Fall had to till the ground in the sweat of his brow—this in itself being no evil, and therefore not a penalty of sin—the tilled ground brought forth thorns and thistles for him, is certainly meant to indicate that nature's opposition to man's moulding handiwork is to be thought of only in connexion with sin. Similarly, the fact that death, hitherto unknown to him, is put before him as the recompense of transgression, and that the first case of death is represented as the outcome of sin, seems to indicate that it is through sin alone that natural imperfections come to be incorporated with social evils. Now, as the Pauline account [1] of the relationship of death, and thus of all secondary natural evils, to sin turns wholly upon that symbolical narrative, and can only be interpreted in the light of it, it too (precisely on the analogy of sin) depicts the evil which befell the first pair after the Fall as 'originating orginal evil,' and this again can be applied to every contribution which the individual in consequence of his sin makes to the deterioration of the world.

§ 77. *The dependence of evil upon sin, however, can be empirically established only as we consider a communal life in its entirety; on no account must the evils affecting the individual be referred to his sin as their cause.*

1. If sin as an organic whole can be rightly understood only as the corporate action of the human race, its causal action relatively to evil can only be understood from the same point of view. In fact, the most definite expression of this conviction lies, for each of us, in the general statement that throughout the human race as a whole, increase of sin is necessarily attended by a corresponding increase of evil (though as the effects of sin naturally ensue only by degrees, it is often the children and grandchildren who first suffer for the sins of the fathers),[2] and that, in like manner, as sin

[1] Rom. 5[12ff.]. [2] Ex. 20[5].

diminishes, so will evil diminish. As the intercourse, however, of the human race is even yet relatively limited, and many groups, being in a manner outside the range of the sins of other groups, form enclosed wholes by themselves, the same principle will hold good of these as well. Following up this line, we shall next be able to say of every nation, and indeed of every social class in it, so far as it seems to stand by itself, that the measure of its sin will be also the measure of the evil it suffers. Nor does this strict correspondence with sin apply to social evils only; for since large bodies of men not seldom affect one another precisely as natural forces do, and external nature obstructs the common efforts of all, these influences are, in every large association of human beings, felt the more intensely as evil, the more deeply it is involved in sin; and, in fact, even common evils not seldom acquire their peculiar cast and character from the nature of the sin that predominates in the society. All this becomes unmistakably clear only when we have in view a circle of homogeneous communal life not too small in extent.

2. Now it would indicate not only a limited and erroneous but a dangerous point of view—even if a view deeply rooted in Judaism and Greek heathenism—were we to make a similar affirmation regarding the individual, namely, that for each the measure of his sin is the measure of the evil that befalls him. For the very conception of the community and fellowship of human life implies, as indeed follows all but self-evidently from the manner in which sin produces evil, that quite possibly only the merest fraction of the common evil may fall upon the author of much of the common depravity. Accordingly, to refer first to natural evils, we find Christ explicitly declaring that, on the one hand, those operations of nature in which the original perfection of the world is most clearly shown are by divine appointment not less active where there is sin than where there is righteousness;[1] and on the other, that natural evils,[2] and accidental evils such as might almost be identified therewith,[3] are assuredly not linked to the sin of the individual—so far as we can isolate it—in such a way as to warrant our measuring his sin by the evil he suffers. And even if we go back to the view that sinfulness and natural imperfections spring from a common root, yet the individual's share in the one seems to be quite independent of his share in the other. Only in this way, indeed, can our assumption hold good without subverting the completeness and constancy of the natural order. Again, as regards social evils: were these to be

[1] Matt. 5[45]. [2] John 9[3]. [3] Luke 13[5].

apportioned to each individual according to his share in the collective wrong-doing, we should often, as by some magic process, have to find justice in injustice.[1] In point of fact, Christ warns His disciples of persecution and suffering in their work for the Kingdom of God, but not assuredly in proportion to their sin. How indeed could such a supposition be squared with the idea—an idea pervading the New Testament, and, if rightly understood, essential to Christianity—that within a common sphere of sin it is possible for one to suffer for the rest, so that the evil due to the sin of many may all converge upon one, and that penal suffering may fall pre-eminently upon one who is himself most free from the common guilt and most resolute in his battle with sin ?

Postscript.—From the point now reached, we find it possible to estimate a position which I would characterize broadly as the Cynical, but which has been maintained repeatedly and in various forms in Christian times—namely, that all evils have sprung from our social life and from men's endeavours, by combining their forces, to explore and dominate nature more effectively, and that in the so-called state of nature these evils would virtually not have emerged at all. In one aspect, this view seems to be a mere corollary of our proposition. For since in social life the individual may have to suffer for the many, it is impossible that evil could be the same in the solitary state as it is in society. Clearly, too, the less a man is inclined to activity, and therefore the less in touch with other men and with external nature, the less exposed will he be to the evils that result from such contact. If this view, however, is advanced, not as a mere observation, but as counsel and warning to the effect that a man would do well to act less in order to suffer less, it conflicts with the spirit of Christianity in that it commends the maxim of the slothful servant, and finds a higher ideal in being passive than in being spontaneously active.

POSTSCRIPT TO THIS DOCTRINE

§ 78. *The consciousness of this connexion does not demand a passive endurance of evil on account of sin; nor does it entail an endeavour either to bring about evil because of sin, or on the other hand to do away with evil in itself.*

1. This proposition, since it does not more exactly determine anything in regard to the origin of the consciousness already eluci-

[1] Cf. Luke 13^1-3.

dated, or further define or analyse its non-active content, can only be dealt with here as an addendum. But as the proposition has to do with the issues of that consciousness in so far as the latter may express itself in an impulse to deeds that react upon it, it is strictly one that verges upon the sphere of Christian Ethics. At the same time it is not taken from that sphere. A system of Christian Ethics formulated independently, *i.e.* not simply in relation to a definite existing system of Christian doctrine, or as a series of practical corollaries drawn from such a system, would hardly be capable of directly combining the points which our proposition summarizes. On the contrary, the question whether the Christian consciousness enjoins a passive acceptance of all evil, or whether, on the other hand, every other task imposed upon us should be laid aside until some evil that we suffer from has been got rid of; or again, the question whether a positive system of penal law is directly derived from religion, and whether the sense of one's own sin should induce one to bring evil upon oneself, would all emerge at quite different points in Christian Ethics. What entitles our proposition to a place here is its distinctively dogmatic combination of the points concerned.

2. In every instant of suffering the consciousness of the connexion between evil and sin is present, and is indeed combined in the unity of the moment along with our God-consciousness; this association of our feeling of absolute dependence with our state of suffering constitutes the mood of religious submission, which is thus an essential element of piety, but an element which wholly disappears if we regard the said connexion as non-existent or as of minor importance, and in face of our present difficulties in life look for corresponding ameliorations in the future. Similarly, should this submission develop into something more positive, and should we become willing that evil should continue or unwilling that it should cease (on the pretext of not desiring to infringe the desires of God or to be found in opposition to Him), then our submission would not be grounded upon the connexion in question. Queer fancies of this type, due to misconception, have always been repudiated by the Christian Church, which has always set itself here against superstition and fanaticism. For the continuance of evil could assuredly not be willed as a hindrance to life, since every such hindrance tends to restrict on one side or another the activity that flows from the God-consciousness. And still less in the sphere of redemption, within which we confidently hope sin will disappear, could we desire

the continuance of evil, since, evil and sin being connected, we should in that case either desire the continuance of sin itself or else not desire the realization of that hope. On the other hand, it is no less certain that the Christian consciousness could never give rise to a moment of activity specially directed towards the cessation of suffering as such—partly, of course, because such a moment would really be determined by the interests of the lower side of life, and partly because (since, in view of the aforesaid connexion, suffering necessarily evokes the consciousness of sin) it is a disposition hostile to sin itself that needs to be aroused. And at the same time, as every restriction of spontaneous activity implies a still defective domination over nature, we are confronted with the task of making that domination effective. These, then, would be the two consistent and practical results flowing from our sense of the connexion of sin and suffering, whereas every activity directed against suffering in itself would, precisely because of the end in view, be a sensuous one, and also would only too easily take on a character of passionate vehemence.

Further, there is thus exposed the unchristian or rather the wholly irreligious nature of a certain other view—namely, that it is evil alone which, from the outset, has evoked all the human activity that goes to subjugate nature and to form social life. For if that activity has been directed solely against evil, and has accordingly sprung up only as a reaction against depressive influences without any spontaneity, then this whole phase of life will be of a purely sensuous kind, and will draw no incentive from the God-consciousness. On such terms the truth would lie with those who think that religion does not express itself in outward acts at all, and who so divorce that entire sphere of things (as merely secular and purely a matter of necessity) from the province of religion, as to make an irremediable cleavage in life.

3. Finally, if on the one hand sin is essentially a corporate thing, since every sin emanating from an individual implies the guilt of others, so that corporate evil can be related only to corporate sin, and on the other hand every increase of sin must be regarded as of itself entailing an increase of evil ; then our consciousness of this divinely ordained connexion can furnish no grounds for our bringing about evil as a result of observed sin ; for by its very nature such procedure could not but interfere with the divine ordinance in question. Whether there may, however, not be other grounds for doing so is, of course, not the question here.

THIRD SECTION

The Divine Attributes which relate to the Consciousness of Sin

§ 79. *Divine attributes relating to the consciousness of sin, even if only through the fact that redemption is conditioned by sin, can only be established if at the same time we regard God as the Author of sin.*

1. To begin with, it is certain that we can arrive at ideas of divine attributes only by combining the content of our self-consciousness with the absolute divine causality that corresponds to our feeling of absolute dependence. That in this manner we trace the annulment of sin by redemption to the divine causality is a fact that we may premise as given universally in the Christian consciousness. But divine attributes that were there conceived as operative would of course be operative primarily in redemption, and it is only through redemption that they would be related to sin. Now, if in relation to sin there are divine activities other than those concerned in its removal, the existence of sin must in some sense be due to the divine causality, and that causality must be determined in a special way with respect to sin's existence. We have already [1] discussed the fact that, in general, sin as an act, besides having always a basis in the natural order (this term being taken here as connoting the historical as well), also comes under the co-operative agency of God; but this points only to the creative and preservative omnipotence of God. If, nevertheless, because sin does exist and in so far as it exists, we feel bound to posit a special divine activity bearing upon it, we must not forget that in thus considering the consciousness of sin *per se,* we are moving in the region of the abstract, and should therefore err were we to look for divine activities bearing upon sin purely by itself. On the other hand, as regards sin in its relation to redemption, we must—if this section is to have any subject-matter at all—be able somehow to show that sin does actually exist in virtue of certain special divine activities ; and what is more, we must do so, keeping in mind the fact that we have

[1] See § 48.

already ruled out as inadmissible any distinction in the divine causality between causing and permitting, or between creating and preserving.

2. Our task, accordingly, is to answer the question whether and how far God can be regarded as the author of sin—sin too as such (not merely, that is, as regards the material element in sinful action)—yet always of sin as linked with redemption. If an affirmative answer can be given, there will then be divine attributes in virtue of which sin is ordained by God—not indeed sin in itself, but in so far as redemption likewise is due to Him. These attributes then will have as their counterpart those which we shall have to look for under the like condition in the second division of this Part—those, namely, in virtue of which God is the Author of redemption, not in itself, however, but in so far as sin too is due to Him. The conceptions of the divine attributes to be formulated here will accordingly, on the one hand, be posited only on the assumption of their being interwoven with those that come to us from an examination of the consciousness of grace; for we assume it beforehand to be out of the question that the two sets of conceptions could in reality be so distinct as the mutual opposition of the two elements of our Christian consciousness, when considered thus abstractly, suggests. On the other hand, the divine attributes in question are to be conceived of as attaching to the divine omnipotence only as this has been described as the eternally omnipresent, for this is the most general expression of that feeling of absolute dependence which is regarded here as forming the basis of this first aspect of the antithesis.

§ 80. *As in our self-consciousness sin and grace are opposed to each other, God cannot be thought of as the Author of sin in the same sense as that in which He is the Author of redemption. But as we never have a consciousness of grace without a consciousness of sin, we must also assert that the existence of sin alongside of grace is ordained for us by God.*

1. If to the power of the God-consciousness in our souls, just because we are conscious of it as not due to our own agency, we give the name 'grace' and (abstracting from the universal divine co-operation without which sin itself were impossible) ascribe to it a special divine impartation; and if, again, the content of a moment which lacks the determining activity of the God-consciousness, just because we are conscious of it as an act of our own cut off from that

divine impartation, is termed 'sin'—this of itself justifies the first part of our proposition. The universal co-operation of God is the same in either domain, but in the case of sin there is lacking that specific divine impartation which gives to every approach to salvation the character of grace. It might, of course, be said that as the disappearance of sin is uniformly proportionate to the inflow of grace, the relation between the two resembles that between two species of animals one of which preys upon the other, the two continuing in that relationship as ordained for both by one and the same divine will. This, however, would be tantamount to denying the specific divine impartation in question, and to affirming that redemption is effected solely by the spontaneous efforts of man, so that in the sphere of grace the human factor would be related to the divine co-operation precisely as in that of sin. But while such a view need not be regarded as in itself unchristian, since it might still leave room for the influence of the specific activity of the Redeemer, it nevertheless would not be the doctrine recognized by the Church and therefore expressive of the Church's corporate feeling. Accordingly, if the antithesis in our self-consciousness really implies a special divine impartation, the question what divine activity in turn underlies the fact of sin as such, *i.e.* as that which evokes redemption, can be answered only by saying that no evidence exists of any such activity.

2. No less true, however, is the second half of our proposition. We are conscious of the said communicated power of being determined by the God-consciousness always and only as co-existing with an incapacity of our own that reveals itself as a co-determining factor, and we also know that, while the power overcomes the resistance, it nevertheless leaves it still there. Hence we can conceive of the divine will that imparts the power only as at the same time having in it something which entails that sin even in the process of disappearing should continue to exist side by side with grace.[1] For if the divine will without any such latent strain were wholly directed against sin, the latter of necessity would vanish altogether and at once. Now, the second part of our proposition rests wholly upon the assumption that everywhere human evil exists only as attached to good, and sin only as attached to grace. Were it possible to speak of a type of sin absolutely unconnected with

[1] Melanchthon, *Loc.*, p. 121: Respondeo de renatis adultis omnes concedere coguntur reliqua esse peccata. Cf. 1 John 1[8].—*Conf. Anglic.* xv.: Sed nos reliqui etiam baptizati et in Christo regenerati in multis tamen offendimus omnes.

redemption, we should certainly not have to assume a divine activity directed to the existence of such sin. But if it is the case that the state of hardening is, strictly, not a human state at all,[1] no such type of sin really exists either within the narrower sphere of Christianity, where everyone is brought into some kind of connexion with redemption, or outside that sphere, where even the most impotent and vitiated God-consciousness belongs to a corporate life that at the same time comprises a morally higher element which finds expression in precept and law; and, as a matter of fact, every such corporate life, imperfect and sinful as it may be, has yet, in virtue of its presentiments and aspirations, an inward link with redemption. Least of all, however, can we imagine that sin could have a place in the creative dispensation of God apart from redemption, since in the divine will bearing upon the existence of the whole human race the two are ordained to stand in relationship to each other. For the mere fact that the emergence of sin preceded the advent of redemption in no sense implies that sin was ordained and willed purely for itself; on the contrary, the very statement that the Redeemer appeared when the fulness of the time was come [2] makes it quite clear that from the beginning everything had been set in relation to His appearing. And if we add the fact that the sin which persists outside direct connexion with redemption never ceases to generate more sin, and that redemption often begins to operate only after sin has attained to a certain degree, we need have no misgiving in saying that God is also the Author of sin—of sin, however, only as related to redemption.

3. The antinomy in these two statements, both of which are expressions of our religious consciousness, is all the more difficult to resolve because it is not in two different relations that they are severally predicated; on the contrary, both are postulated in respect of one and the same relation, namely, as we trace the potency of the God-consciousness to a special divine impartation. It is true both statements are derived solely from the consciousness of the Christian who has been brought into the actual fellowship of redemption, and in this narrower field the antinomy appears easy of solution if we say that, as sin is in fact present and continues to exist prior to redemption, and as the divine impartation can operate only in the forms of human life, we must infer that in the narrower sphere sin can be overcome even by divine grace only in a time-process. We cannot, however, claim to have dealt successfully

[1] Cf. § 74, 3. [2] Gal. 4[4].

with our problem unless we also bring the presence of sin in the human race as a whole into connexion with our God-consciousness. Precisely because the narrower sphere is in process of constant expansion—and that, moreover, in virtue (under God) of the labours of the forgiven—we cannot but have that outer field constantly in view. In this reference, accordingly, our race-consciousness finds expression solely in the antithesis between the Kingdom of God and the world, and this again represents in the most general way both the antithesis of sin and grace and their co-existence ; so that in this necessary universalization of our consciousness we meet again with the same antinomy, which accordingly must be solved for the universalized consciousness as well.

4. Now every attempt to solve the antinomy by accepting one statement and rejecting the other leads inevitably to a result incompatible with the character of Christianity, drawing us, in fact, into either the Pelagian or the Manichæan heresy. We fall into the latter when we put the first half of our proposition in such a way as entirely to exclude the second. Thus if sin is in no sense grounded in a divine volition and is nevertheless held to be a real act, we must assume another will so far completely independent of the divine will as to be itself the ultimate ground of all sin as such. Nor will it matter greatly whether this will is the human will itself or another ; for, if we still assume, what is certainly given in our self-consciousness, the co-existence of sin and grace in the same individual, that state of things can be regarded only as a conflict of these two antithetic wills, which means that every activity of the flesh would be an overcoming of the divine will—a view implying in any case that the divine omnipotence is circumscribed, and therefore abrogated, and that the feeling of absolute dependence is proclaimed an illusion. Or, again, were we, contrary to all inward experience, to advance the opposed and clearly fanatical statement that the influx of divine grace involves the complete disappearance of sin proper, only a semblance of it being left behind, then wherever real sin still existed the divine omnipotence would still be excluded from the entire sphere of free action as such, and the two spheres—that of the divine will and that of its antithesis—would stand opposed to each other, even externally, in the most rigorous fashion.

Just as certainly, however, we should fall into the Pelagian heresy were we to admit the validity of the second part only of our proposition, and so do away with all distinction in the divine causality, which would thus be identical alike in the activities of the flesh and the energy of the God-consciousness. In that case the spontaneous activity of man must be the same throughout ; the antithesis between our native incapacity and the imparted energy of the God-consciousness would disappear ; and, since the most powerful element in us, equally with the power of the flesh, would be the outcome of our own activity, the consciousness of incapacity that forms part of our inward experience can indicate only a transitional and even now evanescent state of the social life of mankind. In such an indistinguishable 'more or less' of flesh and spirit, redemption inevitably comes to occupy a very insecure position, and it is virtually a matter of accident how much or how little special influence is ascribed to the Redeemer, whether more as the Author of redemption or as its occasion. This attenuation of the specific difference between Redeemer and redeemed—this, as we might almost call it, merely figurative use of the term 'grace'—marks the Pelagian heresy. Pelagianism, therefore, on the one hand sacrifices the practical religious interest (which postulates somewhere a perfectly pure impulse) to the theoretical (which demands that every vital activity shall have the same relation to the divine causality), and on the other feebly and through mere stolidity surrenders all hope of perfect satisfaction. Manichæism in turn is a surrender of the theoretical religious interest in the reality of the divine omnipotence, in favour of the practical interest attaching to the idea that evil is real in the most unqualified sense, so as all the more to bring out the necessity that the perfect good should counteract it redemptively. And this, too, is to despair of reconciling the existence of sin with the divine omnipotence.

§ 81. *If ecclesiastical doctrine seeks to solve this antinomy by the proposition that God is not the Author of sin, but that sin is grounded in human freedom, then this must be supplemented by the statement that God has ordained that the continually imperfect triumph of the spirit should become sin to us.*

Conf. Aug. 19 : Tametsi Deus creat et adiuvat naturam, tamen causa peccati est voluntas malorum videlicet diaboli et impiorum, quae non adjuvante Deo avertit se ad alias res.—*Sol. Decl.*, p. 647 : Neque Deus est creator vel autor peccati.—Melanchthon, *Loc.*, p. 72 : Non igitur Deus causa est peccati, nec peccatum est res condita aut ordinata a Deo. P. 76 : peccatum ortum est a voluntate diaboli et hominis, nec factum est Deo volente.—*Exp. Simpl.* viii. : scientes . . . mala non esse quae fiunt respectu providentiae Dei voluntatis et potestatis Dei, sed respectu Satanae et voluntatis nostrae voluntati Dei repugnantis.—*Conf. Hungar.* (Ed. Aug., p. 251) : Sicut impossibile est contrarie inter se pugnantia . . . causam efficientem formalemque esse posse sibi contrariorum . . . ita impossibile est Deum, qui est lux, justitia . . . causam esse tenebrarum peccati . . . sed horum omnium causa Satanas et homines sunt. Quaecunque enim Deus prohibet et propter quae damnat facere ex se et per se non potest.

1. The use of the terms 'Creator' and 'creation,' as bearing upon sin, was made possible only through that scholastic misuse of abstract terms which gave to the controversy about original sin the peculiar turn represented by the question whether it was a substance or an accident. That usage, however, is as it stands quite inadmissible, since sin is not an independent entity, and does not form an independent process. And just as little—least of all if we distinguish between 'creation' and 'preservation'—can we apply the said terms to the sinful nature, since that nature does not start with sin, but sin first makes its appearance in the course of life. If, however, we still keep to the statement that God is not the Cause or the Author of sin, we find that such denial, taken strictly, involves two distinct ideas, one of which stands out more prominently in the first two, the other in the last two, citations given above.

The first is that, as in God thought and creation are one,[1] and as sin cannot be a divine thought or purpose, there cannot be in God any creative will in relation to sin or the sinful nature. But the same might be said of every finite nature. The sinful nature is a blending of the being and not-being of the God-consciousness, but in the same way every finite nature is a blending of being and not-being; and not-being can no more than sin be the divine purpose. Yet in relation to every finite nature there is a creative divine will—not, however, as something existing purely by itself, but as comprised in the will that creates the finite God-consciousness in its entirety, and thus embraces redemption likewise. Hence the first or negative clause of the Church's doctrine requires modification in the sense that the negation is not to be taken as implying that sin must be referred to another creative will which is actually such in the same sense as God is Creator in general, *i.e.* in virtue of a timeless eternal causality; for, were the negation so taken, the same would hold good in every case of individual differentiated being, and ultimately therefore of the entire aggregate of such. In that case we should be forced to choose between a demiurge—distinct from God—as the creator of the world, who created also the sinful nature as such, and an evil primordial being—opposed to God

[1] § 40, 1 and § 55.

—in whom lay the timeless causality of sin, but who must also have been the creator of finite being, and that not merely in part, as some have idly said, but wholly.[1] From this point of view, accordingly, we are shut up to the choice between saying that for sin there is no eternal causality at all, and finding that eternal causality in God.

A transition from the first main idea of our proposition to the second is found, however, in the theory that traces the sinful state in its entirety to the loss of the God-consciousness originally imparted to human nature by God Himself.[2] Thus, while generally the cessation of anything must be due to the same divine will from which it took its rise—otherwise, indeed, there would be no finite being at all—yet it would seem that there must be a difference in the case of the God-consciousness, the cessation of which, *i.e.* of the presence of God in man, could not be due to the divine causality. Now this plea might no doubt hold good were sin a complete cessation of the God-consciousness, and if the sinful nature were wholly sin. But in the sinful nature the bad exists only correlatively with the good, and no moment is occupied exclusively by sin; for sin actually presupposes the God-consciousness, so that the sinful nature always retains the presence of God as something imparted, though only in the most limited degree. Hence in this respect, too, the limitation of the God-consciousness, as well as its impartation, may be grounded in one and the same divine will.

The second thought taken as starting-point is that God cannot possibly have brought about, and therefore cannot be the Author of, what He Himself forbids. Now we must of course admit that the will of God which commands other beings, though we call it will, is not identical with His efficient will.[3] For the divine command does not manifest itself in addition as a will that, in all cases falling under the command, effects what is in conformity with it; in fact, the Scripture actually says that the commanding will of God does not of itself secure obedience,[4] and we are all clearly

[1] It is quite clear that in bringing the devil into the matter our confessional documents had not this in view. For they regard the devil as coming under the same category as man, namely, that of a free finite being, so that his sin, too, is to be thought of as grounded in his freedom, and his relation to human sin is by no means to be regarded as prejudicing the fact that man's sin is grounded in his own freedom. Thus the introduction of the devil brings no Manichæan element whatever into the Church's doctrine, especially as that heresy is none the more easily obviated if we leave the devil out of account.

[2] Cf. § 72.

[3] Calvin., *Inst.* i. 18. 4: Perperam enim miscetur cum praecepto voluntas, quam longissime ab illo differre innumeris exemplis constat.

[4] Rom. $7^{8f. 16-18}$.

conscious of the difference between the state in which what is given us is only the commanding will of God, and that in which God's efficient will is added as well.[1] And we are quite as clearly conscious that the difference between the will of God as commanding and His will as accomplishing what is commanded is altogether unlike that, *e.g.*, in the narrative of the creation, between God's utterance of this fiat and the will that carries it out. A further reason why the commanding will of God is not as such an operative will is that sin is committed only where there exists a commanding divine will to which some active impulse is the opposition. For if sin be committed by one who thinks he is fulfilling the divine will, then what is sin is not the act itself, but only the mistaken thought, and even this is sin only where it has arisen in antagonism to God's commanding will. This holds good likewise when sin is committed inadvertently. Thus all sin lying between the extremes of innocence and hardening [2] presupposes the consciousness of a commanding will. Now, though the commanding is not identical with the efficient will, yet the latter cannot be opposed to the former; for the prohibition could not be genuine if God Himself brought the transgression of it to pass. Here, however, we must not forget that the divine commanding will was posited solely as an absolutely perfect will, to which accordingly even what is effected in us by divine grace as efficient divine will never wholly corresponds. If then this shortcoming in us be described as sin still clinging to us,[3] then even from this point of view the negative part of the Church's doctrine will require modification. We must say that the negation is to be understood only in the sense that a want of conformity to the commanding will of God can none the less be brought about by His efficient will, and that so far sin is grounded in the divine causality.

2. As regards the second or affirmative part of the Church's doctrine, it is no doubt perfectly accurate; but we cannot regard it as fitted to nullify those limitations of the first part which we had to claim on behalf of our religious consciousness. It is, in fact, only in view of these limitations that we are able to interpret the combination of both facts in the sense that sin, so far as there is no divine causality for it, is not grounded in human freedom either. This is the only conclusion that agrees with the relationship we have formulated between the divine eternal causality and the temporal and finite causality.[4] But the fact of sin's being grounded in our

[1] Phil. 2[13]. [2] Cf. § 66, 1; § 74, 3. [3] Cf. § 63, 3. [4] Cf. § 51, 1.

freedom is all the more compatible with its being rooted likewise in the divine causality because, with regard to the feeling of absolute dependence, we recognize no difference between the greater and the less activity of temporal causality.[1] It is only the temporal cause that is stated in this part, and the statement is first and foremost intended to obviate the idea that, if no divine causality can be assumed for sin, the consciousness of sin is a mere delusion. Sin is therefore referred to that highest degree of inward activity which constitutes the distinctive element in our being. What then is here asserted is that in the whole range of life between the inward state of the Redeemer, in whom no break in the supremacy of the God-consciousness could issue from His highest spiritual activity, and those states of human disorder in which the spiritual functions are brought under the power of disease, and responsibility ceases owing to a lack of freedom, free self-development is always attended by sin. Hence if this whole form of existence—the life of the natural man—subsists in virtue of divine appointment, sin, as proceeding from human freedom, has also a place in that appointment.

Next, our proposition affirms for the sphere of finite causality as well, that we cannot truly regard ourselves as merely passive and extraneously determined in our acts of sin.[2] The very phrase ' freedom of the will ' conveys a denial of all external necessity, and indicates the very essence of conscious life—the fact, namely, that no external influence determines our total condition in such a way that the reaction too is determined and given, but every excitation really receives its determinate quality from the inmost core of our own life, from which quality, again, proceeds the reaction, so that the sin proceeding from that core is in every case the act of the sinner and of no other. In like manner, the expression ' freedom of the will ' negatives the idea that the individual is in all cases pre-determined by the common nature of man. In reality, the common elements of our nature are the results of a process of development, and the expression in question marks out each individual as *ab initio* distinct and apart from all others. Hence no one can transfer the guilt from himself to common human nature ; a man's particular sinful self-determinations are his own acts, alike whether they issue from the sinfulness that is part and parcel of the principle of his individual will, or whether by means of them that sinfulness itself becomes more and more confirmed in

[1] Cf. § 49. [2] Cf. Gen. 3[12. 13].

him. None of these cases of determination, however, excludes the possibility of sin being related to the divine causality.

Besides, the proposition must only be interpreted in a sense compatible with the fact that sin is a state of bondage.[1] If the bondage ceases when redemption begins to operate—a process that cannot be conceived as independent of divine causality—but in such a manner that the operation annuls the bondage only by degrees, and is therefore permanently limited in scope by it, then we are again shut up to the conclusion that the sin which is rooted in a freedom thus linked with impotence is as such ordained by God—unless, indeed, we are positively to assume that divine action can be limited by what does not depend upon the divine causality.

3. Since then the Church doctrine, as an accurate expression of our self-consciousness, does not exclude the possibility of God's being in some sense the Author of sin, and since we are drawn by opposed interests to both alternatives ; then in seeking to solve this apparent antinomy we have no choice—if we are to keep the divine omnipotence unlimited and unabridged—than to assert that sin, in so far as it cannot be grounded in the divine causality, cannot in that measure exist for God, but that, in so far as the consciousness of our sin is a true element of our being, and sin therefore a reality, it is ordained by God as that which makes redemption necessary. The more closely these two things are capable of being unified in the sphere of actual fact—in the same way as the diverse elements of our Christian consciousness form a unity within us—and the more definitely we can keep them apart in our thinking, so that neither will seem to involve the contrary of the other, the more completely shall we find all difficulties disappear, and that without our either in Manichæan fashion ascribing to sin a reality independent of and opposed to God, or with the Pelagians minimizing and by degrees annulling the antithesis of sin and grace. Now the latter part of the Church's formula asserts the reality of sin as our own act, while the first declares that sin is not brought about by God. If then, with that formula, and with the problem still set us, we collate the passages cited from the confessional documents, we note that certain of these bring out that the temporal source of sin lies in human freedom, while they do not say that sin involves a divine eternal causality as well ; in others, again, what comes out is that sin cannot have its source in the divine will,

[1] Cf. § 74.

though they do not assert that, in so far as such a source is actually lacking, it does not exist for God. Now the more fully those one-sided views are both developed, the more do the difficulties increase, and we must either resort to over-subtle distinctions in which our immediate religious self-consciousness does not recognize itself, and which cannot be combined in a single organic view, or else we must renounce all deeper inquiry, and so arrest the development of theology.

In endeavouring, therefore, to obviate this one-sidedness by combining the two points of view, we ask first—starting with the former group—what is that element in sin for which, so far as it is rooted in human freedom, we might look to find also an eternal divine causality? Well, in every distinct moment of sin there is for one thing the manifestation of a sensuous natural impulse, in which of course the eternal divine causality is implicated; and, for another, we posit the God-consciousness as capable of being related to that impulse—else there would be no question of sin at all—and the God-consciousness of course goes back to the divine causality in the primordial revelation. But these two elements taken together do not constitute sin; it follows that so far this divine causality does not bear directly upon the sin. In so far as the sin consisted in the impotence of the God-consciousness, it would be a mere negative, *i.e.* something that could be neither a divine thought nor the result of a divine act;[1] however, a mere negation of power does not amount to sin, and, in fact, the mind is never satisfied to have sin explained as simply a defect.[2] The defect becomes sin for us only in virtue of the fact that the God-consciousness, impotent against the sensuous impulse, disavows as consciousness of the divine will that state of defect, whether simultaneously or before or after; for, without such disavowal, which is simply the recognition of a commanding or prohibiting divine will, there is no sin. We shall accordingly be able to say that, as the recognition of the commanding will is wrought in us by God, the fact that the inefficacy of the God-consciousness becomes sin in us is likewise wrought by Him, and indeed wrought with a view to redemption.[3] For the consciousness of an as yet meagre potency of the God-consciousness would be that of a state that must needs be transcended, but the consciousness of a state in which

[1] Melanchthon, *Loci. Th.*, p. m. 76: Etsi enim sustentat naturam, tamen defectus illi in mente non efficiuntur ab ipso.

[2] Cf. § 68.

[3] Gal. 3^{22}.

there is antagonism to the divine will is a consciousness of something that must be wholly annulled.

Taking up now the other standpoint, let us ask what meaning compatible with sin's being our own act we can give to the idea that sin is not brought about by God. If sin is not to be attributed to the divine causality on the alleged ground of its being a negation, we must bear in mind that, in accordance with what has been said above, it shares that feature with all finite being, and may therefore be none the less our own act, as finitude is the very stuff of our experience ; yet negation too is eternally wrought by God within and along with the whole development of the God-consciousness. Again, if the reason why there can be no divine causality for sin is that it is out of harmony with the commanding will of God, let us remember that it has this in common with all the good that is indubitably originated by God, to which sin is always attached, as indeed it is present in association with all good whatever ; and even so it is still our own act, as yet out of connexion with redemption.[1] Only if sin were a thing absolutely contradictory to the commanding will of God, such as would utterly annul sin in us, would it be impossible to think of the efficient will of God as related to sin. Sin, however, is never such, else it would imply the state of absolute hardening which, as we have seen, does not lie within the human sphere at all. Hence our supplementary clause is fully justified, for it is through the commanding will of God present within us that the impotence of the God-consciousness becomes sin for us. By that will, accordingly—though it may be impossible to ascribe any particular act of sin to a divine causality specially pertaining to it —sin has been ordained by God, not indeed sin in and of itself, but sin merely in relation to redemption ; for otherwise redemption itself could not have been ordained.

4. Nevertheless, if it be held that sin arose out of a sinless state of morally perfect activity, we must concede that our proposition does not solve the difficulties. On the assumption of a state of that kind, we must either have recourse to the theory of such a withdrawal of God's hand as would imply a special divine act veritably giving rise to sin, or else we must represent sin as a revolt—surely

[1] Only in this sense can we accept the formula of the *Augsburg Confession* : voluntas non adjuvante Deo avertit se ad alias res. The original German phrase, which, however, has been altered in the revised German Confession, certainly points to a more positive sense : alsbald so Gott die Hand abgethan (' as soon as God withdraws His hand '). For this withdrawal of God's hand, as a special divine act, would then be the primary condition of sin.

least explicable in such a state—directed towards the complete subversion of the commanding will of God. Hence thinkers who proceed on that assumption usually resort to the idea that, as God is not the Author of sin, and nevertheless sin actually exists, it exists by His 'permission.' A term such as this, however, derived as it is from human government and its conditions, is admissible only in a sphere of divided causation. But eternal causality is like no other, and all temporal causality must be uniformly related to it. More confusing still than the idea of permission, however, is the hypothesis that, though God may have ordained sin, He ordained it only as an indispensable means to wider ends of high moment, making the evils consequent upon sin a source of more than countervailing gain, and through Christ completely effacing the mischief of sin itself.[1] But quite apart from the fact that the antithesis of means and end cannot exist for a purely creative and all-creating will, we could not well imagine a more fallacious way of presenting Christianity than to say that Christ came only to make good the mischief arising from sin, while God, looking to the manifold gains to come thereby, could not dispense with sin itself. As against this, our own theory is that sin was ordained only in view of redemption, and that accordingly redemption shows forth as the gain bound up with sin ; in comparison with which there can be no question whatever of mischief due to sin, for the merely gradual and imperfect unfolding of the power of the God-consciousness is one of the necessary conditions of the human stage of existence.

§ 82. *What has been said concerning the divine causality with regard to sin holds good also with regard to evil, in virtue of its connexion with sin.*

Sol. Decl., p. 641 : Poenae vero peccati originalis, quas Deus filiis Adae ratione huius peccati imposuit, hae sunt, mors, aeterna damnatio et praeter has aliae corporales spirituales temporales atque aeternae aerumnae et miseriae. P. 819 : Ut enim Deus non est causa peccati, ita etiam non est poenae.—*Conf. Bohem.* iv. : Insuper docent, omnia incommoda et adflictiones quibus hic quatimur conflictamurque meritissimo iure a Deo ob peccata hominibus infligi.

1. The parallelism expressed in this proposition is for the most part recognized and assented to, but it is only sparingly dealt with in the symbolic documents, and seldom consistently developed in the systems of doctrine. This is more or less due to the fact that the treatment of the subject has had mixed up with it two irrelevant

[1] Cf. Reinhard, *Dogm.* § 75.

matters, and these we would eliminate at once. To begin with, everywhere in the discussion we meet with the misleading assumption that God has conjoined evil with sin in the purely arbitrary fashion exemplified in the penalties of human law; and with this, again, has been combined the idea of eternal penal suffering—a procedure which, though compatible with the assumption just indicated, we for our part cannot follow, since we are here concerned only with what is given in our self-consciousness, and as yet we lack all the data for the discussion of the latter problem. Just as little, however, have we any occasion to suggest the idea of an arbitrary penal law instituted by God. Were we to apply the previously cited Mosaic passages [1] to this point, we should also have to make room for the fantastic notion that the nature of the physical world had been changed by the entrance of sin. In the economy of the world, resting as it does upon the divine causality, it is impossible that one thing should be more and another less arbitrary; everything is equally arbitrary, or else equally not so.

2. Now, keeping to what is given in our self-consciousness on the matter, we find there two opposed interpretations of evil. One is that we ascribe evil to ourselves as the consequence of our sins, thereby denying that God is the Author of evil in the same sense as He is the Author of the original perfection of the world; and this view is amply justified by the fact that the latter conception implies, not that the world is the domain of evil, but rather that everything involved in the relative antagonism between our own life and other things operates merely as a stimulus. The other interpretation is that we acquiesce in all the evils of life as the expression of a divine decree passed upon us. Now, this acquiescence justifies itself most completely in those cases where we can regard evils affecting us as linked up with the atoning sufferings of Christ—as indeed all fellowship with Christ must be capable of being regarded as a fellowship in His sufferings. Observe, however, that the said evils, if viewed purely and exclusively in this light, could not really be regarded as evils in which we must simply acquiesce, but would rather be calls and incentives to a definite spiritual activity—challenges to be embraced with joy. Since, however, we are at the same time conscious of evil, and the said interpretation is also applied in cases where there is no special link between that evil and our participation in Christ's redemptive work; this clearly implies the assumption that evil as such has its origin in God—not

[1] Gen. $3^{14. 16-18}$; cf. § 75, 1.

indeed evil taken purely by itself, but only in its relation to sin, as that which alone runs counter to the simple and unqualified interpretation of the hindrances of our sense-life as being but incentives to action. Here again therefore the true solution is to be found, not in the view that, as evil is grounded in our freedom through the medium of sin, it is not derived from God, but rather in the view that, as we posit everywhere the eternal along with the temporal causality, evil likewise, just in so far as it is grounded in our freedom, is at the same time ordained by God, while if it is not ordained by God, it cannot properly exist at all. It cannot be grounded in God in so far as it takes the form of a conflict of finite beings, for these are ordained by God not in their particularity, but solely in their mutual dependence and measure. So far therefore it does not really exist, but is for us merely a semblance arising from our way of isolating things. God has ordained, however, that the natural imperfections are regarded by us as evil in proportion as the God-consciousness is not yet dominant within us, as also that sin develops into social evil in proportion as it is dominant, while at the same time both sin and evil are likewise grounded in our freedom.

3. The two facts, however—that connexion of evil with sin which is grounded in our freedom, and the divine causation of evil in relation to sin—become explicable only when we look at sin as corporate action and at evil as corporate suffering. The individual cannot say, except incidentally, that the evils from which he suffers are traceable to his own freedom ; the truth is that wherever the sin is with which evil is linked, there too is the freedom from which it issues. But as no sin belongs exclusively to the individual, the said connexion can be exhibited only in the context of a corporate life, and that the more clearly the more independent and self-contained this corporate life is. Taken strictly, therefore, even this explanation only covers those whose existence is due to natural generation and who depend upon a corporate life from the outset ; whereas, with regard to the first human being, considered by himself, it is difficult to represent the divine causality present in evil as combined with the fact that evil originated in his own freedom ; and the difficulty is all the greater the more necessary we find it to assume an initial condition free from natural imperfections. In that case it is, in fact, hardly possible to avoid the thought of an arbitrary decree of God linking evil with sin—and indeed the attempt to explain our present human evils from the natural properties of the forbidden fruit does not evade it either ; in which case

the confessional statement quoted above can claim no sort of validity.

Postscript.—We can exhibit divine attributes only as modes of the divine causality; it follows that, were God in no sense the Author of sin and evil, there could be no divine attributes in virtue of which sin and evil would exist. If, however, we have satisfactorily proved the existence of that causality, we must also enunciate divine attributes or modes of action of a peculiar type and distinct from those hitherto laid down—all the more that sin and evil are on the one hand ordained by God, and on the other are to be done away by redemption. Now, if we had to formulate the concepts of these attributes for the first time, we might hesitate as to whether it were better to propose two—one for sin and the other for evil—or one only, since evil depends solely upon sin. But in point of fact, the religious consciousness has long ago attained to clearness about this situation, and has expressed this aspect of the divine causality in the twin concepts of holiness and justice. This might doubtless be criticized on the ground that in our ordinary language the former concept does not relate to sin alone so much as to the antithesis between good and bad, and similarly the latter not so much to evil alone as to the antithesis between reward and punishment. But in fact the two terms, especially the first, have been defined and explained in so many other ways as well, and even—reward and punishment being simply the outflow of the divine pleasure and displeasure—brought so close to each other in meaning, that the following discussion of them will best show how relevant they are at our present stage, and how no other meaning can be held to than that which we shall attach to them here.

First Doctrine. God is Holy

§ 83. *By the holiness of God we understand that divine causality through which in all corporate human life conscience is found conjoined with the need of redemption.*

1. We use the term 'conscience' to express the fact that all modes of activity issuing from our God-consciousness and subject to its prompting confront us as moral demands, not indeed theoretically, but asserting themselves in our self-consciousness in such a way that any deviation of our conduct from them is apprehended as a hindrance of life, and therefore as sin. In thus limiting our attention to the God-consciousness, we are true to the spirit of our theology

generally. We may certainly assume as a known fact that conscience is elsewhere explained by a corresponding relation to the idea of the good; here we have but to say in passing that the two explanations are in no real sense different. Thus, if it ever were to occur that under the idea of the good the natural conscience made other demands than in the same community are insisted on by the God-consciousness prevailing there, so that the two were in conflict, we should simply have to attribute the fact to a defect in their development or in their application, just as we do where the natural conscience in any one region or period is not identical with that of another, or where different forms of faith differ in the moral demands they make. In the Evangelical (Protestant) Church, however, we are not troubled with any such conflict, for there it is readily admitted that the modes of action emanating from our God-consciousness are identical with those developed from the idea of the good. Now we need give no proof of the fact that, wherever these demands or a law of this kind is referred to the God-consciousness, conscience also is very markedly traced to divine causality, and, as the voice of God within, is held to be an original revelation of God; it is one of those inward experiences which we may assume to be universal in this sphere. None the less, conscience is not identical with the fact of the God-consciousness in man, as constituting the original perfection of his nature; for apart from the discrepancy between the form of the God-consciousness as understanding and its emergence as will, and indeed apart from this discrepancy as combined with a tendency to agreement, there would be no conscience at all; and similarly apart from conscience, nothing that results from that discrepancy would be sin for us. Thus the divine causality, in virtue of which conscience exists, falls wholly within the sphere of the antinomy in which we now live, and is no less certainly the divine causality through which sin exists, though for us it is owing to conscience alone that a given state, and that as something due only to ourselves, becomes sin.[1] And if in addition to this causality, and to the universal co-agency of God we were to postulate another divine causality as the ground of sin, we should have to assume two divine activities antagonistic to each other. It follows, therefore, that the causality we have postulated is the whole and sole divine causality which sin as such implies.

2. Now if our explanation signifies that conscience is present

[1] Cf. 1 Pet. 1[14-16], where the holiness of God is associated with the demand that we should no longer live according to our lusts in ignorance.

only along with the need of redemption, then while this is certainly the purely Christian account of the matter, it must not be taken to mean that we would assume the presence of conscience only where the need of redemption is recognized; on the contrary, treating here as we do of the divine causality, we start from the assumption that redemption through Christ is ordained for the whole human race, and that all mankind are in the state of needing redemption. If, instead of that state, we were to imagine a gradual development in the power of the God-consciousness, then, while even there we might find the discrepancy above referred to, yet, as progress would in that case approximate very closely to the practice of an art, the laying down of a demand such as conscience makes would be superfluous—just as art of every kind develops without any such demand; indeed, as conscience always entails pain, it would be a piece of cruelty. In point of fact, it is with a view to redemption that men are in common held under the power of conscience, which always involves the sense of their incapacity; and so, too, later, it is because conscience still continues to stimulate the sense of sin within them that they are held steadily to redemption. If, however, we could ever think of the will as being perfectly at one with the God-consciousness, so that nothing was striven after but what was prompted by the latter, then—granted that the still remaining defects of performance were due solely to the mental or bodily organism subserving the will—conscience in its distinctive character would cease to exist. Hence, too—to speak here only incidentally or provisionally—if we think it an adequate description of the inward state of the Redeemer to say that He had at all times a perfectly satisfied conscience, we must take the phrase as meaning a conscience that was always silent, so that He can have had a conscience only in the form of fellow-feeling, and not as something personally His own.

What we have said partly explains why we find the proper sphere of conscience in corporate life. For, granted that a single generation of men were to attain to the consummate strength and purity of will above referred to, it would of necessity influence the succeeding generation by awaking conscience in the adolescent; and the same thing would apply to the greater differences in development within a single generation. On the other hand, a conscience manifesting itself solely in each individual by himself would be too variable to secure the certainty of its judgments and of their being attributable to the divine causality. The true conscience, however, emerging in a society as the same thing in all and for all, is law—primarily moral law, though ever finding outward expression in civil law. Thus the holiness of God is the divine causality that legislates in the corporate life of man, and since the law, especially as traced to its inward source, is always for us the absolutely holy, and the whole historical process is ordained by this divine causality, no exception can well be taken to our regarding that causality as a distinctive divine attribute, or to our designating it exclusively by the name 'holiness.'

3. The customary and popular interpretation of the term as used in the liturgical and homiletical field, however, is that the holiness of God consists in His being well-pleased with what is good and displeased with what is bad. That interpretation may be understood in two ways. Its implication is doubtless that the terms 'good' and 'bad' are predicates of the actions of free finite beings.[1] But as taken so, the interpretation can only be given a place in scientific discourse with great modifications. Pleasure and displeasure in their very antithesis always imply an element of passivity, and unless this is eliminated, the attribute of holiness will involve some disturbance of our feeling of absolute dependence, since a divine state would then be determined by human action, and thus the relation between God and man so far become one of reciprocity. Again, the attribute as so interpreted would be a purely inward and quiescent one—such indeed as our immediate religious consciousness gives us no occasion to postulate. Both points might no doubt be disposed of if, of these human states of pleasure and displeasure, we transferred to God only the active aspect, namely, their outward manifestation in the effort to effect or prevent something. But as we find this twofold aim only in redemption, and as it would be altogether a departure from the usage of the Church to say that redemption is grounded principally in the divine holiness, then, unless we are to surrender the term altogether, we must again come back to the view that the manifestation of the divine displeasure, if detached from the effectuation of the good, is simply the effectuation of this displeasure in the acting subject by means of conscience and law. If, however, the interpretation is taken to mean that God's pleasure in the good and displeasure with the bad form the basis of His creative activity and determine it,[2] it follows that the bad, in-

[1] Henke, *Lineam.*, p. 66: Deus ab omni labe et vitio purissimus, omnis pravi osor irreconciliabilis, boni rectique amantissimus.

[2] As indicated by Mosheim, *Th. Dogm.* i. p. 292: Sanctitas est immutabile propositum voluntatis Dei perfectionibus suis congruenter agendi; and

asmuch as being the object of displeasure it is opposed to the good, cannot exist, and so cannot be regarded as a thought of God;[1] in other words, there is no reality in, nor any divine idea of, the bad. This we may lay down without misgiving, with the necessary consequence that in the same sense finite being cannot from itself generate the bad,[2] *i.e.* that the bad as an actual antithesis to the good has no existence at all, and that therefore that displeasure with the bad which is wrought in us by the divine causality is, strictly speaking, only our own displeasure in the fact that the effective power of the God-consciousness falls short of the clearness of our apprehension. Thus what is tenable in both interpretations, when taken together, corresponds exactly with what we have laid down, and we are in this way able to refer the conception of God's holiness directly to His omnipotence and omniscience, and regard these as holy. With this, again, agree those other interpretations which ascribe to God's holiness the function of demanding from His creatures what is perfectly good;[3] for that demand is made upon them only in virtue of the law or the moral feeling implanted in them. Some of these interpretations bring into the conception the inward purity of God as the ground of the demand; such of them, however, as confine themselves to that purity, or go back even to God's perfect self-love,[4] while they might be relevant in a speculative or a so-called natural theology, have no place in a systematic statement of Christian doctrine.

Second Doctrine. God is Just

§ 84. *The justice of God is that divine causality through which in the state of universal sinfulness there is ordained a connexion between evil and actual sin.*

1. This interpretation undeniably is much narrower and more limited than that yielded by the method of other theologians, and therefore requires special vindication. To begin with, here too

Ammon, *Summa Theol. Chr.*, p. 92: Consensus voluntatis liberrimae perfectissimus cum legibus intellectus sapientissimi.

[1] Cf. § 55, 1. [2] Cf. § 67, 2.

[3] Quenstedt, *Syst. Th.* i. p. 420: Sanctitas Dei est summa omnisque omnino labis aut vitii expers in Deo puritas munditiem et puritatem debitam exigens a creaturis.

[4] Buddeus, *Instit.*, p. 252: Quando Deus se ipsum amore purissimo amare concipitur ut simul ab omni imperfectione secretus censeatur amor ille vocatur sanctitas.—Something similar was said by Hilary, on Psalm cxliv.; he would take the divine holiness as signifying especially the non-existence of all self-seeking elements in God.

use is made of the position that justice is of two kinds, namely, legislative (or distributive) and retributive. The former of these, however, cannot be brought under our definition at all. In fact, the thinkers referred to seem to have forgotten that the terms 'law' and 'justice' always imply a relation to something given. Human legislation and distribution can be just, and may be said to be just, only in view of an already given situation to which it is attached and upon which it is based. Divine legislation and distribution, however, is primordial and creative ; it is that from which existent things themselves and their relationships all alike proceed, which needs nothing to attach itself to, and which in its perfection accordingly cannot be described as justice at all, but would more aptly be designated wisdom [1]—a divine attribute that we cannot deal with till a later stage. Hence the divine justice can be retributive only. But even of retributive justice our interpretation covers only the half ; for the term is used to denote not only the punishment of wickedness, but also the rewarding of goodness, while our definition has nothing to say of a connexion between well-being and the power of the God-consciousness, but refers only to that between evil and sin—precisely that connexion, in fact, which we call punishment. Now we might concede the omission, and even excuse it as involved in the very process of abstraction in which we are engaged when discussing one element of our Christian consciousness, namely, the consciousness of sin, and for the time putting aside the other ; but at most we should thereby be exposing an inconvenience of our method, which here forces us to split a divine attribute in two. In point of fact, however, our Christian consciousness recognizes no reward proceeding from the divine justice ; anything that might possibly be called reward is for us something unmerited, and attributable to the divine grace.[2] The rewarding side of the divine justice can have no other object than Christ,[3] and Him only as one who is different from all other men. From our own religious consciousness, therefore, we can know only of God's punitive

[1] Something of this kind seems to have been in the minds of the theologians who apply the term 'internal' justice to the divine holiness, while to justice itself they give the name 'external' justice. On that view, it is holiness itself that is the legislative activity of God ; or else, if external justice is in turn divided into legislative and retributive, the former refers to holiness as the supreme perfection that constitutes the ground of law, the latter to holiness as displeasure at what is bad.

[2] Rom. $4^{4,16}$; cf. Matt. $20^{14,15}$. While in 2 Tim. 4^{8} the conferring of the reward is ascribed to God as judge, yet He is there represented rather as an umpire—a symbol that is not relevant here.

[3] Phil. 2^{9-10}, Heb. 2^{9-10}.

justice ; His rewarding relatively to ourselves we must simply leave out of account. For while Christ Himself seems more often and more variously to portray the rewarding action of God,[1] yet the increase of a man's powers and the expansion of his field of action—two things, be it noted, corresponding exactly to each other—are no more a reward in the proper sense (*i.e.* one that might be contrasted with evil as conjoined with sin) than the increase of wickedness could in the proper sense rank as a punishment.

2. Now, if the conception of divine justice has to do only with the connexion of evil with sin, it would surely seem natural that it can apply solely to the sphere of sin ; and in that case the postscript (p. 341) may well appear superfluous. It is clear that if we formed part of a sinless corporate life we should never have an idea of this side of the divine causality at all, for it is only through our consciousness of sin that we come to the idea of the divine justice. The term itself, however, likewise implies that as sin diminishes the connexion between sin and evil is done away in an equal degree ; and done away, moreover, quite independently of whether there is any change in the material side of man's condition ; and this abrogation, *i.e.* the forgiveness of sin, falls under the very same divine causality ; [2] for it is in this that the recompense of Christ lies. Our restriction of the connexion itself to actual sin rests partly on the fact that, as the original sinfulness still remains unchanged in the corporate life of man, the connexion with evil could not possibly be annulled were it due to that sinfulness ; partly also on the fact that the connexion exists only in so far as it has a place in our consciousness, while the consciousness of the original sinfulness exists in us only in and along with actual sin. Moreover, it is only with actual sin that we must connect not merely the existence of social evil—for it is only definite sinful tendencies of individuals which in corporate life develop into persistent causes of hindrance —but the fact that natural imperfections are regarded as evils. Hence in the measure that sin is done away, not only does evil occur no more, but even the sin which has become actual operates no longer as a hindrance to life, but as a helpful incentive.[3] The formation and annulment of the connexion of sin and evil, accordingly, involves two things : first, that the entire constitution of the world, in so far as evil depends upon it, is related in the most

[1] Matt. 25[21].
[2] Hence in 1 John 1[9] forgiveness too is attributed to God's justice.
[3] Rom. 8[28].

definite way to human freedom as that in which sin is grounded; and secondly, that in our consciousness the two are connected not merely occasionally, but essentially and universally. Since therefore the divine justice, thus regarded, is a form of the divine causality that remains self-identical throughout our whole experience, and covers the whole province of finite intelligence known to us, so that, together with the form of the divine causality treated in the foregoing paragraph, it regulates everything that upon this side of our antithesis bears upon the ethical, we seem to be perfectly justified in setting it forth as a distinct divine attribute.

To deal now with the first element in the attribute, namely, the relation of the entire world-order to human freedom; it will be universally admitted that the relation in question is to be found only in a corporate life. Only to the extent that such a corporate life is a unity complete in itself, and most perfectly therefore in human life considered as an integral whole, does this divine causality reveal itself in such a world-order that the hindrances to life that issue from sin cannot be averted or removed by any circumstances of the external world, however favourable. On the other hand, if we regard the individual as the proper object of the divine justice, we degrade that attribute to the status of a mere counterpart of civil justice, which we so often feel to be injustice. In fact, if we are determined to see the consummate justice of God only in the punishment of every particular offence—or, let us say, in the rewarding of every particular virtue or perfect act of virtue on the part of an individual—then as, *e.g.*, intemperance and falsehood are clearly not always punished by contempt or disease, and as, moreover, the very same evil which, falling upon one person, is interpreted as the punishment of his sin, may also fall upon others to whom without grave injustice we could not attribute the same sin, we find ourselves in a difficulty from which we can hardly escape except by asserting that the divine justice cannot fully reveal itself here below but will attain to completeness only in the life to come. That is an idea which—though attempts have been made to clear it of the charge of involving God Himself in a temporal process—only puts the difficulty further away, for we have no evidence of such disparity of suffering there as would counterbalance the disparities between doing and suffering here. If, however, we posit the idea of a corporate penalty along with that of a corporate guilt, we reach a complete vindication of the principle that all sin is reflected in evil, and that all evil can be explained by sin ; and this is precisely the connexion set forth above.

As regards the second element, namely, that in our consciousness this connexion between sin and evil is actually and even universally made—this is really the consciousness of penal desert, which in the human mind is as truly the creation of the divine justice as conscience is the creation of the divine holiness. The universality of that consciousness, however, manifests itself most unmistakably in the fact that domestic, civil, and social penalties everywhere flow from it, and indeed represent an affirmation of the connexion between sin and evil, just as the gradual mitigation of these penalties in consequence of the progressive disappearance of sin from corporate life represents the abrogation of it ; both features thus appearing as conjoined in the divine justice.

3. The classification of penalties as natural and arbitrary—a classification which indeed could not be fully demonstrated or applied in the realm of finite and temporal causation—is one which we find here no reason whatever to adopt. In point of fact natural penalties, grounded as they are in the creative and regulative divine causality, are arbitrary in the only sense in which that word can be applied to God ; while those which we might most properly call arbitrary, namely, the evils that do not correspond to the actions of those affected by them, are in reality natural ; for this non-equivalence has its source in the world-order as a whole. With a different usage of the terms, again, we apply the adjective ' natural ' to the penalties determined by the relation of the world-order to our freedom, while those that flow from human freedom itself we designate ' arbitrary.' But if we regard both kinds as divine, the distinction disappears ; for penalties inflicted by man, no less than the other group, take place in accordance with the divinely ordained spiritual development of mankind. In fact, the two kinds, as being equally of divine appointment, are essentially correlative and complementary ; for the ' arbitrary ' without the ' natural ' would lack reality, and the latter without the former would lack significance. Of penalties in the future life it is here impossible to say anything whatever ; nor can we determine how far they are to be regarded as ' arbitrary ' rather than ' natural,' or *vice versa*. The idea of these penalties is not taken directly from our self-consciousness ; and only in another section of our work shall we be able to inquire how the distinctively Christian form of this pre-Christian and widely diffused idea is related to a universal ground or reason which we

must certainly assume to exist, and, again, how far it is possible in this matter to go back to the conception of divine justice, whether interpreted as here or otherwise.

The case is different with certain other classifications sometimes applied to the subject, *e.g.* those based upon the various purposes of punishment. (1) To begin with, it seems clear that penalties cannot be ordained by God as reformative. Thus, suppose that an excess of sensuousness is counteracted only by means of sensuous feeling itself, then, *e.g.*, an appeal to fear as against pleasure cannot possibly issue in a higher energy of the God-consciousness and a greater freedom of the spirit ; indeed, all that could be effected in this way would be such a fresh distribution of sensuous motives as would, in accordance with the individual's nature, be felt as less disagreeable. It is also obvious that if the God-consciousness could be strengthened by punishment, a system of divine penalties as perfect as possible could have been made to serve instead of redemption. (2) We have, secondly, just as little right to suppose that the purpose of divine punishment is merely vengeful or retributive. Fundamentally, badness (or wrong) and evil are incommensurable ; it is only when a bad action brings evil upon another person that it is commensurable with a retributive evil. But this retributive evil is inflicted only in so far as the injured person regards his pleasure in the suffering of the injurer as removing or assuaging his own pain. Hence under the conditions of antiquity it is the custom everywhere that a penal evil can be bought off by conferring some other pleasure on the injured person. It was partly in this practice that the criminal jurisdiction of the State took its rise, replacing the vendetta by milder measures. Divine penalties of such a type, however, could be believed in only at a very primitive stage of development —a stage at which the Deity is still thought of as susceptible to irritation, and as not above feeling an injury or having other passive states ; and what has all along been preached, sometimes with apparent profundity, regarding the mysterious nature of the divine wrath and the fundamental necessity of divine retribution, cannot be made clear to the mind. And we can leave the matter there all the more confidently because (3) the consciousness of deserving punishment, as superinduced in us by divine justice, is fully explained by the remaining purpose of punishment, namely, to prevent or to deter. Punishment is, in fact, that which must of necessity be interposed wherever and in so far as the power of the God-consciousness is as yet inactive in the sinner, its object being to prevent his dominant sensuous tendencies from meanwhile attaining complete mastery through mere unchecked habit. Further, what is said, with reference to the Mosaic legislation, as to the people's being kept solidly together under the law applies generally to all criminal jurisdiction among all peoples, and equally to the natural penalties set forth also in the Mosaic legislation. Hence it is only relatively to the dispensation of redemption, and in so far as redemption has still to become operative, that the divine justice can be fully understood.

4. From what has just been said we see, on the one hand, how clearly the divine holiness and the divine justice are connected, and, on the other, how necessary it is to keep them separate. They are connected in the most intimate way as expressions of the divine causality as bearing upon sin in its relation to redemption. On the very same principle, according to which we say of sin that in the sense in which it cannot have its cause in God it cannot exist at all, we say of evil that if it cannot be grounded in God, *i.e.* if it be a real negation of the original perfection of the world for man, it likewise cannot exist at all. Similarly, just as with regard to sin, so too with regard to evil, we assert that so far as it is real, it must have its source in the divine causality. And, again, just as the consciousness of sin as necessarily entailing penalty—a consciousness due to the divine justice—is possible only on the assumption that conscience is due to the divine holiness, so, without that consciousness of penal liability, conscience would have no means of gaining a secure hold in any human soul still under the dominion of the flesh, and thus no means of generating there a consciousness of the need of redemption. But for the same reason it is also necessary that the distinction of the two concepts should be maintained here where, though we are dealing with elements of the religious consciousness which are provisionally abstracted from redemption, we must nevertheless premise the fact of redemption as that on which everything turns. For suppose matters brought to the point that both the natural imperfections and the sins of the world were no longer evils to us, but merely incentives ; that we therefore felt nothing at all to be evil in relation to ourselves, and that accordingly the justice of God was not immediately present even in our own purely personal religious experience ; yet we should still require conscience, and should therefore constantly revive within us the consciousness of God's holiness. Similarly, even while we still need both, we keep them rigorously apart. For our displeasure with what is bad, *i.e.* the reflection in us of God's holiness, is absolutely pure and satisfy-

ing only when not affected by anticipations of punishment; and the consciousness of penal desert is so firmly rooted in our corporate sense that we always acquiesce in punishment, even although our personal moral feeling regarding any particular occasion of it has been entirely corrected and purified, and our will has completely escaped from the bondage it implies. Precisely on this account, therefore, that form of the God-consciousness (*i.e.* the concept of divine justice) is no more transient in us than the form represented by the conception of the divine holiness, for it permanently conserves the same truth for our corporate sense, to which, in fact, it is in its origin specially related. Were it, however, to be said that the two conceptions, having to do merely with the natural imperfection of man, would apart from that sphere be nothing at all in God, and even within that sphere would cease to be of valid application as soon as the said imperfection was finally done away, and that accordingly they are not divine attributes in the same sense as those dealt with in the first part of our system—we should reply as follows. First of all, the same would hold good of the divine attributes which are subsequently to be developed from the second aspect of the antithesis, for to these also it is essential that they refer back to the first aspect; and, in fact, the same objection might be made to all the so-called moral attributes of God so far as they have any reference to the antithesis at all. But we have never attached great importance to these mere general phrases; so I shall only call attention to these special considerations bearing on the conceptions of the two attributes before us. First, as regards God's holiness: apart from its implication of that in virtue of which sin does not exist for God, and from the fact that it forms so far a general characteristic of God's consciousness of His works, and so of His omnipresence and omniscience, holiness is an essential element in our consciousness of God, for we can be cognizant of the absolute power of the God-consciousness only as we are cognizant of the state of sin as removed by redemption. The same is true also of the divine justice, since the Redeemer's merit is only the other side of sin's desert of punishment, and just as the former has always been present in the latter as a premonition of it, so the latter will always be present in the former as recollection. And no less is the relation of God's government of the world to our freedom one with its relation to redemption, while this whole interrelated system of the spiritual and the sensuous is the domain of what is accordingly the equally omnipresent and eternal justice of God.

APPENDIX : THE MERCY OF GOD

§ 85. *To attribute mercy to God is more appropriate to the language of preaching and poetry than to that of dogmatic theology.*

1. For one thing, preaching and poetry can afford to be less precise in their use of anthropopathic terms. And mercy is certainly such a term in a pre-eminent degree, since in the human sphere we apply it exclusively to a state of feeling specially evoked by the sufferings of others and finding outlet in acts of relief. Such helpful ministration is, no doubt, an ethical activity, but here it is conditioned by a sensuous sympathy, namely, the pain produced in us by hampered conditions in the lives of others ; and, in fact, if the help tendered does not spring from such a feeling we do not call it mercy. In this sense mercy is the counterpart of ' kindness,' *i.e.* the helpfulness in which the correlative sensuous sympathy, namely, pleasure in some furtherance of life in the case of others, plays a part ; and here, too, help given without such feeling behind it would not be called kindness. Thus neither of these qualities, as so understood, can be applied to God without our bringing Him under the antithesis of the agreeable and the disagreeable. And even if we were to overlook this and use the two terms solely of the respective acts of helpfulness, yet it would be out of keeping with the character of teleological (ethical) religions were we to admit, in a rigorously formulated system of doctrine, a divine causality bent upon a sensuous furtherance of life simply as such. Nor can the difficulty of finding a place for the conception of mercy in God be due to our looking for it at this particular stage of our inquiry. For, as mercy obviously presupposes evil and the consciousness of evil, the discussion of it could not well come before that of evil ; while, again, as mercy always implies some degree of separateness between the two parties involved—for within a closer group, as between father and children, we do not speak of mercy—the objects of God's mercy cannot be those who are already enjoying, and in so far as they are enjoying, their part in redemption.

2. Again, from a somewhat different point of view, the merciful God is for the most part contrasted with the jealous God. Now, as wrath and jealousy have obviously to do with offence and sin, mercy would in such case be the repression of jealousy by compassion. If, accordingly, we once more set aside the fact that this involves an emotional state, and think only of the withholding of punishment,

we must nevertheless here too set aside the idea that the punishment which is related to redemption is revoked merely on the ground of pain or defect experienced by some other. Thus, these eliminations having been made, all that remains is God's readiness to remit the punishment altogether. Yet, even so, we cannot allow mercy to rank as a distinct attribute, since we have ascribed that remission as well as the enactment of the penalty to the divine justice. Should this procedure be regarded as wrong, however, and mercy in the sense indicated be taken after all as a distinct attribute, then mercy and justice would each delimit the other. Where justice ceased, mercy would begin, and *vice versa*—a relation that cannot subsist between divine attributes. It is true that the classical passage for the use of the word in the New Testament [1] best agrees with that interpretation, for kindness to the unthankful is the suppression of jealousy by compassion. But the point of Christ's saying is the demand made upon the hearers, and in speaking of self-discipline it was natural that the analogous element in God to which He directed their minds should there be referred to by the same term.

[1] Lk. $6^{35f.}$

INDEXES

TO VOLUME I

A. SUBJECTS

B. AUTHORS AND SOURCES

C. SCRIPTURE REFERENCES

72 73 12 11 10 9 8 7 6 5 4 3